PROGRESS OR COLLAPSE

Human progress is heading toward collapse. There are converging ecological crises looming on the horizon: climate change, peak oil, water shortages, fish depletion and food scarcities. The world is on a collision course against the limits of the ecosystem. Modern societies are consuming, polluting and growing as if there is no tomorrow. Indeed, there may not be one.

In *Progress or Collapse*, Roberto De Vogli guides us through the multiple converging global crises of economic progress. He explores the connections between the environmental crisis and the psychological, social, cultural, political and economic emergencies affecting modern societies. It is not a coincidence, the author argues, that global ecological destruction is occurring in tandem with other crises: rising mental disorders, mindless consumerism, rampant conformism, status competition, civic disengagement, startling social inequalities, global financial instability, and widespread political impasse.

In this hard-hitting analysis, Roberto De Vogli identifies the root cause of all these symptoms of societal breakdown: neoliberalism, defined as market greed. He argues that in recent decades, modern societies have been dominated by a suicidal economic doctrine based on two articles of faith: the *greed creed* and the *market God*. The *greed creed* states that people are nothing but selfish profiteers in a perpetual search for status and wealth. The *market God* is the belief that all societal and human affairs are best regulated as market exchanges.

What is to be done? Can we stop progress toward collapse? Given the current distribution of power and wealth, and the state of psychological and political inertia in which we are trapped, our chances of redefining progress around alternative values and embracing a new philosophy of life are slim. Yet, the history of human emancipation has often been shaped by giant leaps forward. In the past, civic struggles have overcome "the limits of the possible." Whether this will happen again in the future is the central question of our time.

This book will be of interest to researchers and students of ecology, psychology, public health, epidemiology, human development, political philosophy, economics, sociology and politics.

Roberto De Vogli is Associate Professor in Social Epidemiology at the University of California Davis, USA. He is also Senior Lecturer in Social Epidemiology and Global Health at University College London, UK.

"Concerned for the future of humanity? Then read this book. Others cover just one aspect of the political, social, environmental and economic challenge facing humanity. But the transformation we so urgently need must start from an understanding of the interlocking system as a whole. With his breadth of vision, fearlessness and unerring eye for the truth, this is what De Vogli provides."

Richard Wilkinson, author of *The Spirit Level*

"If you think the world's current economic problems are just a blip, with normal service soon to be resumed, think again. As De Vogli brilliantly and succinctly reveals in this wide-ranging panorama of a book, the way we live now is simply not sustainable. In the absence of desperately urgent action that redefines our relationship with the planet, the future looks endlessly bleak; that is, of course, if we have any future at all."

Bill McGuire, author of *Seven Years to Save the Planet*

"De Vogli is one of the new ecological thinkers who show that climate change is the most dangerous product of Western corporate capitalism. In a masterful and highly accessible historical review of the development of corporate globalization, he shows that any struggle to save the planet requires a direct confrontation with the Wall Street elites and neo-liberal ideologues who created and now rule our unsustainable world economy. De Vogli shows that the world's prospects for survival depend now on repudiating the 'market greed' driving our elites and our own psyches, recanting the religion of growth, and crafting a new post-consumerist economy based on equality and our non-market needs for social fulfillment."

Charles Derber, author of *Greed to Green*

"The story of our generation is the social destructiveness of markets 'free' to operate in the interests of the few rather than under the control of society as a whole. In *Progress or Collapse* that story is told and analyzed with insight, revealing the depth and breadth of what we have lost due to subservience to the ideology of consumerism and greed. Anyone who hopes for a reversal of the current descent into market barbarism should read this book."

John Weeks, author of *Capital, Exploitation and Economic Crises*

"Roberto De Vogli has written a brilliant book that unveils the destructive nature of the so-called 'free market' and neoliberal doctrines so widely admired in mainstream economic circles. *Progress or Collapse* is a scary, but also stimulating essay that invites reflections, critical thinking and, above all, civic outrage."

Thom Hartmann, author of *The Last Hours of Ancient Sunlight*

PROGRESS OR COLLAPSE

The crises of market greed

Roberto De Vogli

Routledge
Taylor & Francis Group

LONDON AND NEW YORK

First published 2013
by Routledge
2 Park Square, Milton Park, Abingdon, Oxon OX14 4RN

Simultaneously published in the USA and Canada
by Routledge
711 Third Avenue, New York, NY 10017

Routledge is an imprint of the Taylor & Francis Group, an informa business

British Library Cataloguing in Publication Data
A catalogue record for this book is available from the British Library

Library of Congress Cataloging in Publication Data
De Vogli, Roberto.
Progress or collapse : the crises of market greed / by Roberto De Vogli.
  p. cm.
  Includes bibliographical references and index.
  1. Capitalism—Social aspects. 2. Free enterprise—Social aspects. 3. Financial crises. 4. Sustainable development. 5. Social responsibility of business.
  I. Title.
  HB501.D385 2013
  330.12'2—dc23   2012027248

ISBN: 978–0–415–49069–6 (hbk)
ISBN: 978–0–415–51018–9 (pbk)
ISBN: 978–0–203–07331–5 (ebk)

Typeset in Bembo
by Swales & Willis Ltd, Exeter, Devon

MIX
Paper from
responsible sources
FSC
www.fsc.org   FSC® C004839

Printed and bound in Great Britain by the MPG Books Group

CONTENTS

ILLUSTRATIONS

Figures

Tables

PROLOGUE

PROGRESS TOWARD COLLAPSE

A shocking idea explains the end of all life in the universe. It is the entropy theory,[1][2] also known as the second law of thermodynamics. This proposition argues that all systems in the universe are heading toward decay and breakdown in an irreversible fashion. The solar system is going through a process of slow decomposition, and life, no matter how beautiful or miserable, is destined to disappear into the indeterminateness of space and time. We are not sure how or when this may happen. We are almost certain that it will. The entropy theory is not some fantasy of a lunatic mind, but one of the most solid scientific hypotheses ever made.[3] It can be used to understand a large variety of phenomena: the decay of a car, the disorder of forty game cards or the aging of a fly. According to Romanian mathematician, Nicholas Georgescu-Roegen, the second law of thermodynamics can also contribute to explanations of the environmental impact of economic progress. In his book, *The Law of Entropy and Economic Process*, he explains that, although the entropy of the universe increases constantly because of some natural laws, rapid economic development speeds up the process of transformation of order into disorder through ecological degradation.[4] The implications of Georgescu-Roegen's ideas are stark: if we are to still consider this model of development as a form of progress, it is progress toward collapse.

Unlike the entropy of the universe, which increases inexorably regardless of what we do, the acceleration of environmental degradation is not determined by natural laws. It is largely under our control. It is influenced by the way we live, think and feel. It is affected by how much we consume, produce and invest. It is a by-product of how often we dissent, participate and vote. Almost everything we do can speed up or slow down the pace of ecological degradation. It is no coincidence that crises such as climate change and the rapid depletion of natural resources are occurring in combination with other symptoms of social breakdown: rising mental disorders, mindless consumerism, materialistic conformism, status competition, civic disengagement, startling economic inequalities, global financial instability and widespread political inertia. While these crises are usually studied in isolation, they are all interconnected. To some specialists, this claim may sound far-fetched. But this is only because they fail to connect the dots. Specialists have provided invaluable contributions to science, but they are often too attached to their microscopical views of society. They have the tendency "to know more and more about less and less until they know everything about nothing."[5] But to understand how the world works, we need to know more and more about more and more until we know something about everything.

Progress or Collapse is an irreverent journey through the multiple crises of this model of economic development. It is not an original study, but a work of synthesis. It is a conceptual blending of seemingly distant facts and factors. It is an attempt to put a wide variety of disciplines under the same theoretical roof. Drawing on a tapestry of knowledge from a wide range of social and natural sciences, the book provokes the reader to look at the big picture from a critical, lateral perspective.

Of course, in trying to cover all impending and converging crises, this project is set on an impossible task. Some serious global threats, such as the nuclear proliferation crisis, for example, have been left out. Ample details about the global crises described in this book have been omitted. Thoroughness has been sacrificed in the attempt to focus on the common roots of these crises. It required going beyond the analysis of phenomena accessible only to strict empirical investigation and dealing with a rather messy puzzle of information coming from diverse disciplines such as psychology, politics, economics, ecology and philosophy. This book sought to tie together concepts, which at first sight may appear unrelated, through an overarching, underlying theme. Of course, there are multiple underlying causes of these global crises. The assumption in this book is that these global crises are more systemic than specific. They are more societal than individual. And they are influenced by a model of economic progress which is guided by a pathological ideology: the market greed doctrine.

For the past three decades, global economic development has been dominated by a fanatic economic theory based on two articles of faith: the greed creed and the belief in the market God. The greed creed states that people are nothing but selfish profiteers in perpetual competition for profit and wealth. The belief in the market God is the conviction that all social and human affairs are best regulated as market exchanges. In the past, the adoption of the market greed doctrine as a main organizing principle for society has produced disastrous consequences: a notable example is the Great Depression that subsequently resulted in the Second World War. It is exactly for this reason that this ideology was somehow relegated into the tomb of history for more than two decades after the latter conflict. In the late 1970s, however, the market greed doctrine resurrected with a vengeance. First, it gained ground in the most advanced democracies: the US and the UK. Then, it went viral. The globalization of market greed contributed to further escalate the race for profit and wealth among states, companies and individuals. The fight for profit and markets has now become frantic, limitless and without borders.

Unsurprisingly, the past has repeated itself as a tragic farce, and the re-appointment of the market greed doctrine as a guiding philosophy of economic progress has produced, again, disastrous effects. The 2008 Great Recession is a case in point. But there are even more dangerous crises appearing on the horizon. One of them can even threaten our very residence on planet Earth. The environmental consequences of this model of development are now gathering in the air like the clouds of a coming storm. While the ice caps are melting and oil and other precious natural resources are being rapidly depleted, ecological disasters are occurring almost everywhere. From the catastrophic droughts in California and Australia to the devastating hurricanes in the Gulf of Mexico, from the gigantic flooding in Bangladesh to the mass burning of the Siberian and Amazonian forests, extreme events are becoming more violent and increasingly more threatening. Are these glimpses into the future to come?

It would be wrong, however, to assume that these ecological crises are the real causes of a possible future collapse of modern society. They are just symptoms. It is no coincidence that the ecological crises are occurring together with crises of another nature: psychological, social, cultural, civic, economic and political. While poverty has remained endemic and has continued to devastate the lives of countless individuals, especially in the developing world, the lives of people in the West and in emerging economies have been increasingly plagued with mental disorders, stress and alienation. Consumerism, status competition and materialistic values are shaping our lives, thoughts, feelings and behaviors like never before. Social relationships have become less genuine, more divisive and Machiavellian. Communities are increasingly anomic, fragmented and mostly deprived of any real sense of collective spirit. An increasing number of citizens have lost trust in governments, political elections and civic organizations. Many have retreated into their private lives to focus, almost exclusively, only on their everyday business. Inequalities in wealth are at historical heights. Financial instability reigns everywhere and nobody knows whether or when the Great Recession will end.

Worse, the world has plunged into a state of political inertia. Although the last decades have witnessed the spread of democracy to many developing countries, the rapid rise of wealth inequalities has undermined political equality everywhere. A plutocracy of powerful individuals, transnational corporations and financial institutions has accumulated immense economic and political power beyond measure. So much so that national and international policies have been increasingly affected by their vested interests. They are now largely at their mercy. Even within advanced democracies, institutions and politicians hardly act on the basis of public demands, and rather are compelled to serve the interests of those who finance them. So much so that even in advanced societies we are now living in what Greg Palast called "the best democracies money can buy."[6]

Under command of the market greed ideology, the system is now out of control. It is like a train, without a driver, heading toward a precipice. So far, there have been no serious attempts to change course, tackle the converging crises and prevent the risk of collapse. The race for profit and markets is so addictive that corporations, nations and individuals seem to prefer bargaining the future of the next generations to establishing some limits to indiscriminate pollution, economic growth and mindless consumerism. Large corporations are so blindly engaged in a borderless competition for profit that they can hardly pay any attention to social and ecological problems. Governments are paralyzed because of financial blackmail, while politicians seem too preoccupied with extending their privileges and power to worry about the crises and environmental destruction. People as well are too wholly absorbed in the everyday struggle for status and economic security, to be capable of compelling governments to tackle the crises of market greed. In a way, it appears that we are all captives of the imperatives within the system, subjugated by an ideology that prevents us from recognizing the new evolutionary challenges we now face. What is to be done to stop this system from spinning out of control toward disaster? How can we gain control of our society and overcome the global crises ahead? Can we really stop our progress toward collapse?

Although this book does not shy away from condemning the abuses of the market greed doctrine, it is not a critique of economic progress per se. After all, there is no use in attempting to turn back the wheels of history. Rather, the point is to shift them toward another trajectory. There is also no need to advocate for the abolition of markets, either. It is sufficient to make them to work for the pursuit of human goals. Decoupled from greed and guided by social and democratic priorities, markets can be instrumental to social wellbeing, human creativity and self-actualization. There is nothing necessarily wrong with economic progress and markets, however some reforms are urgently required if we desire to move away from the destructive path we are on. This book explores some of these options. Most recommendations are down-to-earth proposals for social change toward an ecologically sustainable and psychosocially fulfilling society. Largely, they derive from real-world examples that can be adapted and emulated. Certainly, this book is not a manifesto for a Bolshevik revolution. There is no use in trying to resuscitate ideologies for a perfectly egalitarian society that have already been buried by history. People are not saints and the Earth will never be transformed into a paradise – we must all know this by now. Nevertheless, an alternative model of development is necessary, not only if we hope to have a future, but also if we hope to have a future worth living.

On this front, only the most radical critics of capitalism have scrutinized the problems of our economy deeply enough to fully understand them. Most of them agree that the strongest argument against a society uniquely based on selfish interests and market exchanges is that it is not humanly interesting. People know that there is more to life than filling pockets with money and inflating egos with futile self-celebrations. They also understand that social relationships are not best regulated by market competition. Regardless of their religious or spiritual orientations, those who have studied the "art of living" well enough to understand it largely agree that personal fulfilment mostly relies on creativity, simplicity and generosity.

The apologists of the market greed doctrine claim that this model of economic progress is the only alternative we have. It is the only model that works because human beings are selfish competitors, uniquely devoted to maximizing their power and profit, they argue. This is not true, of course. Or better, it is not entirely true. Human nature is much more complex than that, and people are capable of exceptional acts of altruism and solidarity that do not fit with the idea of the Selfish Sapiens. Moreover, there are plenty of alternatives for a new society and a different model of economic progress, if we could only bother to try them.

Certainly, this book does not intend to be a compendium of pious illusions for social transformation. Reforms that are deep enough to divert our path away from the global crises we are facing require considerable political support that, in turn, depends on significant human emancipation. Political and personal changes of this magnitude hardly happen overnight. Looking at the world as it stands now, hopes for a swift shift in the fundamental aims of economic progress are rather slim. But there is something that can come to our rescue: human progress is often characterized by great leaps forward. It is a rather irregular, unsteady process of transformation, often characterized by exceptional advances. An epochal shift toward a new mode of progress is unlikely, but not impossible. All in all, we may already be at the front of a paradigm shift, if we really believe that change is possible. Social mutations are more likely to occur in times of crisis. The Greek word "crisis" means, in fact, decision: it is our choice to decide in which direction we go. It is up to us to resolve whether we prefer risking collapse to shifting society's direction toward human, rather than economic growth. But one thing must be clear: we can either have human progress or market greed, but not both.

1

A TURNING POINT OR A POINT OF NO RETURN?

At the dawn of human civilization, some million hunter-gatherers around the planet fought for their survival against ferocious animals, starvation and natural disasters. Thanks to their ability to tame and exploit their surrounding environment, they evolved and prospered. Throughout the millennia, they learned how to make fire, invented spears and arrows, and domesticated animals. They mastered the art of writing, discovered farming and gave birth to the first rudimentary forms of agricultural societies.

Then, came the Industrial Revolution. The horrible working conditions of child laborers, and the massive expropriations of lands from peasants, ruined the existence of countless people. But one thing is certain: without the industrial age, *Homo sapiens* would not have even dreamt of the health, wellbeing, comfort and sophistication enjoyed today. The breakthroughs that followed the Industrial Revolution were impressive: rising wealth, better nutrition, finer medical care, and wider access to goods, services, technologies and medicines. These transformations changed our lives forever. They also changed the way we see ourselves. They made us more confident, aware of our exceptional abilities to discover, create and innovate. They gave us a sense of new security and possibility. They also hooked into our mind an illusion: the thought of being unbeatable, unstoppable.

Overly conscious of our own powers, we have escalated the exploitation of the natural world beyond measure. And we have taken it too far. We are cutting down and burning enormous quantities of forest. We are denuding massive hectares of grasslands to feed our livestock. We are killing most of the wildlife, fish and other forms of biodiversity. We are eroding farmlands to the point of robbing them of their productive topsoil. We are rapidly depleting metals, minerals and other precious materials. We are consuming, wasting and polluting untold quantities of oil, plastic, water and food.

There are multiple ecological emergencies now casting a shadow over the future of our offspring: climate change, peak oil, water crises, and fish and food shortages. It is as if history has reached a turning point where our dream of unlimited progress is turning into a nightmare. Can this really be true?

Cooking up the planet

Some believe that all this is nonsense. They are the so-called environmental skeptics, or those that, for years, have belittled or even ridiculed evidence showing that, because of human activities, the temperature of the earth is getting too high. In 1997, pro-business magazine the *Wall Street Journal*, thundered: "Science Has Spoken: Global Warming Is A Myth."[1] In the United States, Republican Senator James Inhofe argued that "global warming is the greatest hoax ever perpetrated on the American people and the world."[2] Some years ago, the Competitive Enterprise Institute, a right-wing think tank funded by Exxon, aired two 60-second TV ads with the slogan: "CO_2: They Call It Pollution, We Call It Life." Similar claims are still widely heard today. As former wannabe presidential candidate Rick Santorum recently argued: "I have never believed in the 'hoax of global warming.'"[3]

Profusely paid by the fossil-fuel industry,[4] and widely covered by corporate media,[5] many environmental skeptics have grown in popularity in recent years. After the leaked emails scandal of the University of East Anglia Climatic Research Unit, also known as "Climategate," many critics were even more convinced that the science of climate change had been debunked. One wishes that they were right and that global warming is nothing but a fabrication. But it is hardly so. As David Biello wrote, in an editorial in *Scientific American*, "sadly for the potential fate of human civilization, rumors of the demise of climate change have been much exaggerated."[6] Now that massive catastrophic ecological events are multiplying before our eyes, planet heating is becoming more real than ever.

In the last decades, the number of extreme weather events has quintupled.[7] The intensity of hurricanes has sharply increased.[8][9] Since 1976, phenomena like El Niño have become more frequent: the average return decreased from 6 years per cycle to only 3.5 years.[10][11] Heat waves too seem to be becoming more and more dangerous. In 2003, Europe experienced at least 35,000 casualties due to extreme summer heat.[12] Exceptional weather events occur more frequently everywhere. In March 2004, for the first time in history, a hurricane hit Brazil on the South Atlantic coast.[13] In 2010, Russia experienced a fire that wiped out about 20 percent of its grain. That same year, about 1,500 people in Pakistan lost their lives, while half a million lost their homes, to one of the worst floods ever experienced. Although these disasters are disproportionately hitting the poor, and marginalized communities, they can occur virtually anywhere. Recent natural disasters in industrialized countries, such as horrific mudslides in California and the devastating Hurricane Katrina in New Orleans, as well as the worst floods ever recorded in English history, clearly show that there is no safe place to hide. We are all in the same boat. And, by the way, the boat is sinking.

Some scientists believe that extreme weather events are premonitions of how the future will look if the Earth's average temperature continues to rise.[11] Although it is too early to know whether this is true, there is little doubt that the global temperature has risen in an unprecedented way during the last century. Michael Mann, director of the Earth System Science Center at Pennsylvania State University, has investigated the trajectory of the Northern hemisphere's temperature over the last 1,000 years.[14] In a figure named the "hockey-stick," he showed a pattern of 900 years of little or no change, followed by a century characterized by a sharp, abrupt upturn in the average global temperature. Mann's chart provoked ferocious criticisms, not only fired by the skeptics funded by the fossil-fuel industry, but also by scientists criticizing his methods of analysis.[15] Condemnations of the hockey stick have been so serious that they even prompted an inquiry by the National Academy of Sciences. The results of the inquiry, however, supported Mann's general assertion: when considering the past millennium, the temperatures experienced in the Northern hemisphere during the late twentieth century were exceptionally hot.[16]

The warming of the Earth has been documented by numerous other analyses. Some of them are based on the direct planet-wide temperatures over the past 150 years. Available records indicate that 19 of the 20 average hottest years have occurred after the 1980s.[11] According to the National Oceanic and Atmospheric Administration (NOAA), the year 2010 was the warmest since records began.[17] What is more, each of the 10 warmest average global temperatures recorded since 1880 have occurred in the last 15 years. The deadly summer of 2003 was the hottest that Europe had experienced in 1,500 years.[18] In July 2005, the temperature at Ny-Alesund, a little town just 1,000 kilometers from the North Pole, hit a record temperature of 20°C.[11]

The Intergovernmental Panel on Climate Change (IPCC), a group of scientists comprised of the world's most respected experts on climate sciences, displays little hesitation. Already in 2007, their report concluded unambiguously: "warming of the climate system is unequivocal, is now evident from observations of increases in global average air and ocean temperatures, widespread melting of snow and ice, and rising global mean sea level."[19] Climate change is not a hoax. It is real. The planet is truly cooking up.

The slippery slope to hell

Some skeptics agree that planet Earth is warming up, but refuse to believe that human activities are responsible for it. For them, climate change is something attributable to natural phenomena. The skeptics' explanations for the increasing temperature of the Earth include adjustments in the geometry of the planet's orbit, changes in the radiation output of the sun and variations in the composition of the atmosphere. It is a pity – and not only for the skeptics – that none of these explanations has survived rigorous scientific scrutiny.[20] Several papers, including a 2006 study published in *Nature*, convincingly rejected the most popular of these explanations: that climate change is mainly due to variations of solar activities. As the authors of the study concluded: "variations in the sun's total energy output since 1978 are too small to have contributed appreciably to accelerate climate change in the last thirty years."[21] Most scientists, after all, show little disagreement. The most likely culprit for the warming of the planet and the rise of extreme events remains the massive increase of greenhouse gases (such as CO_2) in the atmosphere due to human activities. A scientific review of 928 articles on "climate change," which were published in major peer-reviewed journals over a 10 year period, concluded that "none of the papers disagreed with the consensus position": human activities are causing global warming.[22]

A key principle of the climate-change hypothesis was first proposed by John Tyndall more than a century and a half ago.[23] By studying the absorptive properties of various gases, Tyndall realized that transparent gases were largely responsible for the climate of the planet.[24] His work was later advanced by Svante Arrhenius, who, in the 1890s, investigated the peculiar ability of greenhouse gases to trap heat in the atmosphere.[25] The Swedish scientist demonstrated that greenhouse gases have very important properties; by partially blocking the radiation that the Earth continuously reflects back to space, they allow the sun's rays to heat up the planet. By trapping a portion of the radiation in the atmosphere, greenhouse gases warm it and thus contribute to increases in the Earth's temperature. Arrhenius' work helped us to understand one of the major reasons why we can live on the Earth's surface: the average temperature is about 20°C warmer than it would be without the greenhouse effect.[26] His research was ground-breaking in many respects and has contributed to our understanding of why, in the last few decades, the Arctic and the Antarctic have warmed up faster than any other places on earth.[11] More than a century ago, Arrhenius was already able to affirm that a doubling of CO_2 levels would cause a warming of around 5 or 6°C, a figure quite close to the maximum amount that the IPCC predicts the global temperature may rise by as we approach the end of the century.[19]

The scientific exploits of Tyndall and Arrhenius were later corroborated and expanded by several authors. In 1938, Guy Callendar estimated that a doubling of CO_2 could gradually bring a 2°C rise in the temperature.[23] In 1956, Gilbert Pass re-analyzed the mechanisms by which CO_2 traps heat in the atmosphere and warned that climate change could become a severe problem for future generations.[27] Charles Keeling then took on the task of proving that human activity is the main culprit behind the rise of atmospheric CO_2. In 1958, he started a project at the Mauna Loa volcano in Hawaii where, for the first time, CO_2 concentration levels were monitored continuously over time. In line with the predictions of Arrhenius and other scientists, Keeling detected a gradual year-on-year rise of CO_2 levels in the atmosphere and noted that human activities were raising the concentrations of CO_2 by roughly a third above pre-industrial levels.[28]

Since the pioneering efforts of Keeling and colleagues, an industrial amount of evidence has provided further scientific support to the climate-change hypothesis. In particular, ice cores from Antarctica, holding measurements that date back about 650,000 years, have provided compelling information confirming the validity of the relationship between changes in atmospheric concentration of CO_2 and temperature. They hold data covering six and a half cycles of ice ages and inter-glacials, showing that CO_2 levels and temperatures went up and down together like synchronized dancers.[29] During the last glaciation, the concentration of CO_2 was about 180 parts per million (ppm). It rose to 280ppm after the ice age ended, about 12,500 years ago. Since then, levels remained stable, until the Industrial Revolution when they started to increase, reaching 395ppm in 2012. A more recent study providing an 800,000-year reconstruction of the same variables confirmed these trends (see Figure 1.1).[30]

The significance of this research is startling. For a million years the Earth's climate has had just two states: glacial and inter-glacial – the 100,000-year cycles of ice ages and inter-glacials coincided with minor wobbles in the Earth's orbit. The glacial states have been anchored at CO_2 of roughly 180ppm, while the inter-glacial states have been anchored at about 280ppm.[11] Since the Industrial Revolution, however, human activities have increased the amount of CO_2 by 115ppm. Given that CO_2 levels have reached 395ppm, we have basically contributed to a change in the atmosphere almost larger than the one that usually occurs between an ice age and an inter-glacial. In other words, we are already moving into uncharted territory, a totally new state for planet Earth, or what Nobel-prize winning Paul Crutzen defined as the era of "Anthropocene."[31]

Scientists no longer have any doubt that the increase of 0.6–0.8°C in the average temperature over the last 150 years[19] is the consequence of two centuries of man-made excessive pollution and deforestation. As the IPCC report explained: "Global atmosphere concentrations of carbon dioxide, methane, and nitrous oxide have increased markedly as a result of human activities since 1750 and now far exceed pre-industrial values determined from ice cores spanning many thousands of years."[19]

The IPCC, repeatedly attacked by the skeptics, is not alone in its view. The same conclusion has been endorsed by at least 30 scientific societies, including every one of all the national academies of science in major industrialized countries. Among them, we find the US National Academy of Sciences,[32] the American Meteorological Society,[33] the American Geophysical Union[34] and the American Association for the Advancement of Science.[35] The only exception is the American Association of Petroleum Geologists, of course.[36] Other organizations that disagree with the general consensus include the Science and Environmental Policy Project, the Center for the Study of Carbon Dioxide and Global Change and the George Marshall Institute – all of which receive funding from the oil industry. In fact, their conflict of interest is so wildly apparent that most scientists hardly take them seriously.

What most scientists take very seriously instead are the long-term consequences of climate change, for at least two reasons. First, if CO_2 levels co-vary with temperatures, further increases of CO_2 in the atmosphere will lead to additional rises in the global temperature.[29] Second, the concentration of CO_2 in the atmosphere keeps rising by approximately 20ppm a decade. This means that, in the absence of drastic

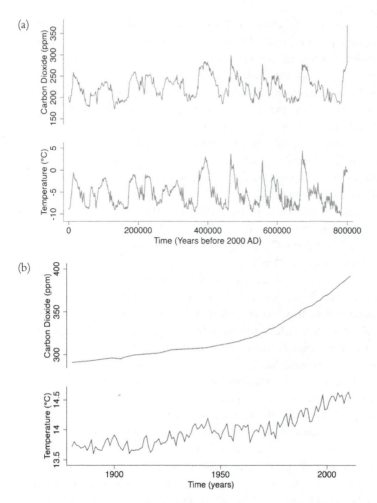

FIGURE 1.1 The road to hell: carbon dioxide concentration and average temperature in the 800,000 years before 2000 (a) and between 1880 and 2011 (b)

Sources: European Project for Ice Coring in Antarctica (2010), the National Oceanic and Atmospheric Administration Earth System Research Laboratory (2012) and the Institute for National Aeronautics and Space Administration (2012).

change, CO_2 is expected to rise to 600ppm or more by the end of the century. If the least optimistic predictions of the IPCC are correct, by this time, planet Earth will experience the same temperature rise that usually occurs between an ice age and an inter-glacial.[19]

What would be the effects of this drastic temperature rise on people's lives and planet Earth? Most likely devastating. Climate scientists have advised that we aim to stop average global temperatures from rising more than 2°C above the pre-industrial levels. The "roof" of 2°C, they believe, is the "critical threshold" of irreversible change,[37] [38] the point after which some of the larger, sudden and unpredictable impacts on the planet are expected to occur. Unless we reduce CO_2 emissions by 90 percent, this point can be reached by the year 2030.[39] As Jim Hansen, former NASA specialist and George Bush's top climate scientist once put it, we are "on the slippery slope to hell."[40]

Points beyond redemption

In spite of the wide scientific support it has gained, the climate change hypothesis continues to be welcomed with derision, not only by the skeptics, but also by powerful economic and political sectors within society. Corporate media pundits often portray the climate-change debate as controversial, by depicting a deceptive impression of weak or inconclusive scientific consensus. An analysis of articles which were published about climate change in the most influential American newspapers (the *New York Times*, the *Washington Post*, the *LA Times* and the *Wall Street Journal*) from 1988 to 2002, showed that more than half of the articles have cast doubts over the actual cause of climate change.[5] The profound knowledge gap between scientists and public opinion was also made quite apparent by a survey involving 3,146 scientists, which showed that while 97.4 percent of climatologists who regularly publish research on climate change agreed that "human activity is a significant contributing factor in changing mean global temperatures," only 58 percent of the general public who participated in an opinion poll were in accord with this statement.[41]

In-between the consensus of climate scientists and the dismissive stance of the skeptics, there is another view, which hardly appears on mainstream media: the position of climate scientists who believe that the scientific consensus on global warming is based on estimates which are far too conservative. For example, an article published in *Nature* in 2005 argued that the doubling of CO_2 concentrations could lead to a temperature increase up to 11.5°C by the end of the century,[42] a much higher estimate than the 6.4°C rise endorsed by the IPCC. Among the climate scientists whose views are rarely covered by mainstream media, there are also those who claim that, even assuming we were to completely stop emitting CO_2 into the atmosphere, the modifications we have already produced are sufficient to generate irreversible climate effects. Supporters of this opinion corroborate it with evidence that the amount of greenhouse gases we have released in over a century will persist in the atmosphere for the next two centuries anyway.[43] As Michael Mann put it, "we are already committed to 50 to 100 years of warming and several centuries of sea-level rises, simply from the amount of greenhouse gases we have already put in the atmosphere."[44]

Some climate scientists also question the validity of mainstream models which assume only gradual changes in the temperature that are proportional to the increase of CO_2 levels for a very simple reason. They suspect the existence of "threshold effects," or radical changes that suddenly occur once a critical line is crossed. These "positive feedbacks" are activated by factors which once altered by climate change, in turn, amplify and reinforce climate change. Historical evidence demonstrates that, in the past, cases of widespread climate change have not followed gradual patterns of modification, but rather have occurred with startling speed. In the Northern hemisphere, half of the temperature changes that have happened since the last ice age occurred in only a decade. As Richard Alley put it, "it is as if climate change were a light switch instead of a dimmer dial."[45] The trouble with these threshold effects of runaway change is that, once trespassed, they are not amenable to interventions of any kind. They are points "beyond which there is no redemption."[40]

On the shoulders of awakening eco-giants

The positive feedbacks that can make climate change irreversible have been visualized by some scientists as the "sleeping giants" of our ecosystem.[46] The only problem with this definition is that they are awakening. There are a number of these "giants," the most consequential being the melting of the ice caps. The disintegration of the Arctic and Antarctica appears to be governed by non-linear responses characterized by exponential increases in the loss of ice, once a certain breaking point is surpassed. This rapid increase occurs because of retroactive loops: the melting of the ice that is induced by the rise of the temperature in the poles creates additional, localized warming that, in turn, leads to even more ice loss. It is exactly for this reason that climate change is particularly amplified in the poles, as demonstrated by the 2–3°C increase in Arctic air temperatures over the past 30 years, which is several times higher than the global average change.

A number of climatologists believe that the melting of the Arctic ice has already passed the critical threshold of irreversible change. Between 1979 and 2003, the Arctic ice shrank by about 20 percent, an area corresponding roughly to that of Texas.[47] In 2005, a group of 21 glaciologists published a gloomy statement in *Eos*, a publication of the American Geophysical Union, which argued that the Arctic system will soon experience ice-free summers, "a state not witnessed for at least a million years."[48] According to some estimates, that are even more discouraging, we can expect the Arctic to completely melt down by 2020. This would be catastrophic not only for the polar bears, but also for the entire ecosystem. The ice of the Arctic covers an area equal to that of the United States and serves as a white reflector for the summer sunlight that falls upon it. It functions as the air-conditioning of the Earth: without the reflective shield of its ice, the whole world would warm by some more degrees.

If the situation in the Arctic is far from rosy, Antarctica does not fare much better. According to Chris Rapley, the West Antarctic Ice Sheet is on a one-way trip toward disintegration. This is not a claim to be taken lightly since this sheet contains sufficient water to raise sea levels by more than 3 meters, enough to inundate New York, London and Tokyo.[49]

Greenland also finds itself in a dire situation. According to Jonathon Gregory and colleagues, if global temperatures rise by more than 2.7°C, the Greenland glacier will enter a phase of instability and will continue to melt until most of it is gone, even if the temperature and CO_2 levels subsequently fall below the threshold of safety.[50] There is some good news, however: some scientists argue that the process can take a very long time, probably thousands of years. Unfortunately, these experts do not take into account either the existence of rivers, or the water flowing across the Greenland ice sheet that causes breaks in its surface. Richard Alley does. As he puts it:

> we used to think that it would take 10,000 years for melting at the surface to penetrate down to the bottom of the ice sheet. But if you make a lake on the surface and a crack opens and the water goes down the crack, it does not take 10,000 years, it takes seconds.[51]

While the Arctic, Antarctica and Greenland are "endangered," an increasing number of mountain glaciers are "committed to extinction." They are retreating virtually everywhere. In Africa, about 90 percent of the ice on Mt. Kilimanjaro has already melted away. In Europe, large glaciers such as "Mer de Glace" have retreated considerably. In Patagonia and in the Himalayas too glaciers are shrinking or disappearing at a worrisome speed.[52]

Another non-linear response to climate change, governed by trigger points and positive feedbacks, is the rise of the world's oceans. While the world's sea levels have been relatively stable for the last five thousand years, they have started to increase quite rapidly in the last decades.[53] The reasoning is simple: if the water becomes warmer and the world glaciers and ice caps melt down, sea levels rise. This is a problem for several reasons. Apart from causing coastal erosion, higher tides are also pushing salt water into fields and underground freshwater reservoirs. If current sea levels increase by more than 40 centimeters, the number of people in danger of saltwater floods, resulting from storm surges, could increase to 200 million.[54] The rise of the oceans will also cause salt water to pollute the drinking water of many major cities including Shanghai, Manila, Jakarta, Bangkok and Buenos Aires.[55] The IPCC predicted a rise in sea levels of up to 59 centimeters by the end of the century.[19] However, a paper published by a team of climatologists led by James Hansen at NASA suggested that the IPCC's prediction might, in fact, be too optimistic. Hansen argues that there is a historical precedent that can inform our understanding of what the rise of oceans is likely to be, if current trends in temperature persist: 3.5 million years ago, when temperatures were 2–3°C higher than they are today, sea levels increased by 25 meters, not 59 centimeters.[56] If a 3 meter sea-level rise can inundate New York, London and Tokyo, how many cities will go under water with a 25 meter increase?

The most paradoxical of all positive feedbacks that can make climate change irreversible is the modification of the oceans' circulatory systems. Scientists have long warned that the current climate conditions in the North Atlantic may depend on the presence of arctic conditions near Greenland. The melting of Greenland, therefore, can produce large changes to the ocean's circulation pattern, including a blockade of the Gulf Stream. If this happens, Northern Europe might no longer prosper from the benefits that this stream of warm water brings. While the tropics would become much hotter, this region may experience a return to Arctic conditions. Currently, Northern Europe is about 8°C warmer than regions occupying the same latitudes in other parts of the world. As Richard Alley once argued, this is a difference that allows "Europeans to grow roses farther North than Canadians meet polar bears."[57] The Gulf Stream has shut down in the past, an event that made the temperature of Northern Europe decrease by 5°C, on average. Apart from the devastating consequences that a repeat of this event may create, another concern is that it took about 1,300 years for the Gulf Stream to recover from the first time that this occurred.[7] As Peter deMenocal argues, a shift in the ocean conveyor, once initiated, is essentially irreversible over a time period of many decades to centuries.[11] A study published in 2005 showed that, since the mid-1990s, the flow of water north of the Gulf Stream into the North Atlantic faltered by 30 percent.[58] However, follow up studies have not confirmed the hypothesis that the Gulf Stream has been slowing down in recent years.[59] And this is good news.

Another awakening eco-giant can be found in the forests of the Amazon. The Amazon is called "the lung of the earth" for a very good reason. It is, after all, the largest living reservoir of CO_2 on the land surface of the Earth. The Amazon also serves as a major engine of the world's climate system, since it recycles both heat and moisture. It has been estimated that trees in some parts of the forest are responsible for as much as 74 percent of local rainfall.[60] As Fred Pearce, author of *The Last Generation* explains, "more than half of the raindrops that fall on the forest canopy never reach the ground, but instead evaporate back into the air to produce more rain downwind." However, as forests start to die from the temperature increases, less water is released into the air, which further escalates the disappearance of trees. The consequence is an increased risk of drought, which may be followed by fires, triggering even more deforestation. Based on the work of forest ecologist Dan Nepstad, Pearce observes: "beyond a certain point, the forest . . . will begin a process of rapid drying" that will result in the overall "savanization" of the Amazon.[61]

The shriveling and dying of plants in massive quantities has the potential to produce disastrous consequences, not only for the inhabitants and eco-diversity of the Amazon itself, but also for the entire world. The reason is simple: when the trees of the Amazon rot or burn, they start to release CO_2 back into the atmosphere. In this case, the Amazon will go from being a store for to an emitter of CO_2. Researchers estimate that the Amazon alone has the potential to release about 10 percent of manmade CO_2 emissions.[62] As a result, the overall temperature of the Earth would increase dramatically.

However, deforestation is obviously not limited to the Amazon: half of the world's tropical and temperate forests are already gone[63] and the rate of deforestation in the tropics continues at about an acre a second.[64] It is predicted that by about 2040, most forests will start to release more CO_2 than they absorb. This means that, before the end of the century, the world's soils may eject the manmade carbon which they have absorbed for the past 150 years.[65] Several climate models estimate that droughts in the Amazon will increase in the future. According to researchers at University College London and the Met Office, "the Amazonian forest is currently near its critical resiliency threshold."[66] Deborah Clark, one of the world's top forest ecologists, holds the same view. As she puts it, "the lock has broken" and now the Amazon "is headed in a terrible direction."[67]

Another natural phenomenon altered by climate change and governed by threshold effects and positive feedbacks is the melting of permafrost and the consequential release of methane that, in turn, contributes to further warming and melting of more permafrost. Permafrost consists of thick layers of frozen peat containing tens of billions of tons of carbon. Potentially, this peat holds a quarter of all the carbon absorbed by soils and vegetation on the land surface of the Earth since the last ice age. Therefore, scientists fear that as the permafrost begins to melt away, the world's largest carbon sink could turn into the world's largest carbon source.[11] The National Center for Atmospheric Research estimated that 90 percent of the top 10 feet of permafrost throughout the Arctic could thaw by 2100.[68] As stated by Fred Pearce, global warming could trigger nature's own "doomsday machine," which currently lies beneath largely inhabited land in Western Siberia. The West Siberian bog alone could contain up to 70 billion tons of gas,[69] which when freed would equate to 73 years of current manmade CO_2 emissions.[7] The melting of the permafrost could be catastrophic for it would release methane, which has a warming effect 23 times greater than that of CO_2.[70] [71]

The awakening giants of the eco-system – the runaway melting of ice caps, the rise of the world's oceans, changes to the ocean circulation systems, carbon releases from the forests and soil, and methane releases from the receding permafrost – are all factors that can change the estimates of planet Earth's future fever. Although they all hold consequences that are potential surprises, they do not appear to be good ones. In fact, it is quite the opposite. Some believe that they can provoke geological events large enough to make the planet uninhabitable by human beings. As written in the final declaration of the Toronto Conference on the Changing Atmosphere in 1985, humanity seems to have engaged in an "uncontrolled globally pervasive experiment" whose consequences can be "second only to nuclear war."[72]

Peak all: is the party over?

The disastrous ecological effects of human activities include not only pollution-induced climate change, but also the rapid exhaustion of natural resources. Since the days in which Reverend Thomas Malthus predicted, incorrectly, mass famine for all humanity, many authors have wondered whether exponential growth of resource usage can be sustained in the future. More than 40 years ago the Club of Rome, a global think tank dedicated to international political issues, attempted to provide an answer. In 1972, Donella and Dennis Meadows published *The Limits to Growth* and argued that, if trends in population growth, industrialization, pollution, food production and resource depletion remained unchanged, the limits to economic growth could be reached in one hundred years time: more or less by 2070.

According to the Meadows, the limits to growth will materialize in sudden and rampant declines in both population and industrial capacity.[73]

Free market economists, neo-conservative think tanks and large corporations dismissed the report and ridiculed the authors as "doomsday prophets." Corporate media led many to believe, including some environmental activists, that the Meadows inaccurately predicted the exhaustion of natural resources by the end of the last century. A precocious George Bush felt obliged to dismiss the study's findings in 1992, eight years before the beginning of the new millennium. In one of his speeches, he declaimed: "Twenty years ago some spoke of limits to growth. But today we know that growth is the engine of change. Growth is the friend of the environment." Ten years later, Exxon Mobil echoed the same view:

> In 1972, the Club of Rome published *Limits to Growth* questioning the sustainability of economic and population growth. *Limits to Growth* estimated that by now we would begin to see declines in food production, population, energy availability and life expectancy. None of these developments has even begun to occur, nor is there any immediate prospect that they will. So the Club of Rome was wrong.[74]

It is a pity that the Meadows did not predict the collapse of the global ecosystem by the year 2000, as the critics maintained. In reality, the authors remained cautiously vague about indicating exactly when natural resources would start to run out. It is still impossible to know whether the Meadows got it right or wrong; perhaps, we will within the next decades. What we know, however, is that consumption of fossil fuels is skyrocketing, pollution of rivers and lakes is widespread, deforestation is continuing unabated, soils are becoming less fertile and overfishing is out of control. The clear impression is that humanity is overshooting the natural limits of the ecosystem beyond irreversibility. But, of course, let us hope that Bush and Exxon Mobil got it right.

Peak oil

Unlike the members of the Club of Rome, a number of writers are convinced that the depletion of natural resources including oil, water and food will never become a problem either in the next 60 years, or in the future. Some even venture to say that the shrinking of natural resources is nothing more than a story fabricated by governments and environmentalists to control and manipulate people's behavior. Lindsay Williams, author of the *Energy Non-Crisis*, is one of them. He argues: "There is no true energy crisis. There never has been an energy crisis . . . except as it has been produced by the Federal government for the purpose of controlling the American people."[75] This is hard to believe: the most vocal concerns over the rapid depletion of fossil fuels do not come from governments, but from energy specialists and independent researchers. Two of them are Colin Campbell, author of *The Coming Oil Crisis*,[76] and Richard Heinberg, author of *The Party is Over*.[77] In their opinion, humanity will soon enter a historical turning point characterized by energy scarcity due to the decline of cheap oil. The reason is simple. The biggest oil fields in the world were discovered more than half a century ago. Since then, there have been a few more discoveries, but none have been as important. The last major discoveries of oil occurred a bit more than a quarter of century ago.[78] As Francis Harper of the Energy Institute observed:

> Worldwide the frequency of finding giant oil provinces and super-giant oilfields has been declining for decades and will not be reversed. We have looked around the world many times. I would say there is no North Sea out there. There certainly is not a Saudi Arabia.[79]

Jeff Rubin, author of *Why Your World Is About To Get A Whole Lot Smaller,* fully agrees. In his view, the world is scratching the bottom of the barrel. As he put it, "if oil sands in Alberta (and deep water oil drilling in the Gulf of Mexico) are more enticing than the next option, one can only imagine the difficulties with what lies next on the list of future oil sources to exploit."[80] Even the International Energy Association (IEA), who once dismissed peak oil whistle-blowers as "doomsayers," has finally joined the choir of Cassandra: "although global oil production in total is not expected to peak before 2030, production of conventional oil . . . is projected to level off toward the end of the projection period."[81]

If even the IEA is accepting the idea of the imminent end of cheap oil, we are probably in deep trouble. Industrial civilization can hardly make it without cheap fossil fuels. Nearly everything we do depends on its availability; 90 percent of all our transportation, 95 percent of all goods in shops and 95 percent of all our food.[78][82] Worse, as newly industrializing countries such as China, India and Brazil require more energy to run their economies and emulate the consumption patterns of the West, oil consumption is expected to sharply increase in the near future. What does this mean? It is difficult to say. It is likely that the increasing demand for oil, together with the prospect of shrinking supply, will generate financial shocks of global proportions.[83] As Campbell argues, once the market recognizes the depletion of cheap oil, it will send harsh signals to the world economy resulting in escalating cycles of economic crises, from which recovery will be difficult. As he put it: "There will be panic. The market over-reacts to even small imbalances. We will enter a volatile epoch of price shocks and recessions in increasingly vicious circles."[84]

Unfortunately, there is little time left to tackle the problem because we have already wasted a lot of it. The theory predicting the end of cheap oil was proposed way back in 1956 by Marion Huppert. During a meeting of the American Petroleum Institute, he forecasted that oil production would have "peaked" in the "lower 48" states of America in five years. Huppert understood that oil is a finite resource, making unrestrained consumption impossible. He envisioned the decline of daily production of oil as inevitable. At the time that Huppert presented his theory, the scientific community ridiculed him. However, in the last decades, quite in line with what he initially forecasted, country after country has followed a crude bell curve in both oil discovery and production. About 60 of the 65 countries possessing oil have passed their discovery peak, while 49 of them have already passed their production peak.[83][85] One of these countries, of course, is the United States (see Figure 1.2).

At the time of Huppert's warning, modern society still had a window of opportunity to plan and begin a gradual transition from an economy based on fossil fuels to a new one rooted on renewable energies. However, this window has almost closed. Western political leaders, under the shadow of financial black-mailing from oil industries and oil-producing countries, have preferred to deny the undeniable. Of course, Huppert could not expect oil industries and oil-producing countries to cooperate and contribute to disseminating the news that the end of their primary source of profit was near. He must have known that those who would know the most about the lifespan of oil reserves are exactly those who have the strongest interest in telling us the least. The last thing fossil-fuel industries want is to create panic among investors and damage business confidence in the oil market system. Oil-producing countries such as Saudi Arabia cannot afford to tell the truth either. By providing honest information on the shrinking of oil production and discovery, they would produce a wave of hysteria in the indus-trialized world and trigger an economic crisis of abominable proportions at home – no way. The problem is that the cover-up strategy only works in the short term. In the long run, information about the decreasing oil supply will inevitably surface and will affect the market, no matter what the stakeholders wish to conceal. The market panic cannot be prevented, but only postponed.

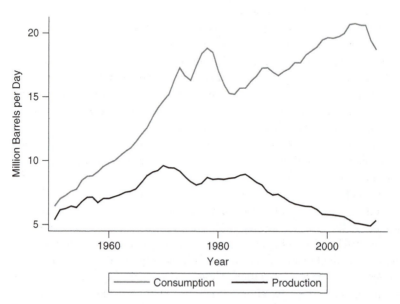

FIGURE 1.2 At the end of the pipeline: oil consumption and production in the United States, 1950–2009

Sources: US Department of Energy (2010) and the Energy Information Administration (2010).

Peak food, fish and water

It is true that the climate crisis and the looming end of cheap oil are casting ominous shadows upon the future of modern civilization. But even more troubles lie ahead. The exponential increases of economic development, consumption and population size are depleting the reserves of other key natural resources indispensable for human survival, including food, fish and water, for example.

Let us start with food. For many years, agricultural productivity represented the cornerstone of unlimited economic growth and consumption. The impressive breakthroughs in agricultural production have allowed humanity to feed increasing numbers of people worldwide and overcome food shortages. Yet, the increase of food production has come almost entirely from yield increases, rather than from expansion of land. American farmers produced four times their own consumption in 1820; this figure increased to eight times by 1987.[86] The rise of food productivity continued until the late 1980s when the trend started to reverse. While grain production peaked in about 1985, it has been slowly falling ever since.[87] Between 1984 and 1992, there was a 6 percent decline in grain output per person. In the three years following, the world produced less grain than it consumed.[88] Although there is still enough food to feed everyone on the planet, the peaks of food production constitute a serious threat to the future of human civilization, especially as the world's population continues to expand. The depletion of grain, which comprises approximately half of the world's agricultural output (measured in calories)[89] has the ability to produce devastating effects on poor countries. This problem can be severely exacerbated by the effects of climate change. The International Rice Research Institute found that rice yields fall by 15 percent with each temperature degree increase.[90] The Food and Agriculture Organization (FAO) has warned that in about 40 poor countries, with a combined population of 2 billion people, crop production losses due to climate change may drastically increase the number of malnourished people worldwide.[91] Moreover, as highlighted by John Gossop in *Famine in the West*, food shortages can threaten the future of affluent societies as well. In his opinion, the entire world is losing over 20 million acres of productive land each year due to desertification, salinization, as well as paving over for urban sprawl, industry and roads.[92]

While supplies of grain, corn and rice are becoming more constrained, the world's major fishing grounds are being exploited beyond their sustainable yields. This has been reported by numerous studies, some of which are covered in *The End of the Line: How Overfishing is Changing the World and What We Eat.*[93] Fish from the seas, rivers and lakes have been a vital part of the human diet for thousands of years. However, in the last century the world's fish catch has increased dramatically – from 22 million tons in 1950 to 101 million in 1994, a rate of 4 percent per annum. Since 1998, in some of the best-known fisheries worldwide, the total fish catch has collapsed. Atlantic stocks of blue fin tuna have fallen by 94 percent. An estimated 90 percent of the large predator fish including swordfish and marlin are gone; meanwhile 75 percent of marine fisheries are over-fished or fished to capacity.[94] A meta-analysis including dozens of studies on biodiversity loss in the ocean eco-systems, which was published in *Science* in 2006, concluded that if fishing around the world continues at its current pace, there will be a "global collapse" of all species in a few decades.[95] The analysts showed that 29 percent of fish stocks have sunk to, or fallen below, 10 percent of their 1950 levels. If fishing practices do not change, all stocks will decline by 90 percent before 2048. Although scientists say that it is not too late to turn this situation around, leading author Boris Worm warned: "we are seeing the bottom of the barrel. Once we do, we will not have a second chance; the situation will be irreversible."[96]

Not only are oil and food productions shrinking, but also the availability of freshwater. It has been estimated that, between 1960 and 2000, freshwater with-drawals doubled globally. Unsustainable groundwater use occurs on every continent except Antarctica.[97] Throughout the twentieth century, water withdrawals rose roughly twice as fast as the population, but the curve of withdrawal is already beginning to slow markedly and is even turning downward in some places. It is expected that increased water scarcity will make withdrawal level off or even drop. In the United States, after doubling approximately every 20 years throughout the twentieth century, water withdrawal peaked around 1980 and has since fallen by about 10 percent.[89] In some cases, water withdrawals are so high in relation to supply, that surface water supplies are literally shrinking and groundwater reserves are being depleted faster than they can be replenished by precipitation.[98] The channels of the Colorado, Yellow, Nile, Ganges, Indus, Chao Phraya, Syr Darya and Amu Darya Rivers are running dry for some or all of the year, due to withdrawal from growing cities and their irrigation demands.[89] It has been estimated that irreversible human withdrawal of water (due to removal without return and incor-poration into crops or products), together with the loss of water to dilution and removal of pollution, add up to 6,780 km^3 of water per year. This is just over half the total sustainable freshwater runoff. If, as expected, the human population grows to 9 billion by the year 2050, humans would need to withdraw 10,200 km^3 per year. This would constitute 82 percent of the global sustainable freshwater runoff.[99] However, if we consider the enormous increase of water demand per capita that will likely occur due to both the continuously increasing consumption of rich countries and the betterment of living standards in the developing world, these figures can be even higher. If so, there will be severe global water limits long before the end of century.

It is estimated that about one-third of the world's population already live in countries that are experiencing moderate to high water stress. But according to some estimates, by 2025 as much as two-thirds of the world population will be under water stress conditions.[100] While contamination and human consumption of water supplies is clearly unsustainable, global warming is shifting the situation from bad to worse. It has been estimated that a rise of just 2.1°C will expose between 2.3 and 3 billion people to the risk of water shortages.[101] Water is the most essential and least substitutable of all natural resources. Its scarcity has important effects on other natural resources including food, energy, fish and wildlife. According to the United Nations

Environment Program, the World Bank and the World Resources Institute, the world's thirst for water is likely to become one of the most pressing issues of the twenty-first century. As the authors of the documentary *Blue Gold: World Water Wars* argue, the planet's dwindling water supplies can end up triggering very serious problems for the future of civilization. "At the worst, a deepening water crisis would fuel violent conflicts," wrote the editors of the *New York Times*.[102]

Endangered species

For many years, environmentalists have warned that, if the current trends of pollution and exploitation of natural resources continue, an increasing number of species will disappear from the face of the Earth. Some will go extinct forever. Although there are no precise estimates of how many species there are in the world and how many have already been lost,[103] available evidence seems to indicate that "mass extinction" is well under way. According to the World Wide Fund for Nature (WWF), the *Living Planet Index*, an indicator of the world's biological diversity status, showed an overall decline of biodiversity by more than 30 percent between 1970 and 2000.[104] The planet has not experienced such a high rate of extinction in 65 million years, more or less since the dinosaurs disappeared.[105] The estimated rates of extinction are now 1,000 times that of what they would be without human impact.[106] About 24 percent of the world's 4,700 mammal species, 30 percent of the 25,000 fish species, and 12 percent of the world's nearly 10,000 bird species are already in danger of extinction. Unsurprisingly, climate change is escalating these trends even more. According to a 2004 article published in *Nature*, if temperatures rise to the expected range, between 15 and 37 percent of the world's species will disappear by 2050.[107] It has been estimated that a rise of 2°C in temperature will potentially lead to devastating effects for sea life,[108] [7] coral reefs[50] and may also result in the disappearance of endangered species like polar bears.[50] But what about *Homo sapiens*? Will the rapid decline of biodiversity affect us?

The extinction of the human species may appear as something quite remote and fantastic, if not impossible. Yet, if the global temperature increases by the upper limit IPCC prediction of 6.4°C by the end of the century, such possibility can become a reality. In a book entitled *When Life Nearly Died*, Michael Benton[109] describes the end-Permian extinction, which occurred about 251 million years ago. This catastrophe left the planet with only 4–10 percent of its previous species. According to Benton, the Permian mass extinction occurred after the release of massive quantities of CO_2 resulting from several volcanic eruptions in Siberia. The subsequent increase in the planet's temperature caused the release of an enormous quantity of methane from the permafrost in the Polar regions – one of the awakening "eco-giants" – which led to an additional increase in the global temperature. The emissions of greenhouse gases and the temperature of the Earth increased together in a feedback loop. The result was the biggest mass extinction ever experienced in world history. Plant life was almost eliminated from the Earth's surface and so were the four-footed animals. The global temperature had risen by about 5–6°C; yes, more or less, the upper limit foreseen by the IPCC to transpire by the end of this century if current trends in carbon emissions persist.[7]

However, if we take decisive action against climate change, or we are simply luckier, we may avoid the worst-case scenario or human extinction. Even so, if the processes that promote the overexploitation of natural resources, population growth and consumption continue unabated, we potentially face economic crises, social unrest and even wars. In 1987, a study entitled *Global Environment Outlook* conducted by the United Nations Environment Program (UNEP) and involving about 1,400 scientists found that human consumption is outstripping available resources. Each person on earth now requires a third more land to supply his or her needs than the planet can supply. As the executive director of the program admitted, "the systematic destruction of the Earth's natural and nature-based resources has reached a point where the economic viability of economies is being challenged – and where the bill we hand to our children may prove impossible to pay."[110] A few years later, a manifesto called *World's Scientists Warning to Humanity* signed by more than 1,600 scientists including 102 Nobel laureates, argued that, "human beings and the natural world are on a collision course. Fundamental changes are urgent if we are to avoid the collision that our present course will bring about."[111] More recently, some other scientists have expressed much less optimism about the possibility of avoiding it. At the release of the 30-year update of *The Limits to Growth*, the authors observed: "sadly, we believe the world will experience overshoot and collapse in global resource use and emissions . . . the collapse will arrive very suddenly, much to everyone's surprise."

> Once the concept of collapse was unthinkable. Now it has begun to enter the public discourse, though still as a remote, hypothetical, and academic concept. We think it will take another decade before the consequences of overshoot are clearly observable and two decades before the fact of overshoot is generally acknowledged.[89]

The great collision

It is typical for free market economists to assume that the resources of the Earth are limitless and the worldwide rise of living standards is the key to sustainable development. According to this view, endless economic growth is not a recipe for global ecological collapse, but instead an essential pre-condition for environmental protection. In *In Defense of Global Capitalism*, Johan Norberg explains: "a country that is very poor is too preoccupied with lifting itself out of poverty to bother about the environment at all," but "when [countries] grow richer, they start to regulate effluent emissions, and when they have still more resources they also begin regulating air quality."[112] Here Norberg sums up the conventional "wisdom" of free market economists who argue that economic growth provides the conditions in which protection of the environment can best be ensured. As the editors of *The Economist* put it, "everywhere, the adoption of more demanding environmental standards gathers pace as income rises."[113] In their view, the fact that in rich societies reductions in air and water pollution have simultaneously occurred with increases of GDP per capita,[114] is sufficient evidence for the validity of their hypothesis.

Rich countries have indeed greatly improved their environmental standards and have overcome many of the ecological problems that are currently being experienced in the developing world. Just to take an example, sulfur levels in the American air went down dramatically in the last decades and lead levels even more.[115] Safety and environmental regulations have also seen continuous improvement during the past few years. Does this mean that, as they develop, China and India will progressively improve their pollution standards too? Possibly. But free market economists entirely miss the point. Pollution is much more a problem of scale, than quality. As noted by Bill McKibben in *Deep Economy*, some of the most urgent ecological problems are not due to pollution caused by "doing something badly," but by pollution caused by "doing too much of something."[116] As people and countries become wealthier they consume and waste more, which produces more pollution, not less. Bigger houses, larger cars, more food and travel in China and India will propel an ecological overshoot, not a sustainable world. No matter how good environmental standards may become, increased consumption means increased energy use produced by burning coal, oil and natural gas that, in turn, means increased carbon emission per capita. It is true that more wealth may bring better energy efficiency; but it is also true that wealthier nations require higher energy consumption and carbon emissions than poorer ones.

The other problem is that the planet is becoming more and more crowded. At the beginning of the nineteenth century, there were about 1 billion people living on the Earth.[117] Now, there are about 7 billion, and the population is forecast to reach about 9 billion by 2050.[118] At the same time, people in low- and middle-income countries aspire to a Western standard of living. This is understandable, but the global pursuit of the American dream is unrealistic. The world simply cannot afford 9 billion "cowboys." The reason is quite straightforward. Exponential growth in population, economic development and consumption are associated with exponential increases in pollution and depletion of natural resources.[119] Consider, for example, the worldwide trends over time in population size, GDP per capita, cropland and pasture use, and water withdrawal, from year 0 to the end of the last century: interestingly, all of these variables showed similar patterns of change characterized by sharp increases of quantities after the Industrial Revolution, after about 1800 years of moderate or no growth (see Figure 1.3).

These growth patterns cannot continue indefinitely. The current model of economic development is based on sustaining infinite growth in a finite planet. But this is impossible, of course. Indeed, as Einstein once observed: "Only two things are infinite: human stupidity and the Universe, and I am not sure about the Universe." In a seminal 1968 paper entitled *The Tragedy of the Commons,* Garrett Hardin explained that the "wish to maintain absolute constancy in a system is deeply pathological," and will inevitably lead to catastrophic consequences.[120] [121] In the opinion of the author of *The Bridge at the End of the World*, James Gustav Speth, the

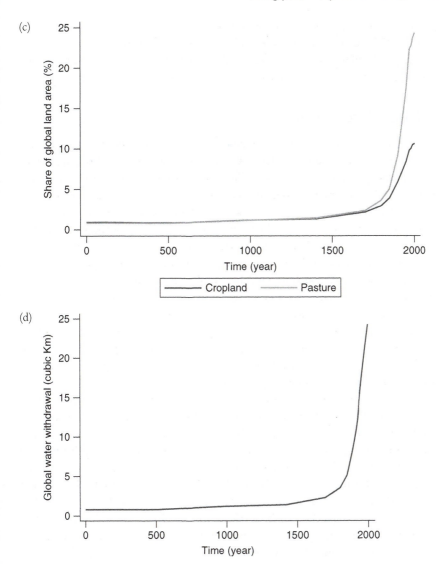

FIGURE 1.3 Infinite growth, finished planet: historical trends in world population (a), GDP per capita (b), cropland and pasture use (c), water withdrawal (d), 1–2000

Sources: (a) and (b) Maddison A. World Population, GDP and Per Capita GDP, 1–2003 AD, 2009; (c) History Database of the Global Environment, Netherland Environmental Assessment Agency. Goldewijk K et al. The HYDE 3.1 spatially explicit database of human-induced global land-use change over the past 12,000 years. *Global Ecology and Biogeography* 2011;20:73–86; (d) Worldwatch Institute from Shiklomanov I. World fresh water resources. In Gleick PH. *Water in Crisis*. New York: Oxford University Press (1993).

global economy and the Earth are moving toward what he called "the great collision."[122] Speth is probably right. If current trends of consumption, economic activities and pollution continue, there is no doubt about whether the great collision will happen or not. It is just a matter of when.

As if there is no tomorrow

Animal species seem to have special abilities to recognize imminent dangers. During the Indian Ocean tsunami that devastated the coasts of Indonesia, Sri Lanka, India and Thailand in 2004, birds, insects, and other wildlife managed to escape the disaster. As for humans, most were unable to perceive the threat, and casualty counts were in the hundreds of thousands. Paradoxically, one of the main consequences of humankind's successful evolution is its inability to accurately recognize ecological dangers. Industrialization has transformed us into a species out of touch with nature, forgetful of the fact that the ecosystem is the fundamental basis upon which our existence depends. Wrapped in our suburban living style, unaware of how rapidly resources such as food, water and oil are consumed, we have stopped perceiving ourselves as part of the natural system. We act like aliens on a planet of endless resources, and we pay no attention to the amount of damage we inflict on our very own ecosystem. We feel entitled to help ourselves to whatever the environment has to offer. As Schumacher noted in *Small is Beautiful*, we have engaged in a perpetual war against nature, a war in which, if we win, we actually lose.[123]

The idea that modern civilization is heading toward collapse was once confined to a few isolated thinkers, who were often dismissed as lunatics, radicals or extremists. Even the authors of the Club of Rome were accused of being catastrophists. Today, the situation is no different. But the number of books arguing that modern society is in danger of a future global ecological catastrophe is becoming larger and larger. From Richard Posner's *Catastrophe: Risk and Response* to Michael Klare's *Resource Wars: The New Landscape of Global Conflict*; from Colin Mason's *The 2030 Spike: the Countdown to Global Catastrophe* to Bill McGuire's *Seven Years to Save the Planet*, there is no shortage of prominent authors seriously concerned about the future ecological crises of human civilization.

Although the idea of global collapse is no longer confined to a few lone wolves, it has not yet entered the public consciousness. It still remains in the periphery of our psyche. It is as if we are living in a state of psychological inertia preventing us from acknowledging the reality we are in. As James Howard Kunstler, the author of *The Long Emergency*, noticed, when facing the prospect of the end of human civilization we enter into a state of "cognitive dissonance," as if our brains are unable to process the bad news. We are incapable of believing that what is happening is actually happening, that what seemed impossible is becoming possible. As Kunstler wrote: "Throughout history, even the most important and self-evident trends are often completely ignored because the changes they foreshadow are simply unthinkable."[124] Indeed, it is extremely hard to live with the prospect that climate change, peak oil, food crises and water shortages and the destruction of natural resources will wreak havoc on our entire society. As a result, rather than figuring out alternative methods of development and strategies to avoid the worst, we live as if nothing is happening. We continue to pollute, consume and destroy as if there is no tomorrow. Indeed, there may not be one.

2

THE GROWTH DELUSIONS

Have you ever wondered why nations are so obsessed with promoting an ever-larger Gross National Product (GNP)? The answer is simple: economic growth has been the major force behind the material improvement of our lives. And not only the wealthy and privileged benefited from these material advances – economic development has enriched the lives of countless people worldwide and across the economic spectrum. The large improvements in living standards are there for all of us to see. In the last 50 years, life expectancy increased more than in the previous two millennia.[1] We have never been better at controlling childhood diseases and deaths. Improved healthcare, new technologies, and effective therapies that make diseases and disabilities more tolerable, are now widely available. We are healthier, taller and more educated than ever. Many of us can now enjoy a wide variety of luxuries: spacious homes, central heating, fancy cars, mobile phones, portable computers, travel and holidays. We can do things that were previously thought to be impossible. As Bjorn Lomborg, author of *The Skeptical Environmentalist*, once wrote:

> children born today, in both the industrialized world and developing countries will live longer, and be healthier, they will get more food, a better education, a higher standard of living, more leisure time and far more possibilities . . . and that is a beautiful world.[2]

If economic growth has been the major driver of human welfare in the past, should not we also assume that it will continue to be so in the future? Most economists think so and argue that the priority must be to promote even more economic growth. This conviction, however, ignores a fundamental paradox: over the last several decades, in spite of the persistent increase of living standards, there have been no signs of improvement in life satisfaction among many affluent societies.

Worse still, rich nations and emerging economies are experiencing a worrisome rise of psychosocial problems, mental disorders and social degradation. Economists insist that human progress should continue to emphasize global wealth accumulation and material production, but – at least in rich societies – the days when economic growth equated to improvements in health and happiness are probably gone. Instead, the indiscriminate focus on unlimited economic expansion and materialism is worsening our quality of life and that of future generations.

Economic growth, human stagnation

Before illustrating why economic growth is no longer the major promoter of quality of life in industrialized societies, let us be clear: some people have not enjoyed the benefits of this model of development. Rather, they have just tasted the bitterness of its distributional failures. The fruits of economic growth are not for all. Both critics and cheerleaders of this model of development have recognized this. As Susan George, author of *Another World Is Possible If . . .*, once explained, this social organization "takes the best and leaves the rest."[3] Canadian development economist and free market apologist, Gerald Helleiner, once observed: "this system brings rewards to all, at least to all who matter."[4] Those "who do not matter" cannot become consumers or producers in a society designed by and on behalf of "the best."

Still today, almost half of humanity lives with less than 2.50USD per day. About 10 million children die of hunger each year.[5] Billions of people do not have access to basic human needs such as water, sanitation, education and healthcare.[6] In Sierra Leone, people are expected to live on average no more than 47 years and almost one out of five children die before reaching their fifth year of life.[7] Shocking inequalities exist even within rich nations. In the Harlem neighborhood of New York City, black youths have a lower chance of reaching age 65 than men living in Bangladesh.[8] In Australia, indigenous people live, on average, 10 years less than white Australians.[9] There are large gaps in life expectancy between aboriginals and white populations in Canada and in the United States as well.[10]

All in all, the world contemplated through the eyes of the poor is not as beautiful as Lomborg describes it. Instead, economic reforms are urgently needed to address the startling inequalities in wealth and health between the so-called "best" and "the rest." Free market economists always prescribe the same antidote to the problem: more economic growth. In their view, when countries grow fast, part of the wealth they accumulate "trickles down" to the poor through the laws of supply and demand. The enthusiasts of "trickle-down economics" ignore a crucial point, however: there is already enough wealth to ensure a decent life for every human being around the world. The real trouble is not lack of wealth, but the reluctance to distribute it and administer it responsibly. Wealth remains unavailable to those who desperately need it and continues to be accumulated by those who do not.

At first sight, this mal-distribution of wealth would seem to create winners (the rich) and losers (the poor). At a closer scrutiny, however, everybody loses. While the lives of countless people in low-income countries continue to be "nasty, brutish and short," affluent societies are affected by psychosocial problems. Rising depression, obesity, mental disorders, stress, anxiety and social alienation: a "prosperous" life requires not only sufficient wealth to live decently, but also a sober detachment from it. Otherwise, instead of controlling wealth, wealth controls us.

Happiness and health are not for sale

Most free market economists disagree with these claims. To them, money can purchase everything, including happiness. We know this to be untrue, of course, as repeatedly argued by numerous thinkers including Tibor Scitovsky, the author of *The Joyless Economy.*[11] While money does buy wellbeing for people who are poor,[12] and wealthier individuals are on average happier than poorer ones, above a certain income level more money does not make people any happier.[13–17] There is plenty of scientific evidence supporting this claim. In rich societies, people have become much richer during their lifetime, and yet their wellbeing has somehow "stagnated."[18] In the last half century, standards of living have more than doubled, but people have not become more satisfied with their lives.[19 20 21] It seems that the capability of money to make rich countries happier has, in some sense, expired. Among affluent nations, economic growth seems no longer very important in promoting better health either. Wealthier nations enjoy, on average, better health conditions than poorer ones, but after a certain threshold of per capita income, more wealth does not necessarily make countries healthier (see Figure 2.1).[22 23]

Economists call this the "law of diminishing returns." A certain amount of wealth is necessary for the provision of basic needs such as food, shelter, medical care and education. The coverage of these basic needs is crucial for happiness[24 25] and health.[26] Imagine living in a poor country with very little to eat, no running water and no sanitation facilities.[27] How happy can you feel? How healthy can you be? Now, imagine living in a safe, healthy and socially cohesive neighborhood, with an income that covers all things required for a decent and fulfilling existence. Would more money really matter? Maybe, but a survey conducted by *Forbes* magazine, some years ago, showed that even the one hundred wealthiest Americans are only slightly happier than the general population.[28] Some philosophers, more than two millennia ago, and without much empirical analyses already understood why: wealth may be useful to reduce human misery, but money cannot buy happiness and, at the population level, it cannot buy health either. The reason is simple. They are both priceless.

Some have even argued that the wealth accumulated in the last half a century has not only been spent in vain, but has actually worsened quality of life. There are various empirical studies showing that this economic prosperity has even resulted in diminishing levels of happiness.[29] Research in England conducted by Clark and colleagues, for example, suggested that the most recent cohorts of Britons are generally less satisfied than the previous, older ones.[30] Similarly, a comparison of

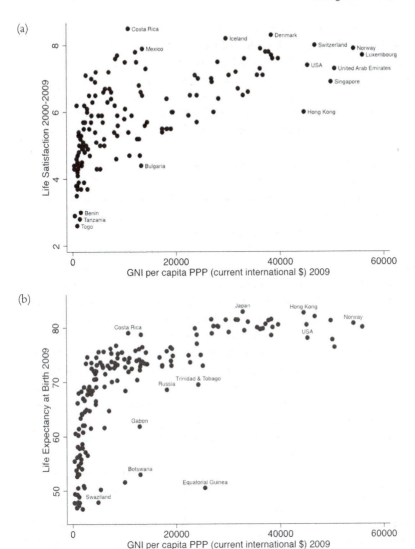

FIGURE 2.1 Out of sale: GNI per capita and life satisfaction in 148 nations, 2000–2009 (a) and life expectancy at birth in 175 nations, 2009 (b)

Sources: World Database of Happiness (2000–9) and World Development Indicators database (2012).

British opinion polls showed that the proportion of people saying they were "very happy" fell from 52 percent in 1957 to a mere 36 percent in 2005.[31] Blanchflower and Oswald indicate that over the last quarter of a century self-reported levels of wellbeing have gradually declined in the United States.[13] According to an Australian survey that analyzed life perceptions by the general population, about 51 percent of the respondents revealed that their quality of life had declined.[32] Unedifying findings on the paradox of declining happiness in times of economic growth have also been observed in Italy, the supposed country of *La Dolce Vita*.[33]

While these results may be counterintuitive, it is not too difficult to see why wealth can make people unhappier. Andrew Carnegie, regarded by some as the second-richest man in history, once revealed: "to continue much longer overwhelmed with business cares and with most of my thoughts wholly upon the way to make money in the shortest time must degrade me beyond hope of permanent recovery."[34]

Of course, although the bulk of evidence indicates that after a certain threshold more income either makes no difference, or worsens, quality of life, there are respectable studies showing exactly the opposite.[35] The research is complicated by the question of whether happiness is reliably measurable. Indeed, the idea of quantifying how happy individuals feel is questionable. Can we really trust people to report their own level of happiness? Can happiness be really quantified like our height and weight? Some philosophers do not think so. "Ask yourself if you are happy," John Stuart Mill once argued, "and you cease to be so." Happiness is not just a subjective status, but a feeling shaped by the cultural and social environment in which we live. For example, in the United States people are culturally encouraged to depict themselves as happy, while the opposite may be true in some Asian countries. Moreover, in a highly materialistic culture, happiness can be confused with social status. Asking people whether they are happy may signify asking them whether they are successful. The problem of measuring happiness across cultures was highlighted by studies comparing the levels of happiness and depression in China versus the United States. Studies have shown that, although the Chinese seem less happy[36] and optimistic[37] than their American counterparts, people living in the US are more depressed than the Chinese.[38] What can explain this paradox? In his book *Affluenza*, Oliver James argues that American culture tends to boost self-esteem at any cost, and is heavily impregnated by the need to harbor positive illusions that sustain emotional wellbeing. These deceptively rose tinted beliefs, however, encourage people to live in optimistic bubbles.[39] In other words, it is possible that some people declare that they are happy when, in reality, they are not. In effect, according to British psychologist Lynn Myers, between 10 and 20 percent of the population are "emotionally repressed."[40] It is also possible that, for some, the pursuit of happiness even turns into an obsession. As Edith Wharton once wrote: "if only we'd stop trying to be happy, we could have a pretty good time."

If happiness is difficult to measure reliably because it is heavily influenced by subjective and cultural factors, and even emotional repression, perhaps a less erratic way to examine whether our lives are better off is to analyze whether people are becoming more or less depressed. Using Schopenhauer's definition of happiness as "freedom from suffering" is less than ideal, but what if the alternatives are even worse?

The price of progress

In one of his most acclaimed works, *Civilization and Its Discontents*, Sigmund Freud wrote that, "the price of progress in civilization is paid in forfeiting happiness."[41] Although Freud could be right for the wrong reasons – he believed that most mental disorders were caused by repressed sexual desires – he was quite a visionary. Studies that report growing levels of life dissatisfaction over time in modern societies are corroborated by research that shows a rising prevalence of mental health disorders. Mental health problems are growing in terms of frequency and length in almost every region of the world. At any point in time, they are present in about 10 percent of the population and affect more than 25 percent of all people at some time during their lives.[42] According to the World Health Organization (WHO), in 2000, mental and neurological disorders accounted for about 12 percent of the global burden of disease, and are projected to account for 15 percent of the same global burden by 2020. At the moment, mental and behavioral disorders cause nearly half of all disability experienced by people living in the United States and Europe, while depression and other neuropsychiatric conditions account for more of the global disease burden caused by either heart disease or cancer.[6]

Depressed, distressed and repressed

Of all mental and behavioral problems that increasingly affect our lives, depression, or the "sense of being dead while our body is alive,"[43] is perhaps one of the most disturbing. Research shows that, overall, depression has increased almost everywhere in the West,[44–46] and in some regions of the developing world.[46] More recent birth cohorts are at higher risk for clinical levels of depression compared to older ones. In a study conducted in the United States, the risk of major depression among people born after 1945 was 10 times higher than those born before.[29] Of people born in 1910, only 1.3 percent had had a major depressive episode over a lifetime period of 70 years, but each succeeding cohort had a higher rate of major depression. Those born after 1960 had a 5.3 percent chance of a major depressive episode, although they were followed only up to 25 years.[47 48]

While the evidence that reports increasing levels of depression in rich societies over time is relatively robust,[49–51] some researchers have questioned its plausibility.[52] Some experts argue that symptoms of depression have always been present, but only in recent times have become fully recognized. According to this view, the rise of mental disorders is attributable to refined diagnostic criteria used by mental health professionals that have increasingly considered healthy emotional responses as pathological.[53] There is some truth in this claim. There is little doubt that there have been profound changes in diagnostic techniques in recent decades and this may well have distorted the results of historical trends. There is also evidence, however, that the rise of mental diseases like depression is not a mere artifact of more reporting or diagnosis.[54] There is sufficient consensus on the hypothesis that rates of major depression rose markedly over the past decades,[55] not only in the US and Britain,[56] but also worldwide, above and beyond the effect of improved diagnosis. According to the WHO, there is little question that depression is growing and will continue to grow in the future. Indeed, it is expected to become the second main cause of disability and years of life lost by the year 2020.[42] By 2030, it will become the top cause of disease and disabilities worldwide.[57]

As it turns out, depression is increasing, but how about other mental disorders? The story is not much different. The authors of the World Health Report 2001, which was devoted to mental health, wrote unambiguously: "from an analysis of trends, it is evident that this burden (of premature death and disability due to mental health problems) will increase rapidly in the future."[58] Research shows that, over the last few decades, people have become more anxious, distressed, worried about their lives and insecure about their jobs.[59][60] Two meta-analyses (summarizing

TABLE 2.1 The rise of misery: depression and other leading causes of burden of disease and disabilities in the world, 2004–2030

2004	As % of total DALYs	Rank	Rank	As % of total DALYs	2030
Disease or injury					*Disease or injury*
Lower respiratory infections	6.2	1	1	6.2	Unipolar depressive disorders
Diarrheal diseases	4.8	2	2	5.5	Ischemic heart disease
Unipolar depressive disorders	4.3	3	3	4.9	Road traffic accidents
Ischemic heart disease	4.1	4	4	4.3	Cerebrovascular Disease
HIV/AIDS	3.8	5	5	3.8	COPD
Cerebrovascular Disease	3.1	6	6	3.2	Lower respiratory infections
Prematurity and low birth weight	2.9	7	7	2.9	Hearing loss, adult onset
Birth asphyxia and birth trauma	2.7	8	8	2.7	Refractive errors
Road traffic accidents	2.7	9	9	2.5	HIV/AIDS
Neonatal infections and other	2.7	10	10	2.3	Diabetes mellitus

Source: Drawn by the author using data from the World Health Organization. *Global Burden of Disease: 2004 Update*. Geneva: World Health Organization, 2008.

Note: DALYs = Disability Adjusted Life Years Lost.

research across many studies) conducted by Jean Twenge, showed that between 1952 and 1993, Americans experienced substantially higher levels of anxiety and neuroticism over time. Although the rise of anxiety reported in the study was generalized across adult and child cohorts, the change was larger among children. So much so that by the 1980s, normal children were scoring higher on an anxiety test than child psychiatric patients of the 1950s.[61] On the basis of other similar findings, some researchers wondered whether the twentieth century could be coined "The Age of Anxiety."[62] While this may sound a bit exaggerated, a growing number of people seem to share a sense of uneasiness about some aspects of modern living: stressful jobs, frenetic lifestyles, crowded roads, noisy cities, broken relationships, sleep deprivation, aggressive careerism and other complaints. A review published in *Evidence-Based Mental Health* showed that, globally, about one out of six persons have suffered from anxiety disorders at least once in their lifetime.[63]

There are different areas of life that have become more and more stressful, especially in the last few decades. Work is one of them. In 1996, the Eurobarometer survey showed that nearly half of the respondents reported their work stress had increased over time. Rising workplace stress levels have been reported in Britain too.[44 64] Psychologists used to say that the most distressed people at work were busy executives of large companies. They were wrong. The Whitehall II Study showed, unequivocally, that people of lower social classes, working in humbler jobs, are far more likely to be distressed than professionals and top executives.[65] Such findings have been confirmed over and over. Yet, successful business people can also suffer from high rates of depression, anxiety[66] and personality disorders.[67] Distressed well-off employees can even be found on Wall Street, as revealed by a study which reported high rates of anxiety and depression among brokers, financial advisers and traders.[68] Clinical psychologist Alden Cass accumulated considerable experience in trying to cure these individuals. As he revealed, many successful brokers have an unhealthy fear of failure and are often referred for treatment by their wives and branch managers due to behavioral problems such as screaming, being overly demanding of co-workers and harassing women.[69] All in all, even people of the financial elites seem to live relatively miserable lives in spite of – or maybe because of – their spectacularly overpaid jobs.

Develop-mental disorders

As mentioned before, the failure of modern society to make people happier is apparent not only from the rise of psychological problems in adults, but also from the deterioration of children's mental wellbeing. An international review of historical trends in psychosocial disorders among young people showed that since the end of the Second World War there has been a troubling rise of mental problems such as depression, crime, alcohol and drug abuse and eating disorders in nearly all developed countries.[70] Conduct disorders, or what are often referred to as "antisocial behaviors," are becoming more and more frequent in most Western societies where the prevalence of such conditions has increased five-fold over the past 70 years.[71] About three decades ago, depression and anxiety in children were almost unknown. More recently, however, they have become a frequent problem,[29] as shown by different studies including a meta-analysis of birth cohorts of young Americans from 1938 to 2007.[72]

Similar trends have also been found in the UK.[73] A paper published in the *Journal of Child Psychology and Psychiatry* reported marked increases of depression and other emotional problems in British girls and boys between 1986 and 2006.[74] Another report published by the British Medical Association portrayed a similar picture. It showed that about 20 percent of children and adolescents have mental health problems at some point in their lives[75] and 1 in 10 children under 16 years of age suffer a clinically diagnosed mental health disorder. Worldwide, the picture is not very rosy. According to the World Health Organization, about 1 out of 5 children in the world suffers from a mental health problem.[58]

Adults go on and on about what is wrong with the way our children feel and behave today, but very few are looking in the mirror to understand and change the social environments that cause these problems in the first place.[76] So far, mainstream countermeasures to address the growing prevalence of psychosocial problems among young people, or what I define as "develop-mental" disorders, mainly consist of biomedical treatments, medicines and psychotherapy. Unfortunately, individual-

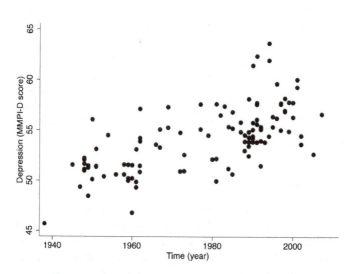

FIGURE 2.2 Develop-mental disorders: prevalence of depression among college students in the United States, 1938–2007

Source: Twenge JM et al. Birth cohort increases in psychopathology among young Americans, 1938–2007: A cross-temporal meta-analysis of the MMPI. *Clinical Psychology Review* 2010;30(2):145–54.

level interventions of this kind do not even scratch the surface of the problem that is largely attributable to problems in society, communities, social relationships and parenting.

Consumed relationships

"Of all things that wisdom provides for living one's entire life in happiness," Epicurus once observed, "the greatest by far is the possession of friendship."[77] Although Epicurus is no longer alive and rarely read, his view on the importance of social relationships for a happy existence is no less important today. When asked to rank the most important possessions in life, the majority of people put friendship and intimate social relationships at the top of their list. Indeed, individuals find meaning and happiness in the people they care for: a child, a spouse, a relative or a friend. Individuals also care deeply about the communities in which they belong. Therefore, it is a pity that the importance of social relationships is not adequately reflected in the policies and priorities of governments and workplaces. On the contrary, these preferences are often utterly ignored. When considering the thirst for power, wealth and profit versus the need for affiliation with and affection for others, the emphasis of modern society is on the former at the expense of the latter.[78] Worse, social relationships have become increasingly commodified, overshadowed by economic priorities, treated as means to pecuniary and materialistic ends.

Gary Becker, a top guru of the University of Chicago School of Economics, and Nobel Prize Winner in Economics, is considered one of the major theoreticians on intimate social relationships. In his theory of marriage, Becker argued that social relationships are to be viewed, more or less, as market exchanges. In his opinion, there is little distinction between a human interaction and a commercial transaction. Marriage is nothing more than an arrangement to secure mutual benefits of exchange between two rational, self-interested agents of different endowments, he explained. It is a rational, self-interested decision to be made after a cost-benefit analysis of available options in what he defined as "the marriage market."[79] In an article published in *The Journal of Political Economy*, Becker wrote that "love and other emotional attachments, such as sexual activity or frequent close contact with a person, can be considered particular non-marketable household commodities"[80] that have the potential to produce more "efficient" marriages.

Becker's theory of marriage and "love" fits very well with the prevailing economic doctrine arguing that society is essentially a big market and people are nothing more than rational, selfish profiteers in perpetual search for wealth and power. Numerous sociologists, long before Becker's intellectual exploits, understood the dangers of these types of doctrines that may turn out to be self-fulfilling prophecies. Authors such as Max Weber, for example, have found that social relationships in industrialized countries have become colder, more impersonal and manipulative, as well as increasingly influenced by utilitarian, materialistic values. According to Weber, whereas in the past social interactions were mainly communal and based on subjective feelings such as a sense of belonging, in recent times, they have become increasingly motivated by rational, utilitarian interests. Although Weber found nothing wrong with the fact that people could harbor a certain degree of self-interest, he believed that rational and utilitarian calculations scorned spontaneous affections and authentic social exchange.[81][82]

In a groundbreaking book, *Studies in Machiavellianism,* Richard Christie and Florence Geis echo a similar concern. In their opinion, genuine feelings of social reciprocity have slowly eroded over time, suppressed by more rational and self-interested patterns of social exchange. The authors show that modern culture promotes what they define as the "Machiavellian Syndrome," a "manipulative attitude toward others that includes a relative lack of affection in interpersonal relations and lack of concern for morality." According to Christie and Geis, this manipulative behavioral style, in which individuals tend to produce many acquaintances, but few close friends, originated with the advent of industrialism.[83] After the Second World War, it rapidly spread across the US and Europe,[83] to subsequently "infect" transitional and developing countries.[84] Virtually everywhere, Macchiavellianism seems more prevalent among the younger, rather than older generations.[83] Manipulative attitudes toward social relationships also seem to have increased over time. A study conducted by Robert Webster and Harry Harmon showed that at the beginning of the twenty-first century US college students demonstrated a significantly higher Macchiavellian tendency compared to students of the late 1960s.[85]

The lonely, the wary and the unfriendly

Perhaps, it is not by chance that the advent of these attitudes has coincided with a progressive deterioration of social relationships in industrialized nations, as documented by Robert Lane in *The Loss of Happiness in Market Democracies.*[29] The increasing penetration of utilitarian and economic values into social and personal relationships has increased diffidence and conflict, and reduced feelings of belonging, affection and genuine sympathy for the plight of others. The impression that there is something wrong with the way social relationships are "evolving" in modern times is corroborated by trends in social isolation and feelings of trust. An increasing number of people in the US report feeling more lonely, disconnected and isolated than in the past.[86][87] It has been estimated that about 60 million Americans, more or less 20 percent of the total population, feel lonely.[88] A study published in the *American Sociological Review* showed that, between 1975 and 2004, the number of people who have someone to talk to about matters that are important to them has declined dramatically.[89] This is not to say that being alone is always necessarily negative. Solitude, silence and peace of mind can be some of the most fundamental traits of creative, healthy living. But as Clive Hamilton, author of *The Growth Fetish,* once observed, the trouble with modern culture is that it promotes too little solitude and too much loneliness.[90] Long before him, Richard Tawney, the author of *The Acquisitive Society,* explained that modern society is turning into "a disorganized dust of (atomized) individuals."[91] Research also indicates that ties with local neighborhoods and community groups have slowly eroded over time. About three-fourths of Americans do not to know their next-door neighbors.[92]

Disturbingly high levels of social isolation were also reported in a survey conducted in France where more than a half of respondents described suffering from loneliness at some time in their lives.[29] A similar picture has emerged in Britain, where one study found that loneliness has increased so much that "even the weakest communities in 1971 were stronger than any community" three decades later.[93] While research on the change in frequency of visits to friends has produced mixed results,[29][89] there has been a general decline in the regularity of individuals visiting family members.[29]

Social relationships have changed not only in terms of quantity, but also in terms of quality. The proportion of people satisfied with their marriage has decreased in the US,[44] Britain and other industrialized countries.[94] In Britain, one survey found that about 35 percent of children don't feel loved by their parents and only 56 percent of them feel comfortable talking to their parents about their problems.[95] When surveying the prospects for the quality of social relationships and their effects on mental health around the world, the WHO observed that, "protective mechanisms of social groups are breaking down, and many people are being exposed to the unsettling effects of uprooting, family disintegration and social isolation."[96]

The commercialization and commodification of social relationships appears to have also produced adverse effects on people's perceptions and sense of trust toward each other. In 1959, about 56 percent of Britons believed that most people could be trusted; by 1998, however, the same figure had fallen to 30 percent. In the United States, interpersonal trust fell from 56 percent in the mid-1960s to 33 percent in 1998.[44] Distrust has become particularly prevalent among younger generations which, in general, tend to be more distrustful than older ones.[97] According to a study conducted by Rahn and Transue, which used data from the University of Michigan *Monitoring The Future Project*, young Americans are increasingly perceiving other people as unhelpful and unfair.[98] In 2005, a survey conducted in Britain also showed that 43 percent of respondents reported their neighborhood as "less friendly" compared to 10 years before.[31]

Addicted to growth: a tale of two states

In fairness to those who stress the importance of economic growth and pecuniary gain, there are some valid reasons as to why governments avoid a decline in GNP like the plague. Economic recessions can have devastating effects in terms of social stability, poverty and employment. The 2008 global financial crisis lucidly illustrated what happens to countries that are affected by economic downturns. Crises can ravage entire societies unless governments intervene boldly to protect the most vulnerable populations from their effects. It is generally accepted that free market economies must grow at a rate of at least 3 to 5 percent annually in order to keep unemployment from rising.[99] This goal is usually achieved by providing incentives to the economy through stimulus packages and economic reforms to promote consumption. This strategy implies that economic and social recovery largely depends on people's ability and inclination to spend more to buy more. As a by-product, a society of satisfied, sober consumers cannot fight unemployment because it can hardly grow at 3 or 5 percent annually. In other words, when hit by a recession, governments are locked between two equally undesirable states: economic instability or ecological degradation. If people consume more, they save the economy, but fail the environment. If they consume less, they save the environment, but fail the economy.[100] This is the dilemma all societies face today as they struggle to recover from the Great Recession.

According to some authors, there may be a way out of this deadlock, however. Reforms are possible that can make economic growth ecologically sustainable. This approach usually implies the adoption of green stimulus packages that can combine economic recovery and ecological sustainability. It relies on the idea of "decoupling" natural resource use and environmental impacts from economic growth. This means "using less resources per unit of economic output and reducing the environmental impact of any resources that are used or economic activities that are undertaken."[101] Various schools of thought in ecological economics have argued that modern civilization can maintain or improve current living standards while reducing its impact on the environment.[102]

But is this really the case? The idea of "decoupling" is potentially promising, but presents two major flaws. First, it does not offer any solution for the psychosocial degradation promoted by conspicuous consumerism and social side effects of "economism." Second, it fails to address a fundamental question: can an economy really grow without increasing pollution and waste? Can economic growth coincide with environmental protections and a sustainable use of natural resources? Hardly. No matter how ecologically efficient free market economies may become, no matter how green consumerism can get, a society devoted to "ecologically friendly" economic growth still requires excessive depletion of natural resources and widespread pollution. While initiatives that promote energy efficiency and a reduction of the material impact of economic growth, such as community energy projects and local farming, are laudable and must be encouraged, they are not enough to avoid ecological collapse. The proposal of "decoupling" economic growth from resource use and environmental destruction is a nice concept, but not much more than that. As Herman Daly, former senior economist of the World Bank, once observed, the expectation that we can overcome the physical limits of economic growth by "angelizing" the GNP is a myth. We would need to become angels before doing so, he explained.[103]

But what is the alternative then? The answer is simple. We need a "post-growth society."[90] A new social system which, instead of emphasizing perpetual wealth accumulation and unlimited consumption, promotes quality of life and ensures a decent standard of living for everyone while protecting the ecosystem.

The most important conversation of our time

The idea of a post-growth society sounds like an impossible, utopian dream. However, this is only because, for years, we have been taught that, in order to rescue the poor from their own misery and create prosperity for all, we need "a rising [economic] tide that lifts all boats." This conviction has become so deeply embedded in modern culture that even some well-meaning ecologists, who advocate for sustainable development, evade challenging it. Another deep-seated conviction sponsored by free market economists is that economic progress is human progress and money can purchase happiness. As discussed earlier, this is hardly the case. In times of persistent economic growth, people of affluent nations have been increasingly affected by depression, stress and anxiety; children are suffering increasing rates of mental illnesses, conduct disorders and behavioral problems; social relationships have become more manipulative, distrustful and Macchiavellian. Given that continuous improvements in material prosperity have coincided with the rise of social and psychological disorders, we must accept that what is good for the economy is not necessarily good for people. Yet, economic growth continues to be worshipped as a secular religion that we are not supposed to question. Those who dare to are treated as fools. But what if the fools were those who support this doctrine? "Nothing is more common than the idea that we the people living in the Western world of the twentieth century are eminently sane," Eric Fromm once wrote. But then he added: "can we be so sure that we are not deceiving ourselves? Many inmates of an insane asylum are convinced that everybody else is crazy, except themselves."[104]

Fortunately, in the last decades, the number of "fools" that question modern society's addiction to economic growth has increased exponentially. Since the publication of the Club of Rome's *Limits to Growth,*[105] and Fred Hirsch's *Social Limits to Growth*, more writers have voiced a common concern: this model of development is socially corrosive and ecologically destructive. It is also unjust. Wealth is not "trickling-down" to the bottom steps of the social ladder, as free market economists promise. On the contrary, most of it remains far up at the top, concentrated in the hands of a few extremely powerful and privileged people. Clearly, an alternative model of development that redefines human progress beyond economic growth is urgently needed.

Ironically, the first political economist who proposed changing the aim of human progress from economic growth to psychological flourishing was not a radical, or an anarchist, but a classical libertarian: John Stuart Mill. In a widely quoted passage of *Principles of Political Economy*, Mill explained: "I confess I am not charmed with the ideal of life held out by those who think that the normal state of human beings is that of struggling . . . trampling, crushing, elbowing, and treading on each other's heels." He continued: "the best state for human nature is that in which, while no one is poor, no ones desires to be richer, nor has any reason to fear being thrust back by the efforts of others to push themselves forward."[106]

Inspired by Mill, Herman Daly refined these ideas and came up with a new model of development he called the "steady-state economy." While this term may sound fancy, the underlying philosophy is rather simple. It refers to an economy of stable (or mildly fluctuating) size that does not require an increased consumption of resources over time, but rather relies on an efficient and adequate distribution of products and services in order to improve quality of human life.[107]

More recently, Tim Jackson, chair of the UK's Sustainable Development Commission, has further developed the idea of a stationary state economy. Jackson made some compelling arguments for a new macro-economic system organized around the promotion of what he defined as "prosperity without growth." After examining various models of development that do not require an "at all costs" capital accumulation, Jackson concluded that there are ways out of the "social instability or environmental degradation" deadlock. He argues that economic *de-growth* can be compatible with the reduction of both poverty and unemployment, provided that a series of reforms are adopted. These policies include the reduction of working hours, the sharing of available work across the labor force,[108] improvement in the wage structure (e.g. the introduction of a basic income for citizens), investments in public assets, a reversing of the culture of consumerism, and a stable and relatively equal earning distribution.[109] [100]

Jackson has engaged us in what he has rightfully defined as "the most important conversation of our time." He has also underlined that a fairer and more reasonable use of resources can go very far in promoting a decent living standard for all and is environmentally sustainable. More than 20 years ago, an international group of scientists estimated that with a better distribution of resources, the entire world population could live at roughly the same level as West Europeans of the mid-1970s. This equates to living in relatively comfortable homes with refrigeration for food, clothes washers, a moderate amount of hot water, and ready access to public transit augmented by limited car use.[110] Clearly, the challenges we face today in a world of 7 billion people, many of whom are committed to emulating the same lifestyle enjoyed in the West, are far more daunting. Yet, we have far more resources and technologies to reorganize society around prosperity without growth. The key is to do it soon.

Toward healthy de-growth

All in all, the idea of moving away from a narrow model of economic development toward a holistic approach to human development is much less utopian than it seems. Health and social conditions can be improved even in times of crises and economic recession. Some countries hit by the latest financial meltdown have actually experienced significant social improvements, not instability and chaos as one may expect. For example, in the years following 2007, Germany and Denmark have experienced a substantial reduction, not increase in unemployment.[100] Even health standards can improve in times of economic recession. Take Japan. In the 1990s, the nation was hit by a prolonged economic recession for more than a decade, but experienced faster reduction in chronic diseases mortality than in preceding years of economic growth.[111] Finland in the 1990s is another case of "healthy de-growth." After the collapse of the Soviet Union, a regime with which Finland had strong economic relations and trade ties, the Finnish GDP dropped by a third. Surprisingly, the Finnish all-cause mortality rate also dropped – more sharply during this recession than in the subsequent economic boom. As incomes fell, alcohol consumption declined by more than 10 percent and road traffic injuries dropped by one-half.[112]

In the low- and middle-income countries, however, financial recessions can have much more serious consequences because there are usually weak or absent welfare policies and unemployment protections. Nevertheless, even some developing countries, such as Chile and Argentina, have managed to improve health in times of recession and stagnation.[100] Another case in point is Cuba, which plunged into an economic crisis during the 1990s, the so-called "Special Period." The sudden absence of subsidized oil from the former Soviet Union produced a sharp reduction of calorific intake (over a third) among inhabitants. Surprisingly, however, the recession did not push the Cuban population to the brink of starvation, but stimulated a change of food habits that improved general health conditions. Cubans returned to their traditional diets consisting of rice, fruits and vegetables, and sharply reduced consumption of saturated fats and red meat. As the price of oil became unaffordable, Cuban people walked more and used bicycles more frequently. The results of this "natural experiment" were astonishing: health standards improved and obesity fell along with death rates attributable to diabetes, coronary heart disease and stroke.[113]

The experience of these countries clearly shows that a new model of political economy, decoupled from endless economic growth, is reasonable and feasible. Policies promoting "prosperity without growth" such as redistributive taxation, reduction of working hours, stable jobs, minimum wages, public education and public services can be adopted easily and realistically. Of course, this does not necessarily imply that such reforms also promote personal and psychological fulfillment. However, a vast body of scientific and practical evidence shows that happiness can be promoted with a relatively moderate amount of wealth. While ensuring access to basic needs and environmental sustainability, a steady-state economy may encourage the pursuit of creative, meaningful and socially satisfactory life goals. By encouraging people to obsess less about money, social position and status symbols, this type of economic system may actually promote psychological fulfillment and healthier social relationships. It can also redirect our attention to more creative and less materialistic life goals. More than two hundred years ago, John Stuart Mill tried to address a question many contemporary free market economists still blissfully ignore: "toward what ultimate point is society tending by its industrial progress?" In Mill's opinion, once assured a decent level of living standards, human efforts need to be directed to mental culture, to the pursuit of social and moral progress, and to the increase of leisure, rather than being caught up in the competitive struggle for material wealth and status.[106]

It is clear that economic growth no longer, if it ever did, represents a reliable measure of human progress. Some of the most miserable human experiences, a war for example, may sharply increase a country's GNP. Yet, this does not necessarily mean that such an event leads to an improvement in quality of life. As Eduardo Galeano once put it:

> From the point of view of the economy, the sale of weapons is indistinguishable from the sale of food. When a building collapses or a plane crashes, it's rather inconvenient from the point of view of those inside, but it's altogether convenient for the growth of the gross national product.[114]

Indeed, riding a bicycle for one mile on a country road surrounded by flowers contributes less to GNP growth than driving in a car for a mile along a crowded freeway. Eating natural, organic foods in reusable containers contributes less to GNP growth than eating processed over-packaged foods imported from another continent. Yet, the former activities make us healthy, not the latter.

There is thriving literature on new indicators of human progress. Some authors have proposed an "enlarged GNP index," an indicator that takes into account not only the accumulated wealth of a nation, but also the proportion of economic growth that comes at the expense of environmental degradation and resource depletion. Others have advocated for a "Happy Planet Index," an indicator that measures the ecological efficiency with which human wellbeing is delivered around the world. Bhutan's former king, Jigme Singye Wangcuck, coined the term "Gross National Happiness" (GNH) later translated into a composite index of indicators of physical, mental and spiritual health such as time-balance, social and community vitality, cultural vitality, education, living standards, good governance and ecological vitality.[115] This new measure of human development has often been proposed in combination with other indicators such as the "Green National Product" for example.[116] There seems to be no shortage of proposals and new ideas to help transform our economic system away from the model of endless economic growth. It is difficult to know whether any of these proposals and ideas for an alternative model of human progress will ever work. They may or they may not. But we will never know unless we try them.

3

UNITED WE SPEND

In 1752, David Hume wrote an influential essay on luxury.[1] In his time, the prevailing Christian doctrine exhorted people to put spiritual and moral values before material wealth. Opulence was considered morally contemptible and inimical to society. For Jesus Christ, it was "easier for a camel to pass through the eye of a needle than for a rich man to enter the Kingdom of Heaven." Hume had a different view, however. In "Of Refinement in the Arts" the Scottish philosopher stated that, "in a nation . . . where there is no demand for superfluities men sink into indolence, lose all enjoyment of life, and are useless to the public."[2]

Hume was not alone in harboring such a view. His friend and compatriot, Adam Smith, actually provided an even stronger justification for the social desirability of luxury: "trickle-down economics." As Smith explained, the surpluses generated by the overspending of the rich provide the means to support others, including the poor. How so? Through the workings of the free market, that guides self-seeking rich individuals to socially beneficial results. In Smith's words: "the rich . . . in spite of their natural selfishness and rapacity, though they mean only their own convenience . . . [and] the gratification of their own vain and insatiable desires, they divide with the poor the produce of all their improvements."

> They are led by an invisible hand to make nearly the same distribution of the necessities of life, which would have been made, had the earth been divided into equal portions among all its inhabitants. . . . Thus without intending it, without knowing it, [they] advance the interest of the society, and afford means to the multiplication of the species.[3]

The wealthy elite merrily welcomed the rising popularity of this doctrine, at times defined as "private vices, public benefits"[4]: the idea that they could further the general aims of society, by simply pursuing their own selfish agenda, provided a moral justification for their lavish spending. Their behavior had no longer to be viewed as a symptom of ephemeral vanity, but as a virtuous contribution to the common good. The collective acceptance of "a virtuous society based on vicious individuals"[5] produced far-reaching ethical consequences that are, in a way, still felt even today. It made the vicious happy to be vicious and left many of those who were virtuous with no plausible reasons to remain so.

Futility unlimited

More than a century and a half after Hume's and Smith's works, Thornstein Veblen published a seminal work entitled *The Theory of the Leisure Class*. This book described the luxurious lifestyle of the elite that emerged in the nineteenth century, following the Second Industrial Revolution. Veblen observed that the super-wealthy, rather than buying goods and services for their intrinsic value and utility, consumed mainly to show off their status.[6] He defined this behavior as "conspicuous consumption," a tendency to seek gratification in frivolous things and pursue happiness through material goods and status symbols. This concept is well captured by the words of Lord Henry, one of the main characters in Oscar Wilde's novel, *The Picture of Dorian Gray*, when he observed he was living in "an age when unnecessary things are our only necessities."[7] Columbia University Professor, Paul Nystrom, defined the idea as the "philosophy of futility," the presumption that individuals have no better purposes in life than concentrating on superficial consumerism and fashionable status symbols.[8]

Initially acquired by the post-industrial elites, conspicuous consumption spread quickly to the general population. It became a mass phenomenon.[9] [10] And now it is one of the defining characteristics of modern culture. Like a virus, it propagates from the top to the bottom of the social hierarchy and infects society through the laws of psychological emulation and cultural assimilation. The mechanisms underlying the proliferation of the luxury fever are easy to explain. As the most affluent people spend lavishly to demonstrate their status, they induce all other social classes to emulate their consumption patterns.[11] Although the people in the poor and the middle classes are not a flock of sheep that are deprived of free will, the more those at the top consume for status, the more the perceived importance of consumerism trickles down to the bottom of the social ladder.[6] This does not happen only through psychological emulation. The wealthy also shape individual behaviors for the rest of society in another way – through the imposition of their worldview and the manipulations of beliefs, values and expectations, or what Gramsci defined as "cultural hegemony."[12] By occupying the "commanding heights" of the information and communication system, the top people of a society set the agenda and establish the social norms that determine collective behaviors. Before Gramsci, philosophers that could not be more ideologically distant, such as Hume and Marx, agreed on this. Hume once explained: "nothing appears more surprising to those who consider human affairs with a philosophical eye than the easiness with which the many are governed by the few."[13] Karl Marx echoed Hume when he wrote:

"the ideas of the ruling class are in every epoch the ruling ideas, i.e. the class which is the ruling material force of society, is at the same time its ruling intellectual force."[14]

Conspicuous consumption did not spread only from social class to social class. It also affected country after country. The global diffusion of the luxury fever came to full fruition with the advent of economic globalization, which integrated nations mainly through trade, capital and finance. Of course, the global race for conspicuous consumption was spearheaded by the US. By the 1970s, Americans were already spending more time in shopping malls than in any other location, with the exception of their workplace.[15] Consumption of luxury goods increased four times as fast as overall consumption.[16] The world's stock of motor and sailing yachts measuring longer than 100 feet doubled in ten years,[17] even though most owners of these yachts spend only a few weeks each year onboard them. Cosmetic surgery rose 178 percent between 1988 and 1993.[18] In 2009 alone, more than 10 million Americans underwent a cosmetic surgical operation.[19] Since the early 1970s, the rich have also been buying more luxury and utility-sport cars than ever before.[20] [11] The sales of sport utility vehicles (SUVs) have grown from slightly under 243,000 units in the 1980s to over 3 million units in 1990.[21] Although sales of SUVs peaked in the 1990s, purchases of luxury cars continued to rise,[22] at least until the 2008 economic crisis.

After taking off in the US, luxury fever went viral. In England, the British Association of Aesthetic Plastic Surgeons found that the number of breast augmentations in 2008 increased by 30 percent from the prior year.[23] Between 1970 and 2003, municipal solid wastes in the United States per person rose by 33 percent.[24] Consumer debt climbed from $525 billion in 1970 to $2,225 billion in 2004.[25] In the Western world, on average we buy a new mobile phone every 18 months; we dump 15 million computers every year; we also throw away our entire weight in rubbish every seven weeks.[26] And a large part of the stuff we buy is never used. According to the United Nations Development Programme (UNDP), the total spending on perfumes in Europe and the US exceeds the resources needed to provide the entire developing world with access to water and sanitation.[27]

Of course, after having deeply affected the Western lifestyle and culture, luxury fever reached emerging economies, especially in recent times. In China and Russia, for example, consumerism became widespread as demonstrated by the sharp increase of SUVs sales over the last decades.[28] [29] All over the world, "the urge to splurge" has conquered the hearts and minds of everyday people. And the consequences of this global cultural transformation are becoming more and more apparent. Although the sharp rise of conspicuous consumption can be seen as a symptom of wider access to goods and services that make our lives more comfortable and happier, the benefits to our quality of life are overstated while the costs are almost completely ignored. The media likes to spin shopping as the way to a happier life, but this is not necessarily the case. A large body of evidence shows that, at best, conspicuous consumption can produce only ephemeral advantages. Most behavioral economists understand why: we continuously evaluate material conditions in our lives via a frame of reference that changes over time, as our social circumstances transform.[30]

People often experience a persistent discrepancy between what they have and what they want; but once they achieve their material goals, they remain unfulfilled because of habituation or adaptation. Put another way, permanent changes in material conditions tend to create only transitory hedonic effects,[31] because we adjust very rapidly to the new standard of living. Once we become accustomed to the fancier mobile phone, bigger television or faster car, the positive effects of the new purchases fade away.

It is the rise of expectations that offset the potentially positive effects of new purchases and luxuries. Habituation or adaptation can also explain why the required income per capita tends to increase over time in proportion with actual average income, as shown by different studies. The reason for this is that, as individuals, and those in their reference group, earn and consume more, their expectations also rise and adapt.[32] Expectations tamper with the effects of rising income on wellbeing[33] and make lasting happiness unlikely. Research shows that people who win the lottery typically report the anticipated rush of euphoria in the weeks after their good fortune, but follow-up studies after several years later reveal that they do not become any happier than before.[34] Rather, tyrannical expectations can make their quality of life even worse. In effect, people striving too much for material goals can actually become more restless, dissatisfied, anxious and unhappy with themselves.[35] According to the University of Chicago's National Opinion Research Center, between 1956 and 1988, the percentage of Americans saying that they were satisfied with their financial situation dropped from 42 percent to 30 percent, even though average wealth increased steadily in the same period.[36] Maybe Oscar Wilde was right then when he wrote that "there are only two tragedies in life: one is not getting what one wants, the other is getting it."[37] As living standards rise, there is a perpetual upgrade of people's wants as well as changes of our perceptions of what we really need. And "what were luxuries for our fathers become necessities for us."[38]

Manufactured wants

There is plenty of evidence showing that people's material expectations have significantly increased in the last decades. In 1970, only 20 percent of Americans considered a second car as a necessity. By the year 2000, this proportion rose up to 59 percent.[39] In *The Overspent American*, Juliet Schor shows that more than a quarter of Americans making more than $100,000 a year declared that they did not have enough money to buy all that they needed.[9] A study conducted in Australia found that among the richest 20 percent of households, about 46 percent declared they could not afford to buy everything they "really needed."[40] In 1973, only 26 percent of Americans considered home air conditioning as a necessity. In 2006, this proportion went up to 70 percent – before decreasing to 54 percent in 2009, following the financial crisis.[41]

These findings can be interpreted in different ways. Some authors suggest that the perpetual transformation of people's wants is a natural phenomenon. The endless desire for new, fashionable goods is nothing more than the result of a built-in motivation to seek status, survive and reproduce. The craving for ever-new goods and fashionable objects, they argue, derives from a natural propensity to maximize genetic success through "sexual selection."[42] Voguish purchases and "positional goods" are a symbolic language people use to communicate with each other.[43] They serve the purpose of showing off and establishing people's status in the effort to attract potential sexual partners.[44] Some neuroscientists even argue that the natural propensity to acquire new fashionable goods without limits is pre-wired into our brain. Our minds, especially those of teenagers, they say, love new objects and release dopamine when they see them. The habit of seeking new things is deeply embedded in our genes because the identification of new resources and potential new dangers (and new partners?) has been crucial to survival[45] and reproduction. Research also indicates that our encephalon is set up to make us perpetually believe that we can have and do everything without limits.[46] These perpetual desires are run by neural circuits buried in the brain called "hedonic hotspots," which have about 30 percent more influence on our behaviors than the circuits of satiety or satisfaction.[47]

Genetic factors clearly do play a role in determining our wants. Yet, are they, alone, sufficient to explain people's perpetual cravings for new status symbols? Can they really account for the rapid obsolescence of our material desires? Hardly so. Genes can contribute to elucidate the mechanisms by which wants are transformed into needs, but they cannot help us to explain the rapid propagation of consumerism over time and across countries. The key drivers of the worldwide diffusion of luxury fever are not in our brain or DNA. They can be found in the way our society is organized, and more precisely, in the deceptive practices of the advertising industry.

The factory of illusions

John Kenneth Galbraith, author of *The Affluent Society*, once wondered: if our basic instinct is to want more and more, why do we need an ad-man to tell us what we need to buy?[48] Galbraith was right. The material pursuit of luxuries is largely a by-product of the massive bombardment our brains are exposed to: the torrent of countless messages and images persuading us that what we have is not enough.[49] Billions of dollars are spent each year to convince us that our necessities are obsolete and that we must update them for the sake of our happiness. For years, we have been the perpetual target of ads and messages that are trying to push the "buy" button within our brains every single time we see a movie, a billboard, surf the net, listen to the radio or go to a sports event. Each day we are bombarded with up to thousands of sales shots; in the US, this adds up to one every 15 seconds of a person's waking life.[46]

According to the 1998 United Nations Human Development Report, the growth of global ad spending outpaced that of the world economy by a third (in that year global ad spending was around $435 billion). Overall spending on ads in the US alone increased from $50 billion in 1979, to about $200 billion in 1998.[50]

Although contemporary corporate advertising is often described as "the soul of the market," most ads are actually based on deception and the withholding of information. The success of marketing campaigns largely depends on techniques of behavioral conditioning that are aimed at conflating the needs of the public.[51] It is true that our genes can make us naturally inclined to seek new things, look for new experiences and unexpected gains, but ads implant within our brains the illusion of scarcity even in conditions of opulence and abundance. Every single day of our lives, we are constantly told that we need more and more of something new. Ads tell us what to eat, what to wear, how to speak, how to walk, where to go and how to live. They prey on our fragility as persons, and leave us continuously unsatisfied with what we have and, more importantly, with whom we are. The trouble is that these ads are not only deceptive, but also effective. Many manufactured needs are now so deeply anchored in our psyche that we are no longer even aware of them. They are like the air we breathe.

There is ample evidence indicating that people are more likely to become prone to excessive consumption if they watch a great deal of television.[52] [53] [54] Juliet Schor found that each additional hour of TV watching per week increases a consumer's annual spending by roughly $200 per year, signifying that 15 hours of TV watching a week equals nearly $3,000 per year. A revealing "natural experiment" that indirectly examined the power of television viewing on people' attitudes was "conducted" in Bhutan. Until 1999, television and advertisements were banned from the entire country. Thereafter, the TV ban was lifted and, for the first time, Rupert Murdoch's Star TV Channel exposed the Bhutanese to ads, soap operas, violent movies and reality TV shows. Large changes in people's behavior and attitudes soon followed: there were sharp increases in family breakdown, crime, drug taking and violence in school playgrounds. After the ban lifted, a third of parents preferred watching TV to talking to their children.[55]

Some of the adverse effects caused by television and advertising may be unintended. Yet, advertisers are quite frank about their motives. They know that it is only when people consider certain products as part of their "extended self,"[56] that they become easy prey of advertising messages. They know that, unless people measure their self-worth in terms of what they possess, they can hardly be persuaded to buy things they do not need. As Nancy Shalek, president of a large advertising agency based in Los Angeles, once put it: "advertising at its best is making people feel that without their product, you are a loser."[57] A survey of presidents of big American companies showed that 85 percent of them admitted that advertising often persuades people to buy things they do not need. About half of them declared that advertising also persuades people to buy things that they do not really want.[58]

The advertising industry's favorite target is a child. Children are the best consumers for at least two reasons. First, they are emotionally and cognitively unprepared to understand and identify deceptive communication. Thus, they can be more easily convinced to attach their feelings to a product. As Shalek remarked: "kids are very sensitive to that [ads] . . . you open up emotional vulnerabilities, and it is very easy to do with kids because they are the most emotionally vulnerable."[59]

But there is a second reason why children are the favorite targets of the public relations industry: once they are hooked, they remain customers for life. As Wayne Chilicki, executive at General Mills, candidly revealed, "when it comes to targeting kid consumers, we at General Mills follow the Procter & Gamble model of 'cradle to grave.' We believe in getting them early and having them for life."[59] Children in the US spend an average of three hours a day in front of a screen. They watch about 10,000 TV ads per year. In *Branded Nation* James Twitchell quotes a study indicating that about 10 percent of a typical two-year-old's known nouns are brand names.[60] About 96 percent of American school children can identify Ronald McDonald and the only fictional character with more recognition seems to be Santa Claus. For them, the "M" of McDonald is more familiar than the Christian cross.

Exposing children to massive campaigns of deception during the early stages of their lives is one of the most powerful arguments challenging the hypothesis of "consumer sovereignty." If it is plausible to assume that adults can exert some degree of control over what they want, and can reject advertisers' suggestions of what to spend on, this is hardly the case for children. Moreover, since every adult is a developed child, how can we be sure that the mental effects caused by deceptive advertisements in early childhood are not still inside our brain once we get older? In fact, we cannot.

The rat race: some win, all lose

There is another explanation for why advertisements are so powerful. People have not only absolute needs, but also relative ones. While the former include the urge for food, water, sex, sleep, and are felt regardless of what the situation of other fellow human beings may be, the latter are particularly satisfying when they leave individuals feeling superior to others.[61] Satisfaction with wealth and material possessions belongs to the last category. It is a feeling influenced by not only what one actually possesses and consumes, but also by how others fare in comparison.

Countless writers have recognized that people have a tendency to evaluate their worth by looking at how well they fare in comparison to their surrounding social environment. Wealth, or lack of thereof, confers a certain degree of social recognition and respect. The rich, at the top of society, may often feel like peacocks displaying their long, colorful tail feathers ostentatiously. They are happy to show off how much they possess and spend. At the bottom of the hierarchy, however, the poor may feel like ugly ducklings. They may feel excluded, marginalized and even ashamed of themselves. Their peers look down upon them and can even make them feel like unworthy, inferior human beings. Both Karl Marx, the father of communism, and Adam Smith, the father of capitalism, agreed on this. Marx once explained that, "a house may be large or small," and "as long as the neighboring houses are likewise small, it satisfies all social requirement for a residence. . . . But let there arise next to the little house a palace, and the little house shrinks to a hut."[62] In a similar vein, when describing the emotions of superiority and inferiority that people feel while standing in different positions of the social hierarchy, Adam Smith observed: "the man of rank and distinction . . . is observed by all over the world. Everybody is eager to look at him. His actions are the object of the public care. Scarce a word, scarce a gesture that fall from him will be neglected." On the contrary, "the poor man . . . is ashamed of his poverty. He feels that it places him out of the sight of mankind. To feel that we are taken no notice of necessarily disappoints the most ardent desire of human nature."[63]

These are not just the intuitions of two of the most influential authors in the history of economics. There is ample empirical evidence showing that human beings deeply care about both their status and that of other people. Vanity is a deep-seated human feeling. Research conducted by Lutmer and colleagues, for example, found that after controlling for personal income, higher earnings by neighbors are associated with lower levels of individual wellbeing.[64] Another study found that participants who earn $40,000 a year are far more likely to be satisfied with their living standards if the people they compared themselves to earn $35,000 rather than $60,000.[65] One is hardly surprised by these results. Saints and angels aside, we are all very sensitive to inequalities in anything that confers us with more or less worth and self-respect.[66] Moreover, in a highly materialistic society like ours, wealth and status symbols are recognized as the most powerful markers of honor and dignity. Consider the value of diamonds, for example. Their worth is hardly proportional to their utility or beauty. Yet, for some people, diamonds can be extremely "useful" to impress others and show off social prestige. Although, on the surface, excessive spending seems all about accumulating fashionable objects and status symbols, on closer scrutiny, it just reflects a low-intensity struggle to gain, maintain or avoid losing social status. It is all about self-worth. As Smith pondered: "to what purpose is all the toil and bustle of this world? . . . what then are the advantages of that great purpose of human life which we call bettering our conditions?" Smith replied to himself: "to be observed, to be attended, to be taken notice of with sympathy, complacency, and approbation, are all the advantages which we can propose to derive from it."[67]

Following Smith's logic, the race for wealth and material possessions is much less manufactured than it seems. After all, if wealth and status symbols are surrogates of social recognition, they are accumulated to fulfill a natural, intrinsic predisposition: the inner desire to feel worthy, useful and appreciated. And is there anything wrong in trying to feel so? Certainly not. The trouble with engaging in a status war based on material pursuits is this: although wealth accumulation may allow one to gain social prestige in front of others, collectively, the level of social prestige remains the same. The reason is simple. In a zero-sum game, no matter how wealthy a population may become, 49.9 percent of it will always remain below the average. Spending for gaining or avoiding losing social prestige is dependent on others' spending. Thus, as wealth standards increase, so do the requirements to maintain the same level of social prestige. This reminds one of the passage in Gilbert and Sullivan's opera *The Gondoliers*: "when everybody is somebody, then no one is anybody."[68] In effect, status competition reminds of a "hedonic treadmill," or a rat running wheel, in which competitors have to go on running faster and faster, in order to keep up with others, even though they never really move forward at all.[65] [69]

The transplantation of dreams

Social determination theory says that people have either intrinsic or extrinsic (materialistic) aspirations in life.[53] Intrinsic aspirations, such as personal growth, relatedness and sense of belonging, can satisfy inner psychological needs.[70] [71] On the other hand, extrinsic, or materialistic aspirations like financial success, fame and physical attractiveness are only instrumental in nourishing deeper psychological needs. The theory also states that high doses of extrinsic, or materialistic values, can engender corrosive feelings of competition, envy, domination and even cruelty. The same values can also cast a shadow on creative and intrinsic impulses – to the point of impairing self-fulfillment and personal realization.[72]

These ideas derive from the groundbreaking work of numerous authors, Eric Fromm probably being the most important. In his best seller, *To Have or To Be?* Fromm placed human motives into two categories: having and being. In the "having" mode, people tend to primarily concentrate on material possessions, power and personal ambition. In the "being" mode, they mainly focus on sharing and engaging in meaningful, creative activities.[73] According to Fromm, only the latter can lead to human realization. Before Fromm, Karl Marx arrived at similar conclusions. As he wrote: "the less you are, the less you express your own life, the more you have, i.e. the greater is your alienated life."[74] Bertrand Russell echoed this view. He divided human aspirations into "possessive" and "creative" impulses. According to Russell, the major difference between these two categories of impulses is that while possessive motives aim at acquiring or retaining private goods that cannot be shared, creative ones strive toward making these goods or products available for use by others and society as a whole.[75] Although the British philosopher recognized that both possessive and creative impulses coexist in all of us, he too highlighted that the sole pursuit of materialistic aims is inherently inconsistent with personal fulfillment.[76] As he put it, "the best life is the one in which the creative impulses play the largest part and the possessive impulses the smallest."[76]

Unfortunately, the diffusion of consumerism, and the status war based on it, has not only changed our perceptions of what we want and need. It has also promoted a progressive modification of our "dreams." Life aspirations have become more extrinsic, materialistic. This may sound like no more than mere speculation, but there is empirical evidence supporting this hypothesis. According to a study conducted by the Higher Education Research Institute, for example, the percentage of American freshmen that found it "essential" or "very important" to become "well off financially" rose from 42 percent in 1966 to 74 percent in 2005. At the same time, the proportion of students that considered it "essential" or "very important" to develop "a meaningful philosophy of life" declined from 85 percent in 1967 to 39 percent in 2003.[77] [78] More recent surveys have revealed that these trends are relatively stable over time and making money remains, by far, a much more popular goal than finding meaning in life.

The rapid diffusion of materialistic aspirations has also been observed in adult surveys, including a study conducted by Roper pollsters which showed that although

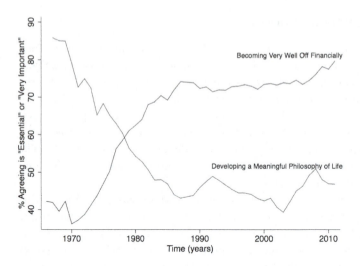

FIGURE 3.1 From meaning to money: changes in life aspirations among American freshmen, 1966–2011

Sources: Data for 1966 to 2006 from Pryor JH et al. The American Freshmen: Forty Year Trends. Cooperative Institutional Research Program, Higher Education Research Institute, University of California Los Angeles, 2007. Data for 2007, 2008, 2009, 2010 and 2011 from Pryor JH et al. The American Freshmen: National Norms for Fall, 2007, 2008, 2009, 2010 and 2011, Cooperative Institutional Research Program, Higher Education Research Institute, University of California Los Angeles.

in 1975 only 38 percent of the population identified "a lot of money" as an essential condition for a "good life," this proportion increased to 63 percent by 1996.[79] Similar conclusions were reached by another study, which estimated that about half of Americans under the age of 30 believed that they would end up rich later in life.[80] Research conducted by Reynolds and colleagues also showed that twice as many American high-school students in 2000 expected to work in a high-status job, in comparison to 1976.[81] Finally, a recent survey of 9- to 13-year-old children in England showed that about half of them believed once they become adults, the only kind of job they would want was one that made them a lot of money.[82]

Let us clear something up. There is nothing wrong with striving for a high-status job and a secure life. An individual's socioeconomic status is the most important determinant of health[83] and, as already explained in the previous chapter, economic resources, at least up to a threshold, play an important role in promoting life satisfaction. Nevertheless, after this threshold is crossed, more income does not buy happiness. Worse, high materialistic aspirations are not beneficial to wellbeing and can even lead to mental health problems.[53][84–88] Most people intuitively recognize that materialistic values can negatively affect their quality of life. A 2005 survey conducted in Sydney, for example, indicated that 83 percent of respondents complained that people in Australia are becoming "too materialistic."[89] Research conducted in the US showed that a large proportion of Americans believe that "materialism, greed and selfishness increasingly dominate American life, crowding out a more meaningful set of values centered on family, responsibility and community."[90] These perceptions are quite correct. An exaggerated focus on materialistic goals can sabotage intrinsic motivations and our ability to identify genuine meanings of life. In *The High Price of Materialism*, Tim Kasser argues that people aspiring to financial success tend to have fewer experiences that are conducive to the free expression of their own interests. As a result, they are less likely to be fulfilled both in terms of autonomy and authenticity.[91] Excessive doses of materialistic aspirations can suppress creative feelings; an observation often made among self-realized people such as artists, poets, scientists or anybody devoted to intrinsically fulfilling activities. People with high materialistic values report feeling passive and even empty as they tend to focus on activities – such as shopping and watching TV – that are antagonistic to the development of intrinsic interests.[92 93]

Materialistic values are also detrimental to healthy social relationships. Little by little, they harden people's hearts.[94] Research has shown that human interactions based on materialistic aspirations, even among family members and close friends, are generally filled with conflicts, envy and jealousies – qualities that disrupt empathy and reciprocity.[95 96] People who put money, success and fame at the center of their lives are not only less likely to be truly happy, but also more likely to make other people unhappy.[97]

Finally, materialism generates alienation and estrangement from the physical and ecological environment in which people live. This has been suggested by studies conducted in Australia[98] and in the United States[99 100] which have found that individuals with strong materialistic values are more likely to harbor negative attitudes toward the environment and report fewer ecologically friendly behaviors.

The failure of success: a love story

There is another major explanation for why materialistic aspirations are unworthy of being pursued. Even the "winners" of status competition, those who are supposed to benefit from the gained social prestige conferred by more wealth, achieve nothing more than a "pyrrhic victory." Why? Because individuals caught in a competition for material status, regardless of whether they are at the top, or at the bottom of the social hierarchy, develop a "contingent self-esteem," or the belief that they are worthy as long as they attain certain material goals (e.g. becoming rich, famous.)[101–103] This type of self-esteem is unhealthy because it is perpetually unstable, continuously challenged by the achievement of ever-new material goals and perpetual social comparisons.[104 105] Put another way, the self-respect gained by accumulating wealth, power and status is based on very shaky foundations. It reflects an inherently fragile self,[91] constantly at the mercy of tyrannical self-evaluation and other people's approval.[106–108]

Although people that strive for status and wealth usually look confident and self-assured, they are, in a deeper sense, the complete opposite. Tim Kasser compared the anxiety associated with the pursuit of status and luxury to the psychological fragility experienced among narcissists, who have personalities characterized by grandiose exterior acts of self-importance that cover inner feelings of insecurity.[91] In both groups, the excessive requirement to show off status, and an exaggerated need to gain the approval and admiration of others through extrinsic achievements, may just reflect a compensatory attempt to obtain a sense of "inner worth" that is lacking among these people. The more insecure individuals feel about the support and approval of others, the more they are in need of wealth, status or material surrogates to obtain the respect and approval that they are lacking, and that they cannot obtain by other means. Perhaps it is no coincidence that the rise of materialistic values in the last decades has coincided with the rise of narcissism, as suggested by a nationwide meta-analysis of American college students between 1982 and 2009.[109]

Psychologists have also found that individuals who aspire for materialistic goals are more likely to have been exposed to hostile parenting styles, characterized by criticism, coldness and disapproval. In *The Origins of Love and Hate*, Suttie explains that the quest to assert power and wealth represents an impulse arising from a deficit in tender reciprocity during the very first social relationships of life.[110] In other words, it is possible that the obsessive search for status and wealth in adult life reflects the attempt to gain the sense of security, love and affection that was missed during early childhood and adolescence. The attempt is futile, of course. Those who strive for love and affection, by showing off their wealth, or by controlling others through their power, end up being loved exactly because of these prerogatives. Thus, they are loved under the proviso that they maintain or even further their power and wealth. In other words, they are conditionally loved or, simply stated, they are just used, taken advantage of.

The age of futilitarianism

For most of human existence, almost everyone everywhere has been living in poverty. Then the Industrial Revolution came and people's lives changed in many ways. Over the years, individuals, generally, have become richer and healthier. Apart from a few nostalgic romantics who dream of the bliss they presume was experienced during the Stone Age, most recognize and appreciate the benefits of material prosperity. The rise of industrialism occurred together with the diffusion of utilitarianism, an ethical theory largely attributable to the ideas of Jeremy Bentham. The British philosopher equated happiness with pleasure or consumption, or what economists later called "utility." Since the Industrial Revolution, the limitless maximization of utility or consumption through fast economic growth has become one of the guiding principles of human progress. In Bentham's time, utilitarianism fit well within the priorities of the epoch. Poverty and indigence were commonplace. People were mostly preoccupied with covering their basic material needs. Utilitarian philosophers and economists could be partly forgiven for confusing happiness with consumption. Today, however, in a time of opulence and extreme wealth, their philosophy is anachronistic. As John Kenneth Galbraith once observed, "to furnish a barren room is one thing. To continue to crowd in furniture until the foundation buckles is quite another."[111]

Some forward-looking authors actually recognized the limits of the utilitarian doctrine early on. Their main criticism was this: life is much more than maximizing consumption and utility. Once material scarcity is overcome, most life satisfactions come from the pursuit of intellectual, social and creative aims, not material consumption. Curiously, one of the early critiques of utilitarianism actually came from a utilitarian philosopher: John Stuart Mill. As discussed in the previous chapter, Mill envisaged a society guided by wider and deeper aims than economic growth. While Jeremy Bentham considered "the game of push-pin . . . of equal value with the arts and sciences of music and poetry,"[112] Mill preferred a depressed Socrates to a happy pig.[113] He thought very highly of Bentham, but found his philosophy too shallow to be used as a guide for human progress.

Almost a century after Mill's critique of utilitarianism, John Maynard Keynes argued, even more persuasively, that the goals of human development must go beyond wealth accumulation and consumption. Keynes envisioned a point in the future in which rich societies had accumulated enough wealth to cover the basic material needs of the entire population. In his view, by becoming eight times better off than in 1930, societies would have reached "the point of enough" three decades into the twenty-first century. The British economist claimed that, upon passing this point, people could finally dedicate themselves to more important life goals than accumulating wealth. As he put it, once out of "the tunnel of economic necessity," individuals could finally "prefer the good to the useful."[114]

Keynes did not live long enough to see his hopes become vain. Just half a century after he made this prediction, the most affluent societies' GDP per capita was much more than eight times the 1930 level. But their exit from "the tunnel of economic necessity" did not affect their goals and priorities. Even today, as the global economy surpasses the threshold of $70 trillion, perpetual economic growth and material consumption remain the unquestioned aims of human development. In fact, such goals are pursued even more aggressively. The editors of *Adbusters*, a cultural jamming organization based in Seattle, argue that life in modern society is nothing but "work, buy, consume and die."[115] They hardly exaggerate. Consumerism is celebrated as a beneficial, even patriotic behavior. In the aftermath of the 9/11 attacks, president George W. Bush exhorted American citizens to go shopping. "We cannot let the terrorists achieve the objective of frightening our nation to the point where we don't conduct business, where people do not shop," he said. "Mrs. Bush and I want to encourage Americans to go out shopping."[116]

Hardly ever in US history had a president delivered a shallower speech. Nonetheless, Bush II should not be blamed more than necessary. He was just mindlessly repeating one of the doctrinal precepts of the public philosophy governing modern societies. Something economists, media pundits and politicians have been preaching for decades. As the editors of the *Financial Times* once pointed out, the "stamina of shoppers" is the driving force of "global (economic) growth."[117]

All in all, a society addicted to growth requires that citizens remain perpetually addicted to consumerism.[118] So much so, that even "the useless," not just "the useful," can be preferred to "the good." Utilitarianism glorified utility. Modern society celebrates futility.

Personal downshifting, political uplifting

More than half a century ago, Eric Fromm argued that modern society had engaged in a grand natural experiment aimed at testing whether unlimited material pleasure made people happy.[73] At the time when he wrote *The Sane Society*, he had already glimpsed at the preliminary findings of the experiment. Now, they are more apparent than ever: materialism and consumerism have failed to make people flourish. The reason is simple. Whatever philosophy, culture or religion one considers, most of them agree that values associated with materialism including greed, vanity and ambition are the antitheses of happiness and self-fulfillment. Since the times of Epicurus, philosophers have understood that excessive material desires thrive in discontented souls.[119] Most philosophers and spiritual leaders have also noticed that the essential ingredients of a happy life are sobriety, humility, sincerity and kindness.[120] Epicurus, for example, believed that happiness could only be found in the stillness of the soul, and suggested that we remain aloof from any process of desire creation and the subsequent striving for desire fulfillment. In his opinion, the true pleasures of life are prudence, serenity, foresight and rejection of immediate gratification.[119] Many other philosophers have arrived at the same conclusions. The Stoics before, and Spinoza later, explained that a life based on material pursuits does not lead to wellbeing for it is eternally unstable and addicted to extrinsic achievements. A key prerequisite for true, deep contentment, however, is freedom from cravings.

These philosophers maintained that, to truly enjoy life and appreciate pleasure, it is necessary to develop a "sense of enough." An essential feature of wisdom and happiness is the ability to appreciate what one already has, rather than continuously crave what one does not have.[121] As David Thoreau once explained, an individual is "rich in proportion to the number of things he can do without."[122] In *Meditations*, Marcus Aurelius echoed the same view. He suggested avoiding the craving of things that we do not possess, and appreciating what we already have. Imagine how much we would crave these possessions if they were no longer ours, he observed.[123] The Roman philosopher was one of the first thinkers to recognize that one of the determinants of happiness is gratitude. Recent empirical evidence provides support to Aurelius' claim. A paper published in the *Journal of Personality and Social Psychology* by Emmons and McCullogh, for example, found that people who recorded daily events for which they felt grateful, showed high levels of enthusiasm, determination, energy and optimism. In explaining these results, psychologists argue that grateful people enter "a circle of kindness," a mechanism in which gratitude leads to happiness which, through a positive feedback loop, leads to even more gratitude and happiness.[124]

The teachings of Epicurus, Spinoza and Marcus Aurelius exude wisdom and sense. Intuitively, we all understand that wellbeing is, at least partially, a by-product of serenity of mind, simplicity, frugality and gratitude. The trouble is that these behaviors are hard to practice in a hyper-materialistic society that praises consumerism, individualism and status competition. Moreover, some frankness is in order here: how many people would accept living in the woods like Thoreau did, for two years, two months and two days? Not many, and this is not surprising. Fortunately, however, there is no need to emulate Thoreau's exploits to be happy and ecologically responsible. A sober lifestyle should be enough to achieve both goals. By living with some, but not too much, people can have a decently happy life while containing waste, pollution and the depletion of natural resources.

In recent years, a growing number of people in the West have felt increasingly disillusioned by the prevailing culture of consumerism that has dominated modern society. A recent survey showed that almost 9 out of 10 Americans feel that the society in which they live is too materialistic. About 80 percent of them also believe their country excessively focuses on shopping.[125] Some, increasingly uneasy with the consumerism and hyper-materialism of modern culture, have began exploring new ways of life that combine ecological responsibility and social fulfillment.[126] While most Americans, on average, consume and pollute far more than individuals living in most other rich nations, some of them have managed to live with less money, switched to lower paying jobs, spent more time at home and have even dedicated themselves to socially fulfilling activities.[127] These lifestyle changes, called *downshifting*, have been observed in many other rich nations. Research conducted in Australia, for example, showed that about 23 percent of its sample, ranging in age from 30 to 60 years olds, decided to spend more time with their families and engage in more personally fulfilling activities by working and consuming less.[89] Similar trends have been reported in Britain.[89]

Personal changes toward a more sober lifestyle are laudable, but they will not stop consumerism or materialism from undermining our happiness and destroying the environment. In the West, lifestyle changes are often viewed as the magic bullet that can transform people's lives into greener, happier and healthier existences. Our bookstores are filled with self-help guides on happiness, health and green living, and many of them are among the very best sellers. Most propose reasonable solutions, but their success is largely based on a myth: the merry assumption that consumerism can be fought at the individual level, or just by changing people's psychology and motivation. This is not going to happen. The behavioral modification of a minority of sober and healthy consumers is futile unless there is a sustained effort to oppose the structural forces, policies and institutions that leave the majority imprisoned in perpetual cycles of dissatisfaction and conspicuous consumption. As Susan George once wrote:

> I have nothing against ethical consumption. Make those individual changes if they make you feel better and healthier, but don't allow them to make you

feel virtuous with regard to the world at large. And please, don't expect the rest of us to applaud: we have more important things to do.[128]

Justin Pudor holds a similar view: "the everyday consumption of the people in the rich countries is an outcome of the system, not the cause." He continues: "If history judges us who live in the rich countries harshly, it won't be for our individual consumption choices but for not fighting the structures of domination and power relations that set the context for those choices."[129]

In effect, the minority of virtuous people that engage in sober and simpler lifestyles will continue to remain a minority unless systemic political changes occur. This is for a simple reason. A "healthy" capitalist system is based on the imperative of unlimited economic expansion which, in turn, relies on the "organized creation of (consumer) dissatisfaction."[130] A functioning capitalist system is mainly driven by corporate profits that, in turn, depend on the perpetual upgrade of consumer needs. In other words, it is based on the hope that we all feel that what we have is not enough.[131] Perpetually. Economic growth cannot be promoted unless people continue to be cyclically unhappy with their material conditions. The more cyclically unsatisfied people are, the more created wants are generated, the more is consumed and the more the economy grows. But the day the citizen-consumers decide to reduce their consumption patterns to only what they really need, the economy shrinks or even collapses.[132] This perpetual engine of misery must be stopped if we want to create a happier and greener world.

4

CHAINS OF THE FREE WORLD

Throughout most of human history, the vast majority of people have been living in conditions of oppression. Poverty has denied individuals the chance to eat or get cured when sick, and the comfort to be adequately clothed and sheltered. It has also deprived people of clean water, sanitation and education. Then, in 1775, James Watt developed an improved version of Thomas Newcomen's steam engine, and the world changed forever. The wealth produced by industrial production, although accumulated through the brutal exploitation of desperate workers, freed countless people from indigence.[1] Industrialism also gave origin to subsidiary revolutions in the areas of technology, transportation, chemistry and medicine. Overall, these epochal shifts have made our lives more comfortable, healthier and safer than ever.

Economic progress has not only promoted freedom from hunger and poverty, but also advanced human emancipation. It provided people with new opportunities to devote their time and efforts to personally and socially fulfilling activities. It developed their capabilities to dedicate their lives to worthy goals.[2] According to Benjamin Friedman, economic prosperity has also provided individuals with the opportunity to become better persons – more tolerant, open, confident and autonomous.[3]

Other authors, however, have been much less impressed by the wonders of economic development. Some have even argued that, far from producing freer human beings, industrial society's obsession with pecuniary prosperity has reduced them to conformists incapable of genuine self-expression. The German sociologist Herbert Marcuse is one of these authors. In his opinion, people in modern society have actually turned themselves into "sublimated slaves."[4] This may sound like an extreme view, but Marcuse's logic is less radical than meets the eye: in a society where economic growth is the only master, who do you think has to play the role of the servants?

Development as unfreedom

Free market societies are widely considered the bastions of individual liberty.[5] Free choice, free markets, free enterprise; these terms are repeated like a mantra by economists, politicians and media pundits. People living in the industrialized world are also considered masters of their own fate. But are they really? The results of two meta-analyses examining trends in people's sense of control in the US suggest that this is hardly the case. The authors of the study, Jean Twenge and colleagues, showed that between 1960 and 2002 a rising proportion of young Americans felt as if their existence was determined by uncontrollable forces rather than their own efforts.[6] Far from enjoying a greater sense of freedom, youths in the US have experienced a growing feeling of alienation and apathy about the direction of their own destiny.

Previously, other authors noticed this same unedifying trend. In 1971, psychologist Julian Rotter observed that as "feelings of external control, alienation and powerlessness continue to grow, we may be heading for a society of dropouts – each person sitting back, watching the world go by."[7][8] One may argue whether findings of a study conducted in the US can be generalized to the rest of the world. This criticism is, indeed, justifiable. Yet, there are plausible reasons to believe that feelings of powerlessness experienced in the US can be indicative of what also happens in other market societies. In our increasingly integrated world, what occurs in America at one point in time is often a glimpse of what the rest of the world may experience later. As the old saying goes: "when America sneezes, the world catches a cold." Virtually all countries are affected by the spread of the American culture, either

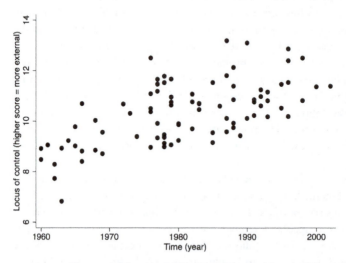

FIGURE 4.1   The age of freedom? The rise of external locus of control among adolescents in the United States, 1960–2002

Source: Twenge J, Zhang L, Im C. It's Beyond My Control: A Cross-Temporal Meta-Analysis of Increasing Externality in Locus of Control, 1960–2002. *Personality and Social Psychology Review* 2004;8(3):308–19.

through economic policies, global communication or both. Think about the diffusion of Hollywood movies, Coca-Cola and McDonalds, for example. What happens in the US does not only affect Americans, but concerns us all. As Thomas Friedman put it, "globalization is in so many ways Americanization."[9] For better or for worse, as long as it remains the most powerful country in the world, the US is the window through which we can imagine our future.

But what can explain the diffusion of a growing sense of impotence in a time of unprecedented freedom and prosperity? There are multiple potential candidates, including changes in expectations about personal efficacy across different generations and changes in the way we perceive the world. According to Twenge and colleagues, however, the main culprit for the growing sense of impotence in America is the diffusion of a culture of cynicism, distrust and social alienation.

The hypothesis that alienation is increasingly affecting modern society is in line with the intellectual contributions of earlier authors. Some have argued that there are subtle forms of social repression in modern democracies. According to Marcuse, people living in what he termed "overdeveloped societies," suffer from "repressive affluence," an illusory condition of freedom proportional to the intensity of economic development. In *One-Dimensional Man*, the author argues that over-consumption and over-production, far from being the results of collective freedom of choice, are tools of social control.[10] Lewis Mumford, the author of *The Conduct of Life*, arrived at a similar conclusion. In his opinion, modern civilization can "produce only a mass-man: incapable of choice, incapable of spontaneous, self-directed activities: at best patient, docile, disciplined . . . a creature governed mainly by conditioned reflexes."[11]

Before Marcuse and Mumford, several other authors expressed the same concerns. The famous theologian, physician and medical missionary Albert Schweitzer denounced the risks of human standardization and the mass conformity of modern living. "There is a tragic alliance between society as a whole and its economic conditions," he once observed. "With a grim relentlessness those conditions tend to bring up the man of today as a being without freedom . . . in short as a human being so full of deficiencies that he lacks the quality of humanity."[12] In the best seller *The Sane Society*, Eric Fromm echoes a similar view. In his book, he cites a number of other writers who highlighted the tendency of free market societies to turn people into mere appendices of the economy. In Fromm's view, although capitalism of the nineteenth century was criticized for its neglect of the material welfare of workers, "this was never the main criticism." As he puts it: "what Owen and Proudhon, Tolstoy and Bakunin, Durkheim and Marx, Einstein and Schweitzer talk about is man and what happens to him in our industrial system." He continues: "Although they express it in different concepts, they all find that man lost his central place in society, that he has been made an instrument for the purposes of economic aims."[13]

Robo sapiens in a material world

It is a conventional opinion among free market economists that the sharp rise of consumerism reflects the increasing sense of freedom people enjoy in modern society.[14] In a narrow sense, this may be true. If one considers our freedom of commercial choice, we have never been freer than today. Never before have we had access to a wider variety of goods, services and technologies. Yet, as Richard Neville once noticed, in contemporary society, while shopping options may have multiplied, lifestyle choices have diminished.[15] In a sense, we are more conformist, and essentially self-repressed, than ever.

Let us examine why. It is true that the enormous expansion of diversity and novelty in consumer choice reflects an increased commercial freedom – for those who can be consumers in our society. But this view ignores a fundamental fact: overspending is not necessarily a symptom of higher "consumer sovereignty." The opposite can be true. Research shows that frequent shoppers often behave as "compulsive buyers" or addicts, not independent human beings.[16] This is especially the case when considering conspicuous consumption that is driven by status competition. About four years ago, an angry mob, obsessed with the bargain buys of the post-Thanksgiving Black Friday Sale 2008, trampled a temporary Wal-Mart worker to death. When buyers were told to leave because of the death of the employee, some customers complained that they had been in line since the morning before and demanded to continue shopping.[17] If this seems pathological, that is because it is.

Shopping may give a sense of choice and power that may be absent from other areas of our life,[18] yet, what we often observe in commercial centers are delirious, hysterical shopaholics resembling anything but free human beings. As British historian Roy Porter once noted, in our increasingly "acquisitive society," people seem rather coaxed to consume and behave as if they are essentially self-enslaved.[19]

For sure, not all shoppers are compulsive buyers. Yet, addictive shopaholism is just the tip of the iceberg of a much deeper epidemic of conformist consumerism. It is a form of social repression on a grand scale. Here is why: the more one consumes, the harder one has to work to keep up with the higher tenor of life. The bigger house, fancier car or new mortgage, that are often acquired to gain, maintain or avoid losing social status, force people to work longer hours and give up more of their free time. People whose entire energies are spent working and consuming for status competition are no longer choosing which activities to focus on. They lose their autonomy and creativity. They lose the capability to do things for their own sake. They live by default. Unless they engage in some form of deep self-reflection, they may not even recognize how little control they have over their own lives. As Rosa Luxembourg once put it, "those who do not move, do not notice their chains."[20]

More than 80 years ago, John Maynard Keynes predicted that the twenty-first century would be called the *Age of Leisure*. This idea became especially popular in the 1970s, when there were high hopes for the power of technology to liberate individuals from long work hours and monotonous labor. Unfortunately, the "technological liberation" envisioned by Keynes did not materialize. It is true that in the last four decades, the annual hours worked by the total employed population in OECD countries has declined.[21] But the advent of new technologies, instead of freeing up manual workers from repetitive, alienating job tasks, has resulted in even higher pressure for faster and more intense production. In the US, since the 1970s, while work productivity has more than doubled, wages stagnated[22] and work stress increased. Work intensity has also risen in Europe, in spite of the more favorable working conditions and increases in annual weeks of paid vacation.[23] Advances in terms of wealth and technology have not promoted a better balance between an individual's work and personal life. Since the late 1970s, there has been a progressive disappearance of the single-income families. While in 1950, there were about 20 percent of American mothers employed, that figure went up to about 70 percent a few decades later. Similar trends have been observed in other industrialized nations. In *The Overworked American*, Juliet Schor shows that the number of work hours per week among women increased an average of 22 percent between 1960 and 1987.[24] In Britain, where full-time employees work the longest hours in Europe, about 46 percent of women work more than they are contracted for.[25] Since 1992, the number of women working more than 48 hours a week increased by 52 percent and the proportion of those working more than 60 hours more than doubled.[26]

No doubt, the increasing participation of women in the labor force offered new opportunities for human emancipation. Through their own employment and salary, many wives "liberated" themselves from economic dependency and maybe from their husbands. Nonetheless, an increased participation of women in the labor force came at a very high price in terms of children's quality of life. Children are the most notable victims of overworked families. They no longer enjoy the luxury of spending a large amount of their time with at least one parent, in a critical time of their development. In 1967, two-thirds of American children had one parent home full-time; by 2009, that figure was only one-third.[27] A study conducted in the US showed that the more time children spent in child care, the more likely their sixth grade teachers were to report behavioral problems.[28]

Excessive work, time pressure, stress and workaholism disrupt work–life balance, undermine wellbeing[29] and disrupt social relationships.[30] The relentless pressure to consume and produce faster can also erode people's ability to enjoy the simplest pleasures in life such as meditating, having a conversation with friends, listening to a song or walking in a forest.[31] Stress and work–life imbalance can sabotage self-actualization and personal expression. According to Aristotle, it is usually during leisure time, while performing activities for their own sake, that are not influenced by any external order or imposition, that we are truly ourselves.[32] It is mainly during free time that our most genuine motives come to the forefront. Of course, some people are able to pursue self-expression at their workplace – but only a few lucky ones. The majority hardly exert any control at work and have little chance to engage in activities that can fulfill their most creative and expressive needs.

While impairing wellbeing, personal fulfillment and social relationships, work-aholism can also generate adverse ecological consequences. This is indirectly suggested by a number of studies conducted in the US,[33] and other industrialized nations,[34] which showed that the more hours people spend at work, the bigger is their ecological footprint.

Just for show

The hypothesis of mass consumerism as a freedom suppressor is in line with the conclusions of numerous studies assessing the effects of materialistic aspirations in life. Research shows that people with high materialistic values are more likely to report feeling a lack of control over their lives.[35] Moreover, some studies indicate that people who prioritize materialistic aspirations often feel as if their quest for material goals is carried out beyond their own wishes.[36] The thirst for wealth seems to trap individuals into self-defeating cycles of ever-increasing new material wants and habituation, which end up undermining their ability to control new desires.[37]

It may sound paradoxical, but those who understand a thing or two about human aspirations know that the process of internalizing materialistic values is hardly governed by free will. Instead, it seems largely mediated by mechanisms of societal pressure and conformity that encourage people to acquiesce to socially accepted patterns of behavior. The prevailing norms in society do not only influence how much we consume and work. They also shape the life goals we aspire to. Furthermore, social norms influence the model of behavior that is admired and emulated in society. During the Renaissance, for example, artists and scientists were regarded as the quintessential expression of human potential. Life in modern society is instead inspired by the exploits of the wealthy celebrity, the attractive showgirl, the business executive or the powerful tycoon. These dominant norms do not only encourage certain life aspirations, but also repress those that do not fit within this prevailing ideology. As Thoreau puts it in *Life Without Principle*, "let us consider the way in which we spend our lives. The world is a place for business . . . It is nothing but work, work, work."

> If a man walks in the woods for love of them half of each day, he is in danger of being regarded as a loafer. . . . But if he spends his whole day as a speculator shearing off those woods and making earth old before her time, he is esteemed as an industrious and enterprising citizen.[38]

Individuals who decide against aspiring to life goals that are heavily discouraged by the prevailing culture can hardly be blamed. The reason is simple. We are all naturally compelled to make a good impression on others. This inclination maybe has something to do with our biology, our evolution and with the way our brain is organized. People tend to conform to the opinion and behavior of the majority in the fear of being ostracized.[39] Social banishment from a group or the exclusion from the herd is, in fact, not a minor nuisance. In the animal world and among hunter-gathering societies, this is tantamount to a death sentence.[40] There even seems to be a neurological basis for an innate "herd instinct." Research shows that popularity makes people feel good because it increases the level of pleasure hormones in parts of the brain. Therefore, it is difficult to partake in ways of living that are radically different from those embraced by the prevailing culture. And when the dominant culture glorifies materialism, aspiring to alternative life goals is even more difficult. Why? Research shows that motivation to adhere to social pressure is particularly strong in cases of social comparisons that are based on conspicuous consumption.[41] [42] As discussed in the previous chapter, relying on wealth and material possessions in establishing self-worth makes individuals' self-esteem perpetually vulnerable to social approval and tyrannical social comparisons.[43]

So, even though people in a highly materialistic society are free to pursue their own aspirations, there are strong social forces working against them. Of course, there are exceptions. There is a minority of independent thinkers who are less prone to follow the mass like sheep, and continue to pursue their own inner goals irrespective of the prevailing societal norms and values. People with a heightened sense of freedom have exceptional capabilities to dissent and refuse to conform to the expectations of others and society. They are only a lucky few, however. The majority prefers to stick to the crowd, even at the cost of losing the freedom to determine their own destiny. Fromm hardly exaggerated when he once observed: "the danger of the past was that men became slaves, [but] the danger of the future is that [they may] become robots."[44]

The unbearable meaninglessness of having

The Boston Museum of Fine Arts holds one of Paul Gauguin's most famous masterpieces. This artwork contains an inscription in the upper left corner with three questions: *Where Do We Come From? What Are We? Where Are We Going?* The French painter considered these the most important riddles of existence. He also believed that solving them is the hardest task of people's lives. Inspired by the same existential torments that have occupied the minds of some of the greatest philosophers in human history,[45] [46] Gauguin also believed that people's mission in life is to find a sense of purpose, a cause that gives meaning to everyday activities. In this, he was at one with Socrates who thought that an "unexamined life" was "not worth living."[47] He would have felt quite at home with Epicurus too who believed that true happiness requires an understanding of the nature of the Universe and our own place within it.[48] So, although happiness may entail light feelings, it is also based on heavy thoughts.

Other philosophers, as diverse as Bertrand Russell[49] and Thomas Aquinas,[50] have reiterated similar views. They also added that the search for meaning requires a contemplative habit of mind, inspiration and even solitude. In effect, existential questions are usually stimulated by our own reflective thinking, an epiphany or a traumatic event that forces us to look into the depths of our journey on planet Earth.

At times, they are evoked by visions of beauty, natural landscapes, the ruins of the past, sculptures, music or anything that fills us with a sense of vastness in time and space. Before these spectacles, we often remain in awe and wonder, as if we entered an ultra-zone of reality, a new cognitive dimension dressed by a deeper under-standing of our existential condition. When confronted with the most profound questions of life, some people turn to religion. Others strive for spiritual ways of living that do not require any extra-terrestrial meanings. People with high mate-rialistic values simply ignore them. For them, wealth, status and power are the only purposes worth pursuing.

In a path-breaking book, *Denial of Death*, Ernest Becker argues that when confronted with the prospect of passing away, some people cope with their anxiety by suppressing their thoughts.[51] Why does this happen? "The real world is simply too terrible to admit," Becker explains. "It tells man that he is a small, trembling animal who will decay and die."[52] The awareness of death's inevitability is pushed out of consciousness, substituted for worldviews that provide a sense of security and coherence.[53][54] This is what Becker defines as "an immortality project," a strategy for coping with the anxiety of existence. Religion is the most typical case of "immortality project." It encourages us to believe in resurrection and to avoid coming to terms with the inevitability of our biological end. Materialism and the belief in unlimited economic progress perform a similar function: they provide people with an even easier way out of the existential anguish tunnel.[55] It is not in resurrection, but in amassing wealth that some people find protection and coher-ence. Like religion, materialism provides individuals with the illusion of being outside the limits of the natural world. It allows people to feel, think and act as if they are immortal. Indeed, wealth and power may confer an image of invincibility, invulnerability as if they could be accumulated without an end.[56]

Becker's provocative hypothesis has been tested by different studies examining the plausibility of what psychologists term the "terror management theory."[57] They show that concerns over death can indeed generate stronger desires for self-distraction, in order to suppress existential concerns induced by mortality reminders.[58] When reminded of their own mortality, some people tend to place more value on status symbols and wealth.[59] They are also more likely to over-consume natural resources.[60] Concerns over death have also been associated with a stronger motivation to engage in compulsive shopping,[61] and longer hours of television watching.[62] Although this evidence can only provide modest support to the Becker theory, it seems clear that the attempt to manage the fear of death through materialistic aspirations is nothing but a "grand illusion."

The pursuit of wealth and status may somehow anesthetize or suppress the pain associated with the inevitability of death. But it cannot eliminate the sense of emptiness that comes with a life devoted to materialistic desires. Wealth and material possessions cannot be meaningful surrogates of deeper psychological needs. Most of us, sooner or later, find ourselves contemplating the most fundamental philosophical questions of life, no matter how hard we may try to suppress them from our consciousness. The *rendezvous* with the riddles of existence cannot be avoided, just postponed. The only way to truly overcome the anxiety of death is not by ignoring the key questions of life, or finding outlets for self-distractions, but by facing them and identifying worthy purposes to pursue.

What matters

If we were like other animals we would not have to ask ourselves where we come from, what we are and where we are going. Food, water, shelter and sex: what else would we need for a living? But we are not like any other animals – we are different. Although we share approximately 98 percent of genes with our chimpanzee cousins, we are the only creatures with the ability to reflect and ponder the meaning of life. We are the only species capable of speculating about the abstract nature of the universe and looking into the abyss of death. Although we can be overwhelmed by the thought of our end, we also have the power to tailor our existence around higher meanings than mere survival and reproduction. In some people, far from stimulating material desires, the awareness that we will eventually turn into scattered dust, motivates deeper reflections about life and its meaning. Research shows that while some people become more materialistic when they are reminded of their mortality, others become more generous, kind and tolerant.[63]

This is not surprising, for many philosophers have long understood that death lucubration brings people in closer touch with the roots of their existence. In their opinion, the authenticity of life springs from the understanding of death. It is in the contemplation of our finite nature and insignificance that we can distinguish what is truly important in life from what is not. It is for such reason that many people who experience a near-death event, or face a terminal illness, life calamities or natural aging, often undergo a shift in values away from materialistic goals.[64] It is not unusual, in fact, to observe people reaching a new level of understanding of the meaning of life when confronted with a traumatic event. Instead of turning to materialism, a near-death experience can promote a new awareness of what life means and how it should be lived fully.[65] It makes people realize that only intrinsic life purposes such as creative expression, social relationships and community contributions are worthy of being pursued.

In *A Free Man's Worship* Russell describes this idea beautifully: "in the spectacle of death, in the endurance of intolerable pain, there is a sacredness, an overpowering awe." In such moments, "we lose all eagerness of temporary desire, all struggling and striving for petty ends, all care for the little trivial things that, to a superficial view, make up the common life of day by day." He continues: "[It is] from that awful encounter of the soul with the outer world, [that] renunciation, wisdom, and charity are born, and with their birth a new life begins."[66]

Spiritual recession

In ancient Greece when someone died, philosophers wondered whether the deceased had lived with passion. Death was viewed as unimportant as long as it happened to a person who had dedicated his or her life to fulfilling his or her inner motives. It was perceived as terrible, however, when someone died without having really lived. For Greek philosophers, the real death was not the last breath that put an end to someone's existence, but the feeling of having wasted an entire life without fulfilling one's own aspirations. The best antidote to an unhappy life was one's dedication to a cause greater than oneself. Aristotle believed that living virtuously was the most important determinant of human flourishing.[32]

Many other philosophers thought in the same way. Spinoza, for example, argued that joy and happiness were determined by worthy living.[67] John Stuart Mill too embraced this view of happiness as a by-product of higher life pursuits. "Those only are happy . . . who have their minds fixed on some object other than their own happiness, on the happiness of others, on the improvement of mankind, even on some art of pursuit," he argued. "Aiming thus at something else, they find happiness by the way."[68] Various psychologists also share the same perspective. Victor Frankl, a Jewish concentration camp survivor and leading existentialist, expressed a similar point of view when he observed: "happiness cannot be pursued; it must ensue."[69]

Of course, this is not to say that people have to uniformly aspire for the same goals or to argue that the search for meaning is, as some religious leaders maintain, an extra-terrestrial enterprise. Exactly the opposite. The meaning in life is defined subjectively; individuals have their own explanations for why life is worthy to be lived. What is important for one person can be completely meaningless for another and vice versa. Instead, it is up to individuals to identify their own motives, through personalized paths, reflective thinking and internal inquiries. As Eric Fromm once explained, there is no meaning in life except for the meaning people are prepared to give to it.[70] Jean-Paul Sartre was at one with Fromm. In his opinion, life is shaped the same way as a piece of art, and people are nothing more than what they make of themselves.[71]

Numerous other philosophers would have agreed on this. They would also most likely concur that a key prerequisite for the discovery of meaning is freedom. Two types of freedom, to be more precise: the freedom to be (oneself) and the freedom to become (what one wishes.) As the father of the theory of human needs Abraham Maslow explained, self-actualization is the tendency of "becoming more and more what one is" and "to become everything that one is capable of becoming."[72] Eric Fromm too viewed self-realization as a by-product of "being" oneself and "becoming" what one wants to be. As he once noted, "man's task in life is to give birth to himself, to become what he potentially is."[73]

The trouble with materialism and consumerism is that they do not encourage any of these freedoms. They actually do the complete opposite. By trapping individuals into a mindless race for status based on conspicuous consumption, materialistic goals repress the innate "freedom to be" and alienate people's identity. By reinforcing the idea that happiness can be purchased through material acquisitions and high status, material aspirations mislead individuals about the most important sources of happiness. But the pursuit and achievement of material goals cannot satisfy the deeper psychological needs of individuals. Only intrinsic life goals such as personal expression, emotional intimacy and community involvement can.[74] As Frankl once observed, what "distinguishes each individual and gives meaning to his (or her) existence has a bearing on creative work as much as it does on human love."[75] Materialism and consumerism do not only stop us from being ourselves; they also limit the "freedom to become," by making us totally oblivious to and unreflective of the deeper meanings of our existence. In this sense, by stopping people's search for meaning and impairing their capability to dedicate their lives to worthy pursuits, materialism and consumerism leave individuals in a sort of existential limbo, a state of spiritual retardation that deprives them of the very qualities that make them humans.

Liberation theosophies

The history of humankind has been shaped by countless battles for freedom. Many have been won and many have been lost. Very often, the price for liberty has been life itself. Throughout the years, countless people have preferred to give up their lives than exist in conditions of slavery or oppression. A large number of intellectuals, activists, philosophers, scientists and religious leaders have insisted that without freedom there is neither happiness, nor dignity in life.

Many of these ideas flourished during the Enlightenment era. One of the first systematic treatises on the importance of freedom is Jean Jacques Rousseau's *Discourses on Inequality*.[76] Rhetorical bursts such as "man was born free, but everywhere is in chains" aside, Rousseau highlighted a very important point: human freedom (and the consciousness of it) is one of the noblest faculties of an individual, and is one of the very qualities that define the state of being human. Immanuel Kant agreed. He once observed that an individual route to happiness is a highly particular individual choice and should not be influenced by any external influence. Wilhelm von Humboldt, one of the founding fathers of classical liberalism, argued that, "the true end of man is . . . the highest and most harmonious development of his powers to a complete and consistent whole." He also added: "freedom is the first and indispensable condition which the possibility of such development pre-supposes."[77]

Following the Enlightenment era, the importance of liberty in human development was reiterated by countless other theorists. In modern times, some of the most insightful essays about freedom have come from philosophers such as John Dewey and Bertrand Russell. Both have embraced a similar idea: love of independence and free thought are characteristics that are unique to productive, creative and happy minds. Scientists of the caliber of Albert Einstein have proposed the same ideas. As he once put it: "everything that is really great and inspiring is created by the individual who can labor in freedom."[78]

Intellectuals that believed in human freedom such as Rousseau, Kant, Dewey, Russell and Einstein have very little to share with the contemporary champions of market liberalism. Today, it is commonplace to hear the word "liberalism" to define a school of thought that promotes the freedom of markets from government interference and the freedom of consumers and producers to buy, sell, acquire wealth and maximize profits. Only a few of today's self-appointed "libertarians," however, bother to wonder whether any of these freedoms are consistent with psychological fulfillment and the expression of intrinsic life aspirations. In fact, far from promoting psychosocial maturation, which is a necessary prerequisite for the actualization of one's inner potential, the commercialized version of liberty promoted by free market ideologues undermines intrinsic expression and personal development. It is no coincidence that, as revealed by Schwartz and colleagues in a study published in *Psychological Inquiry*, the type of economic freedom promoted in societies that emphasize free market competition is actually negatively correlated with an intrinsic sense of autonomy.[79]

It is also very revealing that market libertarians are completely at ease with the undemocratic, hierarchical relationships that prevail in industrial societies. They find no problem with the obedient, knee-jerk behaviors that characterize human relations at work. Their view of liberty has, in fact, very little in common with that of classical libertarians, who opposed hierarchies, subordination and conformity. Even Adam Smith, an author often revered by free market liberals but read only in a hurry, was cognizant of the psychological degradation induced by subordination at work and the division of labor. Smith warned that the division of labor condemned far too many workers to degrading, alienating jobs and deprived them of opportunities for personal growth and social development. Do you hear contemporary free market economists expressing similar concerns? Rarely. As Smith put it:

> The man whose whole life is spent in performing a few simple operations . . . [with] no occasion to exert his understanding or to exercise his invention . . . naturally loses . . . the habit of such exertion, and generally becomes as stupid and ignorant as it is possible for a human creature to become.[80]

Another classical libertarian who is completely ignored by today's "economic freedom fighters" is Wilhelm von Humboldt. Von Humboldt went much further than Smith in highlighting the importance of freedom and the adverse effects of the division of labor. As he explained, "whatever does not spring from a man's free choice, or is only the result of instructions and guidance, does not enter into his very being, but still remains alien to his true nature," and makes an individual more similar to a machine than a human being. As a result, regardless of how good a person may be at creating products, if they are made on the basis of extrinsic motives, or external orders, "we may admire what he does, but we despise what he is."[77]

Given that many market libertarians confuse Marxism with the brutal regime observed in the former Soviet Union during the twentieth century, most are blissfully ignorant of Karl Marx's libertarian ideas. In his fierce indignation and condemnation against the degrading conditions of workers during the early industrial age, Marx complained that alienating working conditions made individuals not only estranged from the outcomes of their labor, but also from their very own nature. According to Marx, an alienating job "mutilates the laborer into a fragment of man, degrades him to the level of appendage of a machine" and reduces workers to the "dependence of an animal."[81]

Another libertarian whose ideas have been completely ignored by today's free market ideologues is Alexis de Tocqueville. The French author underlined the dangers of human alienation, deriving his ideas from the mechanization of work and the division of labor. As he once wrote: "When a workman is unceasingly and exclusively engaged in the fabrication of one thing . . . he loses the general faculty of applying his mind to the direction of the work." He then added: "in a word, he no longer belongs to himself . . . the art advances, but the artisan recedes."[82]

The art of living

When Alexander the Great, the King of Macedonia, asked Diogenes Laertius if there was anything he could do for him, the philosopher replied: "please, step out of my way, you are blocking the sun." Meanwhile, Antisthenes, one of Socrates' pupils, upon learning that in Athens his work was, at last, the object of great admiration, replied sarcastically: "what have I done wrong that I am praised?"[83]

Since the beginning of human civilization, planet Earth has been inhabited by people gifted with a particularly high sense of freedom. Unaffected by the prevailing norms in society, they have managed to think and live as they wish, against the stream of conformity. Unfortunately, this group has always consisted of a tiny minority of exceptional individuals, which is still the case today. However, there is no need for this minority to be the exception, rather than the rule. The unprecedented conditions of prosperity, comfort and technological advancements we enjoy today should allow most, if not all people, to think and live on the basis of their own intrinsic aspirations. We should all be encouraged to express our own creative impulses, instead of feeling compelled to conform to the prevailing values of materialism and consumerism. We are capable of being more than mindless shopaholics and obsessive status seekers. Regrettably, it is because the most social and creative prerogatives of life are neither supported, nor encouraged, that many people's intrinsic motivations in life have descended into a state of dormancy. And until there are more outlets for creative expression and human actualization, too many people will continue to die without having really lived. Many will live without being born. This is a disgrace. In a truly emancipated social system, all people should be offered the chance to fully express their own creative potential. As von Humboldt once argued, even peasants, producers and craftsmen should be given the opportunity to elevate themselves to the status of "artists."

This may sound like a radical idea. But just a few centuries ago, was not the abolition of slavery almost impossible to imagine? In reality, the progression toward a society of creative, independent thinkers is more logical than radical. This ideal has been envisioned by not only classical libertarians, but also by some of the most influential economists who have ever lived: John Stuart Mill, John Maynard Keynes and John Kenneth Galbraith, to name a few. The three Johns recognized the importance of subordinating economic goals to human progress. Far from being attracted to any revolutionary idea, they simply believed that the ultimate aim of society should be to foster "the art of living." As described in a previous chapter, although Mill proposed a post-growth, stationary-state economy, he did not believe that limits to economic growth and consumption implied any limits to social growth and human development. "It is scarcely necessary to remark that a stationary condition of capital and population implies no stationary state of human improvement," he wrote. "There would be as much scope as ever for all kinds of mental culture, and moral and social progress: as much room for improving the art of living."[84]

In a similar vein, Keynes envisioned a future where "the accumulation of wealth" no longer had to be of "high social importance." As he observed, "the love of money as a possession – as distinguished from the love of money as a means to the enjoyments and realities of life – will be recognized for what it is, a somewhat disgusting morbidity."[85] Once human beings are freed from the slavery of needs and oppressive work, Keynes continued, each individual "will be faced with his real, permanent problem – how to use . . . freedom from pressing economic cares, how to occupy the leisure . . . how to live wisely and agreeably . . . and cultivate into a fuller perfection, the art of life itself."[86]

Galbraith struck a similar chord when he imagined that, "sooner rather than later our concern with the quantity of goods produced – the rate of increase in Gross National Product – would have given way to the larger question of the quality of life that it provided."[87]

The lateral society

Unfortunately, the visionary ideas of Mill, Keynes and Galbraith have not materialized. On the one hand, there have not been sufficiently significant steps toward a fairer management of resources and income, and still today a large portion of humanity is struggling with hunger and misery. On the other hand, there have not been any meaningful attempts to reorganize economic activities around the promotion of human fulfillment, genuine social exchange and creative expression. But there are at least two major ways to promote "the art of living." One route regards the way, and how much, we work. The other concerns the way, and how much, we enjoy leisure time.

Let us tackle work first. In the status-obsessed, shopaholic–workaholic culture that prevails, people can hardly find appropriate outlets for human actualization. There are insufficient opportunities to engage in creative expression and social relationships. There is a way out of this, however. One of the major ways to promote a more personally fulfilling society is to re-organize production to ensure that everybody has enough work to live, yet that nobody lives only to work. This can be achieved when people are allowed to choose a reduced work schedule and can spend more time in activities dedicated to self-expression and human development. The trouble with the present organization of production is that while many workers suffer social marginalization and poverty due to unemployment, others that have employment are overworked and overstressed. If the overworked took on fewer hours, there would be enough employment for everyone. And even if this meant fewer goods, services and comforts, it would also provide more time for us to enjoy social participation, personal relationships, creative activities and personal expression.

John Maynard Keynes proposed a 15-hour workweek. In his view, this would be enough to combine material security with social living and creative development. Bertrand Russell advocated for four hours of work a day. In his mind, this would suffice to ensure material security and the free pursuit of personally fulfilling activities.[49] Of course, free market economists find these proposals completely preposterous. For them, a general reduction of work hours would be catastrophic for the economy. They are wrong. A political economic system committed to full employment and a reduced work schedule would allow for an inclusive society where everybody counts and nobody is left behind. This is not utopia – this model has already been applied in the past, during the Second World War, for example. It worked. As Russell once explained: "war showed conclusively that, by the scientific organization of production, it is possible to keep modern populations in fair comfort on a small part of the working capacity of the modern world."[88] Certainly, we do not need to go to war to create a more fulfilling society. It should be enough to learn from history and foster the sense of solidarity and human cooperation that united people in war times, and apply it in times of peace.

The other area that can transform the way people seek satisfaction in life is the availability and use of leisure time. In the *Joyless Economy,* Tibor Scitovsky argues that consumerism makes individuals develop a tendency to seek satisfaction in the wrong things and in the wrong way. Modern living tends to prioritize opportunities and leisure-time activities that increase comfort, but reduce enjoyment. In Scitovsky's opinion, however, in order to create a happier and more fulfilled society it is necessary to educate people on making good use of their leisure time.[89] How? By encouraging them to focus on "creative consumption" – engagement in activities performed for their own sake including sports, arts, music, science, conversations and other forms of non-materialistic activities.[89]

Unfortunately, at the present time, most of the activities that promote creative and social expression seem to be often considered "useless." This mentality must change if we are to develop our society into one that promotes human flourishing. As human beings, we are in need of a considerably fuller expression of creative and emotional powers than our society currently allows. The challenge lies in replacing our competition hunger and self-perfection impulses with forms of expression and social living that are compatible with a happy and sustainable life. While fighting for material status is clearly deleterious from a psychosocial and environmental perspective, competitive impulses should not be completely repressed. Rather, they are essential for the promotion of human flourishing, as they encourage people to go beyond their own limits. The problem is not competition, but what people are competing for. Unlike materialistic aims, competition for intrinsic and social goals is not necessarily affected by tyrannical social comparisons and status anxiety. Research shows that feelings of envy are accentuated when people compete for material rewards, but not necessarily when they compete for other purposes. For example, in an experiment where a group of students were asked to choose between a world in which some subjects earned $50,000 a year while others earned $25,000, and another in which they earned $100,000 while others earned $250,000, about 56 percent of participants chose the first. But when, in the same experiment, students were asked to choose between a world in which they had two weeks vacation a year while others had one, and another in which they had four weeks while others had eight, only 20 percent of subjects chose the first world.[90]

Currently, people's competitive instincts are mostly concentrated on racing for profit and material status. A society promoting human flourishing should redirect these impulses toward the expression of more innocent forms of competition, such as sport, art, science and literature. By reducing emotions of envy and status anxiety, competition for non-materialistic goals can also promote better social relationships and social cohesion. Above all, by changing the focus of the status competition from materialistic to intrinsic goals, the innate sense of rivalry harbored in human beings can be liberated and fully expressed, without causing over-consumption of natural resources and undue harm to the ecosystem.

R-evolution

Our personal aspirations are like a zero-sum game: if the most creative and cooperative expand, the most materialistic and selfish retreat. The development of a happier and ecologically sustainable society relies on a revolution of conscious-ness to liberate our aspirations from materialism, greed and consumerism. In freeing up our lives from the chains of materialistic values we have nothing to lose but the worst part of our nature. If we fail to do so, however, the toll may be insur-mountable.

Countless authors have realized that the ultimate problem with the current model of development is its basis on the wrong ideals.[91–93] There is a need for a revolution of consciousness, a spiritual renewal. Recently, calls for a cultural change toward new values of equity, fairness and solidarity have multiplied. Paul Raskin dreamt of the *Great Transition*.[94] David Korten envisioned *The Great Turning*.[95] Jeremy Rifkin visualized a race to global consciousness and the rise of what he called *The Empathic Civilization*. The bad news is that we do not have much time left to operate a global consciousness revolution. The good news, however, is that in recent years, we have witnessed the rise of counterculture movements committed to changing the world. Perhaps, a silent revolution in our values has already begun. More and more people seem to live "against the stream" of conformist materialism glorified by free market economists and media pundits. In *The Cultural Creatives*, Paul Ray and Sherry Anderson estimate that about 50 million Americans and 80–90 million Europeans are "disenchanted with consumerism, status displays, glaring economic inequalities, hedonism and political cynicism." These "cultural creative" individuals are also increasingly interested in environmental issues, social activism, human relations, spirituality, peace, global justice and self-expression.[96]

Of course, it would be naive to be under the illusion that our social system needs only a change of values. The fulfillment of a new vision of human progress requires much more than the overthrow of conspicuous consumption and status competition. Unless society is liberated from the slavery of an economic system devoted to endless economic growth and capital accumulation, the psychological catharsis of a minority of individuals will be in vain. Indeed, the pursuit of freedom and the realization of human potential are much more than psychological endeavors. To be realized, they require active resistance, peaceful disobedience, and radical political change. Some may feel put off by the word "radical" that is often confused with "extreme." But in reality, radical means "going to the root" and political change that is not radical must necessarily be superficial.

5

MARKET MEDIOCRACIES

The term "civilization" refers to an advanced stage of human and social development. It is also used to indicate the process by which societies reach such stage.
Civilization can occur through advances in culture, art, literature, science, technologies and wealth. Countries also "civilize" themselves by making progress in
political organization. Advanced societies embrace democracy. Backward ones are
under totalitarianism, aristocracies, plutocracies or oligarchies.

If we are to judge humanity by the diffusion of democracy, the world has never
been more civilized than it is today. Although the last century was the deadliest and
bloodiest in history,[1] there were unprecedented advances in civic emancipation. In
many parts of the globe, totalitarian regimes and tyrannies have been defeated. The
rise of social movements, spurred by the active involvement of people in political
affairs, has influenced policies and public opinion almost everywhere. As societies
have developed economically, democracy has become the norm rather than the
exception.[2] These successes are undeniable. At the beginning of the twentieth
century, there were no nations that could be judged as electoral democracies by the
standard of universal suffrage. Women and minorities could not even vote in some
of the most advanced nations, such as the US and the UK. But by the year 2000,
political franchise had spread to more than 60 percent of the world's population.[3]

Civic progress continues today. While in low- and middle-income countries
totalitarian regimes are being dismantled one after another, transparency and
accountability are becoming more common in the most affluent nations. Democracy
is being invoked everywhere as an inalienable right: from the capitals of the Middle
East to Zuccotti Park in New York, from the Chinese sweatshops to the streets of
Athens, people's demands for social justice are growing exponentially. They can
hardly be ignored. Pareto was probably right when he wrote that, "history is a
graveyard of aristocracies." However, that is only half of the story. This chapter is
about the other half.

Uncivil societies

In free market societies, most people believe they live in democracies. Technically, they are right. On paper, citizens of affluent nations enjoy a list of inviolable liberties including freedom of speech, the right to vote and the right of association. Laws are in place to ensure that each resident can take advantage of such prerogatives. But is the existence of these rights sufficient to qualify societies as democratic? This is hardly the case. Democracy is more than a mere juxtaposition of legal arrangements. It also requires the continuous involvement of people in political and civic affairs.[4][5]

Unfortunately, the aspiration of political equality based on the active engagement of all citizens, often flagged as the defining feature of free market democracies, is turning into a mirage. In the last decades, a growing number of people in affluent societies have become completely disaffected by the political process. Faced with the prospect of the unedifying spectacle of political elections run like advertisement campaigns, many do not even take the time to vote anymore. Skepticism toward politicians and governmental institutions is commonplace. Countless individuals have abandoned any hope of contributing to political decisions affecting their countries and communities. Disheartened, disillusioned, they have retreated to their private affairs, choosing to only attend to their own everyday business. Although political rights have never been as widely possessed as they are today, more people seem to act as if they do not have any of them.

The civic crisis of modern societies can be observed from different angles. A case in point is the US, widely considered the blueprint of democracy. In the 1899 novel *Following the Equator*, Mark Twain noticed that, in his country, people had "three unspeakably precious things: freedom of speech, freedom of conscience, and the prudence never to practice either of them."[6] To be sure, since Twain's time, the "land of the free and the home of brave" has become a much more democratic place to live. Nevertheless, Twain's words are still somehow appropriate. There is a disconcerting paradox at the heart of the American democracy: an unprecedented political freedom coexists with an unprecedented political apathy. In 1968, the US voter turnout in parliamentary elections was 89.66 percent. By 2010, it had dropped to 41.59 percent.[7]

The decline in voter turnout has been accompanied by an increase in people's reluctance to participate in public affairs, as documented by various authors,[8][9] including Robert Putnam, author of the best seller *Bowling Alone*.[10] The democratic crisis of America is also reflected in the progressive disengagement of workers from labor unions, one of the most important democratizing forces of society. While in 1970, almost a third of the US workforce belonged to a labor union, by 2007 only 12 percent of workers were unionized.[11]

The US, of course, is an exceptional case. Nevertheless, these changes have not only occurred within the American borders. Civic disengagement has affected the most established democracies,[12] and the entire world.[13] In England, voter turnout decreased from 84 percent in 1950 to 61 percent in 2007.[14] In continental Europe, voting participation peaked in the 1960s only to decline steadily in the decades

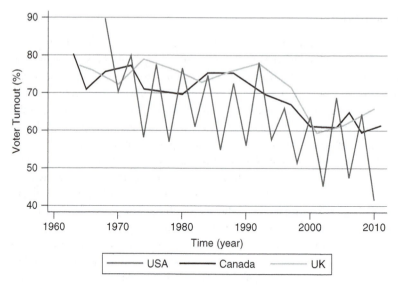

FIGURE 5.1   Democracies in crisis: voter turnout in parliamentary elections in the United States, United Kingdom and Canada, 1963–2011

Source: International Institute for Democracy and Electoral Assistance (IDEA) 2010.

after. Vanishing voter turnouts have been reported in Italy, Spain, Belgium, the Netherlands, Norway, Sweden, Ireland,[15] Japan and Latin America.[16–19] The civic decline has not spared younger generations that are increasingly reluctant to engage in public and political matters.[20][21]

As was the case in the US, in the UK the decline in voter turnout and social participation occurred simultaneously with the eclipse of labor unions. In 1970, about 44.8 percent of wage earners in the United Kingdom belonged to a trade union. By 2007, however, only 28 percent of them were unionized.[11][22] Declines in trade union membership have occurred in most OECD nations[23] and even in Latin America.[24] This leaves us with a crucial question: what is the culprit behind these decreasing trends?

Just for the love of money

There are different explanations for why so many people have become disengaged from social and political activities. David Davenport, a researcher at the Hoover Institution, a right-wing foundation based in Stanford, offered a curious one. In his opinion, the driving force behind the weakening of civic associations in the US is an "unhealthy dependency on government," promoted by "grant programs in education, social welfare (specifically child welfare), and mental and public health."[25] At best, this logic is difficult to follow. Nonetheless, it could be plausible to assume that government interventions are not necessarily beneficial, and can even be repressive to the point of discouraging social participation. Yet, it requires considerable intellectual acrobatics to affirm that welfare policies and public education limit civic engagement. Unfortunately, this claim has managed to garner significant support in the mainstream corporate media – perhaps, because it is in direct line with the cult of blaming "big government" for all wrongs in society. Indeed, orthodox neo-classical economists, and their neo-conservative associates, never miss a chance to reinforce the idea that government interventions limit individual freedom and choice.

The only problem with this claim is that it is entirely wrong. In fact, the evidence shows that the opposite is more likely to be true. Political disempowerment, fatalism and civic disengagement are more prevalent in more unequal societies,[26–31] that are also more likely to have weaker welfare programs and underfunded public education. And why is it that in unequal societies people are more likely to abstain from civic and political action? There are multiple potential mechanisms. As discussed in previous chapters, economic inequality promotes competition for status, reduces feelings of solidarity and encourages people to become more individualistic and materialistic. Consequently, in highly unequal societies, individuals are too preoccupied with looking after their own businesses[32][33] to find time to engage in community, civic and voluntary activities. Although in *Bowling Alone*, Robert Putnam does not specifically concentrate on the rise of economic inequalities in the US as an explanation for the decline of public participation, his analysis offers important insights in the matter. According to Putnam, about half of the reduction in civic engagement is attributable to what he neutrally terms "generational shift." What does he mean by that? Nothing less than a change in the social norms and values of younger Americans that has resulted in a widespread lack of interest in dedicating free time to "non-pecuniary activities."[34]

Putnam is not alone in this view. Other authors have also pointed out the rise of materialistic aspirations as an explanation for the decline of civic engagement. Political scientist Wendy Rahn, for example, proposed that a major contributor to the growing civil decadence of modern societies is "an unhealthy emphasis on making money and acquiring possessions."[35] Psychologist Tim Kasser holds a similar view. In his opinion, a key problem of market societies is that "the main goal of individuals is to get whatever they can for themselves: to each according to their greed."[36] Some authors that we have long forgotten about, however, have previously argued that the rise of individualism and materialism simply reflects a built-in tendency of the capitalist system. To the surprise of some, one such writer was Albert Einstein. In a 1949 article entitled "Why Socialism," he observed: "the position of an individual in society . . . is such that the egotistical drivers of his make up are constantly being accentuated, while his social drives, which are by nature weaker, progressively deteriorate."[37]

In power we distrust

Another major route by which economic inequality is able to depress civic engagement is through mistrust. In highly unequal societies, people are not only more likely to be competitive and selfish, but also to experience feelings of interpersonal and political distrust.[30][38] Both forms of distrust are potential contributors to voting absenteeism and civic disengagement.[39][40] Trends over time have shown that in the last decades, the rise of inequalities and the decline in voter turnout among market democracies has coincided with an endemic diffusion of cynicism toward public institutions and political leaders.[41] This was not the case a few decades earlier. During the 1960s in the US, the percentage of citizens who considered their government trustworthy was about 78 percent. That proportion, however, decreased to less than 22 percent by 2010.[42][43] Louis Harris has developed a composite indicator of powerlessness and feelings of disdain toward people in power, which showed that "alienation" rose from 29 percent in 1969 to 65 percent in 1993.[44] Similar trends have been observed on the other side of the Atlantic, in the UK. In a survey conducted a few years ago, about 72 percent of UK citizens admitted to feeling a high level of "disconnection" from their parliament.[45][46] Civic participation and trust have collapsed in Eastern Europe as well, especially following the economic transition toward free market fundamentalism – resulting in the dramatic increase of the economic gap between rich and poor.[47]

On that note, it must be noticed that the rise of economic inequalities has also coincided with the progressive invasion of corporate money into politics. When we examine this, it is no wonder that people began to merely look after their own

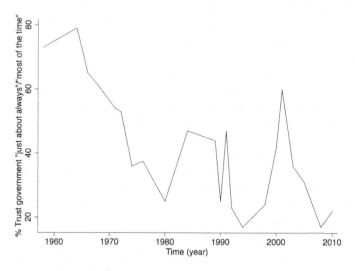

FIGURE 5.2 In power we distrust: changes in public perceptions toward government in the United States, 1958–2010

Sources: Pew Research Center, National Election Studies, Gallup, ABC/*Washington Post*, CBS/*New York Times* and CNN Polls (1958–2010).

Question: How much of the time do you trust the government in Washington? Public trust is measured as a percentage of respondents who answered "just about always" or "most of the time."

business, abandon politics and voting and distrust public institutions. It is not an absurdity that "political abstainers" often mention corruption of politics as a major reason for discontinuing to vote or engage in public politics.[48] [49] In effect, the growing feelings of political disillusionment observed in the last decades may not only reflect a change of values. The belief that governments do not represent public concerns, but serve the interests of the powerful elites, is a justifiable perception.

To some, this might sound like an exaggerated point of view. But there is evidence suggesting that it is not at all. According to the National Election Studies (NES) for example, in 1964, the proportion of Americans who agreed that the government was "run for the benefit of a few big interests," was about 45 percent. Since then, this proportion has continuously increased, reaching 84 percent by the 1990s.[50] Such feelings have remained high until our present day. A survey featured in *Business Week* in 2000 showed that about 75 percent of Americans feel that corporations have too much power over politicians in Washington. In the same survey, roughly 84 percent of the respondents believed that campaign contributions made by big corporations are excessive.

In recent years, numerous studies have also reported growing feelings of distrust and dissatisfaction toward international organizations, as revealed by a cross-national study involving more than a dozen countries.[51] Political distrust is especially high when considering the agencies charged with managing economic globalization: the World Bank, the International Monetary Fund (IMF) and the World Trade Organization (WTO). There may be multiple reasons behind the rise of global political mistrust, but one of them is the growing dissatisfaction with the power imbalances and skyrocketing inequalities in wealth and income that are generated by the globalization of trade, markets and finance.[52] An opinion poll conducted in the US some years ago showed that between 60 and 80 percent of respondents are convinced that the architects of globalization are catering to the interests of big business, rather than those of ordinary citizens and workers.[53]

The revolution of the rich

As previously discussed, from the end of the Second World War to the beginning of the 1970s, voting participation and feelings of political trust were not anywhere near as low as they are today. In 1964, roughly three out of four Americans had confidence that their government did "the right thing most of the time."[54] In the decades following, however, political trust started to erode. Economic inequalities and materialistic values have already been mentioned as the main potential contributors to these trends. But there is more. In order to fully understand why all of these changes have occurred, it is also necessary to examine the "power politics" behind these social and economic transformations. Once again, it is useful to analyze what happened in the US to be able to explain what subsequently occurred with the political economy of the world.

It is no coincidence that civic engagement in America peaked during the mid-twentieth century. During this period, the US government played a wider and stronger role in promoting political participation through social and economic policies. An empirical analysis published in the *American Political Science Review* indicated that the *1944 Servicemen's Readjustment Act*, which extended numerous social benefits including higher education and vocational training to returning veterans of the Second World War, encouraged both political engagement and civic participation.[55] The involvement of the US government in people's civic and political affairs continued throughout the post-war period. In the 1950s and 1960s, the US government actively promoted political engagement through public education and other programs designed to enhance citizens' involvement in community organizations, clubs, associations, unions and political parties.[56] In *How Policies Make Citizens*, Andrea Campbell showed that even social security policies played a key role in promoting civic participation among the elderly of low-income backgrounds.[57] It was out of these social, economic and political circumstances that the civil rights movement was able to gain enough momentum to force Congress into passing both the *Civil Rights Act* in 1964 and the *Voting Rights Act* in 1965. During those years, political activism was vigorous enough to also address some of the social and ecological impacts of economic activities. The *Social Security Act* was passed in 1965. In 1969, it was the time of the *National Environmental Policy Act*.

It is important to remember, however, that during the 1950s and 1960s, both in the US and other advanced nations, human affairs were guided by a political economic approach emphasizing full employment, welfare and social security. In other words, during the post-war era, governments were more inclined to "interfere" with people's lives by providing them with a higher degree of social security and better chances to find a job. At the time the US government put forth "the Great Society," the UK enacted "the Beveridge Plan." In Germany and Northern Europe, governments committed themselves to even more egalitarian and participatory policies. It was a different era, where the political economy of the most developed nations largely reflected the theories proposed by one of the brightest economists ever: John Maynard Keynes. In his magnum opus, *General Theory of Employment, Interest and Money*, Keynes criticized classical, laissez-faire economic theories for placing too much trust in free markets and too little in government interventions. Far from seeing unfettered market competition as the only road to prosperity, Keynes proposed a "mixed economy" approach that emphasized state action, public works, redistributive taxation and welfare policies. In his opinion, governments had to actively intervene in market affairs in order to ensure socioeconomic security, stability and welfare for the most disadvantaged groups of society.

"Social capitalism," as it was called, which sounds a bit "oxymoronic," turned out to be relatively successful in representing the plural interests of the different constituencies of society. Keynesianism also attempted to address the underlying capital–labor antagonism built into the market system. Whether this political economic model ever really succeeded in resolving this rivalry is difficult to say. Even during the post-war age, the business class remained far more politically powerful than the working class. Poverty and hunger were not eradicated. Yet, some of the most unfair and unstable tendencies of the market system were partially offset by counteracting effects of policies, rules and regulations. These reforms also managed to advance democratic interests. The influence of corporations on public affairs was partially counterbalanced by stronger labor unions and popular organizations, which were able to prevent some of the worst manipulations of electoral politics and the legal system that we observe in the present day. There is no doubt that back then, the working class was in a better position to negotiate wages, social protection and job security. By current standards, the mainstream corporate media would view the passage of the *1946 US Full Employment Act* as a subversive act of government socialism. Not at that time, however. Labor unions and public organizations had enough influence to hinder the "freedom" of the business class from shaping policies as they pleased. This balance of power between business and labor also had important effects on people's freedom to exercise civil rights and join social movements. Full employment policies and employment protection legislations impeded arbitrary hiring and firing, as well as allowed workers to exercise the right of association, strike, assembly and dissent.

By the late 1970s, however, the era of "social capitalism" came to an end. The Keynesian economic approach fell into disfavor and a radical version of laissez-faire economics re-emerged from the bowels of history. Every sector of society was affected by the market counter-revolution of the late 1970s. The advent of this new macroeconomic approach coincided with the power falloff of popular democracy, and a decline in institutions working to represent the community and local interests. This paradigm shift changed not only the US, but also the economic policies of the entire world. In *Supercapitalism: The Battle for Democracy in an Age of Big Business*, Robert Reich explains:

> since the late 1970s, a fundamental change has occurred in democratic capitalism in America, and that change has rippled outward to the rest of the world. The structure of the American – and much of the world's – economy has shifted toward far more competitive markets.[58]

Global capitalism unleashed

The shift toward unfettered free markets, and the consequent decline of political participation and labor power was neither a random, nor a natural event. It was the outcome of deliberately strategic class warfare – *A Global Class War*, citing the title of one of Jeff Faux's books.[59] According to Faux, since the mid-1970s, a bipartisan group of large corporations and super-rich who to this day occupy influential positions of power in society, "the Party of Davos," have engaged in a conscious effort to dismantle the social reforms instituted during the post-war period. In what some authors defined as "a revolution of the powerful against the weak,"[60] the Party of Davos redirected policies toward their interest and put an end to the Keynesian consensus. The balance of power between labor and capital shifted. The weakening of labor, however, also had the collateral effect of generating an overall retreat of democracy in society.

The dramatic U-turn toward unfettered free markets is often also called the "neo-conservative revolution." However, this characterization is not entirely accurate for a simple reason: both conservative and "liberal" governments contributed to the market renaissance of the late 1970s. The political and economic ascent of the global business elites was certainly championed by right-wing leaders Ronald Reagan and Margaret Thatcher. Nevertheless, even "left-of-center" political administrations supported it: Bill Clinton in the US, Tony Blair in Britain, Chretien in Canada and Schroeder in Germany, to name a few. Elected by popular will to counterbalance the pro-business agenda of their neo-conservative opponents, they did almost exactly the opposite. They took their stand. They sided with the rich.

As explained before, the main casualties of the class war were labor unions. The turning point of the conflict was the abandonment of the full employment regime and the acceptance of a "physiological rate of unemployment" as an inevitable feature of "efficient" market systems. This was an idea sparked by one of Keynes's fiercest opponents, Milton Friedman, who was awarded the 1976 Nobel Prize in economics. During his prize acceptance speech, Friedman explained: "a highly statist, rigid economy may have a fixed place for everyone, whereas a dynamic, highly progressive economy, which offers ever-changing opportunities and fosters flexibility, may have a high natural rate of unemployment."[61]

Unsurprisingly, the abandonment of full employment policies resulted in increases of unemployment rates in Europe particularly, but in the US as well. In *Capitalism Unleashed*, Andrew Glyn explains how this shift in economic policy provided employers with new opportunities to keep wages in check and use "firing" as a disciplinary measure. From 1960 to 1974, average unemployment was below 3 percent in OECD nations. In such macroeconomic conditions, the business class had only limited opportunities to maximize profit, squeeze wages, increase working hours and determine working conditions at will. High employment created an important obstacle for the business class that could no longer use the "fear of losing employment" as economic ammunition. These labor market conditions also provided trade unions with more freedom to exercise the right of strike and association. At the end of the 1960s, strike days per worker were extremely high in OECD nations. Their increase coincided with higher workers' wages and the implementation of employment protection legislations.[23] As the alternative rock band Radiohead put it: "I wish it was the sixties."

By the early 1980s, the dawning of the "revolution of the rich" was occurring and the labor class and trade unions were forced onto the defensive. In most advanced societies, employment rates and the number of days on strike per worker began to decline. Trade union membership sharply fell in the most industrialized nations, with the exception of Sweden.[62] The right to organize became less tolerated by employers and an increasing number of workers lost their jobs for exercising their right of association.[63] In the US in 1962, about 46.1 percent of union elections occurred with the consent of employers. By 1977, however, only 8.6 percent of the elections were unopposed by employers.[64] The attack against workers was particularly vitriolic in countries adopting the most aggressive version of laissez-faire economics. Major milestones of the class war were two devastating defeats suffered by the labor class: the prolonged strike of air traffic controllers in 1981 in the US, and the miners' pickets of 1984 in the UK.

Already under intense attack by the business class at home, labor unions were further weakened by foreign competition and the globalization of trade. Since the early 1980s, the international financial institutions (IFIs) such the IMF, the World Bank and WTO have promoted a cascade of global agreements that dismantled government regulations and restrictions to trade, especially in the developing world. As production and manufacturing jobs were increasingly outsourced to developing countries, demand for low-skilled jobs have sharply declined. While this was another fatal blow for the working class, big business benefited enormously from the globalization of trade. Globalization provided big business with yet another political gun to the head of the working class. Transnational companies, in particular, were given carte blanche to push down wages and suppress labor rights both at home and abroad. A perverse "race toward the bottom" had begun. At home, commercial treaties provided transnational companies with the opportunity to discipline workers and labor unions by threatening them with the prospect of moving production overseas. Abroad, free trade policies allowed corporations to obtain easy access to cheap labor and exploit the poor working conditions and ecological standards of developing countries. A case in point is the North American Free Trade Agreement (NAFTA). Designed to allow goods, service and money to cross the borders of the US, Canada and Mexico freely, NAFTA has proven to be highly convenient for large American and Canadian companies, but disastrous for the working classes in these countries.

With "the revolution of the rich" and the globalization of trade, the labor class suffered a political defeat from which it has yet to recover. Still today, the power balance between the labor and business classes remains in favor of the latter. Large corporate powers roam around the world in search of profit, undisturbed by national or international laws or ethical standards. Their abuses and suppression of labor and environmental regulations remain largely unaddressed. The global agencies that should be monitoring and enforcing these standards are too weak to counterbalance the overwhelming power of big business. And they are themselves under political attack. This is especially true for international organizations that have tried to protect the rights of workers such as the International Labor Organization (ILO). But it is also the case for other UN agencies that have tried to monitor the activities and abuses of corporations. The examples of the Commission on Transnational Corporations and the United Nations Centre on Transnational Corporations (UNCTC) are revealing.[65][66] After a few years since their inception, both have been practically suffocated in their cradle by the fierce opposition of the business class, and have paid the ultimate price for being on the wrong side of the global class conflict.

Dollars, not bullets

Whistle-blowers who argue that the business class has performed a "global coup" are usually dismissed as conspiracy theorists. It is true that there are a lot of elaborate fantasies out there: Zionist plots against humanity, secret machinations of evil Cabals, masonic ceremonies to establish a "new world order." There is not a shortage of these stories on the net. However, there is also no need to rely on any esoteric conjectures, or obsess over the Bilderberg Group, to recognize what is obvious. As Alasdair Spark, head of American Studies at King Alfred's College in Winchester noticed: "shouldn't we expect that the rich and powerful organize things in their own interests?"[67] Spark is correct. There is no need to believe in any arcane lucubration to understand that large concentrations of wealth tend to produce large concentrations of power. This has nothing to do with conspiracy theories. It is simply how the system works.

All in all, the business elites are not amateurs at arranging political takeovers. Almost 80 years ago, in the US, some of the most powerful corporations in the country attempted one. Unlike the slow, silent attack on democracy carried out by the Party of Davos, in the mid-1930s, a confederation of leading bankers, corporate executives and political reactionaries, enraged by the policies of the New Deal, decided to organize a military coup to overthrow Roosevelt. As revealed by Jules Archer, in *The Plot to Seize the White House*, on August 22, 1934, in a hotel room in Philadelphia, First World War veteran Gerald MacGuire approached former General of the US Marine Corps Smedley Butler to discuss how to raise an army, seize the White House and install a fascist dictatorship in the US.* MacGuire was secretly financed by a pro-business think tank, an ultra-right wing organization called the "American Liberty League," backed by JP Morgan, Du Pont, Rockefeller Associates, Andrew W. Mellon, General Motors and the Chamber of Commerce. Fortunately for the US, and for the entire world, General Butler turned out to be a very poor choice for the job. The coup failed, and Butler reported the attempted act of corruption before Congress.[68]

Of course, this happened almost a century ago. Since the failed coup, many things have changed. However, this is no reason to assume that the desire of the power elites to control policies and democracy has vanished. To be sure, the corporate assault on democracy that began in the late 1970s did not require Generals, First World War veterans or armed forces. As Joe Balkan once put it: "today, seventy years after the failed coup . . . Corporate America's long and patient campaign to gain control of government . . . is now succeeding. Without bloodshed, armies, or fascist strongmen, and using dollars rather than bullets."[69] But there is another method of political control that is even subtler than money: the strategic use of mass media.

---

* At the time, many wealthy corporations found Mussolini's fascism very attractive because of its success in curbing the power of labor unions. Indeed, in July 1934, *Fortune Magazine* even dedicated an entire issue to Mussolini's "achievements." The Italian dictator, after all, never made secret his sympathy for the corporate sector. He even observed that, "fascism should more properly be called corporatism because it is the merger of state and corporate power."

Spinning democracies

November 19, 1863. Gettysburg, Pennsylvania. In one of his most famous addresses, the sixteenth president of the United States, Abraham Lincoln, provided his own definition of democracy. He viewed it as a "government of the people, for the people and by the people." History proved Lincoln a visionary, and democracy is now accepted as the most popular form of political organization worldwide. As Winston Churchill once put it: "democracy is the worst form of government except all the others that have been tried." Yet, while in theory Lincoln's definition of democracy is taken for granted, the reality is that it is also not taken very seriously. Even in the most advanced societies, such as the US and the UK, a peculiarly hierarchical version of democracy seems to prevail. The words of James Madison, one of the founding fathers of the American Constitution, summarize it well. "The few have to decide for the many," Madison once observed, "and government ought to protect the minority of the opulent against the majority."[70]

Unlike Lincoln's, Madison's view of democracy can hardly be qualified as democratic, yet the most privileged circles of society have fully embraced it. A case in point is The Trilateral Commission, a think tank of the super-wealthy founded in 1973 by David Rockefeller. In the first report of the Commission, members debated about what they defined as the "crisis of democracies." What did they actually mean by that? More or less, the "excessive" involvement of civic movements in public affairs,[71][72] and the failure of institutions responsible "for the indoctrination of the young" such as schools, universities and churches."[73] In line with Madison's view, The Trilateral Commission, that represents the interests of the elite, regards public participation, not as an essential pre-condition for democracy, but as one of its very major obstacles.

A basis of this "democratic" theory is the assumption that the "people," or the "many," are unable to decide what is best for them. Consequently, they must be guided in their political choices by what can be defined as the "mediators."

The mediators

Several authors put forth a similar view. The most important of them is Walter Lippmann, an influential American writer and reporter, twice awarded the Pulitzer Prize. According to Lippmann, the general public can be compared to a "great beast" or a "bewildered herd,"[74] a mob not intelligent enough, or too busy with daily activities, to comprehend complex policy issues or make conscious decisions about their political destiny. Therefore, Lippmann believes that the public should delegate representation to the middleman, the so-called "experts." Under this view, democracy and political stability can only be ensured when people, manipulated through "necessary illusions," peacefully assume the "role of spectator[s]." As Reinhold Niebuhr explains, "[while] rationality belongs [only] to the cool observers," the wider public is irrational and incapable of interpreting policies and reality accurately; it must therefore be instructed with "emotionally potent over-simplifications."[75]

It is no coincidence that the interests of the "mediators," who are supposed to "emotionally oversimplify" the world for the "bewildered herd," happen to be strikingly similar to those of the wealthy elite. All in all, the ambition of the aristocrats to make decisions about the distribution of power and wealth in society without any interference from the general population has not transformed very much. In the past, tyrants, monarchs and plutocrats have marginalized public will, often through brutal repression or direct use of force. The trouble is that these methods of social control often face excessive resistance and can even be counter-productive. This is why, more recently, these control tactics are rarely used. Social control is, in fact, much more effective when it relies on the manipulation of thoughts and opinions, not physical coercion.

Perhaps the first thinker who recognized this was David Hume. Echoing the words of James Madison, the Scottish philosopher observed that the "many" (the governed) can be easily kept in order by the "few" (governors) mainly through "opinion."[76] Nevertheless, the first to have come up with a refined theory of mind control, which he named "the engineering of consent,"[77] was Edward Bernays, Sigmund Freud's nephew. Bernays, who inspired Goebbels to develop new methods of mass persuasion in Nazi Germany,[78] was convinced that, "those who manipulate the organized habits and opinions of the masses constitute an invisible government which is the true ruling power of our country."[79] Lenin, who believed that the masses had to be guided by a vanguard of "enlightened" intellectuals or red bureaucrats, embraced a similar view. Of course, the political ideologies they embraced, and the historical circumstances in which they lived, make Bernays, Goebbels and Lenin hardly comparable. Even so, all of them considered propaganda necessary and conceived people as objects of political manipulation. The way they viewed communication is perhaps best summarized by the words of Herbert Marcuse when he argued that the very aim of mass media is to "mediate between the masters and their dependents."[80]

The rise of media oligopolies

As explained before, the advent of the free market doctrine in the late 1970s changed the political and economic landscape of the world. The waves of market deregulation and privatization that have taken place since then have transformed all sectors of society, including the information and communication systems. These transformations provided the business class with even more power to influence policies and public opinion. During the post-war period, when the mixed economy approach was *en vogue*, mass media were very different. Most of them were nationalistic in scope, predominantly governed by state and local interests. In the early 1980s, however, change was on the way and, as usual, it first took place in the US.[72] The shift from public to private media continued in the 1990s and reached a culminating point in 1996, with the passage of the *US Telecommunications Act*. This new law left the US communication system completely at the mercy of market forces,[81] or, more precisely, of the power of big business. After gaining ground in

America, and in the rest of the Anglo-Saxon world, the commercialization of media progressed to other established democracies. Some authors have characterized this grand transformation as the "Americanization" of global culture,[82][83] but this is not entirely correct. The privatization of media has very little to do with the diffusion of American culture. It has much more to do with the growing hegemony of large media companies that have cashed in on yet another major victory for the business elites against labor and the rest of society.

All in all, the global corporate takeover would not have been possible without the occupation of major channels of communication by the private sector. Since the early 1980s, the business class has engaged in a progressive acquisition of media outlets that has dramatically increased its ability to shape public opinion and policies. The business sector has also heavily funded neo-conservative think tanks[84] such as the American Enterprise Institute, the Heritage Foundation and the CATO Institute that flood the information system with business propaganda. Of course, according to most free market ideologues, the rise of commercial media reflects an evolution of communication systems toward more efficient and competitive methods of production and distribution. In their opinion, media privatization has even promoted democracy by providing citizens with a wider variety of options and choices. But is this really the case?

It is true that the corporate sector has somehow promoted dynamism and provided the public with new TV channels, newspapers, magazines and book publishers. Still, the commercialization of media has not promoted the diversity and plurality of political views, as the free marketeers seem to believe. While the world communication system may have increased in size, it has probably decreased in options. A tiny network of mega-corporations that often work together in close partnerships and alliances controls most media channels. Robert McChesney, author of *The Global Media: The New Missionaries of Corporate Capitalism*, explains that the overwhelming majority of the world's film production, TV show production, cable channels, cable and satellite systems, book publishing, magazine publishing and music production is provided by about 50 firms. However, only the top nine thoroughly dominate most of these sectors and three of them in particular: Walt Disney, News Corporation and Time Warner. Rupert Murdoch's News Corporation is a case in point. It includes about 132 newspapers, 25 magazines, 22 US TV stations, Twentieth Century Fox, Fox Broadcasting Network, Fox News Channel, global cable networks including fX, fXM and Fox Sports Net, Asian Star Television, British Sky Broadcasting, Germany's Vox Channel, Sky Italia, Sky Latin America, US Sky TV, Japan Sky Broadcasting, Australian Foxtel cable channel and India's Zee TV.[85][86] Murdoch also partially owns several newspapers such as *The Sun*, the *Sunday Times*, *The Times*, *New York Post*, the *Wall Street Journal*, *Financial News*, the *Daily Telegraph*, the *Sunday Telegraph* and publishers such as HarperCollins. He does not own a media corporation. He owns an empire.

The herd of independent thinkers

Free market ideologues are blissfully at ease with the grotesque concentration of media outlets within a few corporations. But there are many problems with this. In a functioning democracy, far from inculcating "necessary illusions," media outlets are meant to fulfill important public requirements. They are expected to provide people with accurate facts, evidence and plural information without restriction. Media outlets also have the public duty of promoting civic education and citizens' participation in political affairs.[87] They should also play the role of *watchdogs* and expose the potential abuses of power in society. It is for this very reason mass media are sometimes called "the backbone of democracy." In order to perform all of these roles, however, media outlets must be independent. If they protect special interests, instead, they turn into servile instruments of mind control and propaganda. This is actually what happens in totalitarian regimes, where media regularly adopt censorship, distortions and the withholding of information. A notorious case in point is, of course, the former Soviet Union, that inspired George Orwell to write *1984*.[88] But what about major media channels in modern market democracies? Are they fair, credible and objective means of information? Are they really independent?

Most people in the West seem to believe that the word propaganda only applies to totalitarian regimes such as those existing in North Korea and Iran. But this is far from being the case. In *Manufacturing Consent,* Edward Herman and Noam Chomsky define "propaganda" as any media strategies used by powerful elites to "fix the premises of discourse, to decide what the general populace is allowed to see, hear, and think about."[89] According to the authors, the essential ingredients of a "propaganda model" are a series of "news filters" which determine the type of information that is presented in the media. These filters include ownership of the medium, funding sources, advertising as a primary source of revenue and reliance on information provided by governments, business and "experts" funded and approved by primary agents of power.[89] While it is true that media organizations in totalitarian states adopt the most blatant forms of propaganda, mainstream media channels in market democracies also often use filters to conform to the expectations of markets, governments or both. How? While they allow very lively debates around specific issues, media news tend to narrow the scope of such debates within a defined spectrum of politically "acceptable" opinion. This is especially the case of large media corporations that often provide the impression of supporting inherently free discussions, encouraging critical and dissident views. In reality, the opposing perspectives offered in a live debate on corporate media channels often share very similar underlying assumptions. The agenda is fixed a priori, and it is influenced by the political and economic priorities of the shareholders or political leaders that control them.

Of course, the propaganda strategies used by mainstream media in market democracies pale in comparison to those adopted in totalitarian states. Broadcasting corporations in the West rarely recur to outright distortions of information or plain lies (apart from a few exceptional cases). Mostly, they rely on the marginalization or virtual disappearance of certain facts from the news.[90] These strategies are much more subtle and, for this reason, even more effective. Why? Simply because the news filters are much less likely to be identified as strategies of misinformation and deception. Often, they are not recognized at all. As Czech novelist Zdenek Urbánek once argued: "in dictatorships we are more fortunate than you in the West in one respect. We believe nothing of what we read on the newspapers and nothing of what we watch on television because we know it's propaganda and lies."[91][92]

Of course, most journalists working in corporate media portray themselves as independent spokespersons, informers dedicated to free speech and the public interest. And indeed, in a way, they are. Most of them are not deliberately distorting the news and they are not even aware of the filters of information they often adopt in their everyday activities. But the fact they believe themselves to be independent does not make them independent. The opposite can be true. As Johannes Wolfgang von Goethe once observed: "none are more hopelessly enslaved than those who falsely believe they are free."[91] Regardless of what they believe of themselves, columnists and reporters in corporate media have to predominantly act on the basis of the priorities and ideology of the companies that employ them. Unless they share these priorities and ideology, they can hardly advance in their career and can even risk losing their job. Of course, journalists in corporate media may even show and demonstrate different ideas and perspectives. Even so, such differences must remain within a certain framework of "acceptability" established by the company or investors that pay them.

This all may sound extreme. But only when ignoring one simple fact: media companies, by their very nature, are primarily ruled by the need to maximize private profits, not public interests. It is therefore utterly logical that the news they broadcast tends to conform to the expectations of markets and advertisers. As profit-seeking organizations, corporate media are more inclined to attract audiences with buying power than meet the informational needs of the citizenry. It is much more profitable to induce and seduce consumers to buy goods and services,[93] than to inform them about important civic affairs.[94][95] It is also understandable why commercial media marginalize political issues that can threaten their economic interests and profits. Without revenues from advertisers, media companies can hardly hope to survive market competition. As the founder of *Clear Channel*, Lowry Mays, once revealed: "we are not in the business of providing news and information . . . We are simply in the business of serving our customers."[96]

The more you watch, the less you know?

Numerous authors have argued that corporate media, instead of promoting fair and reliable information, spread public deception, political distrust and civic disengagement.[97–100] There is also evidence that viewers of contemporary media channels in the West are often affected by gross misperceptions of important contemporary political issues. A case in point is the "selling" of the Iraq War by Fox News to the American people. A study conducted in 2003 showed that the majority of Americans

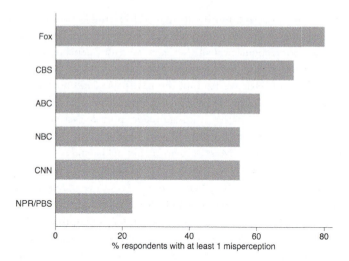

FIGURE 5.3   The more you watch, the less you know: misperceptions about the Iraq
War according to primary sources of news in the United States

Source: *Misperceptions, the Media and the Iraq War* (2003) Program on International Policy
Attitudes (PIPA) and Knowledge Networks.

Questions about misperceptions: (a) is it your impression that the US has or has not found clear
evidence in Iraq that Saddam Hussein was working closely with the al Qaeda terrorist organization? (b) since the Iraq war ended, is it your impression that the US has or has not found Iraqi
weapons of mass destruction? (c) thinking about how all the people in the world feel about the
US having gone to war with Iraq, do you think the majority of people favor the US having
gone to war, views are evenly balanced, or the majority of people opposed the US having gone
to war?

had at least one of the following three misperceptions about the war: first, they
wrongly believed that evidence of the links between Iraq and al Qaeda had been
proven; second, they thought that evidence of the weapons of mass destruction had
been found; third, they assumed that the world public opinion was generally in favor
of the US intervention.

Of course, none of these beliefs was correct. But what is most revealing about
the study is that the frequency of misperceptions varied according to the participants'
main source of news. About 80 percent of those who primarily watched Fox News
had at least one misperception, against 71 percent, 61 percent, 55 percent and
55 percent of respondents whose primary source of news were CBS, ABC, NBC
and CNN respectively (see Figure 5.3).[101]

These findings clearly show that, far from being an example of objective
reporting, Fox News often spreads misinformation and distortions of the truth.
Sheldon Rampton and John Stauber hardly exaggerated when they stated that even
in established democracies, mainstream media are used as *Weapons of Mass
Deceptions*.[102] All in all, this is what the Ministers of Propaganda in totalitarian states
are up to, some may say. For sure, Fox News is just an extreme example and can

hardly be generalized. Murdoch's channels are some of the least trustworthy sources of information we can conceive. Interviews with former employees of Fox News in the documentary *Outfoxed: Rupert Murdoch's War On Democracy* have indeed revealed that the way and how much journalists report is heavily influenced by the interests of the company's shareholders.[103] It is thus not surprising that the people who rely on Murdoch's main TV stations as a primary source of information are the least informed about political and international affairs. As Danny Schechter once put it, "the more they watch, the less they know."[104]

Yet, it would be wrong to treat Fox News as an isolated case. The number of mainstream media that fail to live up to the standards of fairness and integrity goes far beyond Murdoch's media empire. A 2002 study conducted by the University of Glasgow about the coverage of the illegal occupation of Palestine by Israel, found that about 90 percent of young British viewers of television news believed that Palestinians were the illegal settlers.[105]

Free radicals

The occupation of media outlets by private interests presents enormous challenges for democracy. Without a fair and free press, there are only limited ways to understand the world independently from the filters of the power elites. Without accurate news and reporting, it is hard to make informed decisions about political affairs. Yet, there is some good news. Although the increasing commercialization and monopolization of media in the last decades has produced widespread political disinformation and civic apathy, some encouraging signs of change are appearing on the horizon. A growing number of citizens have become more aware that, as long as media remain in private hands, they are left with no voice and no choice. Therefore, new generations of activists and dissidents have taken matters into their own hands by finding new ways to inform themselves about public affairs and engage in political action. It is true, as already observed, that formal political participation and voting has declined in market economies. But there are also counter-trends. Informal political activism, such as consumer boycotts, petitioning, and mass demonstrations has become more common in recent years.[106] A case in point is the organized mass actions of civil disobedience by the Occupy Wall Street movement in dozens of countries in 2011. Hardly before had the world witnessed such massive action by citizens in so many places at once.

There may be at least two major reasons for this civic re-awakening in the face of a global democratic deficit: one is political. It is a paradox, but a system of power that represses people's aspirations so deeply, and for so long, does not only promote the expected outcome of normalizing repression. It can also generate its own nemesis: the spread of dissent. In this sense, political distrust can be interpreted not only as a form of social disengagement, but also as a symptom of civic renaissance. Evidence shows that distrust toward politicians and political organizations is, in fact, not only associated with the decline of institutionalized forms of participation,[107] but also with innovative forms of political dissent and civic resistance.[108] This happens because people come to understand more and better about power, becoming less naive and more cognizant of how wealthy elites operate.

But perhaps the most important reason for the reinvigoration of civic society in recent times is access to new technologies. The rapid diffusion of new information and communication systems has provided citizens with innovative methods of political and civic participation. Activists and social movements have found new, creative ways to access information and disseminate political ideas, making the filters of mainstream corporate or government media less effective than ever. There are hundreds of millions of people using blogs, emails, electronic lists, websites and forums for political and public purposes. The proliferation of these new instruments of information is diversifying voices and opinions, and has given rise to what has been called citizen's journalism.

Of course, new technologies and social media are more likely to be used by relatively wealthy activists and citizen organizations in rich societies. This can create even wider inequality in political participation as the already large "digital divide" becomes even larger. There are still obstacles to reach people who are at the margins of society or without access to any technology. Nevertheless, as more citizens are exposed to these new forms of information and communication, and new technologies become more widely available, opportunities to engage disenfranchised people in civic activities and political action may rise. The current ease with which citizens can access any type of information and organize political activities through a few mouse clicks is truly unprecedented. So are the avenues for democratic participation and political action.

Indeed, the rise of civil society organizations, coordinated through digital network tools of communication, has spurred mass actions and new ways of direct participation.[109] This has not only occurred at the local level, but also globally. Together with direct democracy, the use of new technologies and cosmopolitanism are in fact key features of a new global justice movement that, in the last decades, has performed countless political activities, often organized and publicized through the web. New technologies have been instrumental in coordinating "the battle of Seattle" against the WTO in 1999, for example. Digital communication networks have also been widely used to organize what can perhaps be considered the most massive global anti-war demonstration in history. On February 15, 2003, an estimated 10 million activists took to the streets of dozens of cities worldwide to protest the US-led plan to invade Iraq.[110] Skeptics may argue that all of this did not prevent the war. But this is not because of the failure of the demonstrators, but due to the indifference of the rest of society, and those sitting on the fence. More skeptics, however, can be transformed into activists. And maybe this is exactly what is already happening. In *Blessed Unrest*, Paul Hawken estimates that there must be between 1 or even 2 million non-profit organizations in the emerging global movement of civic society working on a wide variety of issues ranging from ecological sustainability to global economic justice.[111] Environmental groups, trade unions, human rights organizations, community-based initiatives, institutions and students movements fighting for a fairer and more democratic world are rapidly emerging everywhere.[112] Whether they will exert enough political pressure to affect large concentrations of power and wealth is anybody's question. Whether they will ever succeed must be everybody's hope.

6

THE MARKET GREED DOCTRINE

Apart from being two of the most influential thinkers to ever exist, Adam Smith and Charles Darwin have very little in common. Yet, the founder of economics and the father of evolution, respectively, do share at least one similar quality: both gave rise to movements of thought that they would have probably detested. Their groundbreaking contributions to science have not only been used to expand the horizons of knowledge, but have also been distorted in order to justify countless ill decisions. Smith's theory of the invisible hand, combined with Darwin's law of natural selection, unintentionally inspired the two main articles of faith upon which modern economics is based on: the greed creed and the belief in the market God. The first – the greed creed – states that people have no other motivations in life than to pursue their own selfish interests. The second – the belief in the market God – argues that all social and human affairs are best regulated as free market exchanges.

Before the advent of these ideas, the world was not a place of charity, respect for human rights and solidarity. In fact, it was quite the opposite. Nevertheless, the prospect of turning society into a market of selfish profiteers had never before been seriously considered. For better or for worse, religious and spiritual concerns previously played a central role in people's lives and motivations. The birth of the profit-oriented market society, however, radically altered the way individuals viewed themselves, their relations with others and the ecosystem. Karl Polanyi understood this very well. In a widely acclaimed book, *The Great Transformation*, he describes the rise of laissez-faire economics as a social mutation that turned people and nature into commodities.[1] The author was in no way advocating for a ban of the profit motive and free markets – far from it. In Polanyi's view, however, the idea of governing society on the basis of profit and markets could not lead to anything but social and ecological disaster.[2]

Turning Adam Smith upside down

One of the most influential visions in the field of social sciences is Adam Smith's theory of "the invisible hand." The Scottish economist argued that the two major driving factors behind the accumulation of wealth in society are individual self-interest and market forces. According to Smith, if all individuals are left free to pursue their own profit, they unintentionally promote the common good – the wealth of nations.[3] This happens because the "invisible hand" of the market acts as a main regulator of the "collusion of self-interests" among economic actors, as well as allocates goods and services where they are most wanted and needed. In other words, when each producer is free to choose what to sell and each consumer is free to choose what to buy, the "invisible hand of the market" disburses benefits to all. The entrepreneur who desires wealth will in all likelihood commercialize a product that is desired by thousands of customers; thus, by pursuing his or her own profit, he or she unintentionally benefits society. In a famous passage from his masterpiece, *The Wealth of Nations*, Smith observed: "it is not from the benevolence of the butcher, the brewer or the baker that we expect our dinner, but from their regard to their own interest." He then added: "[Every economic actor] . . . is led by an invisible hand to promote an end which was no part of his intention . . . By pursuing his own interest, he frequently promotes that of society more effectually than when he really intends to promote it."[4]

Smith's intuitions on the benefits of the profit motive and free markets are far-reaching, and the implications of his ideas are still deeply felt today. The collective pursuit of profit and the free exchange of goods and services played a crucial role in promoting higher standards of living worldwide. Individual self-interest and an entrepreneurial spirit, assisted by the "invisible hand" of the market, have indeed stimulated dynamism, innovation, specialization and more efficient methods of production. The application of both principles contributed to higher productivity and faster accumulation of wealth, first in the industrialized world, and then in low- and middle-income countries. Within nations, the benefits of efficient productivity and economic growth partially "trickled down" to the general population and freed countless people from poverty and hunger. The application of Smith's ideas made the world a more comfortable and interesting place to live. There is no denying that.

The trouble is that Smith's ideas have been pushed far beyond their original purposes. They have been extrapolated from the context under which they were conceived, and have undergone a process of theoretical mutation. Subsequently, they gave birth to a new doctrine celebrating greed and monopolies, instead of self-interest and free markets. Smith believed that self-interest and market forces could contribute to the common good, so long as they operated within a predefined framework of moral and psychological values. Smith recognized the importance of human empathy in society. In *The Theory of Moral Sentiments* he wrote:

> how selfish soever man may be supposed, there are evidently some principles in his nature, which interest him in the fortune of others, and render their

happiness necessary to him, though he derives nothing from it, except the pleasure of seeing it.[5]

Smith believed that individuals "could safely be trusted to pursue their own interest without undue harm to the community."[6] In his view, moral restraints would have acted as control mechanisms against the possible degeneration of self-interest into greed. In another passage of *The Theory of Moral Sentiments*, Smith observed:

> the agreeableness or utility of any affection depends upon the degree which it is allowed to subsist in. Every affection is useful when it is confined to a certain degree of moderation; and every affection is disadvantageous when it exceeds the proper bounds.[7]

Smith also deplored poverty. He did not blame the poor for their plight, rather he supported universal public education and advocated for a progressive taxation system proportional to one's ability to pay.[8] Some of the early adepts of the theory of the invisible hand, however, had very different political views. They considered any legislation that ensured forms of assistance to the poor as fraud. These laissez-faire economists believed that in a purely free-market society, individuals are solely responsible for their own welfare. States or communities do not hold any moral obligation for the fate of the poor, the sick and the elderly. An outspoken proponent of this view of economics was Reverend Thomas Malthus who, unlike Smith, was notoriously reactionary. A passage of his most important book, *An Essay on the Principle of Population*, clarifies his sense of compassion for the plight of others:

> A man who is born into a world already possessed, if he cannot get subsistence from his parents on whom he has a just demand, and if the society do not want his labor has no claim of right to the smallest portion of food, and, in fact, has no business to be where he is. At nature's mighty feast there is no vacant cover for him.

In Malthus' view, a human being does not possess any "right to subsistence when his labor will not fairly purchase it,"[9] and, "by creating an artificial demand by public subscriptions or advances from the government, we evidently prevent the population of the country from adjusting itself gradually to its diminishing resources."[10]

Malthus was not alone in his views. Another prominent pioneer of laissez-faire economics, David Ricardo, opposed the idea of helping the poor with every bone in his body.[11] In his view, any forms of social protection against poverty interfered with the optimal functioning of free markets and provided the weak with an incentive for idleness, while encouraging irresponsibly large families. Consistent with the theory of the invisible hand (deprived of moral sentiments), Ricardo complained that, "wages should be left to the fair and free competition of the market and should never be controlled by the interference of the legislature." Laws protecting the poor against the full force of the free market, "instead of making the poor rich, they . . . make the rich poor."[12]

One of the first policy reforms based on this aberrant public ethics was the passage of the *Poor Law Amendment Act* in England in 1834. The act repealed the previous *Elizabethan Poor Laws,* which included the *1795 Speenhamland Law,* designed to provide support for people who became unemployed, especially due to sickness or old age. The *Speenhamland Law* provided subsidies to wages in accordance with a scale dependent upon the market price of bread, in order to assure a minimum income for the poor, irrespective of their earnings. In outright contrast with the theories of laissez-faire economics, the *Speenhamland Law* was insurance against starvation. It defended "the right to live."[11] But the law was anathema to the early prophets of the market greed doctrine because it interfered with the rules of supply and demand in determining prices and wages. It had to be abolished. And so it was.

Some, however, were appalled by the cruelty of the anti-poor laws movement. According to Polanyi, the abolition of the *Elizabethan Poor Laws* was a defeat of altruism and a triumph of greed over compassion. As he writes: "never perhaps in all modern history has a more ruthless act of social reform been perpetrated." In Polanyi's opinion, with the passage of the *Poor Law Amendment Act*, people and nature entered into the pricing system, were absorbed into the market process, and were commodified as objects for trade and money exchange. "The *Speenhamland Law,* which had protected rural England, and thereby the laboring population in general, against the full force of the market mechanism, was eating into the marrow of society," he explains. "By the time of its repeal, huge masses of the laboring population resembled more the specters that might haunt a nightmare than human beings."[13]

Polanyi's denunciation of the devastating effects that the abolition of the laws had on the poor was also complemented by a deep sense of indignation for the moral decadence of the rich. As he wrote:

> if the workers were physically dehumanized, the owning classes were morally degraded . . . compassion was removed from the hearts, and a stoic deter- mination to renounce human solidarity in the name of the greatest happiness of the greatest number gained the dignity of a secular religion.[13]

Rolling Charles Darwin over in his grave

Almost a century after the publication of Adam Smith's *The Wealth of Nations,* Charles Darwin made a ground-breaking discovery with the theory of evolution. In *The Origins of the Species,* he compared the progress of humankind to a "struggle for life," a process that allows individuals with certain inheritable characteristics to survive and reproduce more easily than those with less advantageous traits.[14] Darwin revolutionized the field of biology. The theory of "the survival of the fittest" completely changed the way we view humankind within society.

Like Smith, however, Darwin's ideas went through a process of theoretical mutation. His intuitions on biological adaptation and natural selection inspired a reactionary doctrine called "social Darwinism."[15] Darwin seemed cognizant of the importance of social instincts and sympathy in evolution.[16] [17] He opposed slavery, supported the *Poor Laws* and refused to apply his biological discoveries to social living. Herbert Spencer, the founder of social Darwinism, believed exactly the opposite. Spencer was convinced that social reforms were necessary in order to promote "evolutionary success," or the survival and prosperity of individuals with desirable traits and the extinction of those with undesirable ones. It is true that Spencer never really called himself a social Darwinist. But it is also true that his theory clearly implied that humanitarian concerns were subordinate to the laws of nature. In other words, he defended what Thomas Henry Huxley once defined as the "tiger-rights."[18]

According to the social Darwinist doctrine, even war, death and famine are necessary to advance human progress and "biological purification." In a revealing passage of *Social Statics*, Spencer wrote: "under the natural order of things, society is constantly excreting its unhealthy, imbecile, slow, vacillating, faithless members."[19] And although "it seems hard that widows and orphans should be left to struggle for life and death," he continues, "nevertheless, when regarded not separately, but in connection with the interest of universal humanity, these harsh fatalities are seen to be full of beneficence."[20] Spencer concludes: "Beings thus imperfect are nature's failures . . . If they are sufficiently complete to live, they do live, and it is well that they should live. If they are not sufficiently complete to live, they die and it is best that they should die."[21]

The parallels between Malthus' laissez-faire economics and Spencer's social Darwinism are difficult to miss. The concept of "nature" as the major arbiter of the "struggle for life," fits like a glove with the view of the market as the main governor of society's affairs. In spite of their differences, these ideologies share the same philosophical and moral roots. In effect, if Malthus' writings profoundly affected Spencer's ideas, social Darwinism influenced free market ideologies. They inspired one another. Markets were for the laissez-faire economist what the laws of nature were for the social Darwinist. Both doctrines assumed that competition – for life or for profit – need not be restrained. In both philosophies, there is no place for the sick, the weak, the inefficient, the poor and those who lag behind. Both theories also saw no need to limit the exploitation of natural resources. Both assumed that any interference restraining market affairs, such as welfare policies and redistributive taxation, was "a curse in disguise," an obstacle to human progress. For the laissez-faire economist, social security was an impediment to prosperity; for the social Darwinist, it promoted the "survival of the unfittest."[22] The logic is impeccable. As market forces must be left free to reward productive actors with wealth, and punish inefficient ones with bankruptcy, the laws of nature must be left free, and reward individuals who adapt with survival and punish those who fail with extinction. The key distinction between the free market ideology and social Darwinism was this: while the former believed that the failure of the unfit was inevitable, the latter viewed it as even desirable.

This difference aside, the free market doctrine and social Darwinism were a perfect pair. Above all, they served the interests of the wealthy. From 1848 to 1853, when Spencer worked as sub-editor of *The Economist*, it became quite clear that the line separating the two ideologies was rather blurred. The weekly magazine, considered by many to be an oracle for the financial class, celebrated the marriage between free market economics and social Darwinism. In 1848, while expressing objections to the passage of the *Public Health Act*, the editors of *The Economist* wrote: "suffering and evil are nature's admonitions; they cannot be got rid of; and the impatient attempts of benevolence to banish them from the world by legislation . . . have always been productive of more evil than good."[23] The combined popularization of "the invisible hand" and "the survival of the fittest" doctrines provided the business class with persuasive arguments in defense of the "morality of inequality." It allowed the rich to escalate a crusade against welfare, and any other forms of economic redistribution, and still be able to sleep well at night.

In no other country did the corporate elites and their ideologues rave Spencer's doctrine and laissez-faire economics more than in the US.[24–26] Economist Murray Rothbard judged *Social Statics* as "the greatest single work of libertarian political philosophy ever written."[27] Financier, railroad tycoon and "Robber Baron" James J. Hill also invoked the adoption of Spencer's doctrine in economic affairs. As he once observed: "the fortunes of railroad companies are determined by the law of the survival of the fittest."[28] On a similar rampage, one of the richest men on earth, Andrew Carnegie declared: "[The law of evolution] is here . . . We cannot evade it; no substitutes for it have been found; and while the law may sometimes be hard for the individual, it is best for the race, because it insures the survival of the fittest in every department."[29]

If social Darwinism was celebrated as the new secular religion, the immanent righteousness of the "invisible hand" was glorified with ultra-terrestrial connotations. Simply put, the market became God. Decades before the advent of the "Robber Barons" in the US, British manufacturer, and laissez-faire intellectual, Richard Cobden had already inspired the business class to appreciate the divine features of market competition. "[A law which prevents free trade is a] law which interferes with the wisdom of the Divine Providence, and substitutes the law of wicked men for the law of nature," as he once put it.[30] But it was John D. Rockefeller who really pushed the sanctification of market competition to poetic heights. "The growth of a large business is merely a survival of the fittest."

> The American Beauty rose can be produced in the splendor and fragrance which brings cheer to its beholder only by sacrificing the early buds which grow up around it. This is not an evil tendency of business. It is merely the working-out of a law of nature and a law of God.[31]

One would imagine that such fanaticism belonged to a forgotten past buried by a history of moral and civic emancipation. But this is too great a wish. The faith in the market God is still widely popular today. After the 2008 global financial crisis, a reporter asked Lloyd Blankfein, Goldman Sachs chief executive, whether governments should impose limits on the compensations of top executives. The banker replied: "to put a cap on their ambition" is wrong because bankers "serve a very important purpose in society: they are 'doing God's work.'"[32]

The global economic straitjacket

Since the days of Smith and Darwin, the faith in the greed creed and in the market God, as organizing principles of human progress, have been waxing and waning. During the post-war era in particular, modern society remained agnostic about the gospel of market greed. This happened for a very good reason. The devastating effects of the Great Depression and the Second World War were still hard felt, and major industrialized nations were compelled to work together for the prevention of economic crises and trade imbalances. As explained in the previous chapter, the solution was Keynesianism, a political economic theory emphasizing the promotion of full employment, social welfare and economic stability through government interventions in market affairs. However, the popularity of this political economic approach only lasted a couple of decades. Then, the winds of history started to blow in the opposite direction. By the late 1970s, the Keynesian era of "managed capitalism" came to an end. The market greed doctrine was resuscitated from the bin of history with a new name: neoliberalism.

Although the new popularization of the market greed doctrine took over the commanding heights of the economy only in the late 1970s, the origins of neoliberalism can be traced back to 1947, to the meeting of 38 intellectuals at the Hotel du Parc on Mont Pelerin in Switzerland. This group included Friedrich von Hayek and Milton Friedman, later recognized as the fathers of the neoliberal school of thought. Both had very reactionary views about the appropriate role of markets and governments in society. In many ways, their contempt for any form of welfare and redistributive taxation echoed the ideas of Malthus and Spencer. After their meeting at Mont Pelerin, Hayek and Friedman had to wait patiently for almost three decades to see their theories gain political support. By the late 1970s, however, their moment of glory had finally arrived.

The historical and political reasons explaining the emergence of neoliberalism are still widely contested. The ascent to power of two pro-business political leaders in the US and UK, Ronald Reagan and Margaret Thatcher, is often proposed as a key turning point. It is true that the conservative duo significantly helped the neoliberal cause, both in their countries and worldwide. Ronald Reagan was particularly fond of Friedman. He defined him as a "freedom fighter." Reagan's anti-government jokes are still remembered. He once said, "The 10 most dangerous words in the English language are 'Hi, I'm from the government and I'm here to help.'" On the other side of the Atlantic, Thatcher was so inspired by von Hayek that during a British Conservative Party policy meeting, while listening to a presentation, she interrupted the speaker by slamming down one of his books onto the table. "This is what we believe!" she thundered.[33]

The "Acting President" and the "Iron Lady" were professional fighters for the freedom of the deserving rich to own all wealth, the planet and the people in it.

But, as already mentioned, their influence should not be overestimated. The market renaissance of the late 1970s reflected a shift in power distribution that favored the top social classes. During the post-war period, the super-rich had accepted policies that promoted a partial redistribution of wealth downward, from their pockets to those of the poor. They swallowed these policies with large doses of class resentment, however. To their benefit, the macroeconomic instability of the 1970s provided an opportunity to break the post-war Keynesian consensus. At the time, the world economy was hit by a series of global shocks: the aftermath of the Vietnam War, the dismantling of the Bretton Woods system, two oil crises and a sharp rise of interest rates. Big business waged an effective propaganda campaign aimed at persuading political leaders and the public that the only way to overcome the crisis was to abandon the full employment goal, dismantle the welfare state, shrink labor unions and unleash the forces of the free market. One of the major obstacles was to convince lower social classes, which represent a large proportion of the population, to support policies against their own interest. People needed to believe that government interventions were infringements on their own freedom. Even the poor had to be persuaded that their liberty was threatened by social security, a minimum wage, decent labor standards, a universal healthcare system and public education.

Of course, in reality, the only liberty that the business class and the neoliberals were really after was that of American corporations and financial markets – to accumulate unlimited profit and run wild over labor and social restrictions on a global scale. Percy Barnevik, voted Europe's most admired businessman for four straight years during the 1990s, described fittingly what neoliberalism was all about. His words remain memorable:

> I would define globalization as the freedom for my group of companies to invest whether it wants when it wants; to produce what it wants, to buy and sell where it wants and to support the fewer restrictions possible coming from labor laws or social conventions.[34]

The world market trinity

The strategy of the big business class largely succeeded. The market greed doctrine was not only resurrected from obscurity, but chosen as a main organizing principle for worldwide economic integration. It became the basic public philosophy of human development.[24] After taking over the driving seat of the American and British economies, the neoliberal crusade went global. Three powerful international institutions played a pivotal role in the dissemination of the neoliberal dogma worldwide: the International Monetary Fund (IMF), the World Bank, and the World Trade Organization (WTO, initially named the General Agreement on Tariffs and Trade or GATT).

Founded in New Hampshire in 1944, the global financial trio formed the Bretton Woods system, a regulatory framework designed by John Maynard Keynes and Harry Dexter White to promote economic stability worldwide. The scars of the

Great Depression and the Second World War were still visible in the most powerful nations. In order to prevent future military conflicts and avoid the economic circumstances that lead to militarism, Keynes believed it was necessary for the super-powers to engage in global collective actions. However, Keynes would not have aligned with the free market doctrines that the triumvirate sponsored only three decades later. At the time, the conventional economic wisdom was that unregulated competition and free markets inevitably generate economic instability and high unemployment that, in turn, could lead to economic crises, social unrest and even armed conflicts. The idea that the invisible hand of the market can only work if guided by the visible thread of government was relatively popular.

In light of this philosophy, the IMF was supposed to govern the global financial system and protect it from economic crises. Its major goals were to stabilize exchange rates, and promote global monetary cooperation, economic growth and even full employment. The World Bank was born to provide financial and technical assistance to countries in need of reconstruction with the stated purpose of fighting poverty. Keynes had also hoped to add a third organization to the Fund and the Bank: the International Trade Organization (ITO). The ITO was negotiated in Havana, and its charter included provisions such as the use of trade to promote full employment and ensure fair and stable prices for the primary products of developing countries. The ITO was also supposed to authorize poor countries to use subsidies and aid, in order to promote emerging national industries. Unfortunately, the organization was suppressed in its cradle by the US and corporate lobbies in favor of the GATT,[34] later superseded by the WTO in 1995.

Although the IMF, World Bank and GATT turned out to be significantly different from what Keynes had envisioned, and the commercial and financial interests of the US dominated their agenda from the very beginning, Keynes seemed relatively satisfied with the initially proposed plan. He surely had high hopes for the Bretton Woods institutions. As he wrote: "the brotherhood of man will have become more than a phrase." It is important to remember that this was a very particular political age. Laissez-faire economics was considered a failed doctrine. It had promoted enough catastrophes in the past to not be taken seriously again. As Franklin Delano Roosevelt once remarked: "we have always known that heedless self-interest was bad morals, we now know that it is bad economics." Throughout the entire post-war period, Keynes inspired the political economic scene. In 1965, Milton Friedman admitted: "in one sense, we are all Keynesians now." Just a few years later, *Time* magazine featured the guru of the Chicago School as "a pixie or a pest."[35] Even conservative leaders such as Nixon were believed to have succumbed to the spirit of the age. "I am now a Keynesian in economics," he once declared.

All in all, the economic policies of the post-war age proved to be relatively effective in promoting prosperity and stability worldwide. It is for this very reason that this period is often called the "Golden Era" of capitalism. The early 1970s, however, signaled the beginning of the end for Keynes' mixed economy approach and the Bretton Woods system. The policies of the IMF, World Bank and WTO were converting to the neoliberal faith.

fashion. The opportunity to discipline the developing world to adopt these reforms was offered by the outbreak of the debt crisis in the early 1980s. Following the financial instability created by the Vietnam War and two oil crises in 1973 and 1977, the interest rates of US loans increased to 21 percent. This is often remembered as the "Volcker shock." It was a shock indeed especially in the developing world. Many of these countries found themselves knee deep in debt, faced with excessive amounts owed in interest to international banks, on top of the large loan sums they had originally taken out. In desperate need of new foreign loans and financial assistance, many developing countries had no choice but to turn to the IMF and the World Bank for help. The IMF and the World Bank rescue packages, however, were delivered with strict conditionalities. Countries in need of financial assistance were asked to adopt structural adjustment policies and create business-friendly environments, especially for transnational corporations and global financial markets.

The IMF and the World Bank claim that the removal of trade restrictions is absolutely necessary if developing countries are to prosper economically, and reduce poverty and external debt. Therefore, since the late 1970s, poor nations have adopted one or more of these policy packages. The IMF and the World Bank insisted that these reforms would ensure sustainable debt repayment, economic growth and poverty reduction. But has this really been the case? Unsurprisingly, according to the "self-evaluations" of the World Bank, the policies were largely successful.[40][41] Various independent analyses, however, showed quite a different picture.[42][43] Overall, while the rate of GNP growth per capita in the world economy was 2.6 percent during the "Keynesian era" (between 1960 and 1979), in the first two decades of the "neoliberal period" (between 1980 and 1998), the global GNP growth per capita was only 1.0 percent.[44] A panel data analysis of 98 countries between 1970 and 2000 showed that IMF programs and structural adjustment reforms have actually depressed, not promoted economic growth.[43] Neoliberal policies have also increased financial vulnerability and have left economies more exposed to banking and currency crises, a subject that will be analyzed in more detail in the next chapter. The macroeconomic failures of the Washington Consensus policies have been particularly severe in sub-Saharan Africa. Since the early 1980s, most African economies have suffered to the point that their GNP per capita in 2000 was lower than two decades before. But there is more. Since the application of these policies, the developing world debt has skyrocketed. It has become nearly impossible to repay. In 1980, Africa's external debt was about $55 billion. By 1997, it had increased to $210 billion.[45] In recent years, many poor countries have begged for debt forgiveness. Some have obtained it under the World Bank's *Heavily Indebted Poor Countries Initiative*, but in exchange for the usual free market austerity measures.

The Washington Consensus policies also proved to be ineffective in reducing poverty. Although the World Bank depicts itself as an organization whose main dream is a "world free of poverty," it has failed to transform this into a reality. The cadres of neoliberal economists working or consulting for the Washingtonian institution disagree. A policy report of the World Bank argues that, between 1981 and 2005, about 500 million people in the world have been taken out of extreme poverty, presumably because of the policies of the Washington Consensus.[46] David Dollar, a leading World Bank economist, also claimed that the scientific evidence clearly shows that countries that opened up their markets the most since the 1980s (or what he defined as the "winners" of globalization) have largely succeeded in reducing poverty. The "losers" of globalization, on the other hand, have done exactly the opposite, he added,[47] and that is why "they lost." But is this really the case?

There is little doubt that, in the last decades, global poverty has been decreasing. It is also true that those countries that succeeded in their strategy of integration into the global economy, and increased their trade-to-GDP ratio after the 1980s, experienced rapid poverty reduction. But the superficially positive picture painted by the World Bank hides a much less edifying deeper reality. Poverty reduction during the "neoliberal era" is largely attributable to fast economic growth in China, and in the other so-called "Asian tigers," such as South Korea, Taiwan, Malaysia, Thailand, Indonesia and Singapore.[48] As Dollar once admitted, 85 percent of what he defined as the "winners" of globalization are Asian countries. What the cheer-leaders of free market ideologies seem to forget to mention is that the emerging Asian economies have largely rejected the neoliberal dogma. In fact, they have applied a mixed model of protectionism and gradual and selective market liberalization programs. If they really are the "winners" of the neoliberal globalization game, it is only because they have not played by the rules.

Neoliberal crimes against humanity

Orthodox, laissez-faire economists are also reluctant to examine what happened to the "losers" of neoliberal globalization. Free market policies have been particularly disastrous in sub-Saharan Africa, a region that, after the outbreak of the debt crisis in the 1980s, remained under the grip of structural adjustment policies for decades. In the African continent, between 1981 and 2005, the number of people living in poverty has not diminished, but almost doubled.[49]

This sorry record has not produced any crisis of conscience among the neoliberals who, in spite of the evidence of their failures, continue to preach the gospel of market greed. In the opinion of Martin Wolf of *The Financial Times*, for example, neoliberalism is not to blame for the decades of economic recession and the increase of poverty in the poorest continent of the world. In his opinion, "the failure of the state to provide almost any of the services desperately needed for development" is at the root of the "African disaster."[50] In the same vein, the editors of *The Economist* argue that, "corrupt or incompetent governments in the developing countries deny responsibility when they blame the IMF or the World Bank for troubles chiefly caused by their own policies."[51]

While it is difficult to deny that many sub-Saharan African governments have been plagued by corruption and inefficiencies, it is also clear that structural adjustment policies have played a key role in the current state of the region. As the UNCTAD clearly put it, "the least developed countries (many in sub-Saharan

Africa) have actually gone further than other developing countries in dismantling (trade) barriers."[52] Howard Stein, professor at the University of Michigan, observes: "more than any region, Africa has felt the full effects of this shifting agenda [toward neoliberalism] developed by the World Bank and the IMF particularly after the 1980s." "The impact of these policies has been at best disappointing. Virtually every economic and social indicator since 1980 has declined," he adds. "While there has also been an array of other factors such as civil wars and the HIV/AIDS pandemic, the breadth and depth of the decline points to the general failure of the World Bank/IMF strategy." Stein continues that the recommendations offered to Africa by the World Bank, to ensure it "can claim the 21st century," revolved around "three E's": empower citizens, enable governments' capacity and enforce compliance with the rule of law. But, as he puts it, "the only letter that should be discussed is F for the failed agenda of the Bretton Woods Institutions."[53]

These reforms have not failed only in Africa. They have been revealed to be particularly lethal in Eastern Europe as well. After "the fall of the Wall," the former Soviet Union was transformed into a field experiment for a particularly radical version of neoliberalism: "shock therapy." Such reforms were preferred over a more gradual, paced approach that included social safety nets to buffer poor people during the economic transition. In the opinion of the ayatollah of the market greed doctrine, a gradual change was not in the game: shock therapy had to be put into action in the swiftest manner possible. Lawrence Summers explains why:

> despite economists' reputation for never being able to agree on anything, there is a striking degree of unanimity in the advice that has been provided to the nations of Eastern Europe and the former Soviet Union. The legions of economists who have descended on the formerly Communist economies have provided very similar advice . . . The three "-ations", privatization, stabilization, and liberalization, must all be completed as soon as possible.[54]

Jeffrey Sachs, a former enthusiast of the free market doctrine who the *New York Times* called a "shock therapist,"[55] explained:

> the need to accelerate privatization in Eastern Europe is the paramount economic policy issue facing the region. If there is no breakthrough in privatization in large enterprises in the near future the entire process could be stalled for political and social reasons for years to come, with dire consequences for the reforming economies of the region.[56]

The free market choir sang in unison with the voices of the editors of *The Economist*. Quite unsurprisingly, they agreed wholeheartedly with Summers and Sachs. As they observed: "the growing acceptance of . . . gradualism . . . [is] the greatest peril now facing the countries of Eastern Europe."[57] It is a pity that this was exactly the opposite. Shock therapy produced one of the worst economic disasters in recent history. The social misery brought in its wake is still felt today in Russia.[58]

Neoliberal globalization has not only resulted in poor macroeconomic per-formance, but also in adverse health consequences. In spite of the large health improvements in East and South Asia, global life expectancy at birth has been affected by the declines in longevity in both sub-Saharan Africa and Eastern Europe.[59] Although World Bank economists, such as David Dollar, think that neoliberal globalization is healthy,[40] the reality is very different. A regression analysis commissioned by the Globalization Knowledge Network of the WHO Commission on Social Determinants of Health found that, compared to a continuation of trends over the 1960–1980 "Keynesian period," neoliberal globalization policy-driven changes reduced potential gains in global life expectancy at birth by 1.52 years.[60]

The advent of these reforms has also been associated with widening health inequalities between and within countries. After a sustained period of global health convergence between countries in the 1960s and the 1970s, in which low-income countries slowly narrowed the gap in life expectancy in comparison to rich societies, a pattern of divergence began around the early 1980s.[61 62] Increasing inequalities in health have also been experienced within countries as the health gaps between social classes have widened in both developed[40] and developing nations.[63–65]

The deadly effects of the Washington Consensus have become more apparent after the publication of numerous studies that have examined the specific impact of reforms such as financial deregulation, privatization and trade liberalization. These policies have been associated with poverty,[66–68] deteriorating social conditions,[69 70] negative health outcomes[69–74] and even unhealthy behaviors such as smoking[75] and obesity.[76–78] A study that examined trends over a 20-year period in post-communist countries, for example, showed that IMF policies increased tuberculosis mortality by 16.6 percent.[79] When considering structural adjustment programs, although the World Bank claimed that "adjuster countries" generally succeeded in improving health standards compared to "non-adjusters,"[45 80 81] the bulk of evidence shows exactly the opposite.[82–88] These policies have been particularly disastrous in sub-Saharan Africa, as revealed by a review of 76 studies on the health effects of these reforms.[89] Of course, some blame the outbreak of AIDS as the major culprit for Africa's deteriorating health and worsening economic conditions during the neoliberal era. For sure, the AIDS pandemic played a detrimental role. Nevertheless, structural adjustment reforms have also contributed to exacerbate social circumstances potentially conducive to HIV infection such as rapid urbanization, commercial sex and the introduction of user fees for primary healthcare and education.[90]

The inescapable conclusion is that the reforms of the international financial institutions have failed on all fronts. They have achieved the exact opposite of what they were supposed to. The IMF has promoted financial instability and economic stagnation. The World Bank has exacerbated poverty. The WTO promoted unfair trade. Together, these institutions have promoted social unrest, wider inequalities and adverse health outcomes. In reference to the IMF, former chief economist of the World Bank Joseph Stiglitz wrote: "Keynes would be rolling over in his grave were he to see what has happened to his child."[91] The failure of the Bretton Woods institutions was so disastrous that even John Williamson, the coiner of the term

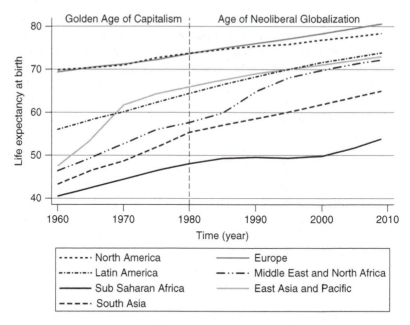

FIGURE 6.1   Keynesianism versus Friedmanomics: regional trends in life expectancy during the Golden Age of capitalism (1960–1980) and age of neoliberal globalization (1980–2010)

Sources: Data on life expectancy at birth for world regions were taken from the World Bank's World Development Indicators database (2012).

Washington Consensus, admitted that these reforms have been "disappointing, to say the least."[92] Far from been structural, adjustment policies have been destructive. But there is even more collateral damage of neoliberal globalization: the planet.

Destructural adjustment policies

The gurus of the market greed doctrine seem convinced that the Washington Consensus promotes not only economic development and poverty reduction, but also ecological sustainability. According to the World Bank, the economic benefits induced by trade liberalization and structural adjustment policies have increased the ability of countries to implement environmental regulations and protect the ecosystem.[93] The World Bank and the neoliberals also argue that free trade and free capital mobility facilitate the transfer of new technologies and the improvement of environmental management practices.[94] As written in the *World Development Report 1992: Development and Environment*, "liberated trade fosters greater efficiency and higher productivity and may actually reduce pollution by encouraging the growth of less polluting industries and the adoption and diffusion of cleaner technologies."[95]

Unfortunately, the need to fit the free trade mantra into the rhetoric of sustainable development has made the World Bank oblivious to the true repercussions of its policies. Ample evidence shows that, far from promoting ecological sustainability, neoliberalism has contributed to environmental destruction on a global scale.[96] From 1992 to 2004, the World Bank approved approximately 128 fossil-fuel extraction projects worth $11 billion that accumulated 43 billion tons of carbon dioxide emissions, one hundred times more than the emissions reductions that signatories of the Kyoto protocol were required to make between 1990 and 2012. In 2004–5, the Bank financed about $7.6 billion in fuel-intensive sectors or 37 percent of its total lending portfolio for the year.[97] The World Bank also urged developing countries to abandon farming for domestic purposes (e.g. rice), and pushed them to grow cash crops for export (e.g. coffee and sugar). The trouble is that high-input cash crops do not feed local people and generate deleterious effects on the ecosystem, much more than small-scale agricultural activities for subsistence. The intensification of agriculture was accompanied by uncontrollable deforestation, excessive use of pesticides and the accelerated decline of soil stability.[98] [99] Structural adjustment programs have also promoted water pollution[100] and increased use of water resources for industries, mining, tourism and irrigation of dams and reservoirs.[101] Furthermore, these reforms have increased energy consumption through more intense processing, packaging and international distribution of food. In wealthy nations, neoliberal globalization pushed polluting industries toward countries with weaker environmental regulations, the so-called "pollution havens."[102] At the same time, increased global competition for markets and profit undermined environmental standards, as countries engaged in a "race to the bottom" to meet the needs of rich foreign investors.[103] Finally, structural adjustment reforms have also compromised environmental protection regulations through cutbacks in public sector spending.[104] As the evidence on the effects of its policies became widely available, even the World Bank was compelled to admit the obvious. A review published by the Bank's Environmental Department concluded that, in spite of some positive effects including the transfer of technologies after trade liberalization and more efficient use of scarce natural resources after removal of subsidies, "the negative environmental impacts of SAPs [structural adjustment policies] exceed positive impacts."[105]

Because of this disastrous social, economic and ecological record, the IMF and the World Bank, together with the WTO, faced intense criticism worldwide. Many in the global justice movement called for their outright abolition. Even after the 2008 financial crisis, which caused public protests to be increasingly focused on Wall Street banks, *The Unholy Trinity* continues to be under fire.[106] Will it survive the storm?

The magic of protectionism

As already stated, the "winners" of globalization have hardly used the prescriptions provided by the Washington Consensus. The "Asian tigers" have refused to elect the self-adjusting market as chief regulator of their economic affairs. They have never really believed in the market God. It is true that Asian economies have become successful exporters, but this is the result of state interventions, subsidies and tariffs, not trade liberalization policies. Initially protected and subsidized markets in Asia attracted foreign investment and were able to achieve sustained economic growth much more successfully than in sub-Saharan Africa, where markets have been widely open since the very beginning of the "neoliberal globalization era." The "Asian model" worked exactly because governments played an essential role in taming markets and capital, provided high-quality education for most citizens, furnished the infrastructure (including the legal system necessary for markets to work effectively), regulated the financial sector, provided a safety net for the poor and invested in new technologies.[107] China, one of the blueprints of what the World Bank called the "Asian Miracle," applied strict capital controls, and rejected the prescriptions of the IMF by leaving more than half of its economy under government ownership. More recently, China reduced its tariffs in order to enter into the WTO. However, at the same time, China has also followed in the footsteps of other rich countries by maintaining all sorts of non-tariff barriers to block foreign imports. Far from hampering economic growth, these policies are at the basis of China's impressive macroeconomic performance, though they have also generated untold ecological disasters. The Chinese communist government created an economy that grew at least 8 percent per year and dramatically reduced the number of people living in poverty. As John Gray notes: "a crucial factor in this success has undoubtedly been China's disregard to Soviet and Western examples and advice. There has been no shock therapy in China. Market reform has been gradual and partial, pragmatic rather than doctrinal."[108] In other words, "free trade" worked well because it was hardly free.

Another country that succeeded economically by rejecting most of the prescriptions of the international financial institutions, is South Korea. In 1961, the nation's yearly income was about $82 per person. In 1996, the country joined the OECD, the club of the richest nations on earth. Contrary to popular belief, the "Korean miracle" was not a free trade success, but the outcome of a clever and pragmatic mixture of state direction and selective and gradual market liberalization. As explained by Ha-Joon Chang in *Bad Samaritans: The Myth of Free Trade*, the Korean government heavily controlled foreign investment, while spending foreign exchange on non-essentials for industrial development was prohibited or strongly discouraged through import bans, high tariffs and excise taxes. By adopting tariff barriers and subsidies, the government protected its most important "infant industries" until they "grew up" enough to withstand foreign competition.[109] Moreover, although South Korea promoted its export and expanded its trade, it actually never removed the impediments to imports. In outright violation of free market theories, government policies heavily subsidized public education, health and new technologies. More recently, South Korea has opened up its markets but, like China, adopted barriers to trade that do not qualify as tariffs in order to block Western imports. In Chang's words: "the popular impression of Korea as a free-trade economy was created by its export success. But export success does not require free trade, as Japan and China have also known."[110] Chang argues that the World Bank's argument for free trade

– that it leads to economic growth – is weak at best. After all, this myth had already been debunked by several other authors including Dani Rodrik who, in an article based on a thorough review of the literature, concluded:

> there is no convincing evidence that trade liberalization is predictably associated with subsequent economic growth. The only systematic relationship is that countries dismantle trade restrictions as they get richer, which accounts for the fact that most of today's rich countries embarked on economic growth behind protective barriers, which they subsequently lowered.[111]

So, the chain of causation runs from economic growth to exports and not the other way round, as the World Bank and the IMF have insisted for years. This explains not only the "East Asia Miracle," but also the economic success of industrialized nations. The lesson to be learned is simple. As Chang wittily observed: "It is not free trade, but trade that works."

Free trade for some

The US and the UK are usually regarded as the true champions of commercial freedom. They are seen in this light for not only encouraging free market policies abroad, but also because they apply them at home. This is true in many ways, but it is only half of the story. Especially in the initial stages of their transition toward industrialization, the US and the UK have protected their markets and infant industries. While they are now preaching the virtues of free trade, the historical record clearly indicates that most of them developed under state-led industrial policies and protective trade laws. These policies are exactly the opposite of those the IMF, the World Bank and WTO prescribe to poor nations.[109] It is true that both Britain and the US opened up their markets at some point – but only after turning themselves into the most powerful players of the free trade game. In another influential book, *Kicking Away the Ladder*, Ha-Joon Chang explains this clearly. Rich countries, after climbing the development steps through protectionism and subsidies, "*kicked the ladder away*," making it more difficult for poor countries to climb up it. This practice was exposed by German economist Friedrich List in 1841, when he criticized Britain for preaching free trade to other countries only after achieving its own economic supremacy through protectionism, high tariffs and subsidies.[112]

In effect, Britain, which is now widely considered a prototype of market liberalism, applied laissez-faire policies only after a long period of initial protectionism and after achieving total supremacy over foreign markets. As Chang explains, the first time Britain pushed for free trade policies was in 1846, with the abolishment of *The Corn Law*; after about 150 years of protection, coercive trade with its colonies and imperial conquests. Before, British policies were generally aimed at capturing trade through colonization, and industrial development was based on measures that protected manufacturing industries from foreign competition.

Subsidies, high tariffs and abolition of export duties, not free market policies, dominated the early phases of economic development in Britain. In 1820, Britain's average tariff rate on manufacturing imports was 54–5 percent, compared to 8–12 percent in Germany and Switzerland and 20 percent in France. Britain also initially banned manufacturing activities in its colonies, in order to avoid competition for manufacturing industries at home. However, as British industries became more competitive, protectionism became less and less necessary and even counter-productive. It was only after Britain achieved market supremacy overseas that Adam Smith attacked Walpole's mercantilist system – arguing that subsidies and monopoly rights were ineffective for the British economy because they restricted competition. In other words, when protectionism was no longer profitable for its manufacturing industries, Britain started its campaigning for free trade.[112][113]

If Britain's road to prosperity was paved with protectionist policies, the US certainly did not embrace free trade during its early years of economic development. Under British rule, America was given the usual colonial treatment. It was denied the chance to use tariffs to protect its own new industries. It was prohibited from exporting products that competed with British commodities. The US was compelled to follow British restrictions on what it could manufacture and produce. Once freed from British rule, however, the US was given the chance to develop its own economic policies that were promptly injected with heavy doses of protectionism. According to Chang, Adam Smith advised Americans against protecting their manufacturing industries, on the grounds that any attempt to stop the importa-tion of European manufacturing would have obstructed the progress of the US. Fortunately for the Americans, however, Alexander Hamilton, who can be con-sidered the first US Treasury Secretary, did not listen. The US adopted policies that would have been considered "heretical" by the IMF and the World Bank. In 1791, Hamilton proposed a program of protection and expansion of US "infant indus-tries," that included protective tariffs, import bans and subsidies. Hamilton's policies also consisted of export bans on key raw materials, import liberalization measures on industrial inputs, prizes and patents for inventions and regulation of product standards. When the War of 1812 broke out, the US Congress doubled its import tariffs from an average of 12.5 percent to 25 percent. By 1820, the average tariff rose to 40 percent. Once elected, Lincoln raised industrial tariffs to 50 percent, the highest in any country of the world until the First World War. Rather than harming the country, protectionist policies turned the US into the fastest growing economy in the world. Although the US is now widely considered a passionate advocate of free markets, it was only after it acquired an unchallenged supremacy at the end of the Second World War that it started to dismantle its barriers on trade.[113]

Not only Britain and the US have become wealthy through the application of "unfree" market policies. Almost all affluent nations, apart from a few exceptions, developed economically through similar macroeconomic strategies. Japan, for example, succeeded in becoming one of the most powerful economies in the world by disregarding prevailing economic wisdom. The Japanese model heavily relied on protectionism, subsidies, tax concessions, price ceilings, controls against capital flight and measures limiting speculations.[114] Like the British and the Americans, rather than applying free market policies which would have caused its corporations to compete against foreign transnational companies, the Japanese heavily subsidized their own "infant industries" and repeatedly bailed them out when necessary. This has been the case for Toyota, for example. The government's involvement in the regulation of market affairs has been so pervasive that some commentators confused Japan with a socialist country. As Chalmers Johnson once put it, "Japan is the only communist nation that works."[115] In reality, there has never been such a thing as a true free market society. And if capitalism really means unfettered free markets, then there has never been a true capitalist society either.

The most successful economies have largely relied on government interventions. And even today, while pushing trade liberalization on developing and transitional economies, they maintain trade restrictions and intellectual property rights to protect their own corporations. The WTO plays a key role in promoting these trade asymmetries that benefit rich nations. Trade liberalization policies are selectively applied to markets where developed countries are traditionally stronger (e.g. technology and high-tech industry). But in those markets where rich nations are traditionally weaker (e.g. agriculture and textiles), protectionism is largely tolerated. It has been estimated that the aggregate agricultural subsidies of the US, EU and Japan amount to about 75 percent of the entire sub-Saharan Africa income. On average, a European cow receives about $2 a day of subsidies, an amount exceeding the income of approximately 40 percent of the world's population. This has led some to joke that it may be better to be a cow in Europe than poor in a developing nation. No doubt, asymmetrical trade policies have resulted in large social and economic costs for developing nations. It has been estimated, for example, that the subsidies which rich countries provide their corporations cost the GDP of sub-Saharan Africa about 2 percent in lost market opportunities.[107] In spite of the rhetoric on free markets and neoliberalism, most developed nations continue to prefer a "mixed approach" that consists of protectionism for themselves and free markets for their competitors.

The invisible hand and the iron fist

It is also important to understand that the rise of a single global free market system dominated by large corporations and affluent societies, with the US at its head, is not a random outcome of history. It is the result of conscious efforts on the part of powerful nations to dominate the trade and economic system. In other words, behind the facade of free markets often lurks a cut-throat competition between imperial nations.[116] History is filled with examples showing that free trade has often been "midwifed" by the use of force. The words of the fourth director of the Dutch East India Company, Jan Pieterszoon Coen, in a letter dated December 27, 1614, are revealing:

you gentlemen should well know from experience that in Asia trade must be driven and maintained under the protection and favor of your own weapons, and that the weapons must be wielded from the profits gained by the trade; so, that trade cannot be maintained without war, nor war without trade.[117]

Almost three centuries later, in 1900, an official of the US State Department made a similar argument: "territorial expansion is but a by-product of the expansion of commerce."[118] A few years earlier, US Senator Albert Beveridge of Indiana explained: "American factories are making more than the American people can use; American soil is producing more than they can consume. Fate has written our policy for us; the trade of the world must be and shall be ours."[119]

To be sure, some of the most naked and brutal forms of imperialism do not exist anymore. Nevertheless, even today, as in the past, trade and war are two sides of the same coin. Samuel Huntington argues that: "A world without the US primacy will be a world with more violence and disorder and less democracy and economic growth than a world where the US continues to have more influence than any other country in shaping global affairs."[120] This is potentially true, but impossible to know. Even so, make no mistake: like any other empire in history, the US has so far been chiefly concerned with advancing its power and economic influence, not promoting freedom and free markets. It is important to remember that, between 1945 and 2001 only, the US "engaged" in about two hundred different "theatres of operation" – including wars, covert operations and single attacks. Many of these "interventions" had nothing to do with promoting democracy or containing the Russians. As Gore Vidal wrote in *Perpetual War for Perpetual Peace*, for the last sixty years the US has engaged in "perpetual wars, cold, hot and tepid."[121] The ayatollahs of free market fundamentalism can insist that neoliberal globalization is a neutral process of economic integration toward a freer and more democratic world. But when they look at themselves in the mirror, they know this is hardly the case. As Thomas Friedman candidly admits: "for globalism to work, America can't be afraid to act like the almighty superpower that it is." He continues: "The hidden hand of the market will never work without a hidden fist – McDonald's cannot flourish without McDonnell Douglas, the designer of the F-15."[122]

The point could not be any clearer. Like all other divinities, the market God never really existed. It is merely an illusion for those naive enough to believe in it.

The self-destructive gene

There is no other economic system besides market greed, the neoliberal gospel says. In the opinion of the free market evangelists, the reason is simple: it is the only model that works. Human beings are inherently acquisitive, self-interested, utilitarian and materialistic. Conclusion: neoliberalism is the sole social order humanity can afford.

No matter how unedifying this picture of human nature may seem, it has found authoritative support, not only among economists, but also from some of the most influential philosophers of Western civilization. The author of *The Prince*, Nicolò Macchiavelli, defined by Bertrand Russell as a "disappointed romantic," once explained: "it may be said of men in general that they are ungrateful, voluble, dissemblers, anxious to avoid danger, and covetous of gain."[123] Then there was Thomas Hobbes. The author of *Leviathan* believed individuals to be naturally inclined to compete against one another in order to advance their own selfish agenda. Life is "a war of all against all," he wrote, and the general inclination of humankind is "a perpetual and restless desire of power after power that ceaseth only in death."[124] Essentially, the only restraints that can stop humans from slaughtering one another are punishments and the rule of law. Friedrich Nietzsche shared a similar view. Human beings are inclined to advance their own power at any cost, he argued. "No act of violence, rape, exploitation, destruction, is intrinsically 'unjust,'" he reflected, "since life itself is violent, rapacious, exploitative, and destructive and cannot be conceived otherwise."[125]

Evolutionary biologists have also provided us with a bleak picture of human nature. In *The Selfish Gene*, Richard Dawkins compares human beings to "survival machines, robot vehicles blindly programmed to preserve molecules known as genes, whose predominant quality is ruthless selfishness."[126] Although Dawkins clearly highlights that we do not need to be selfish just because we are made of selfish genes, his theory unwillingly plays into the market greed argument. Do not be confused here: the Oxford professor is not a reactionary social Darwinist. Quite the opposite. He recommends, for example, that we must be passionate Darwinians when understanding where our moral feelings come from, and that we be passionate anti-Darwinians when it comes to developing a morality for society. His argument, however, has a problem: how can we expect anybody to become passionately anti-Darwinian in politics if his or her genes are hopelessly Darwinian? Can we really persuade a predator to stop pursuing what it is born to pursue? Has anyone ever seen a wolf fasting in front of a sheep? Or a lion turning into a vegetarian? Probably not. If we really are selfish to the core, as some evolutionary biologists seem to claim, the neoliberals may be right after all. A society of greedy profiteers in perpetual competition against one another is the only social order we can achieve.

The end of the story? Not really. For sure, there is some truth to the conjecture that we are selfishly driven. During our long journey on planet Earth, we would not have managed to survive unless we had become the most ruthless of the ruthless. It would be unrealistic to believe otherwise. Unfortunately, the convenient myth that we are pure altruists does not stand the most elementary forms of scrutiny. We are not saints. We must know this by now. We have not become the winners of history because of our compassion. We would not have survived for so long if we had not developed sophisticated ways to kill other animals and exploit the natural environment. We have not even been kind to fellow members of our own species. The story of *Homo sapiens* resembles more of a "war of all against all" than a festival of peace and love. Still, Machiavelli, Hobbes, Nietzsche and the neoliberals have gotten it wrong. Not because such a pessimistic view of human nature sounds too extreme to be true, but because it is untrue.

The view that we are predatory and selfish is an understatement when thinking about Nero, Pope Innocent II, Hitler and Stalin. But history also offered Socrates, Gandhi, Buddha and Saint Francis, to name a few. None of these moral authorities can be reconciled with the theory of the predatory *Selfish sapiens*. An objection is, of course, that these figures are just exceptions to the rule. But this is hardly so. These are, undoubtedly, exceptional cases, but not exceptions. They are just the tip of the iceberg of humanity's vast and deep compassionate potential. Countless individuals who you may not even know have dedicated their lives to altruistic, selfless causes. And even the everyday existences of common people are filled with hundreds of small acts of generosity. There are elements that simply do not square with the *Selfish sapiens* hypothesis.

In stark opposition to the presumption that we are exclusively selfish, numerous experiments have shown that human beings may be prewired for empathy and companionship. Research has found that our brain is endowed with "mirror neurons," or what the popular science press renamed "empathy neurons." We know this from the results of studies that used functional magnetic resonance imaging (fMRI). These found that human beings have neurons that allow them to grasp other people's minds as if their thoughts and behaviors were their own. This was demonstrated by an experiment on a group of individuals who were observing other people's hand movements and facial gestures. A part of the observers' brains activated in the same area as if they were making the hand movements or facial expressions themselves.[127]

The sociability of human nature is also widely supported by psychological research. Since birth, human beings seem to possess an intrinsic need to seek love, affection and warm relationships.[128] The failure to connect emotionally with a mother figure during the early years of life can even promote destructive tendencies or pathological symptoms of isolation, anxiety, anger, abandonment and aggression.[129] [130] We do not necessarily need research to believe this, but it is good when science confirms our suspicions. According to New York pediatrician and author Harry Bakwin, babies deprived of early maternal care and affection can "die of emotional starvation."[131] Several other authors have thought the same way. David Levy observed that, when a child is not loved and nurtured in the early stages of life, he or she usually develops what can be called "primary affect hunger," a severe deficiency of the emotional life reflected in the inability to express the full range of human feelings.[131] This deficiency is clearly observable in some orphans who, deprived of maternal care in early life, experience a deep sense of emptiness. They look and act as though they have no emotion. This is hardly surprising. The love and affection children receive from their mothers is essential for them to be able to love and harbor feelings of affection for others. Empathy may be prewired into our brain, but without parental and social stimuli, the biological circuitry associated with these emotions stops functioning.[127] It ossifies.

Evidence on the sociability and altruism of humans can impress anyone but hard-core skeptical evolutionary biologists. They remain underwhelmed. Cooperative behaviors within members of the same animal group or species, they argue, are not true acts of generosity. They are just sublimated forms of "selfishness in disguise." Nothing more than a different strategy of adaptation aimed at survival and reproduction.[132] Animals cooperate because, together, they are more successful in catching prey and in defending themselves against predators.[133] United they stand, divided they fail. Cooperation enhances their chances to survive and reproduce.[134] But it does not make them altruists. And even if it were true that natural selection promotes social instincts, this occurs for selfish reasons. In the opinion of many evolutionary biologists and psychologists, this applies to humans too. In *Psychology: the Science of Mind and Behavior*, Richard Gross dismissed human altruism as some sort of illusion. In his opinion, cooperative behaviors are likely to be adopted not just because they are functional to survival and reproduction, but because of the emotional rewards that result from generosity. Put another way, people do good not because they are good, but just because they want to feel good.[135]

Is this really the case? Are we really so selfish that, even when it seems that we are not, we actually are? Let us suppose this is true. Let us accept the hypothesis that we are hopeless egotists and genetically programmed to pursue our own profit and power exclusively and unlimitedly. Let us also accept that all forms of altruism human beings can express are nothing more than different versions of "selfishness in disguise." Let us even finally accept that neoliberalism is the best economic system humans can muster. If all this were true, then we are in deep trouble. The neoliberals told us that market greed is the only model that works, and that we can afford. But they are wrong. It does not work, and we cannot afford it. Gandhi provided the reason for this a long time ago. "The earth provides enough to satisfy every man's need," he said, "but not every man's greed." Racing for profit and power may have helped us to survive in the past, but this does not necessarily mean it will allow us to continue to do so in the future. In fact, it will not. Many free market economists and social Darwinists may not have noticed yet, but if the laws of human progress have changed, if adaptation requires more cooperation than predation, in the game of evolution, we will become the unfit. We will turn into the most successful losers of history. And our genes will no longer be called selfish, but self-destructive.

7

DIVIDED WE FAIL

Vilfredo Pareto, an Italian economist, is best remembered for proposing the power–law distribution of wealth. This idea states that, when left to its own devices, or to the will of free markets, wealth tends to distribute itself according to the "80–20 rule." This means that about 20 percent of the population ends up owning approximately 80 percent of wealth.[1] Pareto, who immodestly compared his theory to Kepler's law of astronomy, was proven both wrong and right. Wrong because during most of human history, material resources have not been distributed in the manner that he predicted; right because they have in more recent times. Although people have never been the "noble savages" that Rousseau fantasized,[2] for thousands of years most did live in highly egalitarian hunting and gathering societies that shared food and gifts as a way of life.[3] However, the rise of agriculture changed everything. Since this time, societies started to distribute material resources more consistently with Pareto's guess. During the last century in particular, the worldwide distribution of wealth became strikingly close to the prediction of the Italian economist. In 1992, the United Nations Development Program (UNDP) estimated that the richest 20 percent of the world population received about 82.7 percent of the entire world's income, while the poorest 20 percent only received 1.4 percent.

In more recent years, however, the wealth gap between rich and poor individuals has assumed even more grotesque proportions that not even Pareto could have anticipated. In 2008, according to The United Nations University (UNU) and the World Institute for Development Economic Research (WIDER), the richest 2 percent of all adults owned half of global household wealth, while 50 percent of the world owned just 1 percent. They have also estimated that the Gini coefficient, a popular index of global wealth inequalities ranging from 0 (lowest value) to 1 (highest value), is about 0.89. This is a "value one would obtain in a population of ten people if one person had $1,000 and the other nine had just $1."[4]

All things being unequal

Social scientists have been contemplating for years why some societies have become rich, while others have remained poor. Neoliberal economists have one simple answer. In their opinion, the road to prosperity is paved with the profit motive and market forces. Today's inequalities in wealth, they say, reflect the differential advantage achieved by the countries that have embraced free market reforms, in comparison to those that have yet to adopt them. The neoliberals would have us examine history, and more specifically, the time when the sharpest increase of inequalities in wealth occurred. This was after the Industrial Revolution, when Britain, followed by the rest of Western Europe and the former British colonies, experienced rapid economic growth. It was during this period that today's most affluent societies economically distanced themselves from the rest of the world. Historical data shows that in 1820, the richest country had a real income per head only 4.5 times higher than the poorest. This ratio, however, increased to 15 to 1 by 1913, 26 to 1 by 1950, 42 to 1 by 1973, and 71 to 1 by 2000.[5] According to Martin Wolf, what happened in the early nineteenth century in Britain should be described as a market revolution, not an industrial one. As he puts it, "it was the active force of profit-seeking business people . . . that drove the economic transformation" of the world. "It is they who chose the investments and made the technological innovations," that made our world rich and prosperous.[6] Some decades earlier, in *The Road to Serfdom*, von Hayek arrived at the same conclusion. He argued, "it was men's submission to the impersonal forces of the market that in the past have made possible the growth of civilization which without this could not have developed."[7]

The neoliberal explanation for the origins of the world's current wealth inequalities does have some merit. There is little doubt that the entrepreneurship and the dynamism of some innovators played a crucial role in generating the technological changes that promoted prosperity and wealth. It is also true that market forces and the prospect of pecuniary gain did motivate scientific break-throughs that, in turn, promoted higher standards of living. Nevertheless, the free market enthusiasts have missed some very important pieces of the puzzle. First, the most relevant scientific advances in human history have not been spurred by market forces or the profit motive, but by creativity, intrinsic motivations and through circumstances that promote independent inquiry. Geniuses such as da Vinci, Galileo, Newton, Copernicus and Einstein did not seem motivated by pecuniary motives or the prospect of selling their creations in the marketplace. It was not the search for profit that unleashed their ingenious power and motivation to create. Rather, it was freedom itself. Of course, one of the major obstacles to creative thinking and innovation is poverty, but so is constant preoccupation with accumulating wealth. As Oscar Wilde wrote: "there is no such mortal enemy to genius as poverty except riches."[8]

There is something else to remember. Some of the most important technological discoveries in modern times – semiconductors, optic fibers, satellites, computers and airplanes – were not born from the private sector, but through public support. In *Is*

War Necessary for Economic Growth?, Vernon Ruttan explains this very clearly. In his view, today's global technological landscape would be completely different in the absence of military or defense-related research, the so-called "Pentagon research system."[9] The moral of the story is quite simple: it is "big government," not the "magic of the market," we have to thank for the most important technologies that have made our lives more comfortable, healthier and happier.[10]

Guns, slaves and steal

There are some more important points missing in the neoliberal explanation for worldwide wealth inequalities. The conquest, exploitation and plundering of riches in the New World have no space in the free market economist's equation for the gap between the "haves and have nots." They also turn a blind eye to the role of the slave trade in enriching the lives of those in the West, and impoverishing the "Rest." Some even deny altogether that the latter event ever occurred. Milton Friedman, for example, once affirmed that, "Britain . . . had not had slavery" and it is simply "not true that the enormous increase in the world wealth in the free countries of the West arose out of slavery."[11] The reality, however, is very different. The extraordinary prosperity enjoyed by affluent nations is, in part, attributable to the gold, blood and sweat taken from developing countries. Two of the most historical turning points behind the rise of economic inequalities are both the European colonial expansion initiated in Latin America in 1492, and the emergence of the slave trade that began in Hispaniola in 1501. Adam Smith, himself, most likely would have agreed with these facts. As he once explained, "the discovery of America and the passage to the India Orientals through Capo de Buena Esperanza, are the two most important events of the history of humanity." "The discovery of America," he wrote, "certainly made a most essential contribution to the state of Europe . . . opening up a new and inexhaustible market," leading to "real revenue and wealth."[12] However, Smith added, "the savage injustice of the Europeans rendered an event, which ought to have been beneficial to all, ruinous and destructive to several of those unfortunate countries."[13]

In one of his most acclaimed books, *Year 501: the Conquest Continues*, Noam Chomsky observes that the plundering of the New World "set off vast demographic catastrophes, unparalleled in history: the virtual destruction of the indigenous populations of the Western hemisphere, and the devastation of Africa as the slave trade rapidly expanded to serve the needs of the conquerors."[14] The mass killing and exploitation of Native Americans reached levels of brutality rarely seen before then. When Columbus "discovered" the New World in 1492, there were about 80 million indigenous people living on the continent. By 1650, about 95 percent of them had disappeared, either killed directly by the conquistadores, or indirectly by diseases, poverty and starvation. After the massive disappearance of the "New World's" native population, the Europeans captured 12 million Africans and "shipped" them to South America to work as slaves on plantations. It is believed that between 1750 and 1830,[15] about 15 percent of African slaves died at sea and even more died in Africa before ever reaching the sea – perishing under the initial conditions of capture and transportation.[16] Free market economists are notoriously uncomfortable with notions regarding power and history, but when analyzing the causes of the economic gap between rich and poor nations they must consider this: the "comparative advantage" achieved by the West came at a considerable "comparative disadvantage" suffered by "the Rest." In *Open Veins of Latin America*, Eduardo Galeano expresses this point quite well: "for those who see history as a competition, Latin America's backwardness and poverty is merely the result of its failure. We lost: others won. But the winners happen to have won thanks to our losing."[17]

Countless other writers agree that it was a superior military power, not the work of the free market, that paved the road for the European economy to dominate the world.[18] [19] The first economist who clearly made this connection was most likely Karl Marx. "The discovery of gold and silver in America, the extirpation, enslavement and entombment in mines of the indigenous population . . . the conquest and plunder of India, and the conversion of Africa into a preserve for the commercial hunting of black-skins," he wrote "are all things which characterize the dawn of the era of capitalist production. These idyllic proceedings are the chief moments of primitive accumulation."[20] In Marx's view, all of these historical factors constituted "an indispensable condition for the establishment of manufacturing industry" in England first and in Europe later.[21]

Historian Sergio Bagú had similar thoughts. In his opinion, the accumulation of commercial capital generated by the slavery system in the Americas is "the foundation stone on which the giant industrial capital of modern times was built."[22] Joseph Inikori contends that the rise of commerce and trade-led economic development in the Atlantic system heavily depended on the "forced specialization of enslaved Africans and their descendants in large-scaled production of commodities . . . in the Americas."[23] Similar arguments have been advanced by other writers including the first Prime Minister of Trinidad and Tobago, Eric Williams, author of *Capital and Slavery*.[24] Some analysts even claimed that the Industrial Revolution would not have ever occurred without the slave trade. This is probably untrue. There were multiple other mechanisms that contributed to the rise of the Industrial Revolution beyond the slave trade, including a new trading and banking system that promoted more effective methods of investment. Nevertheless, it is difficult to deny that the exploitation of slaves was instrumental in maximizing profit and accumulating capital in Europe. It is also important to remember that the massive transfer of gold, silver and precious materials from the Rest to the West equaled investing capital in the nascent textiles industries. Between 1503 and 1660, about 185,000 kg of gold and 16 million kg of silver were shipped from Latin America to Europe.[25] According to Ernest Mandel, the value of gold and silver obtained from Latin America until 1600, the booty extracted from Indonesia by the Dutch East India Company from 1650 to 1780, the harvest reaped by the French capitalists in the eighteenth-century slave trade, the profits from slave labor in the British Antilles and from a half-century of British's looting practices in India, exceeded the total capital invested in all European enterprises operated by a steam engine in 1800.[26]

Crusades for civilization

There is more. The conquest of "the Rest" by the West was made possible, not only by a superior military might, but also by an unequal disposition to utilize force. As English journalist John Keay once explained, "warfare in India was still a sport; in Europe it had become a science."[27] The capture of the Inca Emperor Atahualpa by Francisco Pizarro and the Aztec Emperor Montezuma by Hernan Cortez are cases in point. It is true that the American Indians were not pacifists. Nevertheless, as Adam Smith observed, "far from having ever injured the people of Europe, [the Native Americans] had received the first adventurers with every mark of kindness and hospitality."[28] The Europeans harbored very different feelings toward them, however. When describing the first indigenous people he met in the New World, Christopher Columbus observed: "they are so naïve and so free with their possessions that no one who has not witnessed them would believe it. When you ask for something they have, they never say no. To the contrary, they offer to share with anyone." He continues: "they would make fine servants . . . with 50 men we could subjugate them all and make them do whatever we want."[29] In *Short Account of the Destruction of the Indies,*[30] a book that has been ignored for centuries in the West, Bartolome de las Casas argued that the slaughter of Native Americans by Spanish soldiers denoted a level of brutality rarely witnessed before. "I saw here cruelty on a scale no living being has ever seen or expects to see," he wrote.[31]

For hundreds of years, the genocide of the Native Americans has hardly been remembered with sorrow or guilt in the West. Indeed, the "discovery" of America has been celebrated as a major achievement. Moral justifications for the plundering and the pillage of the conquered populations have never been in short supply. And even today, self-serving explanations are still abundant. Some of the most prominent philosophers of Western civilization pictured the geopolitical domination of Europe as an inevitable consequence of its "biological superiority." It was often in the name of a superior race that the European felt justified in engaging in all sorts of brutalities, torture, slavery and genocide overseas. In *Beyond Good and Evil*, Friedrich Nietzsche explained that "hardness, violence, slavery . . . everything evil, terrible, tyrannical . . . serves the enhancement of the species 'man' as much as its opposite does."[32] In his opinion, black people "were representative of prehistoric men."[33] David Hume, in *Philosophical Works*, observed that he was "apt to suspect the Negroes and in general all other species of men . . . to be naturally inferior to the whites."[34] In *Philosophy of Right*, another eminent figure of Western philosophy, Friedrich Hegel argued that, "in Negro life the characteristic point is that consciousness has not yet attained to the realization of any substantial objective existence."[35]

Not only influential philosophers, but also prominent politicians often felt obliged to share their racist beliefs in support of brutal invasions, massacres and conquests by the West around the world. In the opinion of John Quincy Adams, for example, the Native Americans were "destined to extinction . . . a race, not worth preserving . . . essentially inferior to the Anglo-Saxon race" and therefore "their disappearance from the human family would be no great loss."[36] Theodore Roosevelt thought that it was "idle to apply to savages the rules of international morality" because, "the most ultimate righteous of all wars is a war with savages," that needs to be won, "for the benefit of civilization and in the interests of mankind."[37] In 1919, during an Iraqi revolt against the British Empire, Winston Churchill complained that he failed to understand, "the squeamishness about the use of gas . . . against uncivilized tribes."[38]

One would think that racist justifications for the use of violence against non-white populations were no longer tolerated in the West today. One would also assume that no white intellectual still had the "courage" to even attempt to treat the genocide of the indigenous populations as an "inevitable by-product of progress."[39] This is indeed mostly the case. Nonetheless, self-serving myths rationalizing colonization and imperialism as inexorable historical events continue to be reiterated in Western intellectual circles. To correspond with the five-hundredth anniversary of the "discovery" of America in 1992, the editors of *The Economist* observed that, "the demographic catastrophe which befell early Latin America was not an act of genocide, but a genuine tragedy, caused not by wickedness but by human failing and by a form of fate: the grinding wheels of long-term historical change."[40] Small wonder when Gandhi was asked what he thought about Western civilization, he replied that it "could be a good idea."

The flat world myth

"Perhaps you, my judges, pronounce this sentence against me with greater fear than I receive it," Giordano Bruno told the Inquisition after listening to his death verdict.[41] On February 17, 1600, the Italian philosopher, astronomer and mathematician was burned alive in Rome's *Campo dei Fiori* for committing a crime: debunking the myth that the Earth is flat. After more than four centuries, the expression of an original idea is no longer a deadly risk, at least in democratic countries. Yet, the flat world myth is still part of conventional wisdom. Not in the field of astronomy, but in international and economic affairs. Strange as it may seem, when Thomas Friedman published *The World Is Flat* in 2005 and explained that society is becoming more egalitarian because "the global competitive playing field [is] being leveled,"[42] one could plausibly wonder whether he had fallen victim to the same illusion promoted by the Inquisition during the Middle Ages. Indeed, looking at the shape representing today's distribution of wealth, the world more closely resembles a champagne glass or a pyramid, than a level field.

The high priests of free markets, however, revere *The World Is Flat* as one of the sacred scripts of the neoliberal economic creed. The list of those who believe that the world is "flattening" is quite long. Unsurprisingly, it includes the World Bank, which claims that neoliberal policies have reduced inequality and poverty worldwide.[43] It comprises influential columnists, such as Martin Wolf, editor of the *Financial Times*, who are also convinced that the world has become more egalitarian because of neoliberal globalization.[44] Several economists in academia regard the flat world myth as true. In 2006, Professor Xavier Sala-i-Martin at Columbia University

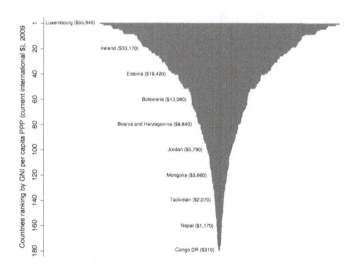

FIGURE 7.1   The world is not flat: the pyramid of world wealth inequalities between 180 nations ranked by GNI per capita PPP (current international $), 2009

Source: World Bank's World Development Indicators database (2012).

List of countries by ranking from richest to poorest: Luxembourg, Norway, United Arab Emirates, Brunei Darussalam, Singapore, Switzerland, United States, Macao SAR China, Hong Kong SAR China, Netherlands, Austria, Australia, Denmark, Sweden, Canada, Germany, Finland, Belgium, United Kingdom, France, Ireland, Japan, Italy, Spain, Cyprus, Iceland, Greece, New Zealand, Korea Rep., Slovenia, Israel, Equatorial Guinea, Oman, Bahamas, Trinidad and Tobago, Czech Republic, Portugal, Malta, Saudi Arabia, Slovak Republic, Antigua and Barbuda, Estonia, Croatia, Seychelles, Hungary, Barbados, Russian Federation, Poland, Latvia, Lithuania, Libya, St. Kitts and Nevis, Romania, Argentina, Turkey, Mexico, Malaysia, Bulgaria, Chile, Mauritius, Botswana, Lebanon, Gabon, Montenegro, Uruguay, Belarus, Venezuela, Panama, Dominica, Iran, Macedonia FYR, Serbia, St. Vincent and the Grenadines, Costa Rica, Palau, Kazakhstan, Brazil, South Africa, St. Lucia, Grenada, Bosnia and Herzegovina, Tunisia, Colombia, Azerbaijan, Albania, Dominican Republic, Peru, Algeria, Suriname, Thailand, Ecuador, Maldives, Jamaica, Turkmenistan, China, El Salvador, Ukraine, Namibia, Belize, Egypt, Jordan, Angola, Armenia, Syrian Arab Republic, Swaziland, Georgia, Sri Lanka, Tonga, Fiji, Guatemala, Bhutan, Bolivia, Paraguay, Morocco, Vanuatu, Samoa, Indonesia, Honduras, Philippines, Cape Verde, Mongolia, Timor-Leste, Micronesia Fed., Iraq, Kiribati, India, Guyana, Moldova, Congo Rep., Uzbekistan, Vietnam, Pakistan, Nicaragua, Djibouti, Yemen Rep., Lao PDR, Papua New Guinea, Cameroon, Kyrgyz Republic, Nigeria, Tajikistan, Solomon Islands, Sudan, Cambodia, Mauritania, Lesotho, Senegal, Sao Tome and Principe, Cote d'Ivoire, Myanmar, Bangladesh, Kenya, Benin, Ghana, Tanzania, Zambia, Gambia, Uganda, Chad, Haiti, Nepal, Burkina Faso, Guinea-Bissau, Rwanda, Comoros, Afghanistan, Mali, Guinea, Ethiopia, Madagascar, Mozambique, Togo, Malawi, Sierra Leone, Central African Republic, Niger, Eritrea, Burundi, Liberia, Congo Dem. Rep.

published a paper whose title did not leave much space for ambiguous interpreta-tions: "The World Distribution of Income: Falling Poverty And . . . Convergence, Period."[45] The "flat world society" includes ideologues covering most of the political spectrum. During a seminar at the London School of Economics, the founder of the "third way" Anthony Giddens dismissed claims arguing that globalization widens the gap between rich and poor. As he told his audience: "does globalization increase inequality? People on the streets seem to think so, but if you examine the evidence, that assertion cannot be supported."[46]

Of course it can. Independent scholarship largely agrees that the world, far from having become flatter, has become grotesquely unequal. It is true that technological advances and increasing economic cooperation have allowed us to travel and communicate much more easily than ever before. In economic terms, however, the world has never been so divided. Within nations, after more than three decades of declining economic inequalities, the gap between rich and poor social classes has gradually widened since the late 1970s.[47] Neoliberal globalization has also significantly widened the economic gap between nations, particularly between the richest and poorest regions of the world.[48-50]

As Robert Wade, professor at the London School of Economics, explains: "world income inequality has been rising during the past two to three decades," and although one particular measure of inequality indicates that inequality has been narrowing over time, "take out China and even this measure shows widening inequality."[51] On top of this, a recent investigation that reviewed various measures of the global economic gap between 1980 and 2007, concluded that inequality has increased irrespective of the indicators considered.[52] Another study showed that the size of inequalities in wealth is actually much larger than previously believed.[53] As Robert Wade remarks: "the Bank's argument about the benign effects of globalization on . . . income distribution does not survive scrutiny."[51] It is ironic that the cheerleaders of neoliberalism attempt to demonstrate that globalization has reduced inequalities by relying on the contribution of China that, as explained in the previous chapter, "got the prices wrong" by interfering substantially with market affairs. The enthusiasts of neoliberal globalization also ignore another "elephant in the room": since the early 1980s, most sub-Saharan African countries have lost ground in economic development exactly because they were forced to adopt structural adjustment policies. As a result, the economic gap between them and the most advanced nations has widened spectacularly. This is very serious because, together with South-East Asia, sub-Saharan Africa concentrates the largest proportion of the poor worldwide. And weren't the poorest nations supposed to see the most improvements by adopting free market policies and utilizing international assistance programs?

The shadow of the West on the Rest

Certainly, the widening economic gap between poor and rich nations experienced in the last few decades cannot be explained by military occupation, slave trade and systematic plunder. The times when large quantities of gold and silver were forcibly

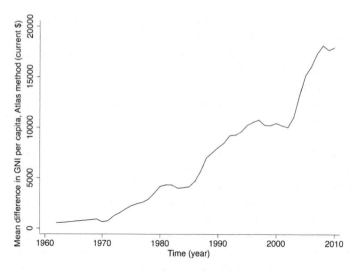

FIGURE 7.2 Divided we stand in the neoliberal world: trend in global wealth inequality (mean difference in GNI per capita, Atlas method – current international $) between 88 nations, 1960–2010

Source: World Bank's World Development Indicators database (2012).

Note: Only countries with less than a maximum of five missing values (out of 49 data points) were included in the analysis.

List of countries: Algeria, Argentina, Australia, Austria, Bahamas, Barbados, Belgium, Belize, Benin, Botswana, Brazil, Burkina Faso, Burundi, Cameroon, Canada, Central African Republic, Chad, Chile, China, Colombia, Dem. Rep. of Congo, Congo, Rep., Costa Rica, Cote d'Ivoire, Dominican Republic, Ecuador, Egypt, El Salvador, Fiji, Finland, France, Gabon, Ghana, Greece, Guatemala, Guyana, Honduras, Hong Kong, China, Iceland, India, Ireland, Israel, Italy, Japan, Kenya, Korea Rep., Lesotho, Liberia, Luxembourg, Madagascar, Malawi, Malaysia, Mauritania, Mexico, Morocco, Nepal, Netherlands, Nicaragua, Niger, Nigeria, Norway, Oman, Pakistan, Panama, Papua New Guinea, Paraguay, Peru, Philippines, Portugal, Rwanda, Seychelles, Sierra Leone, Singapore, South Africa, Spain, Sri Lanka, St. Vincent and the Grenadines, Sudan, Sweden, Syrian Arab Republic, Thailand, Togo, Trinidad and Tobago, Tunisia, Uruguay, Venezuela, Zambia, Zimbabwe.

sent from Latin America to Europe are gone. The slave trade, which enriched European plantations and manufacturing industries, has long been abolished. Most parts of the world are no longer under the grip of colonization, and most empires have already been dismantled. Still, inequalities in wealth continue to widen. Why?

The answer is not completely straightforward. But there is something to consider: just because the West no longer militarily occupies most of its former colonies does not mean that it has stopped exploiting them. In fact, it still does. European nations, along with Britain's most successful former colony, the US, no longer need to occupy foreign nations to benefit from their natural resources and cheap labor. By and large, finance, trade policies and economic reforms now do the job. Although history finds little or no space in the neoliberal explanation for world wealth inequalities, it is important to remember that most colonies, in spite of their political independence, are still under the economic shadow of their former colonizers.[54] [55] Undoubtedly, in the last few decades, and especially after the 2008 economic crisis, the emergence of the "Asian tigers," and other emerging economies, has changed the economic and geopolitical landscape of the world. Yet, many economies of the poorest nations seem to continue to "perform their duty" of supplying raw material and cheap labor to the West. Developing countries' "specialization" in cash crops, such as coffee and sugar, largely reflects the legacy of economic dependency and unfair international division of labor decided by the West. While many former colonies have concentrated on agriculture and primary materials, Western powers have maintained full control of the more lucrative markets of technologies and, at least until a few decades ago, manufacturing production.[56] As Noam Chomsky explains, although European powers are no longer occupying the developing world, in a sense, the conquest has continued during the post-colonial era.[55] Eduardo Galeano has a similar impression. "We are no longer in the era of marvels when fact surpassed fable and imagination was shamed by the trophies of conquest – the lodes of gold, the mountains of silver. But our region still works as a menial," he wrote.

> It continues to exist at the service of others' needs, as a source and reserve of oil and iron, of copper and meat, of fruit and coffee, the raw materials and foods destined for rich countries which profit more from consuming them than Latin America does from producing them.[17]

Of the mechanisms currently used by the West to continue siphoning wealth from the developing world, finance and international loans are perhaps the most sophisticated ones. They are also the least understood. Since the post-colonization era, the West has not only continued to impose unfair trade exchanges on the developing world, but has also dedicated itself to controlling the highly profitable world of finance. The large transfer of financial aid and international loans from Western banks and international financial institutions soon after the end of colonization trapped most developing countries into un-repayable debts and structural adjustment programs. According to the World Bank, the total debt stocks of all middle- and low-income countries increased from virtually zero in the 1970s, to more than $2,000 billion in 1995, to reach about $2,500 in 2003.[57] Between 1980 and 1996, although Africa paid twice its debt in form of interests repayment, it still owed three times more in 1996 than in 1980.[58] The repayment of international loans that were often squandered by enriched, corrupted dictators who were "friendly" to Western policies, has turned out to be an effective mechanism of wealth transfer from poor workers and producers in the former colonies to Western banks and tax havens. The financial flows moving from the Rest to the West exceeds, by far, the financial assistance underdeveloped nations receive from "donor" countries. According to the OECD, between 1982 and 1990, total resources flows in international aid to developing countries amounted $927 billion; during the same period, however, developing countries remitted $1,345 billion in debt service alone, with an income–outflow difference of about $418 billion in the rich countries'

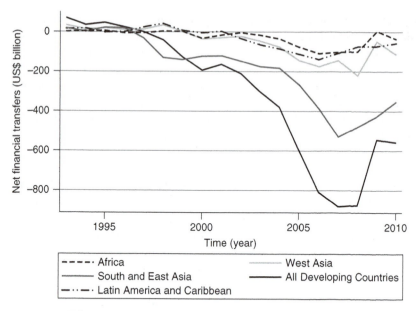

FIGURE 7.3 When recipients become donors: net financial flows to developing countries, 1993–2010

Sources: United Nations Department of Economic and Social Affairs (UN DESA) World Economy and Prospects. United Nations: New York, 2005, 2007 and 2012.

favor.[59] The United Nations Department of Economic and Social Affairs (UN DESA) estimated that from 1993 to 2005, developing countries moved from being net recipients of financial flows to being net losers. In 2005 alone, they were net losers of approximately half a trillion dollars.[60]

This scandal is hardly known of in the West. A survey conducted in 2005 in the US, for example, showed that about 64 percent of respondents felt that their own country was doing, "more than its share in helping less fortunate countries."[61] Approximately 54 percent of subjects interviewed also believed that the US was "spending too much on foreign aid."[62] But it is actually poor nations that are financially assisting the over-developed world. The latter should be named "donor countries." The worst trouble with such massive transfers of wealth from the Rest to the West is its negative impact on their governments' expenditures on health, education and social services. In order to repay their unsustainable debts, which they acquired without benefiting from them, people in developing countries have given up social benefits and opportunities to allow their governments to pay Western banks and global financial institutions. According to UNCTAD, between 1970 and 2002 developing countries had received $294 billion in loans and paid $268 billion, yet they were still left with a debt stock of $210 billion.[63] It has been estimated that in 2004, for every $1 received in grant aid, low-income countries paid $2.30 in debt service.[64] Annual debt-service payment was almost four times Africa's annual expenditure on health and education combined.[65] In 2002, Sierra Leone, a nation with one of the highest child and maternal mortality rates in the world, spent about two and half times more on debt servicing than on health.[66]

Although some low-income countries have received debt forgiveness in recent years, these initiatives have been "too little, too late." More importantly, debt forgiveness has been granted only to those nations that have adopted a new version of structural adjustment policies,[67] the so-called Poverty Reduction Strategy Papers, which some have defined as "new wine in old bottles." Through these policies, many developing countries are still trapped into un-repayable debts, economic dependence and structural adjustment policies. This has not seemed to be a problem for some cynics working in international financial institutions, however. World Bank official Sir William Ryrie described the debt crisis as a "blessing in disguise"[68] probably meaning that while it may have caused untold human suffering, it forced highly indebted countries to accept the "right" economic policies. As World Bank sector manager Steen Jorgensen once said: "If we cancel the debt there will be no World Bank. The World Bank pays my salary."[69]

It is unsurprising that, in the developing world, the imposition of the "golden straitjacket" has reinforced skepticism toward the IMF and the World Bank. It is understandable that they have been accused of a new form of "economic imperialism," or "neo-colonialism" as remarked by the first president of Tanzania and chair of the South Commission Julius Nyerere.[70] He and other writers have, in fact, argued that the policies of the international financial institutions seem quite consistent with those imposed by the former European colonizers, designed to halt poor countries' progress toward industrialization and a higher standard of living. For sure, these reforms are less direct and upfront. As Reverend Jesse Jackson once explained, developed nations, "no longer use bullets and ropes. They use the World Bank and the IMF."[71]

Inequality overkill

In spite of the startling inequalities we have today, some free market apologists dismiss criticism against neoliberal globalization policies as "empty rhetoric."[72] Others, however, accept that inequalities have increased, but do not find anything wrong with a socioeconomic system that systematically redistributes wealth upward from the poor to the rich. This is understandable. From the point of view of investment bankers, insurance companies, hedge fund managers and multinational corporations, however, global free market reforms have been a spectacular success. It is when judged through the eyes of the hungry, the poor, the unemployed, the peasants, manual workers and people on welfare, that we see neoliberalism has been a total disaster.

In the last decades, wealthy elites have accumulated riches "beyond the dreams of avarice." In the US, while the real income of 90 percent of Americans declined from $27,060 in 1979 to $25,646 in 2005,[73] the richest 1 percent of the population increased their share of post-tax income by about 200 percent.[74] As a result, the number of American billionaires increased from 13 in 1982 to about 170 in 1997.[75] In the 1980s, corporate executives of America's largest companies earned about 40 times as much as the average worker. By 1990, they earned 100 times more, and by 2001 their average pay package was about 350 times that of an average worker.[76][77] In 2005, Wal-Mart's corporate executive Lee Scott Jr. earned $15.5 million, about 900 times the pay and benefits of the average Wal-Mart worker.[78]

This is outrageous enough. But it is the bankers and financiers who have pocketed the most stunning salaries of the neoliberal globalization era. In 1997–8, about a thousand Wall Street professionals already received bonuses exceeding $1 million.[79] In December 2006, about 4,000 financial workers in the City of London recorded a bonus of £1.5million.[80] Some of the most "successful" investment bankers, who contributed to the 2008 economic collapse, received compensation packages amounting to tens of millions of dollars. Even after the crisis, they continued to have some of the best years on record. In 2009, Goldman Sachs delivered bonuses totaling $16.7 billion.[81][82] These outstanding compensation packages continue to be disbursed even today while countless people in the world keep losing their jobs, houses, social benefits and their pensions because of the 2008 financial crisis.

There are some neoliberals, however, who view the grotesque inequalities of our era not necessarily as desirable, but simply inevitable. In their opinion, inequalities are by-products of free markets, and any government attempt to redistribute wealth causes harm to everyone, regardless of whether they are rich or poor. In *The Fatal Conceits: the Errors of Socialism*, von Hayek explains that, "mankind could neither have reached nor could now maintain its present numbers without an inequality."[83] Brian Griffiths, one of the top executives at Goldman Sachs, could not agree more. In his opinion, it is important, "to tolerate the inequality as a way of achieving greater prosperity and opportunity for all."[84][85]

This argument is weak at best, and absolute nonsense at worst. Far from enhancing prosperity, excessive economic gaps between the rich and poor tend to depress economic growth,[86] and impair poverty reduction.[87] Worse, these inequalities undermine public health.[88] A cross-national analysis showed that inequality explains about one-eighth of the variability in life expectancy, even after controlling for income per capita. The study also found that changes in wealth distribution during the past 30 years have depressed prior gains in life expectancy and infant mortality worldwide.[89] As former chair of the WHO Commission on Social Determinants of Health, and current University College London professor, Michael Marmot concluded: "social injustice is killing people on a grand scale."[90]

However, equality in wealth may not necessarily promote good health either. In a society where everyone is equally poor and destitute, everyone may also be equally sick and miserable. In fact, most of the critics of neoliberalism do not advocate for a perfectly egalitarian society. The majority supports a social system characterized by what Rousseau defined as a state "where all have something and none too much."[91] Before him, countless other philosophers had long understood that a more egalitarian society is most likely healthier than an unequal one. Plato once noted, "there should exist among the citizens neither extreme poverty nor excessive wealth, for both are productive of great evils."[92] Some economists have identified what they define as an "efficient level of inequality," a distribution of economic resources conducive to economic growth and poverty reduction.[93] Although it is arguable what this level of inequality may look like, healthy levels of inequalities are much more likely to be seen in Sweden, Norway or Taiwan – not in the US, the UK or South Africa.

Free market ideologues and neo-conservatives would like us to believe that the relationship between inequality and health is a preposterous claim made by liberal academics, driven by "an ideology in search of data." However, there is plenty of scientific evidence proving that their accusation is baseless. A review of 155 studies published in *Social Science and Medicine* found that the majority of analyses support the conclusion that health is worse in societies where income differences are larger.

But why does inequality make us sick? There are at least three major explanations. First, unequal distribution of wealth is positively associated with higher poverty which, in turn, leads to poor health.[94] The most unequal societies are characterized by a systematic underinvestment in a wide range of human, physical, health and social infrastructures (e.g. education, health services, transportation, environmental controls, availability of good quality food, quality of housing and occupational health regulations), services that are essential for the poor. Another major cause for how inequality makes people sick is that these disparities are detrimental to both social and psychological wellbeing.[95] As the editors of the *British Medical Journal* once put it, "inequality may make people miserable long before it kills them."[96] In the best selling book, *The Spirit Level*, Richard Wilkinson and Kate Pickett show that,

TABLE 7.1 Inequality kills: evidence on the relationship between income inequality and population health (results of 168 analyses)

	Wholly supportive	*Partially supportive*	*Unsupportive*	*Total*	*Ratio (as %) of wholly supportive vs. unsupportive analyses*
Area level	Only sig. positive findings	Some sig. positive and some null	No sig. positive findings	All studies	
Nations	30 (11)	9	6	45 (11)	83
States, regions, cities	45 (13)	21	17	83 (13)	73
Counties, tracts, parishes	12 (2)	14	14 (1)	40 (3)	46
Total	87 (26)	44	37 (1)	168 (27)	70

Source: Wilkinson R and Pickett K. Income inequality and population health: A review and explanation of the evidence. *Social Science and Medicine* 2006;62(7):1768–84.

compared to relatively egalitarian countries, the more unequal societies rank poorly, not only in terms of life expectancy at birth, but also in terms of mental health, child wellbeing, education, social mobility and teenage pregnancy.[97] Numerous studies have also shown that inequality is associated with stress,[98] mental illnesses,[99] drug abuse and unhealthy behaviors such as obesity.[100]

A third major factor that connects inequality to poor health is violence. An unfair distribution of resources in society is associated with anti-social behavior, crime and imprisonment.[97 101] For one, in highly unfair societies, the poor may feel hopeless and desperate; and when people are left with no choice but to fight for their own survival, that is exactly what they often do. Additionally, high inequalities erode social cohesion and interpersonal trust, and promote a sense of injustice and resentment, making relationships more hostile and even violent.[102–104] It is no coincidence that some of the most unequal cities in the world, such as Johannesburg and Bogota, are also among the most dangerous places to live. A certain degree of equality in society is necessary to protect "the glue that keeps people together," to maintain political stability and a sense of solidarity among citizens. We can either have a healthy society or high inequality, but not both.

Planets apart

After centuries of colonization, exploitation and conquest, followed by decades of unfair economic policies, we are now living in a highly divided world. Almost half of the world's population is often hungry, dies from preventable diseases, lives in shantytowns, begs on the streets, scavenges on rubbish or lives in unhealthy homes with neither water nor sanitation. Meanwhile, a small group of individuals, mostly corporate managers, financial speculators, tycoons and investment bankers, or what David Rothkopf called the *"Superclass,"* lives in formidable mansions, travels in personal jets and spends millions on expensive clothing, yachts, luxury cars and five star hotels. The socioeconomic and emotional distance between this minority of super-wealthy and the large majority of desperate indigents corresponds to what some writers call a global "economic apartheid."[105] In effect, it would be unsurprising to discover that the rich almost feel like they are living on a completely different planet.

Of course, this would be a dangerous illusion. If neither poverty nor the threat of a social revolution appear to be sufficiently good reasons for the super-class to concede to a more humane distribution of wealth, the protection of the ecosystem should be enough. Why? Excessive inequalities are not only associated with negative outcomes in terms of economic growth, poverty reduction, population health, quality of life and social cohesion. They also undermine effective cooperation for the resolution of environmental problems on a global scale.[106–108] This was explained quite clearly by Timmons Roberts and Bradley Parks in their book *Climate of Injustice*. According to these authors, global inequalities in wealth are serious obstacles in the establishment of long-term agreements on climate change, because global inequality erodes conditions of generalized trust and promotes particularistic views of "fair" solutions.[109]

In effect, the history of global climate change treaties thus far has been a pitiful record of broken promises. While international talks about climate change have generated a lot of "hot air," they have led to very little action. Since the first major conference on climate change, the 1992 Earth Summit in Rio de Janeiro, rich and poor nations have failed to take the climate crisis seriously. During the Rio Summit, nations agreed to stabilize carbon emissions at the 1990 levels by the year 2000, and to lower them below 1990 levels thereafter. The talks and negotiations later resulted in the Kyoto Protocol in 1997, which was ratified by 186 countries a few years later. Unlike the Rio agreement, the Kyoto treaty committed developed countries to binding greenhouse gas emissions reductions of 5.2 percent relative to 1990 emissions, by the period 2008–2012.[110] Overall, these targets were completely insufficient to prevent irreversible climate change. Even so, countries have still failed to reach even these goals. Within the EU, apart from Eastern European nations that experienced reductions in greenhouse gases because of poor economic development in the 1990s, only a few countries, including Britain, France, Germany and Sweden, are more or less on course to meet the 2012 target.[110] The US, which initially agreed on a 7 percent reduction, later rejected this target when the Bush administration, heavily connected to the fossil-fuel industry, took office in 2001. One of the main reasons for the US's refusal to sign the Kyoto protocol was a disagreement regarding the involvement of developing countries in the climate target deal.[111]

The lack of progress on environmental agreements largely reflects the climate of self-interest, mistrust and low social cohesion induced by excessive inequalities and a sense of unfairness. While poor nations fear limits on their efforts to grow economically and meet the needs of their own people, powerful countries refuse to cut their own excesses unless developing countries make similar efforts. The US wants poor nations to commit to greenhouse gas reductions, while developing countries such as China and India want to avoid such binding agreements for several very good reasons. First, governors of developing nations claim that rich countries are to blame for climate change; therefore, they should not be expected to forgo development through industrialization. Their belief is that rich societies were not concerned with environmental pollution during their own early stages of development. Second, leaders of developing countries also argue that the average citizen of a poor country pollutes much less than the average European or American. In 2007, the average Chinese citizen accounted for about 16 percent of greenhouse gas discharges emitted by the average American citizen, while the average Indian emitted about 6 percent of the US average. Third, in the developing world, the imposition of binding greenhouse gas emissions is viewed as a new form of imperialism and colonization. The widespread distrust and sense of injustice toward rich societies and international financial institutions, after years of structural adjustment and debt repayments, have made them more reluctant to accept any deals with the West. The unfairness blocking progress toward environmental agreements was well summarized by the Brazilian president Ignacio Lula da Silva, who once remarked: "if the Amazon is the lung of the World, then the debt is its pneumonia."[112]

Understandably, from the perspective of poor nations, unless rich countries are prepared to tackle issues of past injustices, poverty, inequalities and take equal responsibility for pollution in the atmospheric common, little progress can be expected. On the other hand, developed societies refuse to take action unless developing countries do the same.[113] It is a classic example of "tragedy of the commons" in which unless the players start to cooperate and move beyond their narrow short-term interest, everybody loses.

A race against us

What can be done to surpass this impasse then? In order to strike a global green deal, we must learn to live together. In this sense, the ecological crisis is not just a threat, but can also be seen as an opportunity to initiate a process of global cooperation. If globalization shrunk national borders, the ecological crisis has the potential to tear them down completely and facilitate combined efforts to create a greener and fairer world order.

To develop effective and equitable agreements on climate change, developed countries must first acknowledge their responsibility for "historic pollution.[114] [115] As Elazar Barkan, author of *The Guilt of Nations*, argues, rich countries should abandon the usual "realpolitik" in international relations and promote a philosophy of fairness and global responsibility. A key step toward a safer and healthier world is the reparation of past injustices, through financial contributions that support green technologies. This can help developing nations to do their share and commit themselves to stop climate change, in spite of the pressing developmental problems they still face. South America, Asia and Africa are responsible for over 90 percent of carbon emissions due to deforestation. If this process continues unabated, a future ecological disaster is inevitable. With help from rich countries and international organizations, developing nations should commit to reducing their fertility rates, especially through massive investments in women's education and reproductive health services.

Developed nations must not only help poor countries with these issues, but also commit to the principle that each world citizen has an equal entitlement to the atmosphere. This means that everyone must accept that we all have an equal right to emit the same amount of carbon dioxide. In recent years, there have been various proposals to tackle climate change on the basis of this principle. More than two decades ago, Aubrey Meyer, founder of the Global Commons Institute, proposed a model called "contraction & convergence" to reduce greenhouse gas emissions enough to ensure "safe and stable" concentrations in the Earth's atmosphere. The deal is this: first, the scheme sets a cap for greenhouse gas concentrations worldwide and a date by which targets should be achieved (e.g. 350 ppm by 2050). Then, it ensures that the mechanism used to accomplish this target is fair by dividing the sum of greenhouse gas emissions between all the people of the world, and allocating to each nation, on the basis of its population, a respective quota (contraction). The model foresees that, over time, the carbon targets of developed and developing countries converge to a common per capita pollution level, with all countries accepting the same emission goal consistent with a safe target of 350 ppm globally (convergence). The global "carbon cake" would be shared between the different nations of the world in the form of "tradable entitlements," with individual countries negotiating their own quotas proportional to national populations. While converging toward equality of pollution, nations that want to produce more carbon dioxide than their share would be obliged to buy unused quota from other nations.[116] The mechanism also permits trading so that developing countries unable to use up their entire entitlements can sell them to rich nations in exchange, for example, for projects of development, health and education.

Some free marketeers and neo-conservatives, while recognizing that climate change is not a hoax, find the "contraction & convergence strategy" too "biased" toward the developing world's priorities. This is understandable. All in all, they have never made a secret of their predisposition to have the interests of the elite in rich societies at heart. Their argument, however, blissfully ignores that rich countries account for only 15 percent of the world's population, yet emit about 50 percent of carbon dioxide emissions worldwide.[117] Others have also criticized "contraction & convergence" for being utopian and unrealistic. It is true that nobody knows whether this scheme will ever work. What we do know, however, is that rich countries must play a leadership role in the fight against climate change. As former dean of the Yale School of Forestry and Environmental Studies James Gustav Speth once explained: "The lion's share of the blame must go to the wealthy, industrial countries and especially to the United States." He then added, "if the United States and other major governments had wanted a strong, effective international process, they could have created one. If they wanted treaties with real teeth, they could have shepherded them into being."[118] It is true that a binding agreement, such as the one proposed by Meyer, would require a massive political and economic undertaking at the global level. But there are no other choices left if we are to prevent irreversible climate change. As the American libertarian eco-socialist, Murray Bookchin, once put it: "If we do not do the impossible, we shall be faced with the unthinkable."[119]

Global climate change agreements such as "contraction & convergence" must be adopted with reforms to reduce poverty and inequalities. One does not need to be a Marxist to understand why. Calling for a more equitable distribution of resources is not a wish for a classless society where all wealth is equally shared or is concentrated in the hands of a big government. Instead, it is a pragmatic strategy to overcome the climate change impasse. Affluent nations must recognize that any global environmental treaty that is perceived as unfair, or that does not take into account the urgent needs of people in the developing world, is destined to fail. With the world facing an ecological crisis without borders, nothing has become more practical for the West than turning its past wrongs into rights by assisting developing nations in assembling their ecological programs,[120] eradicating poverty and educating women. This would not just be an act of generosity, but also of enlightened self-interest. The reason is simple. As Dipesh Chakrabarty once observed, "unlike the crises of capitalism, there are no lifeboats for the rich and the privileged" that will save them from a future climate disaster.[121]

Unfortunately, thus far the US, and to a lesser extent the EU, have failed to lead by example. Not only have conservative administrations, such as those of the two Bushes, opposed international treaties on climate change. Even center-left political leaders have often watered down the issue. The foot-dragging of the Obama administration, during the negotiations on the climate deals at the 2009 and 2011 conferences in Copenhagen and Durban, is a case in point.[122] Even worse, there have been no attempts to reconcile the resolution of the climate change crisis, through programs to reduce poverty and population growth, with the developing world. There have also been no new proposals introduced that aim to re-establish some fairness in the global economic system. This is because reforms aiming at "redistribution," taxation and global solidarity are considered utopian. Yet, history has already proven these claims wrong. During the Second World War, in both the US and the UK, free markets and the rule of profit were temporarily suspended. Most governments applied controls on consumption and planned industrial production and adopted a very progressive tax system. In 1942, Roosevelt was able to pass a super-tax of 94 percent on all income above $200,000 ($2.5 million today) in the US.[123] In England too the government heavily taxed the income of the wealthiest individuals, as well as all superfluous goods. At the same time, it rationed consumption while ensuring access to food and basic items to everyone, irrespective of social class. No citizen consumed excessively during the war, but none risked starvation either. In an effort to gain cooperation against a common enemy such as Nazi Germany, government policies in the US and the UK were deliberately targeted at making everyone count.[124] [125]

The wartime political economic model showed, quite unequivocally, that it is possible to change an entire society fairly quickly. It also revealed that it is possible to strive for a more sober and egalitarian consumption and distribution of wealth. Of course, the Second World War is an extreme historical example: a brutal enemy threatened the freedom of the entire world. In a sense, however, the enemy we are fighting today is even worse.

Mostly animals, but still humans

The ultimate reason why neoliberal economists argue that we must accept the astronomical inequalities in wealth we have today is this. As explained in the previous chapter, they believe that neoliberalism is the only viable social arrangement, the only system that works. At the basis of this presumption, there is a very cynical view of human nature. It states that people care only about their own interests or anything that can advance their own profit and power. It also maintains that even acts of altruism are mere manifestations of "selfishness in disguise." Conclusion: a more egalitarian and compassionate system than the neoliberal society is unrealistic and cannot be developed out of selfish citizens.

Although this picture is often proposed with an air of certitude resembling inevitability, it is not only too dark, but also too simplistic to be true. Let us see why. First, people do not do good just to feel good, but because they are good. Different research studies have plausibly shown that feelings of pleasure are more likely to be by-products of altruistic acts, rather than primary motivating causes of these acts.[126][127] Second, the behavioral assumptions implied in neoliberal economic models are more appropriate to explain animal conduct, rather than human experience. As Godwy and colleagues put it, "the axiomatic rationale choice model [glorified by the free marketeers] strips away everything that makes humans unique as highly intelligent social animals."[128] In reality, there is much more to human motivations than the "rational" pursuit of selfish interests. As the closing remarks of the documentary, *The Trap*, "The Lonely Robot," sarcastically observed: "the only people who really fit the simplified mathematical model of self-interested rational behavior at all times are economists and psychopaths."[129]

Just instincts

Although human beings have unique predatory prerogatives – they are the only creatures willing to commit mass murder, torture and genocide – they also have distinctive social, cooperative and moral abilities. As explained previously, humans are endowed with mirror neurons and the ability to empathize with other members of the same species. In *Biophilia*, evolutionary biologist Edward Wilson argues that people have an instinctive sense of connection toward not only other human beings, but also animals and plants.[130] Neuroscientists have even identified areas of our brain that can be activated by feelings of justice and injustice.[131] To be sure, we are not alone in our ability to empathize and perceive unfairness. Scientists have shown that there are rudimentary mirror neuron systems in the brain circuitry of elephants, dolphins and dogs.[132] They have also demonstrated that social animals, such as monkeys,[133] can clearly perceive inequities and respond negatively to them. Nevertheless, we are probably the only species endowed with a very sophisticated sense of fairness. It is not completely understood, but we may be the only ones that clearly feel a sense of indignation, both when we experience direct acts of unfair treatment and when we witness acts of injustice toward others. Numerous experiments using game theory have shown that people are willing to punish others in order to restore fairness or to sanction unfair behavior.[134][135] This body of evidence clearly contradicts the idea of a fixed human nature based on selfish and utilitarian instincts. We are not just greedy competitors, but also generous cooperators. We can feel the plight of others. We can punish what we perceive as large inequities and injustices. There is no question that self-interest is an innate characteristic of individuals, but so are altruistic and empathic qualities.

After all, so many writers have recognized that sense of fairness is a deep-seated human quality. In *The Dialogues*, Plato claimed that human beings "are just by nature."[92] Thomas Jefferson believed that "man is a rational animal, endowed by nature with rights, and with an innate sense of justice."[136] More recently, the subject has been examined by numerous researchers from a wide variety of disciplines.[137] [138] A moderate degree of sense of fairness can even be observed in children.[139] It is all too common to hear a child crying, "that is not fair!," when treated unequally or less favorably than others. In *Great Expectations*, Charles Dickens observed that, "In the little world in which children have their existence . . . there is nothing so finely perceived and so finely felt, as injustice."[140] Intuitively, we realize when our sense of justice is violated. It happens when we experience small acts of inequity in our everyday life. We expect people to be honest and play by the rules. We are deeply disappointed when we feel that we are betrayed or cheated. When we treat other people fairly, we expect that they will reciprocate.

But our sense of fairness is also violated when we are victims of grander injustices, such as unequal power and wealth distribution within society. We deeply care about who gets what, and how resources are dispersed within a community. It is not by chance that fictional heroes like Robin Hood and Zorro, both of whom stole from the rich to give to the poor, are so deeply entrenched in our popular culture. They appeal to our innate sense of fairness. Throughout human history, feelings of unfairness springing from unequal treatment and social injustices have inspired countless literary works, poems, songs and social movements. When distribution of power and wealth becomes too unjust, the resulting indignation can be explosive. It can break down the social construction that keeps society together. It can trigger social instability and even revolutions.

Neoliberal economists argue that the global inequalities we experience today should be accepted as they are. Like the market greed ideology, they say, inequalities are inevitable and cannot be changed. This hypothesis implicitly assumes that human nature is fixed and that there is homogeneity in terms of social preferences across societies. Luckily for us, the evidence shows exactly the opposite. Far from being fixed, our sense of fairness can be influenced by social conditioning. It can even be manufactured. An economic experiment conducted in 15 small-scale societies clearly showed that people's generosity widely varies across cultures. The study relied on the *Ultimatum Game*, an economic experiment with two players, the "proposer" and the "receiver." The proposer is allotted a divisible "pie" (usually money) and asked to offer a portion of the pie to the receiver, who can either accept or refuse the offer. If the receiver accepts, he or she obtains the amount offered and the proposer receives the remainder; if the receiver rejects the offer, however, neither player receives anything. The results of the experiment were quite interesting: while in the seminomadic Machiguenga living in the jungles of Southeastern Peru, the majority of people gave between 15 and 25 percent of the share, and kept the rest for themselves, the residents of Lamalera Island in Eastern Indonesia gave away on average 57 percent of the pie. According to the authors of the study, these findings can be explained by the heterogeneity in social norms between societies. In those societies where there is a system of rewards for cooperation and punishment for selfishness, people are more likely to be altruistic.[141] In those where greed is widely acceptable and altruism ignored, people tend to be less generous. These results are hardly surprising, and do not only apply to small-scale societies. In industrialized nations, there are also large-scale societal differences in views of economic equity and social justice,[142] as well as people's levels of altruism.[143] Research has found that people in Scandinavian universalistic welfare states are generally more supportive of redistributive taxation and feel a stronger sense of obligation toward others than in countries such as the US and the UK.[144] A cross-national analysis revealed that in Finland, a relatively egalitarian nation, people are more likely to judge the income gap between rich and poor as excessive than people in the UK and US,[145] even though economic inequalities are much wider in the latter two countries.

This evidence seems to indicate that human nature is quite malleable and so are societies. Clearly, there is a feedback loop between collective perceptions of fairness, and redistributive taxation and social policies.[146] On the one hand, people's sense of fairness is heavily influenced by the social environment in which they live; on the other hand, the policies and social conditions where people live are shaped by citizens' attitudes toward inequalities, social welfare and redistributive taxation.[147] What better proof do we need to believe that neoliberalism is *not* the only social organization we can afford? It is perfectly reasonable to aspire for a new society where fairness is nurtured and rewarded, while greed is stigmatized and shamed. As Christian socialist Richard Tawney once explained, even though no change of system can completely avert selfishness, egotism and quarrelsomeness, we can create an environment where these prerogatives are not promoted.[148] This may not only be a desirable choice, but the only one left to stop humanity's journey toward self-destruction. As poet, writer and activist Audre Lorde once put it, "our future survival is predicated upon our ability to relate within equality."[149] Zoologist Alfred Emerson shared a similar view. "The issue is clear," he observed a few months after the drop of the atomic bomb in Nagasaki: "it is cooperation or vaporization."[150]

8
OUT OF CONTROL

In 2008, the world began sliding into the abyss of one of the worst financial crises in history. Everything started in the US with the crisis of subprime mortgages – high-interest loans given to people who would otherwise be considered too risky for conventional lending. Millions of Americans found themselves unable to repay the subprime mortgages they had taken out years beforehand from brokers without scruples. These subprime mortgages included the so-called NINJA loans that required "no income, no job and no assets." Some of them were offered with "teaser rates," initial low interest rates that sharply increase after a few years. Predatory brokers assured borrowers that housing prices always go up and that loans can be refinanced at any time. For the creditors, it did not matter whether the borrowers were actually able to repay these loans. The scheduled repayments were sold to Wall Street investment firms that securitized, insured and re-sold the risk attached to these securities to other financial institutions. Upon owning the scheduled repayments, investment banks pooled the risky loans and re-packaged them into "mortgage-backed securities." Then, they insured the securities through forms of protection against bad loans called "credit-default swaps." Finally, they re-sold these credit-default swaps to other banks and investors, such as mutual funds and pension funds. Managers of these funds were largely unaware of the risk they were inheriting. After all, credit-rating agencies such as Standard & Poor, Moody and Fitch judged the risk associated with these securities as manageable and even rated some subprime loans with a triple "A."[1]

The indiscriminate proliferation of subprime mortgages and credit-default swaps, which Warren Buffet called "financial weapons of mass destruction,"[2] resulted in a large housing bubble. A sharp rise in housing prices is generally recognized as a potential source of economic instability, but not for the neoliberal technocrats who govern our institutions with a free market ideology that is aligned with the interests of Wall Street. All in all, investment banks made spectacular profits from the skyrocketing housing prices. Between 2004 and the beginning of 2007, Angelo Mozilo, executive of Countrywide Financial, the largest subprime lender, made more than $270 million in profits.[3] Compensation packages worth over a hundred million dollars were also cashed by Stan O'Neal (Merrill Lynch), Dick Fuld (Lehman Brothers), Lloyd Blankfein and Hank Paulson (Goldman Sachs.) These pay packets would have appalled Adam Smith, however. He once revealed: "all for ourselves, and nothing for other people seems, in every age of the world, to have been the vile maxim of the masters of mankind."[4]

Everything was working out just fine for the banksters and the free market bureaucrats, until the inevitable took place in 2007. The housing market ran out of buyers and the subprime mortgages' financial casino started to crumble, along with the entire US economy. A domino effect unfolded – housing prices began to fall and those unable to meet the loan repayments no longer had the option of selling their houses to get out of trouble. Then, the defaulted mortgages (and securities associated with them) created panic in financial markets, since nobody knew which financial institutions were holding the "toxic assets." As a result, banks stopped lending to each other, and companies could no longer borrow any money. Indebted consumers stopped spending, and finally housing prices collapsed. Ultimately, the stock market crashed and some banks virtually disappeared overnight. These failures sent waves of shock throughout the entire economic system. Even now, more than four years after the crisis, the US economy is still in very poor shape. Nobody knows if, or when, it will ever recover.

The promised crash

After hitting the US, the crisis moved across borders, infecting country after country. From the world of finance, it quickly spread to other economic and social sectors. It dissolved millions of jobs, generated countless foreclosures, increased poverty, reduced spending and consumption, and pushed innumerable companies into bankruptcy. The World Economic Forum estimated that about 40 percent of the world's wealth evaporated because of the crisis.[5] Since the eve of the meltdown in 2007, global unemployment has increased by more than 30 million people. At the same time, in low-income countries, between 60 and 100 million people have been pushed into severe poverty.[6] Nobody really knows how many more people will lose their jobs, their houses and their lives because of the crisis.

Recessions do not necessarily lead to social disintegration and mortality crises, especially if governments intervene to protect the most vulnerable populations through social protection and labor market programs.[7] But make no mistake: economic crises can kill. Since the eruption of the global financial meltdown, there has been a general increase in the suicide rates of Europe, reversing a decade of steady declines.[8] In Greece, suicides have increased by 17 percent.[9] In Italy, between 2008 and 2010, there were about 290 suicides and attempted suicides in excess because of the Great Recession.[10] In the past, economic crises have also been associated with increasing suicide rates in Eastern Europe,[11] Japan, New Zealand, Russia and the

US.[12] Economic shocks have also increased adult and child mortality rates in Russia, Thailand, Mexico, Peru, Indonesia and other developing nations.[12] [13]

The wake of social and economic disasters generated by the crisis required prompt government interventions in order to save the failed banking system and to help those who had lost their jobs and houses. For the bankrupted banks, the countermeasures were immediate. Governments were forced to buy the toxic mortgage debts that had accumulated from reckless investments during the "pre-crisis orgy of speculation" years. IMF economists estimated that, worldwide, the bailouts cost taxpayers a staggering $11.9 trillion, about a fifth of the entire globe's annual economic output.[14]

We were told that the rescue packages for the failed banks were absolutely necessary to prevent an even worse economic scenario. But why was it not also a priority to save those who had already lost their jobs and houses because of the crisis? Those who suffered the consequences of the meltdown had to foot the bill for the bank bailouts. Unlike the "too-big-to-fail" banks they were "too-small-to-be-bailed." To add insult to injury, the revenues of the bailouts were used to pay obscene bonuses to the very banksters that caused the crisis.[15] Goldman Sachs, after receiving about $6 billion in rescue funds from the US government, paid $2.6 billion in bonuses in 2008.[16] Two years later, the Wall Street firm was found guilty of fraud and financial deception.[17] None of its executives went to jail, however. Will they ever be brought to justice? It is too difficult to say. So far, the large banks that have created the 2008 financial crisis continue to be considered not only "too-big-to-fail" but also "too-big-to-jail."

Certainly, the decision to save the architects of the crisis and fail its victims was not only shamelessly unjust, but also inept. The massive bailouts could have been used as leverage mechanisms to develop a new regulatory framework. This could have helped us to prevent future crises and put an end to the predatory, reckless activities of speculators. The bailouts could have been disbursed with conditionalities, such as regulations that would break up the "too-big-to-fail" banks, into ones that are "small-enough-to-succeed." At the very least, the US government could have nationalized the banks that required the most extensive bailouts.[18] Even Alan Greenspan, after mustering up crocodile tears about the failure of the neoliberal market experiment, agreed with the idea of temporarily nationalizing some of the banks.[19] After all, the bankrupted Citigroup, AIG, and Bank of America had received so much public money that, in a way, they had become "public institutions." As Paul Krugman once observed, "Wall Street is no longer, in any real sense, part of the private sector. It's a ward of the state, every bit as dependent on government as recipients of Temporary Assistance for Needy Families."[20] In effect, even the British had nationalized Northern Rock after the financial collapse. Why did the US not do the same? Because nationalization is anathema for Wall Street bankers that continue to make the rules. Therefore, banks had to remain in rich, private hands: theirs.

In June 2010, the Obama administration approved various reforms of the financial system. These included regulations and restrictions on troubled companies, and new rules on consumer protection.[21] Fox News characterized the bill as "the stiffest restrictions on banks and Wall Street since the Great Depression."[22] In reality, these reforms did very little to shut down the financial casino we still have today. The bill failed to regulate the very derivatives at the root of the crisis, such as the credit-default swaps, and lacked any measure to impose size limits on large financial companies. The bill also failed to re-establish the barrier between the deposit and investment activities of banks, a measure adopted as a part of the *Glass–Steagall Act* in 1933 that was later repealed by the Clinton administration in 1999.

In Europe as well, in spite of the proposals for new regulations such as those listed in the *de Laroisiere Report*, the derivatives market still represents a menace for global stability. As in the US, it is the financial industry that continues to run the show.

International Monetary Failure

The "blank check" approach was applied to not only the failed banks, but also to rescue the very institution in charge of the economic stability of the world: the IMF. A few years after the crisis, the IMF, already navigating in troubled waters, was provided with $750 billion in financial assistance by the G-20.[23] In a sense, this was the "bailout of the bailouts": for decades, the Fund had been using taxpayers' money to rescue failed, bankrupted lenders that had engaged in risky investments in the developing world. From 1995 to 2004, it gave emergency crisis-stemming loans totaling $312 billion to Mexico, Thailand, Indonesia, South Korea, Russia, Brazil, Turkey and Argentina.[24] Unlike what the Washington-based institution usually does to bankrupted countries in need of financial help, however, the G-20 did not enforce a structural adjustment program on the IMF in return for its assistance. By bailing out the IMF without conditionalities, the G-20 did two things: first, it encouraged speculators to take even more risks. Second, it ensured the continuation of the same failed neoliberal market policies that had led to instability in developing countries for almost half a century.[25] Instead of fulfilling its original mission of preventing financial crises, the IMF has mostly exacerbated them and worsened the pain of economic recovery,[26] by imposing reforms that even wealthy nations usually avoid when hit by a crisis.[27] After an economic downturn, advanced nations usually try to relax monetary policies and implement stimulus packages even at the price of increasing budget deficits. This is exactly the opposite of what the IMF asked developing countries to do after experiencing a crisis. Poor countries were forced to raise interest rates and balance their budgets abruptly, even when it was apparent that these policies would have increased unemployment and prolonged the recession. During the 1997 Asian crisis, for example, the IMF allowed the Korean government to run a maximum budget deficit equivalent to 0.8 percent of GDP. But when Sweden had been hit by a crisis in the early 1990s, its budget deficit was allowed to increase by up to 8 percent of GDP.[28] What can be the reason behind this double standard?

The answer is straightforward. The IMF provides a different "economic treatment" on the basis of a country's power and influence in the global financial and geopolitical system. Instead of acting as the guardian of global financial stability, the IMF operates more as a debt collector for Western banks. Therefore, it is no surprise that the Fund generates so many opposing views. In the rich financial sectors of the most affluent societies, the Washington-based institution is respected and admired. In the developing world, it is mainly despised. But the failures of the IMF are not limited to the disastrous economic reforms imposed on poor countries. Just some months before the beginning of the Great Recession, IMF economists assured that "notwithstanding the recent bout of financial volatility, the world economy still looks well set for continued robust growth in 2007 and 2008."[29] They could not have been more wrong.

The blame game

When the global crisis started to unfold in 2008, some of those who had been celebrating the virtues of financial deregulation since the birth of the Mount Pelerin Society were taken by surprise. "How could this have happened?" they wondered. Since the advent of neoliberalism, free market economists had harbored a delusional belief that crises were problems of the past. During the years leading up to the meltdown, whistle-blowers who warned about the trouble of the housing bubble were treated with derision. The free marketeers preached that there was no need to worry about the high concentration of speculative capital, both in the economy and in the housing sector. For decades, they contended that financial markets tend toward equilibrium and take care of themselves. As Alan Greenspan once put it: "markets are an expression of the deepest truths about human nature and . . . as a result, they will ultimately be correct."[30]

After the crash, the faith in the free market doctrine started to crumble. At last, the neoliberals were forced to look at themselves in the mirror. A few renegades admitted that, when completely unleashed, free market forces do generate crises. The majority, however, continued to deny the obvious. The possibility that free markets could fail just did not occur to them. The neoliberals thus pointed their fingers at a usual suspect: big government. In an article published in the *Journal of Banking Regulation*, Mark Nichols and colleagues concluded that the major drivers of the first financial crisis in the twenty-first century were excessive regulation and poor policy choices.[31] In the same vein, Mark Calabria, a free market enthusiast of the Exxon-Mobil funded CATO Institute, argued that the last crisis was caused by "a failure of regulation, not mythical deregulation."[32] For more than half a century, exponents of the Rockefeller-founded-and-funded Chicago School of Economics used to reiterate similar clichés depicting "big government" as the only culprit for all troubles that have occurred with the economy. The eminent guru of the School, Milton Friedman, claimed that even the Great Depression was caused by undue government intervention in the economy.

However, the exact opposite is true. Although each crisis happens in its own way, in some sense most crises do resemble one another and are more likely to occur when there is too little, not too much, government intervention. The risk of financial crashes is augmented by insufficient controls and regulations on capital

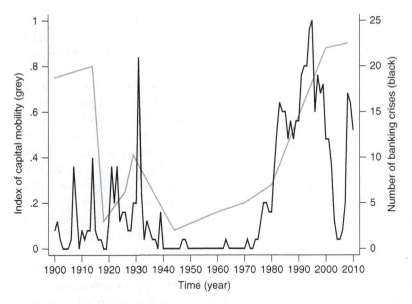

FIGURE 8.1   From the Great Depression to the Great Recession: index of capital mobility and banking crises, 1900–2010

Sources: Reinhart CM and Rogoff KS. From Financial Crash to Debt Crisis. NBER Working Paper 15795, 2010. Forthcoming in *American Economic Review*. Reinhart CM. This Time is Different Chartbook: Country Histories on Debt, Default, and Financial Crises. NBER Working Paper 15815, 2010.

List of countries: Australia, Austria, Belgium, Bolivia, Brazil, Canada, Central African Republic, Chile, China, Colombia, Costa Rica, Denmark, Dominican Republic, Ecuador, El Salvador, Finland, France, Germany, Ghana, Greece, Guatemala, Honduras, Hungary, Iceland, India, Indonesia, Ireland, Italy, Japan, Kenya, Korea, Malaysia, Mauritius, Mexico, Morocco, Myanmar, Netherlands, New Zealand, Nicaragua, Norway, Panama, Paraguay, Peru, Philippines, Poland, Portugal, Romania, Singapore, South Africa, Sri Lanka, Sweden, Switzerland, Taiwan, Thailand, Tunisia, Turkey, United Kingdom, United States, Uruguay, Zambia and Zimbabwe.

movements, and they are usually preceded by periods of rapid and excessive capital expansion and speculation. A review of the historical association between international capital mobility and banking crises, published by Kaminsky and Reinhart, revealed that both the 1929 Great Depression and the 2008 Great Recession were anticipated by years of excessive capital flow.[33] Like the 2008 recession, the era that preceded the 1929 stock market crash, often remembered as the "Gilded Age" of "high finance," was characterized by large-scale global investments and indiscriminate financial movements. As occurred in 2008, the unleashing of speculative financial markets at the end of the 1920s produced a gigantic bubble (in this case in the stock market) that burst and caused one of the worst epidemics of banking crises and economic depression in history (see Figure 8.1).[34]

It is important to remember that the massive transfer of capital and financial instruments across borders has caused more harm beyond the Great Recession and the Great Depression. Rapid emigration of capital has also been a key cause, or exacerbating factor, for most crises that have occurred since the 1970s. This applies to the 1999 Russian financial meltdown, for example.[35] The rapid and indiscriminate flow of short-term capital was also the origin of the 1997 Asian financial crisis.[36] The ease with which money moved in and out of national borders was at the root of the economic breakdowns that occurred in the Nordic countries and Japan too.[26]

No matter what free market economists may think, it was financial deregulation, not government intervention, which caused the last Great Recession. The most recognizable culprit of the 2008 collapse was the introduction of complex financial innovations, such as the mortgage-backed securities (derivatives of asset values), and credit-default swaps (derivatives of insurance contracts on derivatives of asset values). The proponents of "financial innovation" justified the introduction of these extremely risky instruments on the grounds that they were conducive to stability and wealth creation. Alan Greenspan, for example, claimed that the derivatives were not risky bets but "a useful vehicle to transfer risk from those who shouldn't be taking it to those who are willing to and are capable of doing so."[37] In the same vein, Timothy Geithner explained: "these developments (the proliferation of derivatives) provide substantial benefits to the financial system. Financial institutions are able to measure and manage risks much more effectively. Risks are spread more widely, across a more diverse group of financial intermediaries, within and across countries."[38]

Unfortunately, contrary to the claims of Greenspan and Geithner, these derivatives, far from promoting stability and wealth creation, did the exact opposite. They have filled the world economy with newer risks and dangers and transformed it into a global financial jungle.

More than 30 years of economic follies

In order to understand the origins of the crisis and the advent of financial deregulation policies, it is useful to go back first to the post-war or "Golden Age" of capitalism. As already mentioned in previous chapters, this period was characterized by relative economic stability and prosperity. Government interventions promoted high employment and reduced vulnerability to crises through laws and regulations that were inspired by the work of Keynes. Banks were highly controlled by government, and were viewed as public utilities whose mission was to protect people's deposits and provide loans for individuals and companies. Usury and reckless investing were limited and discouraged. Wild fluctuations of exchange rates were repressed. Of course, these regulations were deeply resented by the financial elites. In their eyes, the "financial repression" of the post-war age was an intolerable attack on their freedom. Indeed, these regulations reduced the volatility of the global financial system and limited opportunities to profit from market fluctuations.[39]

For economists concerned with the welfare of people, the set of rules which kept speculation in check during the post-war exerted enormous benefits. They reduced systemic risk, and prevented the emergence of new crises. The empirical evidence clearly shows this. In the US, during the period following the approval of the 1933

Glass–Steagall Act, there was the fewest number of banking failures in American history.[40] The effects of government interventions in regulating markets were deeply felt worldwide, too. Between 1945 and 1971, developing countries experienced no banking crises, 16 currency crises and only one "twin" crisis (a simultaneous banking and currency crisis).[41] At the time, there was the Bretton Woods system of fixed exchange rates, in which every nation agreed to exchange its currency at a fixed rate for a certain amount of US dollars – the US government exchanged dollars on demand for gold at a rate of $35 per ounce. This system was not perfect, of course. Nevertheless, during the time in which the Bretton Woods system operated, as revealed by a review of 120 years of financial crises,[42] there were no abrupt fluctuations of exchange rates. The system did not work for the speculators, but it ensured some degree of economic stability for the people.

By the beginning of the 1970s, however, something happened that would change the world. On August 15, 1971, Richard Nixon abruptly dismantled the fixed exchange rate system and re-wrote the rules of the global financial system. The age of economic stability came to an end and a new era of "high finance" and speculations gradually re-emerged. The reasons for the "Nixon shock" are still contested. The US was running large deficits due to the Vietnam War and was losing its competitiveness relative to Europe and Japan. Instead of cutting military expenditures, reducing imports and devaluing the dollar against gold, the US administration found it more convenient to abolish the Bretton Woods system. In other words, when the American super-power found itself losing, it changed the rules of the game. British academic, Susan Strange, called this "a deliberate act of sabotage." In effect, the Nixon shock undermined the stability of the entire global economy. With the fixed exchange rate system gone and done, national currencies were no longer tied to anything of real value. They were linked to the expectation that others would accept paper dollars in exchange for real goods and services. Currencies were free to float and economies became more prone to wild fluctuations in their exchange rates. Additionally, they were also much more vulnerable to speculative attacks and rapid capital flight. Unsurprisingly, since the 1970s, currencies have become three times more volatile on average.[43] Currency transactions increased 200-fold, reading a daily volume of $3.2 trillion in 2007.[44]

Yet, the "Nixon shock" was just one of a long series of reforms toward the re-election of the market God as governor of society's affairs. After the dismantling of the Bretton Woods system, financial deregulation went viral. It first gained momentum in the US and the UK, and then spread rapidly to the rest of the world. Reforms included lifting controls on international capital movements, the privatization of national banks, the deregulation of interest rates, the elimination of credit controls and the escalation of financial innovations (including the derivatives that caused the 2008 crisis). Deregulation policies created a playing field for the rapid, undisturbed and untaxed movement of capital worldwide. At the same time, they indirectly encouraged the concomitant proliferation of offshore financing. Cayman Islands, Andorra, Monaco, Bermuda and Switzerland became paradises for the wealthy speculators. The free market globalizers freed themselves once again from "the dead hand" of government interventions and tax policies. By the late 1980s, it had become crystal clear that the era of financial repression was over. A new age of market greed had begun.

Masters of disasters

As explained before, the US and the UK were the spearheads of the financialization movement that started in the 1970s. It was also in these two countries that the financial instruments, which ultimately flooded international markets and crashed the global economy in 2008, originated.[45] The movement toward deregulation was not an exclusive neo-conservative plan, as some writers argue. There is little doubt that Margaret Thatcher and Ronald Reagan were fanatic political crusaders for financial "freedom." As soon as she assumed power in 1979, Maggie Thatcher promoted a radical agenda of liberalization, in order to free London speculators from the "evil" of government regulations. With the approval of the *UK Banking Act* in 1979 and the 1986 *Big Bang Day*, which together deregulated the London Stock Exchange, she basically helped transform the City of London into an offshore haven.

A few years later, on the other side of the Atlantic, Ronald Reagan approved the *Garn–St. Germain Depository Institutions Act*. This bill eliminated regulations on the savings and loans industry, allowing banks to start commercial lending programs and to invest in corporate bonds. The act authorized large banks to offer subprime loans and mortgages with adjustable interest rates. In 1984, the Reagan administration escalated the deregulation campaign even further. Securitization was born. The *Secondary Mortgage Market Enhancement Act* provided investment banks with new opportunities to buy up mortgages, combine them into pools, and resell them in slices with varying levels of risk. They could, then, issue securities backed by these pools to the lenders, who could then sell them to investors. By the time this act was approved, the building blocks of the global financial casino were in place.

Although Reagan and Thatcher gave origins and impetus to the reforms that ultimately caused the financial collapse, the race for deregulation was a bipartisan political effort. The administrations of Tony Blair and Bill Clinton equally contributed to escalating the policies of creative financial destruction. What can perhaps be considered the most disastrous piece of deregulation legislation since the Great Depression was the *Gramm–Leach–Bliley Act*, passed by Clinton in 1999. This bill marked a watershed in the proliferation of the financial products that caused the last global crisis. It repealed the *1933 Glass–Steagall Act* – which was developed in response to the 1929 crash – to dismantle several banking regulations as a means of controlling speculations. In particular, the bill abolished the wall separating an investment bank from a commercial bank, and an insurance company. It also repealed any rules requiring banks to hold specific levels of cash reserves.

Although the *Glass–Steagall Act* was revealed to be very effective in ensuring financial stability it was, nonetheless, fiercely opposed by Wall Street bankers. Of course, gambling with market securities is far more profitable than providing loans and securing deposit accounts. The bankers strongly supported the passage of the

1999 *Gramm–Leach–Bliley Act* for this exact reason. The burial of the *Glass–Steagall Act* allowed large commercial lenders, such as Citigroup, to finally underwrite and trade very profitable new speculative instruments. However, it was the passage of the *Futures Modernization Act* in 2000 that completed the financialization of the US economy. This act basically repealed all bans against single-stock futures, and prohibited federal regulation of over-the-counter derivatives including the infamous mortgage-backed securities.

In the end, the financial gamblers got what they wanted. But the undoing of the New Deal's most important regulations and the introduction of new financial innovations caused radical changes beyond the US and UK economies. The global economy was also transformed into a gambling house. Everywhere, the "real" economy, consisting of the production and exchange of goods and services, was gradually overshadowed by a virtual economy of fictitious capital and speculative investments. In 1970, about 95 percent of the capital in international exchanges was related to the real economy in some fashion (that is they were either investments or trade of goods and services). Only 10 percent involved speculations. By 1990, however, the proportion of foreign exchange transactions that involved speculations or short-term investments reached about 98 percent, while only 2 percent involved the exchange of goods and services.[46] Avalanches of new financial products such as currency derivatives, credit-default swaps and mortgage-backed securities have quickly proliferated since the 1990s. Particularly in the new century, the market of derivatives began to spiral out of control. It embraced almost anything at hand, from trading the future value of currencies, food and oil, to gambling with the prospect of weather conditions. By 2008, over-the-counter derivatives grew to a staggering $680 trillion.[47] In the same year, credit-default swaps reached over $50 trillion,[48] while mortgage-backed securities rose to about $3 trillion in 2007.[49]

Since the abandonment of the Bretton Woods system and the beginning of a new financial liberalization era, the world has become more exposed to stock crashes, economic recessions, banking suspensions and banking failures.[40] Between 1973 and 1997, developing countries experienced 17 banking crises, 57 currency crises and 21 "twin" crises.[41] In the years following, crises continued to strike all over the world, especially in Latin America and Eastern Europe. As long as they affected developing countries and transitional economies, free market economists and media pundits could easily point their fingers at the inefficiency and corruption of national governments. "It is easy to draw up a checklist of what went wrong," wrote the editors of *The Economist* in explaining the sequel of financial downturns in Mexico, Thailand, South Korea, Indonesia and Russia. "Financial systems in many emerging markets were weak, badly supervised, and inadequately regulated and exchange rate regimes were inappropriate," they wrote. "All hit trouble because their firms, banks or governments borrowed too much short-term money."[50] In a unique showcase of cynicism, Thomas Friedman remarked: "I believe globalization did us all a favor by melting down the economies of Thailand, Korea, Malaysia, Indonesia, Mexico, Russia and Brazil in the 1990s, because it laid bare a lot of rotten practices."[51] When, at last, in 2008, the "financial clockwork orange" hit like a boomerang the very countries that designed it, these delusional allegations could no longer be sustained with a straight face. The inefficiencies and corruption of developing countries' governments could not be used as scapegoats anymore. It became clear instead that there was something rotten at the very heart of the global financial empire.

The crises of inequality

As shown before, the economic conditions that preceded the Great Depression and the Great Recession present some important similarities. The years preceding both crises were not only characterized by rapid capital movement and indiscriminate financial speculations, but also by extremely high economic inequalities. The links between financial deregulation, inequality and crises can be appreciated by looking at fluctuations over time of a "financial deregulation index,"[52] and the percentage of wealth owned by the top 1 percent of the population over the last century in the US. When looking at a combination of these trends, it is quite easy to recognize some striking parallels: peaks of economic inequalities coincided with peaks of financial liberalization, and both occurred before the two largest economic crises in recent history. Are these associations coincidental? Probably not.

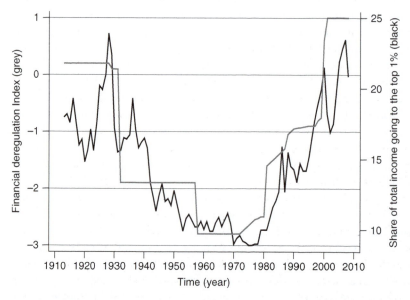

FIGURE 8.2 When history repeats itself: the rise and fall of financial deregulation and the share of total income going to the top 1% in the United States, 1913–2008

Source: Share of total income for the top 1% families are from the World Top Incomes database (2010) and financial deregulation index from Philippon and Reshef. Wages and Human Capital in the US Financial Industry: 1909–2006. NBER Working Paper 14644, 2008.

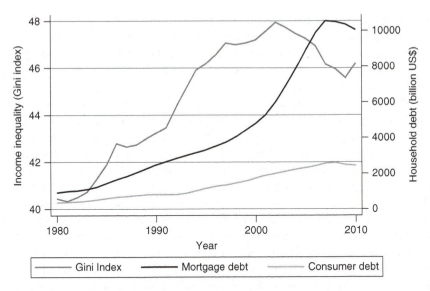

FIGURE 8.3 In debt we trust: the increase of income inequality and household debt in the United States, 1980–2010

Sources: Data on the Gini Index come from the Standardized World Income Inequality Database (SWIID); data on household debt (mortgage and consumer) come from the Federal Reserve Bank. Debt growth, borrowing and debt outstanding tables. Federal Reserve Bank: New York, 2012.

Both the "Gilded Age" of high finance and the new era of hyper-financialized neoliberalism were times of stagnating workers' wages and skyrocketing profits for a minority of rich investors and corporations. But how exactly have these conditions led to the Great Depression and the Great Recession? Numerous economists have actually explained, quite convincingly, how excessive inequality can increase vulnerability to economic crises.[53][54] Now, even the IMF seems more inclined to recognize the causal nexus between these two factors. A recent IMF paper concluded not only that the association between inequality and crisis is plausible, but even argued that the most effective strategy to prevent future meltdowns is to restore "the lower income group's bargaining power."[55] This may sound like the IMF and the Industrial Workers of the World now share the same political agenda. But one does not need to be a socialist to understand that an excessively large concentration of assets and wealth leads to financial vulnerability.

One of the most important mechanisms connecting inequality and crises is this. As the wealth gap between rich and poor widens, more money flows to the top social classes, while workers' wages stagnate or decline. This means that the rich have more opportunities to overspend on luxuries and fashionable goods, while workers struggle to maintain basic standards of living. When the wealthy escalate their spending, however, they induce the rest of society to do the same. This occurs because those at lower and middle steps of the socioeconomic ladder, in order to keep up with the status race or to simply defend their sliding standards of living, have to spend more of their income. The trouble is that stagnating wages and the declining purchasing power of the poor and the middle class force them to over-borrow money, especially when interest rates are very low. Between 2003 and 2007, US consumer debt more than doubled.[55] The same also occurred from 1925 to 1929.[56] Is this just another coincidence?

While promoting consumers' indebtedness, high inequalities in wealth and income provide the wealthy with large amounts of surplus capital to invest in short-term gains and highly speculative financial assets. Together with the financialization of the economy, both heavy borrowing at the bottom and over-investment in short-term profiteering at the top promote price distortions and asset bubbles, or discrepancies between the price of something and its real value. This is risky business. Asset inflations can lead to financial meltdowns for a very simple reason: prices of assets cannot go up forever. Like all bubbles, sooner or later, asset bubbles burst.

Furthermore, there is another major way by which high inequalities have promoted financial instability: through "regulatory or policy capture," a subject that will be examined in detail in the next chapter. This happens when governments, instead of making decisions on the basis of public priorities, advance the special interests of certain groups in society, typically the very wealthy. This is exactly what happened. Since the beginning of the neoliberal globalization era, governments have been increasingly dominated by the vested interests of powerful financiers, who have acquired enough economic and political power to dictate policies at will. Since the late 1970s, they have engaged in massive efforts of advocacy and political pressure in support of financial deregulation. This is hardly surprising. Although financial liberalization has proven to be disastrous for the general population, these policies have also resulted in very high concentrations of wealth in the top social classes.[25] [57-62] It is small wonder they have worked so hard to promote these reforms.

Shock and cut

Yet, there is something that does not add up in this story. Why would the super-rich support financial deregulation that has proved to create financial crises and stock market crashes? Why would they want to bargain the stability of the entire system that has provided them with so much profit over time? Did not the global financial crises of 1929 and 2008 negatively affect even their profits and assets? Indeed, some rich people and large corporations have lost impressive amounts of wealth because of the two largest financial crashes in recent history. There is little doubt that these economic shocks can hit even them, in terms of absolute wealth. In relative terms, however, economic downturns tend to benefit the rich and powerful handsomely.[63] As Andrew Mellon, banker and US Secretary of the Treasury from 1921 to 1923, once put it, "in a depression, assets return to their rightful owners."[64] Crises can be exploited to promote upward redistributions of income, from the poor and the middle-class to the rich. The reason is simple. When prices fall sharply, those that have surplus capital can easily "buy on the cheap." This was the case of Carlos Slim, one of the richest men in the world, who took advantage of the *Tequila Crisis* in

1994 to buy up large sectors of the Mexican industry and consolidate an economic empire.[65] The crisis that exploded in Russia after the transition in 1991 was also a "blessing in disguise" for wealthy tycoons, who bought large stakes of major state enterprises for ridiculously cheap prices. The 26 billionaires that ended up acquiring about 19 percent of Russia's GDP in 1994 had very little to complain about after the economic collapse of the former Soviet Union.

In the best-selling *The Shock Doctrine*, Naomi Klein explains how wealthy elites tend to gain even more relative wealth and power following an economic crisis. After a shock, governments are often forced to impose harsh austerity programs that further reduce the bargaining power of the working class and the poor. With the excuse of striving for security and economic stability, these governments are usually in a better position to impose "emergency" reforms that would otherwise be considered unacceptable. Even violence is, oftentimes, tolerated more in times of shocks. Indeed, in crisis-stricken developing countries, many IMF austerity programs have been imposed through the use of force in order to suppress popular uprising. Only coercion allowed the governments of Bolivia, Chile and Argentina to impose IMF-style draconian policies on their populations.[35] In the eyes of financial elites, the crises occuring in the developing world provided a great opportunity to force entire regions into applying neoliberal market policies and financial deregulation. Of course, the official excuse for imposing austerity was to "save" these countries from even worse economic scenarios. It was with this unspoken assumption in mind that, in 2000, *Time Magazine* featured US Treasury Secretary Robert Rubin, Deputy Treasury Secretary Larry Summers and Federal Reserve Chair Alan Greenspan as "The Committee To Save The World."[66] It is unfortunate, however, that austerity and budget cuts, far from preventing worse economic scenarios, exacerbate them. Indeed, instead of saving the world, the "three marketeers" have contributed to ruining economies and the lives of countless people on a global scale.

Some neoliberal ideologues do not see anything wrong with the "shock and cut" strategy, however. On the contrary, they are quite candid in admitting that crises can be useful. As Michael Bruno, chief economist of the World Bank, once confessed: "a large enough crisis may shock otherwise reluctant policy makers into instituting productivity-enhancing reforms (such as structural adjustment policies)."[67] More recently, former White House Chief of Staff of the Obama administration, Rahm Emanuel, explained: "You never want a serious crisis to go to waste. And what I mean by that is an opportunity to do things you think you could not do before."[68] In the same vein, in *The Political Economic of Policy Reform,* the designer of the Washington Consensus, John Williamson, with his colleague Stephen Haggard, revealed: "these worst of times give rise to the best of opportunities for those who understand the need for fundamental economic reform."[69] In a later chapter of the same book, Williamson added: "one will have to ask whether it could conceivably make sense to think of deliberately provoking a crisis . . . so as to scare everyone into accepting those changes."[70] Bruno, Emmanuel, Williamson and Haggard were surely inspired by the profound insights Milton Friedman exposed them to. As the guru of the neoliberal doctrine once put it, "only a crisis, actual or perceived, produces real changes . . . When a crisis occurs, the actions that are taken depend on the ideas that are lying around." He continued: "That, I believe, is our basic function: to develop alternatives to existing policies, to keep them alive and available until the politically impossible becomes politically inevitable."[71]

Free market monopolies

In the aftermath of the banking sector bailouts, it has become quite clear for large companies that there is no such thing as free market competition. First, big banks and giant corporations are quasi-monopolies that own large sectors of their market of influence. Second, almost anytime one of these big banks and large corporations go bankrupt, governments rescue them. Put another way, they are "too big to beat" and "too vast to bust." A question comes natural, however: how have these banks and corporations become so powerful and invulnerable? Why cannot they compete in the market like any other smaller firm? Why are they not free to fail like all other market actors?

The answer is straightforward. In spite of the rhetoric on free trade and free enterprise, the unstated goal of neoliberal globalization is the concentration of massive amounts of power and wealth in the visible hands of big business. It is not by chance that the most blatant examples of solid and stable oligopolies have materialized in countries that have applied "free market" policies more diligently than others. The US, for example, is once again a case in point. No other nation in the world has "liberated" itself more from the most significant regulations that are supposed to nurture free market competition and liberalism. But how did this happen? According to Barry Lynn, author of *Cornered: The New Monopoly Capitalism and Economics of Destruction*,[72] the transformation of the US economy into an oligopoly state began with the suspension of the anti-trust laws, around the 1980s. The race toward oligopoly was then escalated by the "merger revolution" of the 1990s, to reach new heights in the first decade of the twenty-first century, just before the Great Recession. Mergers, acquisitions and the progressive relaxation of rules and regulations took place diffusively and indiscriminately. David Korten, author of *When Corporations Rule the World*, calls these practices "corporate cannibalism." Waves of buyouts and takeovers ended up destroying countless corporations, which were swallowed by more profitable and competitive rivals. At the same time, they pushed local enterprises, family farms and smaller firms out of business.[73]

Virtually every sector of the US economy has been affected by the advent of "corporate cannibalism." The banking system is the most notable case. During the 1990s, in just a few years, hundreds of US banks merged or closed down, resulting in immense concentrations of economic activity among a few powerful companies.[74] Some of the largest financial institutions – Bank of America, JP Morgan Chase, Wells Fargo and Citicorp – are all combinations of previous large banks. The rise of free market monopolies has not only affected the banking sector. Consider the food industry, for example. Between 1982 and 1990, the US experienced more than 4,000 mergers and leveraged buyouts.[75] Three companies – Tyson, JBS and Cargill

– now control more than 70 percent of the US beef industry. Large food companies such as Monsanto, Kraft Foods, Pepsi-Co and Nestlé set prices at will and determine the terms and conditions of their own market sectors. The TV industry too is an oligopoly with seven companies controlling most of the market shares. Four wireless providers – AT&T, Verizon, T-Mobile and Sprint Nextel – control almost 90 percent of the cellular telephone service market. Concentration has also proceeded apace in the retail sector. Four firms, including Wal-Mart, dominate more than 70 percent of the general merchandise stores sales.[76]

Started in the US, the anti-trust laws crusade went global. The increasing pressure emanating from the global market and finance made governments more receptive to new mergers and acquisitions. Ideas such as "monopoly capitalism" and "big is bad" vanished almost completely from the vocabulary of economics.[76][77] Soon after the US began to dismantle its anti-monopoly laws, England, another champion of big business-friendly market policies, followed suit. Unsurprisingly, the effects were quite similar. There are now four megabanks controlling the British banking sector: Barclays, HSBC, Lloyds and Royal Bank of Scotland. The UK food industry is dominated by four large corporate giants: Tesco, Sainsbury, Asda and Morrisons. They control up to 75 percent of the grocery business. The British detergent market is also an oligopoly. It is managed by two main players: Unilever and Procter & Gamble.

From the US and the UK, free market monopolization spread to other English-speaking countries including Australia and Canada. The Australian banking sector is now dominated by four companies: Australia and New Zealand Banking Group, Westpac, National Australia Bank and Commonwealth Bank – though the latter is owned by the government. When considering the food sector, grocery retailing is controlled by two large companies: Coles and Woolworths.[78] Most Australian media outlets are owned by either Murdoch's News Corporation, Time Warner or Fairfax Media. In Canada too, most economic sectors are in the hands of a few big companies. About six of them control the banking industry. Three corporations (Rogers Wireless, Bell Mobility and Telus Mobility) share over 94 percent of Canada's wireless market, and two dominate the Internet service provider market (Rogers and Bell).

The globalization of monopolization has also affected the developing world. Mexico is a case in point. After the passage of the North American Free Trade Agreement (NAFTA), Carlos Slim, otherwise known as "Mexico's Mr. Monopoly," gained control of more than 7 percent of Mexico's business, including 92 percent of its fixed telephone lines and 73 percent of its cell phone business.[65] Before NAFTA, there were already startling inequalities in wealth and power in the country. Now, they have become grotesque. As Porfirio Díaz, former president of Mexico, once remarked: "Poor Mexico. So far from God, and so close to the United States."

One would assume that the rise of global monopolies, which dominate such large chunks of the economic sector, would outrage the champions of free trade. Surely, the displacement and disappearance of small producers and sellers before the rise of powerful companies would have disappointed Adam Smith. The Scottish economist deeply hated monopolies. He could not stand the East India Company, for example. The main reason he was so wary of power and wealth concentrations in the hands of a few was pragmatic: monopolies pervert the operation of free markets by increasing prices and reducing wages, distorting investments and disrupting peaceful relations between countries. Unfortunately, today's free marketeers share very little, or nothing, with Smith's views. As Lynn once put it, "the Chicago School of Economics' definition of free markets enabled the rich and powerful to use their corporations and their banks to actually destroy markets, not make them free." He continued: "*Capitalism and Freedom* deserves to be recognized for what it is: the most effective profeudal manifesto in the English language since the restoration of monarchy in Britain."[78]

The rules of the gain

The increasing monopolization of the global economy under a competitive, free market regime sounds paradoxical. But this may not surprise economists who have studied the inherent contradictions of capitalism. They know that unfettered competition naturally degenerates into monopoly. Socialist writers already understood this more than a century ago. In Engels' opinion, although competition seems, on the surface, to be the opposite of monopolies, it is, in reality, just a precursor of them. To him, the antithesis between competition and monopoly was quite hollow. As he observed: "competition is based on self-interest, and self-interest in turn breeds monopoly. In short, competition passes over monopoly."[79] In effect, it is not hard to imagine that in a competitive system, the winners of a competition actually try to suppress the very competition that made them win. It is natural that the most profitable companies, once they become successful, try to purge other small competitors out of the market. This is exactly what happened during the neoliberal globalization era. Neoliberal policies that were supposed to promote free competition and free markets worldwide ended up generating almost the opposite result: concentrations of power and wealth in a few hands.

Of the market actors who benefited the most by the mutation of the market system into a global oligopoly, transnational corporations are, by far, the most powerful ones. Freed from government regulations and invited to compete for profit worldwide, they have adopted all possible strategies to advance their profit. Their influence has now become immense. They set prices and dictate methods of production and market conditions at will. They blackmail trade unions, drive down wages and outsource production to wherever they prefer. They lobby governments, fund politicians and overspend on advertisements. They own TV stations, newspapers and magazines. They fund think tanks, academicians and entire universities. They have their wealth in tax havens and plenty of lawyers to avert rules and tax legislations. They are tied to one another in a dense network of partnerships and business ventures. Simply put, they rule the world.

Corporate social irresponsibility

In recent years, the social and ecological ravages that were produced by global corporations have generated considerable public outcry and civic opposition in countless nations. Companies such as Goldman Sachs, Exxon Mobil, Enron, McDonald's, Coca-Cola and Nestlé have been the center of public protests and civic indignation. Corporate abuses are being exposed for how they adversely affect public health, the environment, the economy and the social fabric. In recent years, the anti-corporate movement has compelled corporations to respond to public requests and become more socially responsible, transparent and accountable. They have triggered massive demonstrations, consumer boycotts and other types of anti-corporate activities. Part of the anti-corporate movement lobbies in the hope of transforming the business practices of these corporations and making them more in tune with the social, ecological and economic needs of societies. In some cases, these campaigns have succeeded and generated positive changes. Some firms have taken public issues seriously by attempting to make their business practices more ecologically and socially friendly. Yet, although the anti-corporate movement should be widely praised and supported, in a sense, it is still missing the point. The reason is simple. It is futile to indict transnational corporations for the abuses they commit. As David Vogel once put it in *The Market for Virtue*: "there are important limits to the market for virtue . . . [and] . . . the main constraint . . . is the market itself."[80]

Vogel got it right. It is naive to expect enough social responsibility from market actors who are in perpetual competition for profit and power. In a system guided by perpetual capital accumulation, market actors have just one task: compete and innovate. They cannot give up profits or market opportunities for the sake of making the planet a happier and safer place to live. If they do, they risk going out of business. In other words, they have just two ways to go: expand or die. As some writers have argued, business is simply war by other means.

This may sound extreme, but so is the reality of market competition. In this sense, the free marketeers cannot be blamed for recognizing the obvious. In an essay published in the *New York Times* in 1970, Milton Friedman explained: "the [only] social responsibility of business is to increase its profit."

> In a free-enterprise, private-property system, a corporate executive is an employee of the owners of the business. He has direct responsibility to his employers. That responsibility is to conduct the business in accordance with their desires, which generally will be to make as much money as possible.[81]

Along the same lines, Martin Wolf observed: "companies are servants of market forces . . . if they do not meet the terms of market competition, they will disappear."[82] Roberto Goizueta, former executive of Coca-Cola, could not agree more: "businesses are created to meet economic needs," and when they "try to become all things to all people, they fail." Like all other private companies, Coca-Cola has only "one job: to generate fair returns for . . . [their] owners,"[83] he added.

Ironically, when considering the concept of corporate social responsibility, the views of the free marketeers are peculiarly aligned with those of Marxist economists. In *Understanding Capitalism*, economist Samuel Bowles writes: "competition for profit arises because the only way a firm can stay in business is to earn a profit. Each business owner has no choice but to engage in a never-ending race to avoid falling behind." He adds: "if a firm does not grow, others that do grow will soon outpace it. In a capitalist economy, survival requires growth, and growth requires profits."[84] Paul Sweezy, economist and editor of the *Monthly Review,* explains that the proliferation of monopolies and globalization that started in 1974–5 was a by-product of "the always expansive and often explosive capital accumulation process."[85] Henry Magdoff, another influential Marxist economist, observes that, "the growth of the multinational corporations is merely the latest emanation of the restless accumulation of capital and the innate drift towards greater concentration and centralization of capital." He continues: "the problems arise not from the evils of the multinationals or the presumed diminution of the sovereignty of the advanced industrialized nation states: the problems are inherent in the nature of a capitalist society."[86]

One could argue, however, that the problem is not the system, but individuals of flesh and bones, who fail to be morally responsible for their actions. The trouble with this argument is that individuals do not live in a vacuum. The culture that compels corporations to behave ruthlessly in the market is inevitably transmitted to the individuals who are employed by them. Joel Balkan, author of *The Corporation*, explains that:

> the people who run corporations are, for the most part, good people, moral people . . . Despite their personal qualities and ambitions . . . their duty as corporate executives is clear: they must always put their corporation's best interest first and not act out of concern for anyone and anything else.[87]

In Robert Hare's opinion, when people act as corporate operatives, they are compelled to become competitive, manipulative, ethically irresponsible and selfish. They must turn themselves into psychopaths.[87]

Put another way, there is no use in blaming corporate executives for being ruthless and ice-hearted. They have little choice but to play according to the "rules of the gain." Their mission is to maximize the price of their companies' shares, no matter what social, economic or environmental disasters their activities may cause. If they refuse to play by the rules, the next executive in line, who is ready to satisfy the requirements of their post, easily replaces them. As Peter Drucker, an expert in management theory, once exhorted: "If you find an executive who wants to take on social responsibilities, fire him. Fast."[88]

The system imperatives

The "rules of the gain" do not only explain why free market competition eventually leads to monopolies and why transnational corporations cannot be socially responsible. They also help us to understand why free market societies are crises-prone and cyclically unstable. Different authors, largely ignored by mainstream media, have long understood that, left unchecked, financial markets have an inherent predisposition to excesses. Unless governments step in to control them, they crash. In a book published in 1978, *Manias, Panics and Crashes*, Richard Kindleberger provides an overview of the financial crises since the South Sea bubble. He concludes that bursts of speculation, economic bubbles and crashes are common features of capitalism.[89] In a similar vein, Hyman Minsky argued that unfettered market economies tend to be periodically exposed to surges of speculation and cycles of boom, bust and depression.[90] In other words, these fluctuations are almost inevitable, he argued. Many other authors have underlined these tendencies. Almost all of them have, directly or indirectly, a debt of recognition to a notable ancestor: Karl Marx.

Marx was the first to provide a systematic, critical account of capitalism and describe its inherent predisposition to be in trouble, seasonally. Although Marx did not develop a full theory of crises, and seemed to have given only marginal attention to financial markets, he clearly identified the key sources of the system's instability. First, he recognized that capitalist societies are inexorably affected by continuous revolutions of the "mode" and "means of production."[91] This happens because market actors are involved in a perpetual search for new strategies to maximize profit and out-compete rivals. In the *Communist Manifesto*, Marx and Engels argue that capitalism cannot function "without constantly revolutionizing the instruments of production, and thereby . . . the whole relations of society."[92] The imperatives of a "constantly expanding market," and capitalism's "universalizing tendency . . . to go beyond its limiting barriers," inevitably promote a continuous metamorphosis of the economic order.[93] This is what Joseph Schumpeter later defined as "creative destruction," a process of unlimited business innovation, in which old markets are continuously destroyed and perpetually replaced by new, emerging ones.[94] Indeed, the last global crisis was triggered by the indiscriminate proliferation of financial innovations, and various authors have explained their diffusion through the inherent tendency of market societies to modernize and devise new methods of accumulating capital.

Marx seems to have also recognized that in the monopoly stage of capitalism, the exploitation of the working class becomes especially acute. This leads to wage repression and "underconsumption," which are serious predisposing factors to inadequate aggregate demand and stagnating economic activity. In *Capital*, Marx explains that:

> the ultimate reason for all real crises always remains the poverty and restricted consumption of the masses as opposed to the drive of capitalist production to develop the productive forces as though only the absolute consuming power of society constituted their limit.[95]

Several economists, especially of the Keynesian school, are persuaded that the stagnation of wages and the consequent increase of consumer debt were crucial predisposing factors to the 2008 financial crisis. Some Marxist economists, however, disagree. In their view, it was what Marx defined as "the law of the tendency of the rate of profit to fall," that best explained the origins of the last global crisis.[96]

Perhaps the most important contribution Marx left to posterity is his insights on the inherent "anarchy of the market." As underlined in the *Communist Manifesto*, he and Engels believed that, "modern bourgeois society, with its relations of production, of exchange and of property . . . is like the sorcerer, who is no longer able to control the powers of the nether world whom he has called up by his spells."[97] Capital is inherently uncontrollable, they argued. One has to admit that today's world, dominated by hordes of hedge funds, mutual funds, investment banks and futures, which strike country after country and cause countless bankruptcies, massive layoffs, cuts in social spending and civic unrest, fits quite well with Marx and Engels' hypothesis.

Many mainstream economists consider the 2008 financial crisis as an unforeseen error of an otherwise well-functioning economic system. But, this is hardly the case. In a system completely at the mercy of the laws of profit maximization and creative destruction, crises are unavoidable – in fact, inevitable. The reason is simple. Oligopolies of corporations who are competing for profit without borders, on the surface, may seem like the ultimate rulers of the world. But, in reality, they are not even in charge of their own actions. It is the system imperatives – profit maximization and perpetual innovation – that control them. Thus, they are, in a sense, out of control. And so it is the entire system that they dominate.

The crisis within

Never again! This is what many hoped to hear from economists and pundits, in the years following the collapse of the global financial system, on October 29, 1929. In the years after the Great Depression, many hoped that the free market ideologies, which crashed the world economic system, had fallen from grace forever. Many wished that they would never again hear pompous celebrations of the magic of laissez-faire economics. But the future did not live up to their hopes. Half a century after the Great Depression, the world engaged in yet another grand free market experiment. It began in the late 1970s, and has yet to end. Nobody even knows when it will. The new free market experiment has already produced adverse outcomes, which are before our very eyes. Overall, they look quite similar to those observed about eighty years ago. Writer and historian Santayana once explained that, "those who do not remember the past are condemned to repeat it."[98] Have we really learned nothing from history? Are we to repeat the same mistakes again and again?

The 2008 global economic crisis should have taught us all a lesson. It should have shown us, once and for all, that unregulated markets naturally fail. Regardless of what neo-classical economists have conjured up in their mathematical models, they must come to terms with the delusional vacuity of the "efficient market hypothesis." The other grand fallacy, that individual self-interest always benefits the larger society, should have been debunked a long time ago. Private vices cannot ever become virtues – they remain vices. Even some of the most radical ideologues of neoliberalism have finally realized that the free market doctrine is grounded on completely unrealistic assumptions about a world that has never existed. A riveting moment of truth was experienced when Alan Greenspan, grilled by a US congressional committee about his direct role in causing the 2008 financial crisis, admitted to being in a state of "shock disbelief." As he pathetically declared: "I made a mistake . . . [there was] a flaw in the model that I perceived [to be the] critical functioning structure that defines how the world works."[99] Another former champion of financial deregulation, Lawrence Summers, finally recognized that the assumption regarding the self-stability of the market system has been "dealt a fatal blow."[100]

Although Greenspan and Summers may have reconsidered their creed, probably for opportunistic reasons, the world of politics and economics is still, by and large, dominated by free market illusionaries, who persistently defend the indefensible. Former managing director of the IMF, Rodrigo de Rato, sums up their position quite well. In his opinion, although the crisis needs to be fixed with some mild regulations, this has to be done "without renunciating to financial liberalization and financial globalization, because that is at the heart of the success of the global economy."[101] De Rato is not alone in this view. The faith in the neoliberal gospel is still profoundly rooted in our society. Those harboring hope that the last financial crash could be the beginning of the end for neoliberalism have been disappointed so far. The market greed doctrine is far from dead. It is still alive and kicking.

Disarming the markets

The economy now resembles a leaky balloon, uncontrollably floating around the world. If governments fail to fill it up in one way or another, global economic depression is the future. After cashing in some trillions in bailouts, the "masters of mankind" at the head of big banks have learned an important lesson: in times of prosperity, they make outstanding profits; in times of crisis, taxpayers rescue them. The financial companies that caused the 2008 financial collapse are now larger and more powerful than ever. They are still totally unregulated, full of toxic assets and reckless. So far, the timid attempts to introduce financial regulations "with teeth" have been easily neutralized. The banksters know what they are doing: they do not want any of them. They have no intention to stop gambling with the deposits and pension funds of everyday people. They have no interest whatsoever in conceding to any real change of the system. They like it the way it is. This may seem smart of them, but it is far from it.

Without a new set of global economic rules and regulations, the risk of another financial collapse remains extremely high. Even Paul Volcker has recognized it: "the obvious danger is that with the passage of time, risk-taking will be encouraged and efforts of prudential restraint will be resisted. Ultimately, the possibility of further crises – even greater crises – will increase."[102] But there is more. There is a serious possibility that the global recession will eventually degenerate into something worse. There are clear signs of rising social unrest almost everywhere in the world. Between nations, diplomatic relations are being strained by trade disputes, national rivalries and currency wars. Within nations, epidemics of bankruptcies, unemployment and poverty are undermining the fabric of society. Worse, there are other, even more threatening, looming ecological and energetic crises on the horizon. If ignored, they could turn into a perfect storm. In the past, economic collapses have created new opportunities for political extremists and fanatics who are eager to stir popular uprising and resolve social problems through totalitarian solutions.[103] The 1929 Great Depression ended with the beginning of the Second World War. History can, indeed, repeat itself as a tragic farce. Economic historian Niall Ferguson hardly exaggerated when he observed that, "in mid-2008 we witnessed the inflationary symptoms of a world war without the war itself."[104]

The financial system is in urgent need of re-regulation. We must adopt special policies to meet the needs of those who have lost their jobs and their houses. Reforms must also include *ad hoc* legislations that nurture and protect small businesses and local enterprises. Together, with a democratization of workplaces and progressive taxation regimes, reforms that protect workers and small firms from the ravages of the crisis may, indirectly, contribute to a fairer distribution of wealth. This can prevent future crises at the same time. It is also an imperative that we repeal laws such as the *Futures Modernization Act*. Fast. Regulations that separate real banks from speculators and investors, such as the *Glass–Steagall Act*, urgently need to be re-enacted. There are numerous historical examples that can be useful to sketch new reforms of the financial system: Sweden after the crisis of the 1980s, for example. The US historical record has also offered important lessons in this regard. Roosevelt's reforms during the New Deal proved to be quite effective in curbing speculations, regulating banks and promoting economic stability. Simultaneously, they promoted employment, social security and a more egalitarian distribution of wealth. The New Deal also consisted of a series of anti-trust laws that were designed to keep trade and industry divided among as many different parties as possible.[105] This was revealed to be very effective in preventing the formation of monopolies, and in limiting the power of corporations to shape policies and control democracies. The importance of splitting the "too-big-to-fail" banks into smaller institutions cannot be overemphasized. New Deal regulations also included the *1934 Securities and Exchange Act*, which empowered small investors in search of stable and safe returns on long-term welfare of companies, as opposed to large investors ready for big sellouts for short-term profit. Another New Deal regulation, the *1936 Robinson–Patman Act*, even outlawed or controlled giant trading firms and retailers, in order to protect the smaller ones and the public. This law also empowered an anti-trust team with the task of developing policies that could, whenever possible, break large enterprises into smaller pieces and establish regulations to avoid the influence of large speculators on prices. Companies that were too big were decentralized and split into smaller entities. At the same time, Roosevelt promoted mild forms of democratization of corporations by empowering small investors to participate in the management of corporations, and protected labor unions through reforms such as the *1935 Wagner Act*. This law gave workers more freedom to form labor unions, and have a real say in how the work was done, how the profit was distributed, and even whether an enterprise could be sold and to whom.

Naturally, we also need global policies to put an end to the anarchy of free markets, and to limit the damage global financial speculators have already caused worldwide. This can be done though a set of comprehensive and stringent regulations of global finance and taxes on international financial transactions. John Eatwell and Lancet Taylor, authors of *Global Finance At Risk: the Case for International Regulation,* proposed a new economic architecture regulated by a new "World Financial Authority," specifically designed to manage the threat of systemic risk and financial contagion.[106] Recently, a group of economists have lent their support to the *Robin Hood Tax,* a new Tobin Tax on speculative dealings in foreign currencies, shares and other securities of 0.05 percent.[107] The European Union and some political leaders, including France's president Hollande, have expressed their support for the initiative.

These are some of the measures to prevent future crises, but it is also necessary to address the inequalities at the root of financial instability. Even some IMF economists have finally recognized that, "redistribution policies that prevent excessive household indebtedness and reduce crisis-risk ex-ante can be more desirable from a macroeconomic stabilization point of view than ex-post policies such as bailouts or debt restructurings."[55] Mainstream policy proposals to end the Great Recession continue to be narrowly focused on two options: budget cuts or deficit spending. But the best way to get out of the mess is to embrace a third option: austerity for the rich.

For sure, financial regulations and redistributive policies will continue to be fiercely opposed by the wealthy, the banksters, the speculators and the free market economists that dominate mainstream neoliberal institutions. Yet, the impression is that words such as "regulation," "redistribution" and "capital controls," once dismissed as cardinal economic sins, are now regaining some political attention, even respectability. A key lesson we must all take from history is that unless governments take steps to stabilize economies, the invisible hand of the market produces disasters. In the 1930s, it was government spending and a war-like economy with full employment and fixed targets, not free markets and parasitic financial products, which pulled societies out of the depression. Of course, there is not any need for an outright abolition of markets or trade either. Markets can be agents of prosperity and human progress. They can provide dynamism and incentives to generate new ideas, goods, services and technologies. Yet, there are limits to what markets can do.[108] As Arthur Okun observed, "the market needs a place, but the market needs to be kept in its place."[109]

9

STATE OF POLITICAL INERTIA

"A fashionable strand of skepticism," argue the columnists of *The Economist*, "[asserts that] the world's biggest companies are nowadays more powerful than many of the world's governments . . . These claims are patent nonsense."[1] Advocates of neo-liberalism, including the editors of the British magazine, are dismissive of any allegations contending that large transnational powers have eroded democracy and national sovereignty. They find it a symptom of paranoia to suspect that big business is shaping global and national economic policies. Large corporations have not limited the right of independent development and political choice, they argue; they have, instead, promoted more democracy and more freedom. The neoliberals also assert that nobody is really responsible for neoliberal globalization,[2] this is simply how it should be. In their opinion, the best "government" is the one "which governs (the) least" (a quote they often attribute to Thomas Jefferson, but that was first proposed by David Thoreau).[3]

Have the neoliberals got it right? Has the diffusion of global corporations really promoted democracy and freedom as they say? And is it true that nobody is really in charge of neoliberal globalization?

A large number of authors would respond with three "no's." In their view, the rise of transnational corporate giants has generated profound political imbalances within and between societies. In effect, even the policies of the most advanced democracies are now largely influenced by the vested interests of global corporate and financial companies. The reason for this is simple: as already mentioned in previous chapters, a large concentration of wealth in a few hands tends, almost automatically, to generate a large concentration of political power in the same hands. Consider this: in 2010, transnational corporations generated a valued added of approximately $16 trillion, accounting for more than a quarter of the global GDP.[4] They are believed to control about two-thirds of the world's trade, most of which consists of intra-company transactions.[5] Global companies have acquired so much wealth that any government decision that does not favor their interests is considered "politically unrealistic." *Top 200: The Rise of Corporate Global Power*, a pioneer study conducted by Sarah Anderson and John Cavanaugh in 2000, estimated that of the 100 largest economies in the world, 51 are corporations and 49 are countries. According to their study, in 1999 General Motors had annual sales of about $176 billion, two billion more than the yearly GDP of Denmark. In the same year, Wal-Mart obtained about $166 billion in sales, about three times more than the annual GDP of Bangladesh ($45 billion), a country of more than 150 million people. As some critics say, it is true that the gross sales of a company can hardly be set side by side with the GDP of a country: it is almost like comparing apples and oranges.[6] Nonetheless, even when considering companies' annual added value instead of gross sales, 29 corporations still make the list of the top 100 economies in the world.[7]

Many of these corporations, in actuality, are more powerful than governments. This is even truer when considering global financial actors such as hedge funds, private pension funds, mutual funds, investment banks and insurance companies. In 1996, the world's top 20 banks had assets worth more than $8 trillion (one-fourth of the world's GDP at the time). In the same year, the total assets of US mutual funds stood at $3.4 trillion,[8] while about 900 hedge funds, 75 percent of which are registered offshore, managed $2 trillion worth of assets.[9] In 2010, six banks – Bank of America, JP Morgan Chase, Citigroup, Wells Fargo, Goldman Sachs and Morgan Stanley – controlled about 60 percent of US GDP.[10] A recent analysis revealed that 1,318 global companies collectively own, through their shares, the majority of the world's largest manufacturing firms and blue chip, representing about 60 percent of global revenues. The same study also revealed that a "super-entity" of 147 companies, less than 1 percent of the total, controls about 40 percent of the entire wealth in the network.[11]

These figures are astonishing. Yet, two questions may be pending: how do transnational corporations and global financial markets erode democracy?; and how does neoliberal globalization place limits on national sovereignty?

The shadow world government

The waves of trade liberalization, financialization and deregulation, which started in the late 1970s, provided transnational corporations and global financial actors not only with immense amounts of new wealth, but also with new opportunities to affect national and international policies. Global financial markets have acquired the ability to influence political decisions on interest rates, exchange rates, budget deficits and redistributive taxation. They can compel national governments to follow "fiscally responsible" policies in fear of "financial retaliation." How?

Around the world, transnational corporations are organized through merges, acquisitions and partnerships. They often make decisions collectively.[8] When they decide to leave a country, they usually make everyone else rush for the door.[12] Wherever governments apply policies that are not in their interests, they just move elsewhere, posing a threat to national security.[13] As Harvard University professor and author Dani Rodrik observes, as large investors and corporations have become more and more "footloose," they have acquired the ability to vote "with their feet."[14]

Global financial actors are even more powerful. By simply, and abruptly, withdrawing investments and capital from one country, they can create enough instability to trigger a financial crisis. This may sound hard to believe. But with the advent of new technologies facilitating rapid communication and connectivity worldwide, conglomerates of global financial powers can easily move massive amounts of capital across borders very quickly. If they decide to move their investment out of a country, they can determine the economic destiny of millions of people.

Numerous authors have lamented over the destabilizing effects of financial markets and the democratic deficit caused by the threat of short-term capital flight.[15][16] In *False Dawn: The Delusions of Global Capitalism*, British political philosopher John Gray claims that global financial markets have engaged in a war of competitive deregulation against sovereign states. In his view, the increased global mobility of capital and production has left the welfare policies of European social democracies unworkable. It is the specter of political instability and long-term economic depression, Gray explains, that keep governments disciplined and attuned to the demands of speculative capital. Indeed, restoring the confidence of rich private investors has now become the overarching priority of national governments, irrespective of the wishes of the public and political parties.[13]

Two recent cases in point are Greece and Italy. Both countries are now under economic treatment. They have been compelled to give up national sovereignty and apply austerity programs that are desired by foreign investors, under the leadership of technocrats such as Papademous and Monti. Both political leaders have not been elected, but chosen because of their close ties with the financial industry – including Goldman Sachs. The tragic irony is that the ability to keep foreign capital and corporations within national borders by dismantling the welfare state does not actually protect nations from financial crises – it does quite the opposite. Finance-friendly policies may save a nation from an immediate economic downturn, but they also leave it perpetually at risk of future ones. Moreover, economic austerity programs, usually applied in exchange for rescue packages and foreign investments, tend to prolong recessions. This, in turn, further increases budget deficits, and pushes a country in a downward spiral toward disaster. This is exactly what both Greece and Italy may risk in the near future.

If global financial markets can dictate policies in rich democracies, imagine what they can do in the developing world. In the last decades, the political self-determination of poor countries has been severely restricted, sacrificed on the altar of the market God. This has happened not only because low-income countries have much less economic and geopolitical power than affluent nations; there is more. After the 1980s debt crises, most developing countries were forced to swallow the bitter medicine of the "golden straitjacket," designed by the IMF and the World Bank. With the profit of wealthy investors at heart, these international financial institutions compelled them to adopt the usual package of austerity, which included abandoning restrictions to capital flow and trade, leaving these countries even more susceptible to crises, unfair competition and financial blackmailing by corporate and financial powers.

Regardless of what the editors of *The Economist* may believe, both developed and developing countries' policies are now virtually at the mercy of oligopolies of transnational corporations and financial institutions, which are moving around the world in search of short-term profits. As the editors of *Business Week* observe, "global forces have taken control of the economy. And governments, regardless the party, will have less influence than ever."[17] In a later editorial, the columnists of the magazine compare the unconstrained flow of hot money across borders to a "shadow world government."[18] This is hardly an exaggeration. Global financial conglomerates have an enormous influence over governments and hold "veto power" over national regulations. From their computers, by deciding whether or not to move large amounts of investments across borders, they can perform real-time referendums over policies.

The best democracies money can afford

The democratic deficit created by the speculative attacks of global investors, or what Bill Black defines as the "sovereign raiders" of the financial system, is hardly analyzed in depth by mainstream media.[19] At times, however, we hear candid statements about the impotence of politicians before the overwhelming power of finance. The words of the former president of the German Bundesbank, Hans Tietmeyer, could not be more revealing. "Politicians have to understand that they are now under control of the financial markets and not, any longer, of national debates," he once declared.[20] Under the threat of economic instability, even the so-called center-left political leaders have prioritized the interests of financial industries and "disciplined" their policies to please the "sovereign raiders." This was the case with Labour Prime Minister Tony Blair in England, for example, whose reforms have actually sustained the wealth gap between the rich and poor; a gap that he inherited from the previous Conservative governments.[21] On the other side of the pond, Bill Clinton, instead of reviving the political agenda of the Left, organized his deficit reduction strategy to please large corporations and gain the "credibility" of Wall Street firms.[22] Both Blair and Clinton served the priorities of financial powers, not the needs of the people in their countries. In a moment of truth, Clinton admitted: "by the time you become the leader of a country, someone else makes all the decisions. You may find you can get away with virtual presidents, virtual prime ministers, virtual everything."[23]

Even the politicians who are genuinely committed to social justice and redistribution of wealth usually succumb to the pecuniary urges of the financial superpowers. A notable case in point is former anti-apartheid leader – whom Baroness Thatcher once defined as a terrorist – Nelson Mandela. When, after a life of struggle for freedom and racial justice, Mandela finally became the president of South Africa, he had little option but to abandon his egalitarian ideals and adopt the Washington

Consensus policies. The reason for such an abrupt political "U" turn is obvious. As Mandela himself explained: "The very mobility of capital and the globalization of capital and other markets, make it impossible for countries, for instance, to decide national economic policy without regard to the likely response of these markets."[24] A similar case in point is the former leader of the Brazilian Workers Party, Ignacio Lula da Silva. Once elected president of Brazil, after a lifetime struggle for social justice and land reforms, Lula too had little choice but to follow the orthodox policy prescriptions of the IMF and the World Bank.

Mandela and Lula cannot be blamed too much for abandoning their egalitarian agenda under the pressure of foreign powers. Political leaders in the developing world are reminded, as soon as they are elected, that they have no choice but to swallow the bitter pill of the neoliberal "golden straitjacket." The threat of capital flight and the "veto power" of global financial markets can produce devastating social consequences, which are further aggravated by the absence of welfare policies and social security. Disobeying the "sovereign raiders" is not an option – it would be like committing social and economic suicide for the country. It would also be a suicidal move for the careers of the political leaders. As noted by William Greider in *The Soul of Capitalism*:

> if an activist president sets out with good intentions to rewire the engine of capitalism – to alter its operating values or reorganize the terms of employment and investment or tamper with other important features – the initiative would very likely be chewed to pieces by the politics.[24]

In recent years, there have been promising steps toward more autonomous political agendas, especially in Latin America. Yet, for many low-income countries, which are still under the grip of the financial powers, the right to independent development remains a mirage. As Thomas Friedman cynically, yet accurately puts it: "As your country puts on the golden straitjacket," political choices "get reduced to Pepsi or Coke."[25]

Sovereign raiders in (tax) havens

There is something else that has advanced the power of global financial investors and has diminished that of national governments over the last decades: the rise of offshore tax havens. As regulations and national controls on the movement of capital have been gradually dismantled, tax paradises have proliferated as financial centers of the world. According to Brittain-Cattlin, author of *Offshore: the Dark Side of the Global Economy*, in 2005 about one-third of the wealth of the world's "high net worth individuals" – more than $14 trillion – was legally held in offshore havens. He also explains that about 80 percent of international banking transactions and half the capital of the world's stock exchanges were parked in tax havens.[26] Large corporations have taken advantage of the deregulation policies to move their taxes away from their country of operations to fiscal paradises. The Cayman Islands, the fifth largest banking center worldwide, have about 40,000 inhabitants and 65,000 registered firms and banks.[27] For 1999 as a whole, US multinationals had $400 billion of untaxed earnings in offshore havens. By the end of 2002, this figure reached $639 billion.[26] A congressional study estimated that, in 2000, about 63 percent of US corporations paid no taxes, while 6 out of 10 reported no tax liability from 1996 to 2000.[28] Between 1987 and 1999, Rupert Murdoch's News Corporation, with its 152 offshore subsidiaries, earned profits over $2.3 billion, but paid no British taxes.[29]

As explained by Nicholas Shaxson, author of *Treasure Islands*, the proliferation of tax havens since the early 1970s has created new opportunities for tax evasion.[30] Offshore centers have been turned into weapons against states that desire to tax capital. In order to keep wealthy investors within national borders, governments have transferred the burden of taxation on workers' wages and local industries. They have also often provided big corporations with large tax breaks.[31] In 1957, corporations in the US provided about 45 percent of local property tax revenues. By 1987, their share went down to 16 percent.[18] Between 1975 and 2005, the headline tax rate on corporate income of advanced OECD countries fell on average from around 50 percent to around 30 percent.[32] In the US, in 2004, corporate income taxes amounted to 8 percent, compared to 34 percent of personal income taxes.[33] In 2002 and 2003, the 275 most consistently profitable *Fortune 500* corporations paid less than half of the 35 percent statutory rate at least one of those years. About 80 of them paid no federal taxes at all.[34]

Make no mistake: while large firms have been gifted with enormous help, small firms have been left to compete "freely" with subsidized corporate giants. It is no coincidence that small firms pay a higher percentage of their profit in income tax than transnational companies. In 1999, US companies with assets equaling $250 million or more paid a real tax rate of 20.3 percent. In the same year, however, companies with assets between $25 and $50 million paid a real tax rate of 36.7 percent.[26] There are also startling tax inequalities between super-rich individuals and the rest of us. Trends over time on top marginal tax rates, and the share of total income going into the hands of the top 10 percent of the population, show that the rich have never had a better tax regime since the end of the Second World War.

In 1992, the 400 Americans with the highest incomes paid 26.4 percent of taxable income ($46.8 million on average) in federal, state and local taxes. In 2007, although their average taxable income rose to $344.8 million, their effective tax rate fell to 16.6 percent.[35] Warren Buffett, believed to be the third richest man in the world, complained that in 2007 his secretary paid more taxes than he did. This is no joke. While his secretary earned approximately $60,000 and paid about 30 percent tax rate, Buffett earned $46 million and was taxed only at 17.7 percent.

Welfare incorporated

Global corporate and financial conglomerates are not only paying less tax than small businesses and the general population. They also receive massive subsidies and other forms of government support, or what Ralph Nader once called "corporate

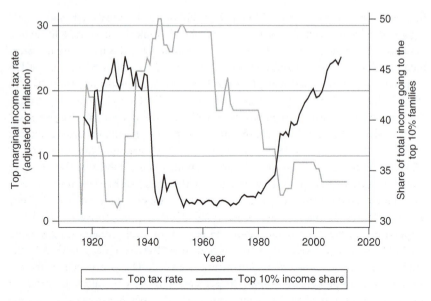

FIGURE 9.1   Tax the rich: share of total income going to the top 10% families and top marginal tax rate in the United States, 1913–2012

Sources: Data on top tax rate were taken from the Tax Policy Center (Urban Institute and Bookings Institution) Tax Facts, 2012; data on the income share of the richest 10% of income groups came from the World Top Income Database, 2012.

welfare." This is probably one of the main reasons why large firms, instead of moving offshore completely, just transfer their fiscal residency into tax havens. By standing "with one foot onshore and the other offshore," they can exploit the best of both worlds. The former helps them to socialize the costs, the latter to privatize the gains. This may sound exaggerated, but only if one ignores a simple fact: without taxpayer money, many successful companies would not have become or remained successful. There is no such thing as "free market discipline" for giant corporations. As observed in a study conducted by Winfried Ruigrock and Rob van Tulder, "virtually all the world's largest core firms have experienced a decisive influence from governmental policies and/or trade barriers on their strategy and competitive positions." They add: "at least 20 companies of the 1993 *Fortune 100* would not have survived at all as independent companies, if they had not been saved by their respective governments."[36] This is not the exception, but the rule. One must not forget the massive bank bailouts following the 2008 crisis. What's more, countless corporations were saved from sure bankruptcy through massive government bailouts before the crisis.[37] In 2006 alone, the US government spent about $92 billion on corporate welfare to companies such as General Electric, Boeing, Xerox, IBM, Motorola and Dow Chemical.[38] In a book entitled *Perverse Subsidies*, authors Myers and Kent estimate that each year, globally, environmentally unfriendly corporations, including those in the coal, auto and oil industries, receive about $2 trillion in subsidies from governments. This is about 4 percent of the world economic output in 2001.[39]

This is enough to raise all eyebrows, but not those of the neoliberals and neo-conservatives, who are completely at ease with these forms of "socialism for the rich." It is not rare to hear free market advocates ranting about the "nanny state" when social policies provide for the poor, the unemployed, the sick and the hungry. But they do not find anything wrong with blatant violations of the free market doctrine when government help is directed to their beloved corporations. The welfare state only creates "dependency" when it supports public education, public housing, better sanitation, control of water, air pollution regulations, roads and infrastructures.[40] But not when it subsidizes big business to avoid bankruptcy. All in all, some of the most radical advocates of free market doctrines were, in reality, welfare champions for the corporate sector. A case in point is Ronald Reagan. While praising the wonders of market efficiency, his administration rescued troubled industries, such as Chrysler, using taxpayer money. Another example is George W. Bush, a free market devotee who saved AIG and other bankrupted banks during the 2008 global financial meltdown. Ronnie and George were also very keen on letting taxpayers foot the bill for military technologies and war operations from which the corporate sectors benefited enormously. Both supported peculiar cases of "neoliberal conservatism," an oxymoron to define a political economic doctrine advocating for free markets for the poor and welfare policies for the rich. All in all, the two have never made a secret about which social class they side with. As George W. Bush observed at The Alfred E. Smith Memorial Foundation Dinner, a white tie "charity" fund-raising event in 2000, "this is an impressive crowd. The haves and have-mores. Some people call you the elite. I call you my base."[41]

Politics for sale

As written before, those who criticize the harmful influence that global corporations have over democracies are often dismissed as extremists. But there is no need for extreme theories to explain why wealth and power go hand in hand. When the rich and powerful can dispose of large amounts of wealth to control politics and politicians, and to acquire even more power and wealth, that is oftentimes what they do. It is natural for them to seize the opportunity to transform wealth into power and power into wealth.

Some of the mainstream political figures of recent history understood this reality a long time ago. Thomas Jefferson, for example, believed that large corporations and banking institutions were "more dangerous than standing armies."[42] Andrew Jackson was at one with Jefferson. In his opinion, large banks and big business, if given too much power, were capable of subverting the proper functioning of democratic governments. In Jackson's opinion, "the rich and powerful too often bend the acts of government to their selfish purposes."[43] Theodore Roosevelt shared the same skepticism. He defined large corporations as "malefactors of great wealth."[44] In a similar vein, Woodrow Wilson claimed that, "the combined capitalists and manu-facturers of the United States" were the real "masters of the government."[45] Franklin Delano Roosevelt expressed a similar concern. In his view, the major sources of his nation's economic problems were the pernicious practices of "economic royalists" sitting atop giant corporations.[46]

Thomas Jefferson, Andrew Jackson, Theodore Roosevelt and Franklin Delano Roosevelt were neither extremists, nor conspiracy theorists. They themselves were part of the wealthy elite. Nevertheless, they understood power politics. They foresaw the dangers that await democracies in which a vast amount of economic power is concentrated in the hands of a small number of super-rich people. As Associate Justice on the US Supreme Court, Louis Brandeis, called "the Robin Hood of the Law" by *The Economist*, once declared: "when the economic power is all in the hands of a few (plutocracy), it doesn't matter whether the people can vote or not. The government is bought, the media is wholly owned, the police repress dissent, and the poor suffer." He added:

> no, the reason great inequality is a problem is not because they don't pay their "fair share" (whatever that means), or even because the poor are starving. The problem is that they control the society and the economy for their own purposes, to their own ends, and to the detriment of the masses. When there is great inequality in wealth, democracy is a joke.[47]

In effect, there are multiple ways economic inequality affects political inequality. A key consequence is the resulting shift of political priorities among elected officials. When there are extreme economic inequalities, public priorities become skewed toward the interests of those at the top of the economic hierarchy. This, in turn, can result in "policy" or "regulatory capture" – a form of legal political corruption in which government policies, instead of being designed on the basis of public deliberations, end up being "dominated" by vested interests, usually those of large corporations. Simply put, in a highly unequal society, governments risk being turned into the executive branch of the big business party. While the latter dictates the policies, the former executes them.

The problem with prioritizing the interests of the wealthy elite is that this comes at the expense of those of the general public. Programs that can benefit the majority and the poor, such as social security, healthcare, unemployment benefits and environmental protection, become marginalized.[48] What is worse, the association between economic inequality and democracy can turn into a vicious cycle: inequality erodes democracy which, in turn, results in even more inequality. Once large inequalities in political power are established, and policies are regularly "captured" by powerful corporate elites, the potential for the democratic process to redress the growing inequalities through taxation is significantly weakened.[49] And, thus, the system spins out of control, only to be moved by cravings for power and wealth of the elite of the country. This is more or less what is happening today. As Robert Dahl once explained, "powerful international and domestic forces push us toward an irreversible level of political inequality that so greatly impairs our present democratic institutions as to render the ideals of democracy and political equality virtually irrelevant."[50]

When money rules

In the last decades, the rise of economic inequalities has largely transformed the political process. It has gone from a battle of words to win the hearts and minds of the electorate, to a hunt for money – by conquering the pockets and grants of rich donors. While political ideas are still important, at the end of the day – and even at the beginning – it is all about money. The reason is easy to figure out. Political campaigns have become astonishingly expensive, where success largely depends on how much money a politician can spend in terms of advertising, television appearances, professional advice, billboards and travelling. A study conducted by Ansolabehere and colleagues showed that in the US in 1972, total campaign spending was about $200 million. By 2000, however, candidates, parties and organizations raised and spent approximately $3 billion in the national elections.[51] Over the past three decades, corporate political action committee spending increased from $15 million in 1974 to $222 million in 2005.[52] The winners of House elections in 1976 spent an average of about $87,000 on campaigns, an equivalent value of about $308,000 in 2006 dollars. Forty years later, however, the average Senate winner spent an astonishing $9.6 million.[53] What is worse, in 2010, the US Supreme Court ruled that corporations are now allowed to spend unlimited amounts of money on election campaign advertising.[54] According to *USA Today*, the Democrat and Republican presidential candidates will each raise and spend about $2 billion on the 2012 campaigns.

The natural question is: from where is an ambitious politician expected to raise such startling amounts of money? It does not take a genius to figure it out. The largest part of the financial contributions to political campaigns comes from big corporations and extremely wealthy individuals. It is no coincidence that the most important contributor to the last US presidential election was Goldman Sachs. It has been estimated that in the US, the richest 0.25 percent of the population makes approximately 80 percent of financial contributions to political elections. In the 2000 presidential campaign, about 86 percent of campaign contributions over $200 came from people with household incomes of $100,000 or more, representing about 34 percent of Americans.[55]

On the surface, there may seem to be nothing wrong with such startling inequalities in financial contributions to political campaigns. But the trouble for democracy is that when large companies and wealthy elites decide to finance a politician, it is rarely for humanitarian purposes. They expect to be paid back. Elected officials, increasingly in need of securing funds for their next election campaign, are compelled to attend to the interests of their donors.[56] In effect, it is not an exaggeration to say that the chief business of politics has now become to "beg for bucks," and that politicians have now turned into "cash cows." As the author of *Earth Odyssey*, Mark Hertsgaard, once noticed, "the legal bribery known as campaign contributions . . . has turned so many politicians in the United States (but also in other modern democracies) into spineless corporate suppliants unwilling to bite the hands that feed them."[57] In countries that heavily rely on private donor funding such as the US, over half of political candidates spend at least one-fourth of their time on fund-raising.[58] Once elected, most of them start their next election fund-raising campaign on their very first day in office. The reason is obvious. They are well-versed in the rules of the game: whoever raises the most corporate money, by promising the most to corporations and wealthy individuals, stands a better chance of winning an election.

Inequalities in political financing have, indeed, completely changed the rules of the political game. In the best seller, *The Golden Rule*, Thomas Ferguson put forth what he defined as the *Investment Theory of Party Competition*. In his opinion, the fundamental market for political parties is no longer voters, who have limited resources and power, but coalitions of major investors. According to his theory, big donors have very good reasons to invest in politics: if they rent the best "political horse" they can gain favors, which they may profit from handsomely.[59] The more companies invest, the more they obtain in return. Between 1991 and 2001, the top 41 transnational companies in the United States (including Microsoft, General Electric and Disney) contributed $150 million to political parties and campaigns. They also enjoyed $55 billion in tax breaks in three years alone.[60] In the last few decades, after accumulating massive amounts of wealth from trade deregulation, financial industries have become top contributors to political campaigns. Most of them include the too-big-to-fail corporations that enjoyed the massive bailouts footed by taxpayer money after the 2008 financial collapse: Goldman Sachs, Citigroup, Bank of America, UBS, JP Morgan Chase and Morgan Stanley. Of course, to this day, they are still the main funders of political activities. Between 2007 and 2008, the chair of the Senate Banking Committee, Christopher Dodd, received $2.9 million from the securities industry.[61] As US Senator Richard Durbin once said, "the banks – hard to believe in a time when we're facing a banking crisis that many of the banks created – are still the most powerful lobby in Capitol Hill. And they frankly own the place."[62] After the 2008 bailout, some naively believed that we would finally control the banks. They were wrong: the banks *still* control us.

The idea that one must simply follow the money to identify the winner of an election may sound too simplistic to be true. In effect, campaign contributions do not always influence the political process to the point of determining the electoral victories. There are cases in which political candidates who are provided with more funding actually succumb in the election. Yet, only a few exceptional politicians can afford to be outspent by their rival candidates. More importantly, without a large amount of money to fund a political campaign, a wannabe politician cannot even dream to be in the running for an election. In the US, the amount of campaign funds has been predictive of electoral success in 2002, 2004 and 2006, where more than 90 percent of House winners outspent their opponents.[53 63 64] Even in the 2008 presidential election, Barak Obama largely outspent John McCain in campaign finance contributions. It was not without merit that Obama was awarded the "Marketer of the Year" prize.[65] He was also far better off in terms of television advertising. As Wall Street correspondent Karl Rove put it: "He [Obama] buried Mr. McCain on TV."[66] However, during the 2010 mid-term election when the

employed them. After participating in public office, some former businessmen and lobbyists return to their previous employees. Legally, there is nothing wrong with this. However, the problem with having former private managers in public office, and then former public officials in private corporations, is that they often advance special interests at the expense of public priorities.[72] Some of the major architects of deregulation policies that prompted the 2008 financial collapse have entered and exited through this system of "revolving doors." A revealing example is the Enron scandal. Before becoming the symbol of financial corruption in 2001, *Fortune* magazine featured Enron as "America's Most Innovative Company" for six consecutive years. The company's economic success was largely due to the proliferation of the highly profitable, but extremely risky, energy derivatives. In 1992, Enron had successfully lobbied the US Commodity Futures Trading Commission, chaired by Wendy Gramm, to exempt energy-derivatives trading from government oversight. At the time, Enron was a significant source of campaign financing for Wendy Gramm's husband, US Senator Phil Gramm, the "high priest of deregulation" who spearheaded the *Gramm–Leach–Bliley Act*, which, ultimately, caused the 2008 subprime mortgage crisis. Just six days after providing Enron with the exemption it wanted, Wendy Gramm resigned her position as a chairwoman of CFTC. Five weeks later, Enron appointed her to its board of directors. According to Public Citizens, between 1993 and 2001, Enron paid her between $915,000 and $1.85 million in salary, attendance fees, stock options and dividends.[73]

But the Enron scandal is not an isolated case of a few "bad apples." It is a symptom of a legally corrupt system. In the past decades, the flow of top executives from the financial sector to government offices has increased exponentially. In the US, a survey of 20 leading firms in the financial sector showed that 142 lobbyists, employed in various industries between 1998 and 2008, had formerly worked as top government officials.[74] The crony relationship between corporations and politicians can be also appreciated when examining the flow of former senior elected officers toward the corporate sector. According to the Centre for Public Integrity, between 1998 and 2004, in the US, more than 2,200 former high ranking federal officials, from both Republican and Democratic administrations, registered as federal lobbyists, as did over 200 former members of Congress.[75] Unsurprisingly, most of them became lobbyists for large corporations. Reagan's first Treasury Secretary Donald Regan, one of the very first crusaders for the deregulation of the US economy, was a former executive of Merrill Lynch. Henry Paulson, George W. Bush's Treasury Secretary, and major architect of the massive bailout that rescued the Wall Street banks after the crisis, was head of Goldman Sachs from 1999 to 2006. Robert Rubin and Lawrence Summers, both of whom contributed to dismantling the regulations of derivatives and other complex financial transactions at the time of the Clinton administration,[76] were previously employed in or tied to Wall Street. Once out of office, they both went back to work as financiers in the private sector, only to later be re-appointed by Obama to "clean up the mess" that they had helped to create.[77] Of the two, Robert Rubin is perhaps the most revealing prototype of the revolving door phenomenon. A key opponent of regulating the derivatives that brought down the economy in 2008, Rubin worked for about 26 years at Goldman Sachs before becoming US Secretary under Clinton. The forty-second president of the US once called him the "greatest secretary of the Treasury since Alexander Hamilton." After his political appointment in the Clinton administration from 1995 to 1999, Rubin returned to Wall Street to work as an investment banker at Citigroup. In 2008, reappointed as a top economist in the Obama administration, he advised the US president to hire his protégée, Timothy Geithner, for the position of US Treasury Secretary. Rubin also made sure that Obama hired Lawrence Summers as the new director of the National Economic Council (NEC). While a director of the NEC in 2008, Summers was also paid more than $5.2 million as a managing executive of the hedge fund DE Shaw. He pocketed an additional $2.7 million in speaking fees from a smorgasbord of future bailout recipients, including Goldman Sachs and Citigroup. The Obama economic team also included Jamie Rubin, who happened to be Robert Rubin's son. Wonder of wonders, the very first act of legislation passed by the Obama administration was an economic reform, which provided Citigroup with a $306 billion bailout.[78] As leading economist Dean Baker pointed out, when he first heard that the three financiers had been appointed by Obama to fix the economic system after the 2008 collapse, "selecting Summers, Geithner and Rubin to solve the crisis" is like "selecting Osama bin Laden to run the war on terror."[79]

The vicious connection between the financial industry and government through the "revolving door" is not only an American phenomenon. It is also widespread in Europe, East Asia, Australia, Brazil, India and Russia.[80] The "revolving door" is even apparent when examining the connections between financial investors and international institutions such as the IMF, World Bank and WTO. A notable example is the previous president of the World Bank, Robert Zoellick, appointed by the Bank in 2007, after a spectacular career as the managing director of Goldman Sachs. Another example is Stan Fischer who, after a successful stint in the corporate sector, became number two in the IMF, only to join Citigroup once again, when out of office.

Beyond political inertia

At the time of Socrates' execution, Athenian democracy was on the verge of collapse.* Greed, mistrust, narrow self-interest and political corruption were wide-spread.[81] Plato noticed all of these troubles at once. Although quite critical of democracy, he saw the re-awakening of a sense of justice and civic virtue as the only remedy against Athens' social and political decadence.[82] Plato most likely over-estimated the importance of these moral values. No matter how fair, virtuous and responsible Athenian citizens and politicians had become, stronger, more powerful enemies such as Sparta would have most likely put an end to the Hellenic civilization regardless.[83] Nonetheless, Plato had a point. The political ineptitude and civic

---

* Athens was not really a democracy: slaves, women and non-residents were not allowed to par-ticipate in any political and civic processes.

breakdown afflicting Athens before and during the Peloponnesian Wars helped to push the city onto the path of disaster.

More than two millennia later, Plato's antidote for Athens' social and political ills may be the remedy we need to halt the decline of modern civilization. Without a resurrection of some form of public integrity and civic responsibility, political decisions will continue to be made on the basis of individual opportunism and special interests. And with the global challenges we face ahead, the situation can turn very nasty. What to do then? Simply asking politicians to stop both chasing corporate money and using deceptive marketing strategies to maximize their chances of political success, would be naive. Inviting corporations to transform themselves into good Samaritans, who act on the basis of public interests and humanitarian concerns, would be futile. Counting on individuals to adopt more sober and altruistic behavior, while the very rules of society compel them to be more materialistic and greedy, is a pious hope. As already stated in the previous chapters, it is clear that the solution is to change the "rules of the gain": reform the system at its root, even if this implies giving up some of the privileges that politicians, corporations and individuals have enjoyed for so long.

But how can we do this? It is obvious that quick fixes would not suffice to address the deep, underlying problems of our political system. There are, however, some reforms that can help to reduce the democratic deficit in our societies. One of the main interventions needed to stop the transformation of democracies into "govern-ments of the few, by the few, and for the few" is the reform of campaign and political financing. In the US, one of the pivotal decisions that gave corporations the power to transform politics into a "commercial circus of political horses" was the ruling by the US Supreme Court in the mid-1970s, which extended the First Amendment constitutional protection to corporate financing of elections. This law, and similar ones, must be repealed. In a report entitled *Breaking Free with Fair Elections: A New Declaration of Independence for Congress*, a group of civic society organizations presented numerous valuable ideas on how to change the rules of political elections financing. The conclusion of the report is quite straightforward: in order to restore honesty, and to end the chase for campaign money, political elections must be supported by public funding,[53] and must be regulated by principles of fairness and political equality to foster public interests, not private priorities. Another important reform that can contribute to changing "the rules of the gain" is the reform of mass media and broadcasting. As underlined in a report written by UNESCO and the World Radio and Television Council, neither commercial media, nor state-controlled broadcasting can truly promote public interests and democracy. As discussed in a previous chapter, the emergence of independent media and Internet-based journalism is a promising development in this regard. However, so long as the bulk of mass media remains in the hands of market forces or state control, the majority of citizens will continue to be poorly informed about important civic affairs. The solution proposed by UNESCO and the World Radio and Television Council is this: "public service broadcasting . . . a forum where ideas should be expressed freely . . . and financing is independent from both commercial and political pressures."[84] Other reforms that can contribute to overcoming the political deadlock that we are currently experiencing include rules and legislations that limit the employment of former corporate lobbyists in government offices and vice versa. In other words, in order to develop a functioning democracy, the "revolving door" between big business and governments must be shut down. Last, but certainly not least, it is crucial to create a system of environmental, economic, cultural and legal incentives, which promote the active re-engagement of people in civic and political affairs. Without passionate, well-informed citizens and vigorous civic organizations committed to public causes, hopes to limit the shadow cast by big business over society will remain slim.

From corporatized democracies to democratized corporations

It will take more than simply changing the rules of the political game and the media for us to overcome our current democratic deficit, however. While increased regulation of corporate practices would be helpful, alone they would be insufficient to create a true democracy.[85] The reason is simple. As explained before, political inequality is, by and large, a by-product of economic inequality. Even the strongest government intervention pales in comparison to the overwhelming wealth and power of big business. As Mark Hertsgaard explains:

> in theory, governments are supposed to police corporate greed, channeling it . . . away from the corner-cutting that threatens public health and safety. But regulation is an iffy thing. Corporations are constantly pressuring governments to relax . . . regulations if not eliminate them altogether.[57]

Political analysts David Levy and Peter Newell express a similar concern. As they put it, "government negotiating positions in Europe and the United States have tended to track the stances of major industries active on key issues, such that the achievement of global environmental accords is impossible if important economic sectors are unified in opposition."[86] What is the solution then?

A number of authors have attempted to tackle the issue. In *Red Sky at Morning*, James Gustav Speth outlines a series of interesting proposals. Some of them include the revocation of corporate charters and expulsion of a corporation when it grossly violates public interests. He also suggests rolling back the limited liability that leaves corporate directors and top managers personally unaccountable for gross negligence and major failings. Above all, his list of recommendations involves nullifying the state of "corporate personhood," or the ability of corporations to claim the same legal status and institutional rights intended for people.[87] These reforms can be important steps toward the transformation of corporations into more socially and ecologically responsible institutions. Companies do have the potential to be instrumental in promoting the general interests of society. In the US, before the *1886 Santa Clara Act*[88] [89] that sanctioned their right to be "private enterprises," companies were required to demonstrate their public usefulness. Their charters could even be dismantled if they failed to show a sufficient commitment to the common good. Unfortunately, the era of corporations as public entities ended at the beginning of the Gilded Age when the "Robber Barons," such as John D Rockefeller and JP Morgan, finally succeeded in turning corporations into private bodies. This ideological shift is well captured by the words of railroad tycoon William H Vanderbilt when he explained: "The public must be damned . . . I don't take stock in this silly nonsense about working for anybody's good but our own . . . Railroads are not run on sentiment, but on business principles."[90]

But corporations can work for the good of everyone. According to Allen White, author of *Transforming the Corporation*, "the corporation of the future" will move away from the "gladiatory culture that deifies competitive advantage" toward a new business philosophy. As he once argued:

> whereas scale, growth and profit-maximization were previously viewed as intrinsic goods and core goals of the corporation, the new corporation marches to a whole different set of principles: namely, those serving the public interest, sustainability, equity, participation and respect for the rights of human beings.[91]

Part of the problem is that, to be effective, these changes are to take place at the global level. This requires effective international cooperation and global democracy, a subject to be detailed in the next chapter. White advocated for a "multi-tiered structure in the form of global, regional, and local agents, norms and powers that enables the exercise of citizen rights and democratic control over the corporation."[92] This may be a long shot, but it is needed to effectively tackle the global crises we are facing today. There is no plausible reason why corporations should be run as "unaccountable private tyrannies." There is no rational explanation for why they should be left free to corrupt politicians, and destroy the ecosystem and the fabric of society. More importantly: if it is true that corporations used to operate as public entities in the past, why should we assume that they cannot function similarly in the future?

Some authors believe that the only way to overcome the democratic deficit caused by global corporate powers is to turn them into workplace democracies. As Allen White put it, "shareholder primacy is the single greatest obstacle to corporate evolution toward a more equitable, humane and socially beneficial institution."[93] White's hopes for a democratic transformation of corporation are not original. They echo the ideas of countless writers and political thinkers that for years have advocated for workers' control, democracy at work, employees' assemblies and self-management companies. Many of these ideas are gifts of socialist and anarchist thinkers, now marginalized, ridiculed or forgotten in contemporary political discourse. But whatever political inclination one prefers, one thing is clear: at the social level, political equality or true democracy cannot happen unless we democratize corporations. As John Dewey once put it, "until industrial feudalism is replaced by industrial democracy, politics will [continue to] be the shadow cast on society by big business."[94] Clearly, the world is not moving in the direction it needs to go: corporations are less and less democratic, and democracies are more and more corporatized.

The best of all impossible worlds

"It is demonstrable that things cannot be otherwise than as they are," said Dr. Pangloss, "for all things have been created for some end, they must necessarily be created for the best end."[95] Dr. Pangloss, one of the main characters of Voltaire's novel *Candide, or the Optimist*, epitomizes Gottfrieb Leibniz's famous motto: "this is the best of all possible worlds."[96] More than three centuries later, Leibniz's aphorism has revived and mutated into a different, yet similar mantra. "I do not know whether [neoliberalism] will work or not," said Baroness Margaret Thatcher. "Why is there no critique of it? Because no one has an alternative. There is nothing else to try," she thundered.[97] "There is no alternative," or TINA, is an idea that Voltaire would have probably laughed about if he were still alive. But Voltaire is dead; along with the critical spirit of most contemporary intellectuals who have resigned themselves to the myth that neoliberalism is the only show in town.

Unlike the clumsy naiveté of Dr. Pangloss, Thatcher showed to be a quite vitriolic and heartless politician. Yet, she should not be held responsible more than necessary for having resurrected Leibniz's axiom. Countless writers, before and after her, have repeated a similar refrain, often with the same air of inexorability. The guru of economic liberalism von Hayek, for example, was completely convinced that our only option was to submit to the laws of the market. "The only alternative to submission to the impersonal and seemingly irrational forces of the market is submission to an equally uncontrollable and therefore arbitrary power of other men," he once proclaimed.[98] But no one has re-evoked the spirit of Leibniz's mantra more than Johns Hopkins University professor Francis Fukuyama, author of *The End of History and the Last Man*. In his view, the worldwide diffusion of neoliberalism corresponds to nothing less than, "the endpoint of mankind's ideological evolution . . . the final form of human government . . . the end of history."[99] The same sense of immanent historical inevitability infected Thomas Friedman. In his opinion, "the historical debate" over viable economic systems is "over": the only possible political model is "free market capitalism."[100]

The inexorability of global neoliberalism relies on an unspoken assumption: all other political economic systems have failed. According to the supporters of the TINA dogma, this has been clearly proven by history. What happened to the former Soviet Union, a centrally planned economy by definition, taught everyone a hard lesson: dream heaven on earth and you will wake up in the worst of all possible worlds. As Martin Wolf explains, "intelligent critics are prepared to accept that a sophisticated market economy works far better than any other economic system." He continues: "Those who condemn the immorality of liberal capitalism, do so in comparison with a society of saints that never existed and never will."[101] Another victim of the same historical delusion is Anthony Giddens, author of *The Third Way: the Renewal of Social Democracy*.[100] He too saw the triumph of "free marketism" as a success of "pragmatic politics" that supersede sterile ideologies.

It is a pity that the shrinking of political alternatives to "Pepsi or Coke," far from reflecting "the end of ideology," implies an unconditional surrender to another ideology: that of big business. Gore Vidal could not be more on target when he wrote that the American government has only one political party, the business party, which has two right wings: the Republicans and the Democrats. The neoliberal society glorified by the free marketeers is often described as a paradise of innovation and ingenuity, but politically, it shows the same level of conformity of a close-minded bigot. The lack of political imagination in which our collective mindset leaves us is preventing us from recognizing the alternatives. But there are plenty of them. And even if there were not any, we had better find one soon. Although a fairer society is still considered utopian by the neoliberal pundits, the real utopia is harboring the illusion that the current system can go on forever. Even if this were the best of all worlds, it is still an impossible one.

10
PROGRESS OR COLLAPSE

In the best seller *Collapse: How Societies Choose To Fail Or Survive*, Jared Diamond proposes two lists of factors explaining why civilizations have fallen in the past. The first includes: excessive deforestation, habitat destruction, soil erosion, water mismanagement, overhunting, overfishing, the adverse effects of introducing new species on native species, overpopulation and increased per-capita impact of people. The second list comprises: climate change, the build-up of toxins in the environment, energy shortages and the human utilization of the Earth's entire photosynthetic capacity. Diamond argues that roughly 10 to 20 civilizations have ultimately collapsed because of one or more of these factors.[1] A civilization now appears to be threatened by most factors in both lists: ours. And the risk of breakdown is global. As Diamond observes: "for the first time in history, we face the risk of a global decline" for "globalization makes it impossible for modern societies to collapse in isolation."[2] About 15 years ago, Joseph Tainter, author of *The Collapse of Complex Societies*, expressed a similar concern. In his view, modern civilization is at risk of "deep collapse," a cascading implosion of the entire system, being triggered by concatenating problems that are chained together and reinforce one another.[3]

So far, the global ecological crises we face today have failed to stimulate any serious political action. Modern society is still trapped in a state of immobility, inertia. Our collective mindset seems unable to picture the prospect of global breakdown, maybe because the idea challenges our capability to accept the reality we see. And as Carl Jung once noted, human beings cannot stand too much of it. But there is another possible reason explaining our state of psycho-political apathy. After centuries of progress and breakthroughs, the human species has acquired an intoxicating sense of confidence in its ability to solve problems. We have been so good at overcoming so many obstacles in the past that we may now falsely believe that any crisis, regardless of its severity, can easily be overcome. A particularly dangerous illusion that we glorify is the presumption that markets and human ingenuity are able to automatically address ecological problems as soon as they surface. In this, neoliberal economists have no peer. They persist in believing that humanity can continue expanding, consuming and polluting without restraints. Whenever ecological troubles such as excessive deforestation, climate change or the depletion of natural resources begin to occur, they tell us that markets automatically promote a response by signaling the need for price adjustments, reallocation of resources, innovations and new technologies. Peter Huber, the author of *Hard Green: Saving the Environment from Environmentalists*, enlightened us with a sample of this wishful thinking: "Markets as a whole 'know' things the rest of us don't," he once explained.[4] As the economic mantra goes, "they know best."

Free market devotees also charge climate scientists and environmentalists with misplaced gloomy prophecies that history has repeatedly proven wrong, citing examples such as Malthus' incorrect predictions about mass famine and population decline.[5] In their view, the problem with the Greens – often addressed as "watermelons" because they are "green" on the outside, but "red" on the inside – is that they ignore the adaptive capacity of societies and individuals to generate creative solutions for the ecological problems we face. In *Small Is Stupid: Blowing the Whistle on the Greens*, Wilfred Beckerman accuses eco-scientists of fabricating "melodramatic disaster scenarios," that are not only unfounded, but also harmful to prosperity and economic growth.[6] Similarly, in *Hard Green*, Peter Huber explained: "cut down the last redwood for chopsticks, harpoon the last blue whale for sushi and the additional mouths fed will nourish additional human brains, which will soon invent ways to replace blubber with olestra and pine with plastic." He concludes, "humanity can survive just fine in a planet-covering crypt of concrete and computers."[7] The columnists of *The Economist* have also felt obliged to fill our minds with similar fantasies. As they once wrote, "human ingenuity, energized by sensible policies creates resources faster than people use them; people learn to substitute sand (in the form of microchips) for sweat, and fuel cells for petrol engines."[8]

These proclamations, which exhibit blind faith in the omnipotent power of free markets and new technologies, are nothing new. In 1972, a few years after Donella and Denis Meadows wrote *Limits to Growth*, Herman Kahn and colleagues dismissed their warnings about the depletion of natural resources as groundless. In *The Next 200 Years*, Kahn and colleagues even argued that with the technologies available at the time that the book was written, it was already possible to support about 15 billion people at $20,000 per capita for a millennium.[9]

The logic of the "free market technologues" is clear. Climate change? Peak oil? Water crises? Food shortages? There is nothing to worry about. As Lawrence Summers once pontificated, "there are no . . . limits to the carrying capacity of the Earth that are likely to bind any time in the foreseeable future. There is not a risk of an apocalypse due to global warming or anything else." He then added: "the idea that we should put limits on growth because of some natural limit, is a profound error and one that, were it ever to prove influential, would have staggering social costs."[10] While this argument may be popular, it is neither wise, nor original. Most empires and civilizations that have disappeared did so virtually overnight,[11] and believed themselves to be exceptional and invulnerable. At least, right up to the time they collapsed.[12]

All right or no one left?

Countless ecologists, intellectuals, researchers and even reactionary organizations such as the Pentagon and the Bilderberg Foundation have expressed serious doubts about the future viability of modern society.[13] Some scientists have even claimed that the aftermath of climate change may result in the extinction of the human race. In the opinion of Frank Fenner, director of the Centre for Resources and Environmental Studies at the Australian National University, our species will be gone within the next one hundred years.[14] Martin Rees, former president of the Royal Society, gives the human species about 50 percent odds of surviving the century.[15]

These predictions may sound too gloomy to be true. But they are not completely far-fetched. As explained in the first chapter, if the worst-case scenario predicted by the IPCC materializes, the end of the century will mark a 6°C increase in the mean temperature of the earth. This means that our planet is at risk of approaching the same conditions seen at the end of the Permian era, when about 96 percent of marine species and 70 percent of terrestrial vertebrate species disappeared.[16–18] Like most of the massive extinctions that took place in history, "the mother of all mass extinctions" was preceded by a rapid increase of the global temperature, following the release of massive quantities of greenhouse gases into the atmosphere.[19]

It is hard to say whether a world that is 6°C warmer would be habitable. We would expect that hurricanes, heat waves and other catastrophic natural disasters would strike more frequently and more severely. Large parts of the Earth would most likely turn into barren deserts. In a world that is 6°C warmer, most of the major cities and even entire nations could be submerged in water. In all likelihood, freshwater shortages would become widespread. It is likely that there would be frequent severe droughts, floods, famines and epidemics. Hundreds of millions of people could become refugees. It has been estimated that a rise of 3.5°C in the world's temperature would be sufficient to make almost half of the world's population face droughts and water shortages.[20] With the same increase of temperature, about 2 billion people in 40 poor countries would be expected to suffer large crop losses, malnutrition and even starvation.[21] But there is more. In times of crisis, things can turn very nasty. Global shocks could ignite civil conflicts and wars between people and nations that are left to contest for the shrinking natural resources.[22] These crises could even trigger nuclear conflicts. If this were to happen, the risk of our extinction would become all too real.

The potential state of affairs just described is obviously a rather extreme, worst-case scenario. If we are lucky and smarter, modern civilization will avoid the most severe forms of collapse. Numerous authors think so. In their view, humanity will not follow the fate of civilizations like Easter Island and Mesopotamia, which completely disappeared.[23] Instead, our civilization will experience a milder version of collapse, more similar to that faced by the Roman Empire and the Mayans. Thomas Homer-Dixon, author of *The Upside of Down*, embraces this view. To him, although the breakdown of modern society is inevitable, we still have time to manage a "graceful" collapse, a controlled demolition in which damage can be limited and options for recovery can be preserved in order to build a new society. As Homer-Dixon argues, rather than hoping to avoid an inevitable downfall, "we need to allow for breakdown . . . in a way that does not produce catastrophic collapse."[24] Even in this more favorable scenario, our future would still be filled with enormous challenges to say the least. As Homer-Dixon explains, "in coming years, I believe, foreshocks are likely to become larger and more frequent. Some could take the form of threshold events – like climate flips, large jumps in energy prices, boundary-crossing outbreaks of new infectious disease, or international financial crises."[25] The intensification of these conditions could drag humanity down to barbarous living standards, he explains. We may be forced to live with a minimal diet, multiple economic shocks, wars over basic resources and mass migrations. It would not necessarily be the end of the species, rather "the end of modern civilization as we know it."[26]

There is another possibility, however. Let us imagine that climate change does not strike planet Earth as harshly as environmental scientists expect. But even in this case, the world would still be confronted with the depletion of oil. For this reason alone, unless we will quickly transit toward a new system based on renewable energies, the risk of facing disastrous consequences in the future remains high. All comforts of modern life are based on cheap energy supplies: shelter, clothing, electric lighting, cars, airplanes, medications, chemicals, central heating and air conditioning are all partially supported by fossil fuels. Without oil, modern ways of living, travelling, eating, dressing, working and communicating would no longer be possible. There is more. Expensive oil supplies and the rise of energy prices would also result in multiple economic crises and food shortages. The end of cheap oil would make it more difficult to grow food on a large scale and obtain fresh water, leaving us with potentially devastating repercussions on our ability to meet basic human needs. A global oil crisis can also generate massive civil unrest, social instability and violence – maybe even wars. Of course, there is also the possibility that a new path-breaking discovery will replace oil as a main source of energy and avert all of these problems at once. However, nobody knows whether new technologies will come to our rescue before the end of cheap oil. For now, this remains a pious hope rather than a reasonable expectation.

Free market technologues can continue to believe that market forces will automatically address the ecological crises we face ahead. But after the 2008 global financial meltdown, it has become painfully clear that their ability to project future trends is underwhelming. All in all, we are still paying the price for their sorry record of bad guesses. Therefore, it would be unwise to trust their theories again. Indeed, if we continue pretending that all is right, we risk a future in which no one will be left.

Planetary emergencies

Urgent action is clearly necessary. Scientists argue that in order to avoid reaching "the point of no return" of irreversible climate change, the average global temperature should not be pushed more than 2°C above the pre-industrial level.[27–29] This means that we need to remain under the atmospheric threshold of 350 ppm of greenhouse gases, a target achievable by reducing carbon emissions by about 90 percent by 2050, relative to 1990 levels. Undoubtedly, this is a very ambitious target. But a paper published in *Geophysical Research Letters* estimated that even with a 90 percent global cut of carbon emissions by 2050, the 2°C seal of irreversible climate change could eventually still be "broken." As the authors of the article clearly point out, "if a 2°C warming is to be avoided," measures such as CO_2 capture from the air and subsequent sequestration "would have to be introduced in addition to 90 percent global carbon emissions targets by 2050."[30]

Other authors claim that we can afford less ambitious targets. Nicholas Stern, professor at the London School of Economics and author of the *Stern Report*, thinks so, or he used to. According to Stern, in order to prevent runaway climate change, it is sufficient to decrease annual emissions of greenhouse gases by 60–85 percent by 2050.[31] Critics of the *Stern Report*, however, consider this target completely inadequate.[32] Nevertheless, even the achievement of this less ambitious goal would require epochal global economic, behavioral and political changes. It would require large energy efficiency gains in the areas of electricity generation, transportation and residential and commercial buildings. It would also demand a massive development of renewable energy sources, especially wind and solar energy, and a rapid shift to low-carbon fuels. It may also require massive sequestration of carbon dioxide, sharp reductions of greenhouse gas emissions – beyond cuts in carbon dioxide emissions – and enhanced forest and soil management practices.[33] [34] It will be no walk in the park, that's for sure.

Unfortunately, as the current political situation stands, even the most achievable targets are a mirage. The concentration of greenhouse gases is already over 385 ppm, and continues to rise at about 2 ppm per year.[26] According to the National Academy of Sciences, between 2000 and 2006, the growth rate of carbon emissions accelerated more rapidly than in any prior period.[21] About four times faster than in the preceding decade, to be precise.[35] Developed countries, with the US at the head, are not doing enough to change their economies and way of living. At the same time, the growth rate of pollution in the developing world is increasing steadily. China alone is building, on average, two power stations every week.[36] At the same time, global deforestation proceeds unabated. Between 2000 and 2005, the world lost forest acreage equal to the size of Germany.[37]

Free market apologists and environmental skeptics dismiss all proposals for a low-carbon economy. In their view, sharp reductions of greenhouse gas emissions are unnecessary, and would entail unacceptably high costs to economies that are already at risk of another global recession. This argument ignores at least two major points. First, as underlined by the *Stern Report*,[31] present inaction will generate much larger economic costs in the future. Second, even without considering the effects of climate change, the end of cheap oil and the shrinking of natural resources would make it impossible to maintain current patterns of development, consumption and economic growth.[25] But there is a third and even more important argument that they ignore: is there any higher cost to pay than the collapse of modern civilization or even the extinction of the species?

Green revolutions

Oil has become the Achilles' heel of modern civilization. Not only because it is the main instigator of the Earth's fever, but also because it will inevitably run out. The priority must be to break humanity's addiction to the "black gold" and find alternative sources of energy. Soon. All of this must happen before we reach the point of no return and we find ourselves scratching the bottom of the oil barrel. An obvious question is whether, without oil, humankind will still be able to produce enough energy to sustain modern living standards. Will new sources of energy such as solar, hydrogen and wind power be enough to sustain modern lifestyles? Can we really turn the entire economy over to renewable energies?[22]

Some prominent writers do not think so. In their opinion, it is simply impossible to run society without abundant, cheap oil. James Howard Kunstler, author of *The Long Emergency*, believes that energy alternatives such as natural gas, solar, wind, water and tidal power will not make up for the depletion of oil. This is because all of the non-fossil fuel energy sources actually depend, to some degree, on an underlying fossil fuel economy. Put another way, clean and green technologies will not work without petroleum.[22] Oil is an exceptionally versatile, convenient and still relatively cheap fuel. It provides a vast amount of energy and no other substance even comes close to matching its properties. Echoing Kunstler's view, Homer-Dixon argues that solar, wind and hydrogen powers would not meet the growing energy needs that we will face in the future. While our energy efficiency efforts – turning off lights, fluorescent light bulbs, reductions in heating and cooling of buildings, gas-electric hybrid cars and public transportation – are crucial, they are insufficient.[38] Matthew Simmons, an investment banker interested in the energy industry, agrees with both arguments: there is no alternative energy that can replace oil, he explains – "The world economy has no plan B."[39]

Other authors, however, disagree. According to them, peak oil and the climate crisis can both be tackled without incurring major shocks to economic development and human consumption. In George Monbiot's view, the entire energy system can be run on renewable sources, and the economy can adapt to the use of electricity and regional super-grids, grid balancing and energy storage. The major exception, Monbiot argues, is flying, as there is no expectation whatsoever for the invention of battery-powered jetliners anytime soon.[40] Before him, many other writers, such as the authors of *Factor Four: Doubling Wealth, Halving Resource Use*, dispensed optimism about a smooth transition toward a world run on renewables. As they argue, "a new efficiency revolution" with new technologies will be sufficient to cut the use of natural resources by half, all while doubling our total economic value.[41] Another study, conducted by Greenpeace, claims that renewable energies, combined with energy efficient strategies, can deliver half of the world's energy needs by 2050.[42] Lester Brown, director of the Earth Policy Institute, asserts that aggressive policies on new wind turbines can generate up to three million megawatts of wind power by 2020, enough to meet 40 percent of the world's energy needs.[43] The European Union, which plans to derive roughly 20 percent of its energy from renewable sources by 2020, has already started to support projects that turn the sunlight of the Sahara desert into electricity.[44] Even small actions that are implemented globally can produce large savings of energy. For instance, it has been estimated that if every household in the UK double-glazed its windows, insulated its attic and used the most efficient appliances, total domestic energy use would fall by 40 percent.[45]

In recent years, the idea of moving toward a green global economy has become something more than just an aspiration. Some affluent nations have made outstanding improvements, in terms of eco-efficiency and the use of renewables.[46] The rising popularity of solar panels, the growing use of low-energy light bulbs, the emphasis on public transportation, and even the reduction in sales of SUVs in rich societies – although they are increasing in China and Russia – are encouraging signs of change. In the worldwide transition toward clean energies, European countries are leading by example. Take Sweden and Switzerland, for example. Both are among the wealthiest and healthiest countries on earth. And they still manage to emit almost four times less carbon emissions per capita than the United States, Canada and Australia.[47]

Sweden – along with Finland, the Netherlands and Norway – was one of the first countries to adopt a carbon tax. In Denmark, an impressive 25 percent of energy consumption comes from wind power. This figure is expected to reach 50 percent by 2020. Germany, while not quite gifted with the most sunlight on Earth, still generates about 44 percent of the world's production of photovoltaic power.[48] In recent years, various governments have adopted green stimulus packages, which are able to address climate change and the effects of the global financial crisis at the same time. These are forward-thinking ideas. Many countries now engage in these types of "green economic new deals": Germany, Denmark, the United Kingdom, Spain, India and China.[49] Unfortunately, many governments are also hampering progress toward a greener and healthier society by subsidizing large oil and coal industries.[21][50] Moreover, the most powerful country, the United States, continues to drag its feet and remains one of the worst polluters and stubborn over-consumers of oil and other natural resources. For sure, without its geopolitical and technological leadership there is little hope for a global transition toward a low carbon future.

Some countries in the developing world are also getting serious about the ecological transition to a green economy. Many of them – certainly not Saudi Arabia

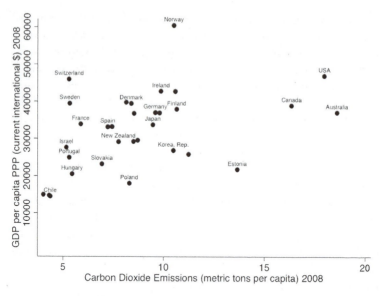

FIGURE 10.1   Wealth and green: GDP per capita and carbon dioxide emissions per capita among OECD countries, 2008

Source: World Bank's World Development Indicators database (2012).

Note: Countries with population size less than 1,000,000 people (Luxembourg and Iceland) excluded from the analysis.

or Kuwait – are on track for the advent of a de-carbonized world. Costa Rica, a nation that operates with 54 percent renewable energies, has had a carbon tax since 1997. India and China have both made important advances and large investments in renewable energies.[49] China, once defined by the *New York Times* as "a green energy superpower," is making giant strides in the fields of solar energy and wind production. Between 2005 and 2008, state-owned Chinese companies have doubled their wind power capacity, and have also built the sixth largest wind power station in the world.[51]

Not only countries, but also corporations have shifted toward eco-efficiency and renewable energies. Monte Vibiano, a farm of about 60 employees in Umbria (Italy) that is famous for its olive oil and wines, has recently become even more popular for another reason: it is the first Italian farm that achieved the target of zero greenhouse gas emissions. Its secret is simple: it heavily invested in biodiesel-fueled tractors, organic fertilizers, electric vehicles and solar panels. But there are also large companies that have joined the movement toward sustainable business. Ray Anderson's Interface Inc., one of the world's largest manufacturers of modular carpet for commercial and residential applications, has distinguished itself by significantly reducing its reliance on petroleum and its improved eco-efficiency.

While Monte Vibiano and Interface are rare examples, the number of firms committed to reducing greenhouse gas emissions is growing. There is a thorny obstacle to overcome in the revolution toward corporate sustainability, however: what to do with the automobile and fossil fuel industries? Understandably, car and oil companies will never volunteer to go out of business in order to "save the planet." For this reason, government interventions, coupled with forms of diversification and production redirection, are necessary. For the automobile sector, the obvious option is a transition toward the production of "ecologically friendly" cars. This transition is already under way. Since 2003, Toyota has been selling hybrid cars that combine gasoline engines with an electric drive. In July 2010, the total worldwide sales of hybrid electric vehicles passed three million.[52]

If the changes witnessed in some of the most future-looking countries and corporations go viral, a global green transition is possible. It could trigger a new technological revolution. According to James Martin, author of *The Meaning of the 21st Century*, the recent "breakthroughs in fuel-cell technology (fuel cells replacing petrol engines) have made a 'hydrogen economy' seem practical." In his opinion: "by the second half of the 21st Century we will reach an era of abundant energy without pollution." He continues:

> the many-decades-long effort to create fusion power will probably have paid off. Fuel cells will become inexpensive and mass-produced in great quantities. There will be widespread use of large-field solar generators and multi-megawatt wind generators, and pebble-bed energy. Third World countries may use fuel-cell motor bikes or three-wheelers on a massive scale, rather than cars.[53]

Breaking humanity's addiction to oil would be a giant leap ahead. However, new technologies, alone, are not a panacea; they are just not enough. They may help us win some battles, but without deeper and broader changes within our socioeconomic system, we will ultimately lose the war.

Saving progress from itself

The top challenge blocking our global conversion toward a greener economy is reconciling two aims that are in potential conflict with one another: poverty reduction and ecological protection. For years, neoliberal economists have insisted that the only way to reduce poverty is to promote fast economic growth through "free" trade. Neoliberals claim that in order to enlarge the wealth pie and distribute slices to the poor – most often the crumbs – countries need to liberalize trade as much as possible. Global neoliberal institutions such as the IMF, the World Bank and the WTO have preached this free trade mantra for decades. They contend that an export-led, big-business-focused, large-cities-centered model of development is the only way forward.

In *The End of Poverty*, "clinical economist" Jeffrey Sachs offers a series of prescriptions to defeat misery worldwide, based on this economic creed. Although

Sachs has recently turned himself into an environmentalist of sorts, at the time that he wrote the book, he endorsed the typical view of human "progress" embraced by neoliberal institutions. The argument goes like this: in order to end poverty and hunger, poor nations must exploit their countrysides as much as possible, by industrializing agriculture and displacing "deeply inefficient" small farmers from the most productive lands. According to this strategy of development, small peasants are left with no other choice than to move to urban slums and work in factories that specialize in export goods. Sachs contests, or at least he used to, that this is necessary because in cities the poor can enjoy "higher wages that, in turn, reflect the higher productivity of work in densely settled urban areas."[54]

Needless to say, this approach generates immense environmental costs. Export-led economic growth promotes rapid deforestation, degradation of agricultural soil, excessive pollution of rivers and lakes, urban decay and the rapid development of shantytowns. Moreover, the neoliberal policy recipe, while failing the environment, does not necessarily reduce poverty either. In fact, quite the opposite. The evidence is before our very eyes. As noted in a previous chapter, the insistent emphasis on free markets, free trade and indiscriminate export promotion has yet to deliver a world without poverty and hunger. Instead, it has "succeeded" in doubling the number of poor people in sub-Saharan Africa.[55] For sure, the forceful eviction of peasants from fertile lands to make way for export plantations,[56][57] far from putting an end to socioeconomic misery, has left the lives of many even worse off.

But there is another reason that should persuade developing countries not to emulate the "overdeveloped" world: Western culture is psychologically and spiritually unfulfilling. It distracts people from the finer things in life, such as social relationships, community contributions and creative expression. It forces individuals to focus on materialistic aspirations, conspicuous consumption, status competition and "futilitarian" values. As Emile Henry Gauvreau once explained, modern society is based on "a system that persuades us to spend money we don't have to buy things we don't need to create impressions that will not last in people that we do not care about." Indeed, it is not just the failure to defeat poverty and protect the ecosystem that makes neoliberalism a political economic model not worthy of pursuit. It is also the sense of futility and emptiness that it inevitably promotes.

An obvious question now is this: If neoliberalism does not work, then what are the alternatives?

A brand new world

Although it is doubtful that a perfect society will ever be created, there are real-world examples of nations that have succeeded more – or failed less – than others, in promoting wellbeing and a decent standard of living, while minimizing their impact on the environment. The countries that have the best combination of economic, social and ecological outcomes are the "mixed economies" of Northern Europe. Their success is easy to explain. As underlined by Peter Corning, social democracies, such as Sweden and Norway, are the closest examples of what can be defined as "fair societies."[58] Corning is right: Northern European nations are unique. By blending the benefits of market liberalism with the virtues of social egalitarianism, they have succeeded more than others in subordinating economic interests and market forces to equity and social concerns. It is their mixed model of economic development, oriented toward human and social goals, that have made them role models for the rest of the world.[59] Nevertheless, make no mistake: even Northern European countries have been affected by the advent of global neoliberalism since the beginning of the 1980s. Yet, these nations have somehow managed to preserve some of the most important elements of the mixed economic approach of the post-war period and resist the worldwide pressure toward neoliberal policies.

The developing world also offers interesting lessons and concrete examples of how to advance social and economic goals, while imposing a smaller burden on the environment. Cases in point are low-income countries and states that have achieved health standards comparable to those of wealthy nations, but with a much lower level of income:[60] Costa Rica, Kerala (India), Cuba and Sri Lanka. These countries and states have followed quite different economic development pathways. Yet, they all seem to share a similar predisposition to oppose the idea of governing society around a self-regulating market. Instead, their economies have been heavily influenced by government interventions. This is clearly the case of Sri Lanka, Cuba and Kerala, which have all undertaken developmental paths radically different from neoliberalism, and have adopted a socialist-oriented political economy. Of course, the case of Costa Rica is more complex. Free market economists often praise the Central American nation as a "neoliberal miracle." This is hardly the case. It is true that Costa Rica opened up its markets, but liberalization reforms have been implemented partially and gradually. More importantly, although Costa Rica has applied liberalization policies, at the same time it has also maintained a strong welfare state and universal access to primary healthcare.[61 62]

It is no coincidence that, like Northern European countries, Costa Rica, Kerala, Cuba and Sri Lanka have proven to be good at not only promoting social and human goals, but also environmental policies. Kerala has been described as a model of "participatory, community-based sustainable development."[63] Costa Rica and Sri Lanka have been recognized as leading developing nations in terms of renewable energies. Their greenhouse gas emissions are lower than those of other nations with a similar national income per capita.[64] Cuba also holds a relatively successful environmental record, in spite of its past neglectful policies. The island has now become a leading example of environmentally sustainable agriculture, and has made substantial efforts in both reforestation and the protection of biodiversity.

Sober egalitarianism

Former US President George W. Bush once declared that, "the American way of life is not negotiable."[65] This statement demonstrates the suicidal spirit of modern civilization. The current consumption patterns of natural resources are not sustainable. As Lester Brown long ago noticed, if the Chinese ate meat, milk and eggs in the same quantities as Americans, they would have consumed two-thirds of the world's entire grain harvest in 2004; they would have used more steel than all Western countries combined; they would have consumed 303 million tons of paper; and they would have also used 20 million more barrels of oil than the entire world currently consumes.[66] A transition toward a greener society is not only about renewable energies, eco-efficiency and higher environmental standards. It is also about a more sober consumption of natural resources. As living standards and pollution rise everywhere, the rapid depletion of oil, food and water can become a major threat for world stability. Left uncontrolled, this problem can ignite conflicts and wars that may push modern civilization back to the Dark Ages. Bluntly stated, if the American way of life is truly not negotiable, in the future there may no longer be an American way of life left to negotiate.

Curbing our voracious appetite for material wealth and profit is not just a feel-good personal choice to be made. It is a survival mandate. The good news is that while transitioning toward a soberer and greener world, modern society can also improve quality of life. By finally giving up our obsessive addiction to material consumption and infinite economic growth, the forced transition toward a green economy can become a "blessing in disguise." A soberer and greener world does not mean we will all have to become Tibetan monks. Green technologies, public transportation, eco-friendly cars, new local farming techniques, fishing and recycling regulations and a more efficient use of water can go a long way. Moreover, although some large changes in consumption patterns, travelling, eating and transportation will probably be unavoidable, this does not mean that life has to be any less fulfilling or enjoyable. Quite the opposite. A transition toward a sober pattern of consumption can actually leave society healthier and happier.

As mentioned in the first chapter, a drastic reduction in living standards does not necessarily result in worsening health conditions. There are numerous historical examples that can prove this. After the collapse of the former Soviet Union, Cuba faced a serious oil and economic crisis that severely undermined its food production system. In spite of the sudden reduction in its oil supply and the deterioration of its economy, the health of the Cuban population did not worsen. In fact, it actually improved.[67] Between 1989 and 1993, while the Cuban Gross National Income (GNI) in international $ per capita decreased by almost 20 percent – from $2,539 to $2,040 – life expectancy at birth did not decline, but steadily increased from 74.4 to 74.7 years.

How did Cuba perform such a "miracle" of healthy de-growth? As the reserves of oil shrank, the country performed a quick transition toward sustainable agriculture. Cuban farmers abandoned the use of fertilizers and pesticides, and specialized in organic farming, using bio-fertilizers and bio-pesticides. Farmers stopped growing sugar for export and started to produce food for local consumption, organizing themselves into small cooperatives or local farming communities. They raised their own food in small private firms and urban gardens. The results were impressive. According to the authors of *The Power of Community: How Cuba Survived Peak Oil*, about 80 percent of Cuban agriculture is now organically grown. As leading

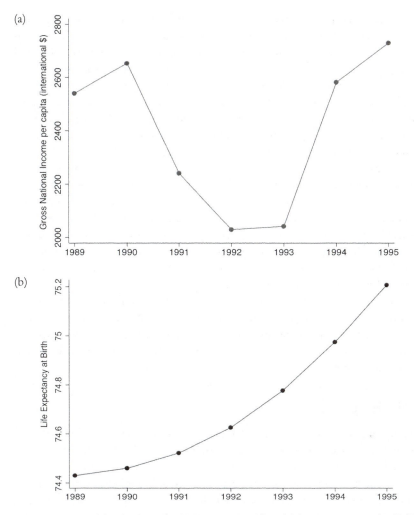

FIGURE 10.2 Healthy de-growth: GNI per capita (a) and life expectancy at birth (b) in Cuba during the Special Period, 1989–1995

environmentalist Bill McKibben writes: "Cubans have created what may be the world's largest model of a semi-sustainable agriculture, one that relies far less than the rest of the world on oil, on chemicals, on shipping vast quantities of food back and forth."[68] Even the World Bank praised the Cuban transition toward organic agriculture as an experiment that "may hold many of the keys to the future survival of civilization."[69]

There are other interesting historical cases of declining consumption and health promotion: Britain in the 1940s, for example. During the Second World War, a time of drastic reduction in food supplies, England and Wales experienced large reductions in mortality and malnutrition. Surprisingly, longevity increased faster than it had during peaceful times. This is still a puzzle that many researchers and economists have difficulty making sense of. Amartya Sen attributes this paradox to the "more effective use of public distribution systems associated with war efforts and more equal sharing of food through rationing systems."[70] Other authors emphasize the exceptional spirit of sharing and the willingness to cooperate that usually characterize social environments during war times.[71] Both hypotheses sound plausible; cohesive and cooperative social relationships do make a difference. However, policies make an even bigger difference. During the Second World War, the British government adopted egalitarian economic reforms characterized by full employment and a fairer distribution of resources. Luxury items were heavily taxed and private cars almost disappeared from the roads. Even the cultural climate was different. Unlike what happens today, media propaganda discouraged consumerism and motivated people to enjoy moderate consumption. Local authorities were active in organizing cultural activities such as dances, concerts and open-air theaters to nurture collective engagement and discourage unnecessary travel. People's attention was directed away from materialism, and toward a philosophy of life centered on solidarity, family life and enjoyment of leisure time.

These historical events are revealing. The cases of the Cuban transition during the "special period," and the metamorphosis of Britain during the Second World War, clearly show that a swift shift toward a more egalitarian and sober society is not utopia. In fact, if we are to avoid climate change, peak oil and a rapid depletion of natural resources, similar transitions are a necessity.

Modest proposals

A popular myth reiterated by free market intellectuals, states that the critics of neoliberal globalization have neither suggestions, nor solutions for the problems of the world. Of course, this is not true. For decades, countless activists, writers and development specialists have advanced new ideas and lobbied governments and international organizations for alternative policy reforms. The issue is not the lack of alternatives. The real problem is that the powerful elite does not like any of them. Most people who take part in the alternative globalization movement find that the destructive anarchy of hot money, unregulated financial markets and global wealth inequalities are incompatible with social progress, economic stability and ecological sustainability. How can we blame them for believing that? Since the late 1970s, the speculative activities of rich investors, moving massive amounts of capital very quickly across borders, together with the diffusion of offshore financing, have generated crisis after crisis, and turned the democratic process into a farce. In the opinion of the supporters of an alternative model of globalization, the worldwide financial casino must be shut down. As long as the economic system remains at the mercy of the global "financial raiders," governments will have limited capability to prevent crises, tax capital and companies, redistribute wealth, adopt a full employment regime, apply environmental regulations, enforce labor standards and raise revenues to fund social security, health and education.

Since the suggestion of the American economist James Tobin "to throw sand in the wheel of global finance" by raising transaction costs on foreign exchange,[72] there have been numerous proposals to limit speculation and capital movement across borders. Recently, a coalition of civic society organizations that are supported by UNICEF and 350 economists has re-popularized the same idea. It is now called the *Robin Hood Tax*, a package of financial transaction taxes that can be used to address multiple global problems.[73] Some authors have proposed that we use the revenues resulting from the taxation of short-term money flows to support a global fund for environmental protection, poverty reduction, health and education. In 2003, an organization called The Leading Group came up with a scheme of 10 global taxes on financial assets, transnational corporation (TNC) profits, currency transactions and Internet traffic that could be used to fund global ecological projects. The organization estimates that the revenues liberated by these multiple taxes would amount to about $1 trillion annually, nearly 20 times the allocated resources available for the achievement of the Millennium Development Goals.[74] Other authors have also suggested using potential revenues, which could accrue from the recovery of taxes unpaid by corporations and wealthy individuals in offshore centers, to fund environmental and social justice programs worldwide.

Of course, although taxes are important, they are not the panacea for all problems. As already underlined in Chapter 8, a new system of regulations at the national and global level is even more important. Anti-trust laws, stringent restrictions on capital flow, the limitation or abolition of derivatives and other risky financial instruments are urgently necessary. These ideas too are already on the table of advocates who are for an alternative globalization. New global taxes and the elimination of tax havens can be promoted together with institutional reforms aimed at re-designing the rules of the global economic system. One of them is a new set of rules and regulations similar to those designed by Keynes for the Bretton Woods system, which would include fixed (yet changeable) exchange rates, strict capital controls, full employment regimes and welfare policies. Others comprise the resurrection of the International Clearing Union that was proposed by Keynes in 1944, to correct payment and trade imbalances.[75]

Another idea proposed by the alternative globalization movement is to address the policies of the world market trinity: the IMF, World Bank and WTO. A key question confronted by the movement is this: should these institutions be abolished or merely reformed? Is the triumvirate deserving of any space in a future global economic system based on fairness and social justice? Advocates for a new world order are divided on this matter. Some prefer their outright abolition, while others call for their reconstruction and transformation. With or without the IMF, World Bank and WTO, a global system of agencies devoted to maintaining economic stability and international cooperation is clearly necessary.[76] Charles Derber, author of *Greed to Green*, proposes that we shift many of the functions of these international financial institutions to the UNCTAD, which has distinguished itself through a reasonably decent record of policy proposals and economic analyses. Other authors have called for the reinvigoration and redefinition of the Economic and Social

Council of the UN (ECOSOC), originally placed at the apex of the IMF, World Bank and GATT. Meanwhile, activists of the *International Forum on Globalization* have proposed a new agency in lieu of the IMF: the International Finance Organization. With regard to the WTO, some have suggested restructuring the organization around the same principles as the ITO. This means, for example, reconsidering the Havana Charter,[77] and advancing equitable trade policies that are no longer biased in favor of rich countries and powerful corporations. This would also include a political shift toward a new idea of free trade, to be viewed as a means to promote health and wellbeing, rather than as an aim in itself.

Another proposal of the alternative globalization movement regards the abolition of structural adjustment conditionalities, that have now mutated into the so-called *Poverty Reduction Strategy Papers*. Several non-governmental organizations have called for an end to these reforms on the grounds that they reduce national sovereignty and harm national economies. Some affirm that, if conditionalities must be attached to loans or foreign aid, the IMF and the World Bank should use them to promote a more equitable distribution of wealth, investment in health, education and the environment, instead of the interests of private investors and corporations.

It is also necessary that proposals to reform global finance, taxation, international institutions and their economic policies be complemented with measures to protect national democracies against the abuses of transnational corporate powers. As explained in the previous chapter, a wall that separates governments and big business from each other can be erected through a series of legal constraints that regulate political campaign financing, corporate lobbying, revolving doors and media owner-ship. However, this alone is not enough. Global agencies that are charged with monitoring and regulating the practices of transnational corporate powers are also necessary. Although the idea of multilateral agreements on TNCs is often considered unrealistic and unfeasible, just a few decades ago it was not. As explained in a previous chapter, in 1974 the UN established the UN Center on Transnational Corporations (UNCTC). One of its specific aims was to monitor and address the impact of TNCs on labor standards, environment practices and human rights. The agency even tried to enforce a UN Code of Conduct for TNCs. The problem was that big business did not like this kind of oversight; and it resisted. In 1993, the UNCTC was dismantled and reduced to a division of UNCTAD.[78] Global justice activists, such as Kevin Danaher and Jason Mark, authors of *Insurrection: Citizen Challenges to Corporate Power*, have advocated for a revival of the UNCTC.[79] They have very good reasons for doing so. Indeed, if there is any hope to create a fairer global economic system, a regulatory framework on transnational powers and their impact on democracy, human rights and the environment is necessary.

Glocal democracy

"Everything has been globalized except our consent," writes *Guardian* columnist and author George Monbiot, in his book *The Age of Consent*. "If you consider this distribution of power acceptable," he continues, "that is your choice, but please do not call yourself a democrat."[80] Monbiot has a point here. The global policies that are now shaping the lives of 7 billion people from London to Calcutta, from New York to Sao Paulo, from Dar es Salaam to Tokyo, have not been designed with the interests of the public in mind. They have not been developed after democratic debates, public forums and civic disputes. They were planned by a few technocrats, elected by none, who just so happened to work in Washington, DC, at some of the most powerful institutions on Earth. Numerous authors have recognized this problem of accountability. They have therefore proposed that we create new democratic decision-making processes that extend beyond the level of nation-states. This is what is often called "cosmopolitan democracy" or "globalization from below," a model of democratic governance that aims to promote political representation of all citizens in global political affairs by emphasizing participation and equality of access to information worldwide.[81–83] Clearly, it is a very ambitious idea. It is based on a model of direct democracy and direct methods for the expression of consent, such as referenda and petitioning at the regional and global levels. One of the main proponents of this model, Monbiot, even proposed the formation of new global governance institutions that include a democratically elected world parliament, an International Clearing Union, a Fair Trade Organization, and a democratized United Nations General Assembly.

Some have argued, perhaps with some merit, that these ideas are as good as they are unrealistic. Others have dismissed them on the grounds that new global agencies could create even more asymmetrical concentrations of power. To say the least, the challenges of creating a new world order on the basis of direct democracy and the rule of law are daunting. "Cosmopolitan democracy" would require impressive coordination and communication efforts worldwide. The idea would also be difficult to materialize if people are unwilling to develop a sense of cosmopolitanism and solidarity that goes beyond the borders of their own nations. However, in spite of these obstacles, the democratization of globalization is too important to be so quickly dismissed. The reason is this: most of the ecological, economic, political and social crises we face today cannot be tackled through national policies. Without some form of political authority beyond the level of nation-states, there is little hope for us to coordinate converging political actions and adequately address these crises. Global problems require global solutions. As Monbiot points out, "there is little point in devising an alternative economic policy for your nation . . . if the International Monetary Fund and the financial speculators have not first been overthrown." He continues: "issues such as climate change, international debt, nuclear proliferation, war, peace and the balance of trade between nations can be addressed only globally."[84]

For sure, the road toward global democracy would be lengthy, bumpy and twisty. However, cosmopolitan democratization would be best conceived as a process rather than a one-shot aim.[85] So, on the one hand, it is important to strive for large-scale global changes in the decision-making process. On the other hand, however, it would also be useful to adopt a piecemeal approach based on the achievement of smaller, more feasible reforms, to be accomplished one step at a time. For example, one of these policy changes toward a gradual democratization of globalization includes the reform of the structure and voting system of the international financial institutions (IFI). Currently, both the IMF and the World Bank are undemocratic. Not only because they prioritize the commercial and financial interests of rich countries and their corporations, but also because they use a voting system based on the "one dollar, one vote" rule. In both institutions, the US owns more than 16 percent of the voting share, while the entire sub-Saharan African region accounts for less than 6 percent.[76] A democratic voting system in the IFIs would not solve all problems, but it could bring more volume to the feeble voices of poor countries. Undeniably, the inequality that exists within the IFI's voting power is largely a by-product of inequality in economic power among members of the IFIs. The WTO could not make this any more visible. Unlike the IMF and the World Bank, the WTO utilizes the "one country, one vote rule." Yet, this does not prevent the WTO from holding remarkably strong biases toward the interests of the US and other powerful countries. As it is often joked: "the WTO is ruled by the one country, one vote rule, but the country is the United States."

In effect, high concentrations of political power cannot be addressed effectively without also addressing the grotesque global economic inequalities. Even if member states of international organizations are treated equally in political terms, some of them continue to be "more equal than others" – as they are able to use their economic power to disrupt the democratic process. The corruptive power that money holds over politics does not apply only at the national level, but also globally. The shadow cast by inequality over democracy affects the IFIs just as much as it does other UN institutions. This is why, for example, some development specialists have proposed a series of reforms to make UN agencies less vulnerable to financial blackmailing from rich nations and corporate powers. Suggested reforms have included new schemes to fund the UN on the basis of revenues that are derived from global taxes on currency transaction, carbon pollution, arms sales, air travel, the UN world lottery and the UN credit card.[86]

Some of the critics of globalization, however, would not invest a penny into the "financial liberation" of the UN agencies. To them, the UN is already a lost cause. In their opinion, a stronger and larger UN system would promote an even more dysfunctional centralization of decision-making power.[87] The solution, they say, is not to empower global agencies by transferring wealth at the top, but to promote "localism" or the decentralization of power. This is a fair point. In order to be effective, policy decisions need to be made at smaller political units. Without a very high degree of devolution, as well as huge coordination and communication efforts to ensure accountability at the local level, a world government would probably end up undermining, rather than promoting, democracy. Nevertheless, although the skepticism of the "localists" is understandable, the other side of the argument is that, without some global governance, local democracies are of limited effectiveness. The reason is simple. Global financial markets have proven to be a threat to national democracies. If they are powerful enough to subvert state policies, global financial markets can also overrun local interests and community-based decision-making processes. Only global regulations can limit their power. The good news is that efforts to establish global democratic institutions do not necessarily have to undermine local accountability if a high degree of devolution is ensured.[88] This can occur if local political units are deeply integrated into a coherent network of democracies at multiple levels of the governance hierarchy. In this sense, local and global democracies can become two sides of the same coin. As Charles Derber noticed: "democracy at any level depends on democracy at all levels."[89]

Overthrow capitalism?

Some writers believe that it is quite naive to hope for a fair, green and democratic society. It is the nature of capitalism, they argue, to be unfair, un-green and undemocratic.[90] According to Marxist thinkers, a capitalist system cannot be reformed, but only overthrown.[91] In *Beyond Capital*, Istvan Meszaros explained that any calls for limits to economic growth and the exploitation of natural resources are vacuous. In a society solely regulated by free market competition, the rule of capital always asserts itself in its expansionary nature.[92] Along the same lines, American economist William Baumol explains that, a "capitalist economy can usefully be viewed as a machine whose primary product is economic growth."[93] Therefore, calling for limits to growth without calling for an end to capitalism is senseless. Libertarian eco-socialist Murray Bookchin puts it even more bluntly: "capitalism can no more be 'persuaded' to limit growth than a human being can be 'persuaded' to stop breathing."[94]

Although these authors may be right, the trouble is that as of now, there are no signs of any socialist revolutions on the horizon. Capitalism has spread to nearly 90 percent of the world's population[95] and prospects for its imminent demise are, for the time being, statistically insignificant. As Fredric Jameson once put it, "it seems easier for us today to imagine the thoroughgoing deterioration of the earth and of nature than the breakdown of late capitalism."[93] Possibly. But the stubborn position of those who argue that only by overthrowing capitalism we can stop the current ecological crisis sounds just as rigid as those who argue that there is no alternative to neoliberalism. This is the reason. Within capitalist societies, there are large variations in terms of economic policies, social conditions and environmental standards. The extent to which governments promote redistributive taxation, financial regulations, renewable energies, full employment policies and welfare programs varies dramatically by country. Some societies have come a long way in regulating market forces and limiting corporate abuses, which helps to promote or maintain health, wellbeing and ecological protection. Others have done very little. There are polar differences between the political economic models of Northern European countries and the US, for example. And there are no resemblances between the environmental policies and records of Costa Rica and Saudi Arabia. Clearly, these examples show that capitalism is remarkably flexible. Therefore, a complete abolition of the market system may not only be unrealistic, but also unnecessary.

That said, the ideological divisions between those who advocate for sweeping social changes versus those who champion gradual reforms, though intellectually important, are politically futile. The reason is simple. The financial and corporate elites that rule the world oppose even the mildest of reforms.[25] Revolutionaries and reformists, if they harbor any hope of success, must move beyond the "narcissism of small differences" and identify common areas of political struggle. They have little option but to join forces and resist "globalization from above" through global civic resistance "from below."[96][97] This sounds futuristic, but a mass social movement aimed at democratizing globalization and decoupling it from neoliberalism is already under way.[98]

The critical "mess"

Since the late 1990s, collaborative acts of civil protest against globalization and neoliberalism have multiplied around the world.[99–101] The global justice or solidarity movement first materialized at the "battle of Seattle," during the 1999 meeting of the WTO. Throughout the years, it has developed and matured into a vast global network of organizations and activists that some have defined as "the movement of the movements."[102][103] Members of the network meet every two years at the World Social Forum to discuss ideas and proposals for peace, justice and ecological sustainability. The forum, sometimes called "world parliament in exile," was born in opposition to the World Economic Forum, the annual meeting of the financial elites in Davos. Although it experienced a temporary decline at the beginning of the twenty-first century, especially after the 9/11 attacks, the movement has been slowly regaining momentum. In 2011, three years after the outbreak of the Great Recession, the movement reincarnated into Occupy Wall Street, which has now spread to more than 80 countries. The movement comprises thousands of decentralized, fragmented, multi-head sub-movements and networks of activists, trade unionists, public intellectuals, community organizers, indigenous populations, religious groups, artists, writers, students, diplomats, and academics. Although it was inspired by diverse philosophies and charismatic figures such as Noam Chomsky and Susan George, the movement does not respond to any leader, hierarchy, ideology or doctrine. It is loosely organized, with no central or formal structure. It is still something of a mess.

Of course, free market apologists have depicted the global solidarity movement as violent, radical and anachronistic. Jagdish Bhagwati, a devotee of neoliberalism, has dismissed the movement as mindless anti-capitalists, hard-core protesters, "whose fears and follies" merely reflect their deep-seated antipathy against globalization.[104] Thomas Friedman defined the demonstrators as "a Noah's ark of flat-earth advocates, protectionist trade unions and yuppies looking for their 1960 fix."[105] When covering the movement, mainstream media outlets tend to focus on the violent acts of some demonstrators, rather than covering the issues that the movement is attempting to raise. Mainstream media also tend to ignore police brutalities and security services' collusions with infiltrated violent groups, such as the Black Block.[106] This is an unfair depiction, of course. In reality, the global solidarity movement is predominantly peaceful and its aims largely reflect ideas proposed by moderate economists and intellectuals. One of the slogans of the movement, "people before profit," for example, merely reiterates ideas already proposed by renowned economists such as John Maynard Keynes, John Kenneth Galbraith and John Stuart Mill. The three Johns believed that profit and money need not be the goals of human development, but just their means. The movement's aims are also in line with the ideas of Nobel-laureates in economics such as Joseph Stiglitz and Paul Krugman, who both support a mixed approach in political economy. Far from advocating radical social change, the World Social Forum Manifesto is a call "against the concentration of wealth, the proliferation of poverty and inequalities, and the destruction of our earth." It is also an indictment against "the hegemony of finance, the destruction of our cultures, the monopolization of knowledge, mass media, and communications, the degradation of nature, and the destruction of the quality of life by multinational corporations and antidemocratic policies."[107] In her book entitled *Another World Is Possible If . . .,* Susan George explains that the global justice movement is not advocating for a red revolution or a violent overthrowing of capitalism. As she observes: "most of what the global justice movement is proposing amounts to a universal European model based on taxation, redistribution, and democratic participation like the one developed in Western Europe from the 1930s onwards, particularly during the post-war period."[108]

Although free market advocates and corporate media never miss an opportunity to dismiss the movement as foolish "anti-globalizers,"[109] most of its members are deeply internationalist, both in their spirit and in the way they look at the world. The movement is not opposed to globalization, but rather to the social injustices, wealth inequalities and ecological abuses of global neoliberalism. As George Monbiot puts it, "globalization is not the problem. Our task is surely not to overthrow globalization, but to capture it and to use it as a vehicle for humanity's first global democratic revolution."[110]

The limits of the impossible

As the entire world now struggles with the consequences of the Great Recession, social unrest is becoming a common concern. In the last years, there has been a proliferation of new revolutionary movements worldwide. From Tahrir Square in Cairo to the streets of Athens, from Zuccotti Park in New York to the roads of Santiago in Chile, from Porta del Sol Square in Madrid to the neighborhoods surrounding the Iceland Parliament in Reykjavik, since 2008 the world has been in tumult. The multiple emergencies caused by the financial breakdown have united distant activists and organizations against a common "enemy": market greed. Although mainstream media dismiss Occupy Wall Street as mindless protesters with no aims and no alternatives, the aims and the alternatives of the movement could not be any clearer. Redistributive taxation, full employment, a revival of the *Glass–Steagall Act*, reforms of political elections financing, revocation of corporate personhood and a global tax on foreign transactions. The global justice movement also has a very clear target. Unlike the global campaigns of the 1990s aimed at policy changes in the IMF, World Bank and WTO, the outrage of Occupy Wall Street is directed at the ultimate planners of the global neoliberal project: the "top 1 percent."

Not literally, of course. Some in the top 1 percent have even joined the Occupy Wall Street movement to protest "against themselves." Rare cases aside, however, there are very good reasons why the movement holds the very wealthy responsible for the economic, social and environmental crises that we are experiencing today. In the last decades, the "super-class" has spearheaded a very regressive political movement that has changed the world for the worse. It has contributed to the escalation of environmental pollution and the destruction of the ecosystem. It has resisted and suppressed meaningful international agreements on climate change and renewable energies. It has promoted the diffusion of mindless consumerism and the rapid depletion of natural resources. It has led a crusade against full employment, the right to organize, social security and universal healthcare. It has pushed for draconian policies in the developing world that undermine efforts to reduce poverty and hunger. The "super-class" has also helped with the dismantling of public education and the transformation of media outlets into corporate propaganda apparatuses that are filled with disinformation, deceptive advertisement and idiotic entertainment. The top 1 percent has opposed reforms that are aimed at economic redistribution, and have exploited every possible opportunity to promote policies that widen the wealth gap between them and the rest of society. They have also turned the world economy into a global financial casino, by drowning it in toxic financial assets and risky bets that ultimately caused the Great Recession. Now, after having been rescued by massive government bailouts, and having virtually transformed national sovereignty into an illusion, the top 1 percent is pressing governments to adopt austerity programs that force taxpayers to foot the bill caused by their fraudulent practices.

It is little wonder that the top 1 percent has become the number one target of the Occupy Wall Street movement. Far from being purposeless nihilists, the global justice movement represents, in the words of Paul Hawken, "humanity's immune response"[111] against the neoliberal attack to our health, quality of life and the environment. The obvious question is whether the movement will be able to stop the top 1 percent from spinning the world out of control toward self-destruction. Whether it will be able to dethrone the super-class and redirect the wheels of history toward a new path of progress. The future of modern society and the fate of the human species may depend on this. As Noam Chomsky once observed:

> modern industrial civilization has developed within a certain system of convenient myths. The driving force of modern industrial civilization has been individual material gain, which is accepted as legitimate, even praiseworthy, on the grounds that private vices yield public benefits.

> Now, it has long been understood, very well, that a society that is based on this principle will destroy itself in time . . . at this stage of history, either the general population will take control of its own destiny and concern itself with

community interests guided by values of solidarity and sympathy and concerns for others, or alternatively there will be no destiny for anyone to control.[112]

It is unclear whether global civic society will succeed in turning human progress in a new direction. Looking at the world as it is, without the consolation of any illusory shortcuts, prospects for a swift paradigm shift away from the market greed doctrine appear slim. After all, the Occupy Wall Street movement, and all who try to shake the hearts and minds of humanity, represents a tiny minority of the Earth's citizens. The movement has no power, money or authority. It is only equipped with a willingness to change the world. This may not sound like much, but it is something that has the potential to come to our rescue. Virtually all social changes in history have occurred because of a small group of courageous, visionary dissidents who challenged conventional wisdom and organized systematic forms of civic resistance. Movers and shakers have often been ignored first, then vilified, and then finally praised. As Russell once put it, "progress comes through the gradual effect of a minority in converting opinion and altering custom."[113] Changes introduced by a few dissidents can snowball to the rest of society, expand the horizon of acceptable practices and transform acquired knowledge. According to Saul Alinsky, the world only needs 2 percent of committed people to move, inform and inspire the larger population toward social change. Maybe this is an exaggeration. But a group of scientists at the Rensselaer Polytechnic Institute found that when 10 percent of the population holds an unshakable conviction, their beliefs are ultimately adopted by most members of the society.[114] So, Alinsky was right, just a bit imprecise.

Nobody knows whether a critical mass of conscious citizens can reach a turning point before the world passes the point of no return. What we do know is that human progress has often been shaped by abrupt, unpredictable events. Historical shifts have usually been characterized by tipping points, threshold effects and small changes that end up generating large-scale social transformations.[25] Many historical breakthroughs, that we take for granted today, appeared unimaginable at first, before being accepted as part of conventional wisdom. In 1787, when a few activists began to meet in London to organize a movement for the abolition of the slave trade, almost no one took them seriously. Just 60 years later, slavery was abolished in England. When Gandhi exhorted Indian people to liberate themselves from the oppression of the British Empire, only a few believed that they had any chance in succeeding. Years later, India broke free and kicked the British out of the country. When Rosa Parks refused to leave the front seat of a bus in Alabama and unwillingly started a campaign against racial inequities in America, many thought her insane. Just a few years later, the US government approved a civil rights bill that sanctioned, at least in principle, equality between black and white. When Nelson Mandela, in the early years of his revolutionary activities, engaged in a lifetime fight against racial apartheid, it looked like he had embarked on an impossible mission. Decades later, apartheid was abolished and he became the first democratically elected president of South Africa. These historical occurrences may sound like exceptions, but they are the rule. As anthropologist and activist Margaret Mead once argued, we should "never doubt that a small group of thoughtful, committed citizens can change the world. Indeed, it is the only thing that ever has."[115]

Although the net impression is that we are driving blindfolded at high speed toward disaster, it is still up to us to decide where we go. There is still a window of hope left ajar. Crises are like crossroads: they can take us in one direction or in another. In the past, they have either triggered a recrudescence of totalitarianism or promoted radical shifts in human emancipation. In the future, nobody knows. What we do know is that, more than ever, true progress depends on our deliberate attempt to embrace a new model of economic development, based on values of cooperation, solidarity, empathy and creativity. Contemplating society in light of nobler ideals than markets and greed can no longer be dismissed as radical or utopian. In fact, the ideal of sisterhood and brotherhood of humankind has never been so pragmatic.[116] The challenges are now unprecedented, but so are our capacities to overcome boundaries. As British author and futurist Arthur Clarke once observed: "the only way of discovering the limits of the possible is to venture a little way past them into the impossible."[117] History has made it clear that these limits are not fixed. They can change, adapt and accommodate. They can also be trespassed. If what seemed impossible in the past has now become possible, why should we assume that what seems impossible today will not become possible in the future? In fact, we should not.

NOTES

Prologue

1. Clausius R. On the application of the theorem of the equivalence of transformations to interior work. *Philosophical Magazine* 1862;xxiv(4):81–201.
2. Frost R. Fire and ice. *Harper's Magazine* December 1920.
3. Klein M. Thermodynamics in Einstein's universe. *Science* 1967;157:50.
4. Georgescu-Roegen N. *The Entropy Law and the Economic Process*. Cambridge, MA: Harvard University Press, 1971.
5. Wright R. *A Short History of Progress*. Cambridge, MA: Da Capo Press 2004:29.
6. Palast G. *The Best Democracy Money Can Buy: The Truth About Corporate Cons, Globalization and High-Finance Fraudsters*. New York: Plume, 2003.

Chapter 1: A turning point or a point of no return?

1. Robinson A, Robinson Z. Science has spoken: Global warming is a myth. *Wall Street Journal* December 4, 1997.
2. BBC. Climate havoc cost $60 billion. BBC News December 11, 2003.
3. Huffington Post. Rick Santorum: I've never believed in the "hoax of global warming." *Huffington Post* February 7, 2012.
4. Hoggan J. *Climate Cover-Up: the Crusade to Deny Global Warming*, 1st ed. Vancouver: Greystone Books, 2009.
5. Boykoff M, Boykoff J. Balance as bias: Global warming and the US prestige press. *Global Environmental Change* 2004;14:125–36.
6. Biello D. Climate change cover-up? You better believe it. *Scientific American* November 24, 2009.
7. Monbiot G. *Heat: How to Stop the Planet from Burning*. London: Penguin, 2006.
8. Webster P, Holland G, Curry J, Chang H. Changes in tropical cyclone number, duration and intensity in a warming environment. *Science* 2005;309(5742):1844–6.
9. Emmanuel K. Increasing destructiveness of tropical cyclones over the past 30 years. *Nature* 2005;436:686–8.

10. Cromie W. El Niño found to be 124,000 years old. *Harvard Gazette Archives* August 19, 1999.
11. Pearce F. *The Last Generation: How Nature Will Take Her Revenge for Climate Change.* London: Eden Projects Books, 2006.
12. Bhattacharya S. European heatwave caused 35,000 deaths. *New Scientist* October 10, 2003.
13. Berbardes J. First South Atlantic hurricane hits Brazil. *USA Today* March 29, 2004.
14. Mann M, Bradley R, Hughes M. Northern Hemisphere temperatures during the past millennium: Inferences, uncertainties, and limitations. *Geophysical Research Letters* 1999;26(6):759–62.
15. McIntyre S, McKitrick. R. The M&M Project: Replication Analysis of the Mann et al. Hockey Stick. Toronto, 2005.
16. Brumfiel G. Academy affirms hockey-stick graph. *Nature* 2006;441:1032–3.
17. Vidal J. Last month was the hottest June recorded worldwide, figures show. *The Guardian* July 16, 2010.
18. Stott P, Stone D, Allen M. Human contribution to the European heatwave of 2003. *Nature* 2004;432:610–14.
19. IPCC. *Climate Change 2007: The Physical Science Basis – Summary for Policymakers.* Geneva: Intergovernmental Panel on Climate Change, 2007.
20. McGuire B. *Seven Years to Save the Planet: The Questions . . . and Answers.* London: Weidenfeld & Nicolson, 2008.
21. Foukal P, Fröhlich C, Spruit H, Wigley T. Variations in solar luminosity and their effect on the Earth's climate. *Nature* 2006;443:161–66, 161.
22. Oreskes N. The scientific consensus on climate change. *Science* 2004;306:1686.
23. Weart S. *The Discovery of Global Warming.* Boston, MA: Harvard University Press, 2006.
24. Tyndall Center for Climate Change Research. Who was John Tyndall. Online, 2007.
25. Arrhenius S. Ueber den Einfluss des Atmosphärischen Kohlensäurengehalts auf die Temperatur der Erdoberfläche. *Proceedings of the Royal Swedish Academy of Science, Stockholm* 1896;22(1):1–101.
26. Maslin M. *Global Warming: A Very Short Introduction.* Oxford: Oxford University Press, 2004.
27. Guardian. The father of climate change. *The Guardian* June 30, 2005.
28. Keeling C, Pales J. Mauna Loa Carbon Dioxide Project, Report No. 3, 1965:183.
29. Siegenthaler U, Stocker T, Monnin E, Lüthi D, Schwander J, Masson-Delmotte V, et al. Stable carbon cycle-climate relationship during the late pleistocene. *Science* 2005;310:1313–17.
30. Brook E. Palaeoclimate: Windows on the greenhouse. *Nature* 2008;453:291–2.
31. Crutzen P. Geology of mankind. *Nature* 2002;415(6867):23.
32. Committee on the Science of Climate Change National Research Council. *Climate Change Science: An Analysis of Some Key Questions.* Washington, DC: National Academy Press, 2001.
33. American Meteorological Society Council. Climate change research: Issues for the atmospheric and related sciences. *Bulletin of the American Meteorological Society* 2003;84:508–15.
34. American Geophysical Union Council. AGU position statement on human impacts on climate. *Eos.* Washington, DC: American Geophysical Union, 2003:574.
35. American Association for the Advancement of Science. AAAS Atlas of Population and Environment: Climate Change: American Association for the Advancement of Science, 2000.

36. American Quaternary Association. Petroleum geologists' award to novelist Crichton is inappropriate. *Eos* 2006;87:364.
37. Hare B. Relationship between increases in global mean temperature and impacts of ecosystems, food production, water and socio-economic systems. In: Schellnhuber H, Cramer W, Nakicenovic N, Wigley T, Yohe G, Pachauri R, et al., editors. *Avoiding Dangerous Climate Change*. Cambridge: Cambridge University Press, 2006.
38. Grassl H. Climate protection strategies for the 21st century: Kyoto and beyond. *WBGU Special Report*. Berlin: WBGU German Advisory Council on Global Change, 2003:11.
39. Forrest C. The Cutting Edge: Climate Science to April 2005: Global and UK Emissions Reductions Targets for 2030, 2005.
40. Hansen J. A slippery slope: How much global warming constitutes "dangerous anthropogenic interference"? *Climatic Change* 2005;68:269–79.
41. Doran P, Kendall-Zimmerman M. Examining the scientific consensus on climate change. *Eos* 2009;90(3):22.
42. Stainforth D, Aima T, Christensen C, Collins M, Faull N, Frame D, et al. Uncertainty in predictions of the climate response to rising levels of greenhouse gases. *Nature* 2005;433:403–6.
43. The Royal Society. A Guide to Facts and Fictions about Climate Change, 2005.
44. Appell D. Behind the hockey stick. *Scientific American*. February 21, 2005:34–5.
45. McFarling UL. Scientists now fear "abrupt" global warming changes. *Los Angeles Times* December 12, 2001.
46. Steffen W. The Anthropocene, global change and sleeping giants: Where on Earth are we going? *Carbon Balance and Management* 2006;1(1):3.
47. Connor S. Global warming "past the point of no return." *The Independent* September 16, 2005.
48. Overpeck J, Sturm M, Francis J, Perovich D, Serreze M, Benner R, et al. Arctic system on trajectory to new, seasonally ice-free state. *Eos*, 2005;86:309, 312–13.
49. Rapley C. West Antarctic Ice Sheet: Waking the Sleeping Giant? American Association for the Advancement of Science, 2006.
50. Metereological Office. International Symposium on the Stabilisation of Greenhouse Gases: The Tables of the Impacts. Exeter: Hadley Centre, 2005.
51. Calvin WH. Ship locally, crash globally. In: Calvin WH, editor. *Global Fever: How To Treat Climate Change*. Chicago: University of Chicago Press, 2008:120.
52. World Glacier Monitoring Service. Glacier Mass Balance Data, 2004. Zurich: United Nations Environment Programme, 2006.
53. IPCC. Summary for Policymakers to Climate Change 2001: Synthesis Report of the IPCC Third Assessment Report. Geneva: IPCC, 2001.
54. Patz J, Campbell-Lendrum D, Holloway T, Foley J. Impact of regional climate change on human health. *Nature* 2005;438:310–17.
55. Pearce F. Cities may be abandoned as salt water invades. *New Scientist* April 16, 2005.
56. Hansen J. Climate change and trace gases. *Philosophical Transactions of the Royal Society* 2007;365:1925–54.
57. Alley RB. Fast forward. In: Alley RB, editor. *The Two-Mile Time Machine: Ice Cores, Abrupt Climate Change, and Our Future*. Princeton, NJ: Princeton University Press, 2000:15.
58. Bryden H, Longworth H, Cunningham S. Slowing of the Atlantic meridional overturning circulation at 25° N. *Nature* 2005;438:655–7.
59. Willis J. Can in situ floats and satellite altimeters detect long-term changes in Atlantic Ocean overturning? *Geophysical Research Letters* 2010;37:L06602.

60. Cowling S, Betts R, Cox P, Ettwein V, Jones C, Maslin M, et al. Contrasting simulated past and future responses of the Amazonian forest to atmospheric change. *Philosophical Transactions of the Royal Society* 2004;359(1443):539–47.

61. Pearce F. *The Last Generation: How Nature Will Take Her Revenge for Climate Change.* London: Eden Projects Books, 2006:113–16.

62. Cox P, Hungtinford C, Jones C. Conditions for sink-to-source transitions and runaway feedbacks from the land carbon cycle. In: Schellnhuber H, Cramer W, Nakicenovic N, Wigley T, Yohe G, Pachauri R, et al., editors. *Avoiding Dangerous Climate Change.* Cambridge: Cambridge University Press, 2006.

63. Millenium Ecosystem Assessment. Ecosystems and Human Well-Being: Synthesis. Washington DC: Island Press, 2005:31–2.

64. FAO. Global Forest Resources Assessment 2005: Progress Towards Sustainable Forest Management. Rome: Food and Agriculture Organisation of the United Nations, 2006.

65. Jones C, Cox P, Essery R, Roberts D, Woodage W. Strong carbon cycle feedbacks in a climate model with interactive CO_2 and sulphate aerosols. *Geophysical Research Letters* 2003;30:1479.

66. Cowling SA, Betts RA, Cox PM, Ettwein VJ, Jones CD, Maslin MA, et al. Contrasting simulated past and future responses of the Amazonian forest to atmospheric change. *Philosophical Transactions of the Royal Society* 2004;359:539.

67. Lean G, Pearce F. Amazon rainforest "could become a desert." *The Independent* Sunday, 23 July 2006.

68. Lean G for Atmospheric Research. Most of the Arctic's Near-Surface Permafrost May Thaw by 2100, 2005.

69. Pearce F. Climate warning as Siberia melts. *New Scientist* August 11, 2005.

70. Cited by the House of Lords Select Commitee on Economic Affairs on 6 July. *The Economics of Climate Change.* London: Stationery Office, 2005:24.

71. Pearce F. *The Last Generation: How Nature Will Take Her Revenge for Climate Change.* London: Eden Projects Books, 2006:135.

72. Boyle S, Ardill J. *The Greehouse Effect: A Practical Guide to Our Changing Climate.* Sevenoaks: New English Library, Hodder & Stoughton, 1989:298.

73. Meadows D, Meadows D, Randers J. *The Limits to Growth.* New York: University Books, 1972.

74. Meadows D, Meadows D, Randers J, Behrens W. *Limits To Growth: The 30-Year Update.* White River Junction, VT: Chelsea Green Publishing, 2004:204.

75. Williams L, Wilson C. *The Energy Non-Crisis.* Green Forest, AK: Master Books, 1980.

76. Campbell C. *The Coming Oil Crisis.* Essex, UK: Multi-Science Publishing, 2004.

77. Heinenberg R. *The Party's Over: Oil, War and the Fate of Industrial Societies.* Gabriola Island, BC: New Society Publishers, 2003.

78. Leggett J. *Half Gone: Oil, Gas, Hot Air and the Global Energy Crisis.* London: Portobello Books, 2005.

79. Harper F. Oil peak – a geologist's view. Presentation given at *Oil Depletion – No Problem, Concern or Crisis?* London: Energy Institute, November 10, 2004.

80. Rubin J. *Why Your World Is About To Get A Whole Lot Smaller.* London: Virgin Books, 2010:52.

81. Monbiot G. When will the oil run out? *The Guardian* December 15, 2008.

82. Skrebowski C. Joining the dots. Presentation given at *Oil Depletion – No Problem, Concern or Crisis?* London: Energy Institute, November 10, 2004.

83. Campbell C. The essence of oil and gas depletion. Multi-science: PowerPoint presentation in CD accompanying the summary booklet CJ Campbell, "The truth about oil and looming world energy crisis," 2003. Available from www.info@eagleoffice.net.

84. Leggett J. *Half Gone: Oil, Gas, Hot Air and the Global Energy Crisis*. London: Portobello Books, 2005:88.

85. Straham D. *The Last Oil Shock: A Survival Guide to the Imminent Extinction of Petroleum Man*. London: John Murray Books, 2007.

86. Todaro M. *Economic Development*. London: Longman, 1994.

87. Brown L, Flavin C, French H. Feeding nine billion. In: Starke L, editor. *State of the World 1999: A Worldwatch Institute Report on Progress Toward a Sustainable Society*. New York: WW Norton 1999:118.

88. Brown L. *State of the World*. New York: WW Norton, 1996.

89. Meadows D, Randers J, Meadows D. *Limits to Growth: The 30-Year Update*. London: Earthscan, 2004:xxi.

90. Peng S. Rice yields decline with higher night temperature from global warming. *Proceedings of the National Academy of Sciences* 2001;101:9971–5.

91. Fischer G, Shah M, Velthzuinen Hv. Global Agro-ecological Assessment for Agriculture in the 21st Century: International Institute for Applied Systems Analysis and the Food and Agriculture Organization, 2001.

92. Gossop J, Wilcox L. *Famine in the West (Peak Food)*. Goole, UK: Peak Food, 2007.

93. Clover C. *The End of The Line: How Overfishing Is Changing the World And What We Eat*. London: Ebury Press, 2004.

94. Myers R, Worm B. Rapid world-wide depletion of predatory fish communities. *Nature* 2003;423:280–3.

95. Worm B, Barbier E, Beaumont N, Duffy J, Folke C, Halpern B, et al. Impacts of biodiversity loss on ocean ecosystem service. *Science* 2006;314(5800):787–90.

96. Dean C. Report warns of "global collapse" of fishing. *New York Times* November 2, 2006.

97. Gleick P. *The World's Water 1988–99*. Washington, DC: Island Press, 1999.

98. Bozzo S, Barlow M, Clarke T. *Blue Gold: World Water Wars*. USA: PBS, 2008:89 min.

99. World Water Assessment Programme. *The United Nations World Water Development Report 3: Water In A Changing World*. London: United Nations World Water Assessment Programme, 2009:318.

100. UN Comprehensive Assessment of the Freshwater Resources of the World. CSD, 1997.

101. Parry M, Arnell N, McMichael T, Nicholls R, Martens P, Kovats S, et al. Millions at risk: Defining critical climate change threats and targets. *Global Environmental Change* 2001;11:181–3.

102. Dugger C. Need for water could double in fifty years, UN Study Finds. *New York Times* August 22, 2006.

103. May R. How many species inhabit the Earth? *Scientific American* October 1992;267:18–24.

104. WWF. *Living Planet Report, 2002*. Loh J, editor. Gland, Switzerland: World Wide Fund for Nature, 2002.

105. Radford T. Scientist warns of sixth great extinction of wildlife. *The Guardian* November 29, 2001.

106. Species Survival Commission. *2000 IUCN Red List of Threatened Species*. Gland, Switzerland: International Union for the Conservation of Nature, 2000.

107. Thomas C, Cameron A, Green R, Bakkenes M, Beaumont L, Collingham Y, et al. Extinction risk from climate change. *Nature* 2004;427:145–8.

108. The Royal Society. *Ocean Acidification Due to Increasing Atmospheric Carbon Dioxide*. Policy Document 12/05 (June 2005). London: The Royal Society, 2005.

109. Benton M. *When Life Nearly Died: The Greatest Mass Extinction of All Time.* London: Thames and Hudson, 2003.

110. Hodgson M. Environmental failures "put humanity at risk." *The Guardian* October 26, 2007.

111. Union of Concerned Scientists. *World's Scientists Warning to Humanity.* Cambridge, MA: Union of Concerned Scientists, 1992.

112. Norberg J. *In Defense of Global Capitalism.* Washington, DC: Cato Institute, 2001:225–6.

113. *The Economist. Globalisation: Making Sense of an Integrating World.* London: St Edmundsbury Press, 2001:9.

114. Grossman G, Krueger A. *Economic Growth and the Environment.* NBER Working Paper N. 4634. Cambridge, MA: National Bureau of Economic Research, 1994.

115. Friedman B. *The Moral Consequences of Economic Growth.* New York: Knopf, 2005.

116. McKibben B. *Deep Economy: The Wealth of Communities and the Durable Future.* New York: Times Books, 2007.

117. US Bureau of Census. *Historical Estimates of World Population.* Washington, DC: US Department of Commerce, 2009.

118. US Bureau of Census. *World Population Summary.* Washington, DC: US Department of Commerce, 2009.

119. Stepphen W, Sanderson A, Tyson P, Jager J, Matson P, III BM, et al. *Global Change and the Earth System: A Planet Under Pressure.* Berlin, Heidelberg, New York: Springer, 2005.

120. Hardin G. *Stalking the Wild Taboo.* Los Altos, CA: Kaufmann, 1973.

121. Hardin G. The tragedy of the commons. *Science* 1968;162(3859):1243–8.

122. Speth JG. *The Bridge at The Edge of the World: Capitalism, the Environment, and Crossing from Crisis to Sustainability.* New Haven, CT: Yale University Press, 2008.

123. Schumacher E. *Small is Beautiful: A Study of Economics As If People Mattered.* London: Vintage, 1973.

124. Kunstler JH. *The Long Emergency: Surviving the Converging Catastrophes of the 21st Century.* London: Atlantic Books, 2005:20.

Chapter 2: The growth delusions

1. Riley J. *Rising Life Expectancy: A Global History.* New York: Cambridge University Press, 2001.

2. Lomborg B. *The Skeptical Environmentalist: Measuring the Real State of the World.* Cambridge: Cambridge University Press, 2001:540.

3. George S. *Another World Is Possible If . . .* London: Verso, 2004:6.

4. Chomsky N. What is globalization? *Politics in Action Series.* Online, 2000.

5. Black R, Morris S, Bryce J. Where and why are 10 million children dying each year? *Lancet* 2003;361(9376):2226–34.

6. WHO. *The World Health Report 2002 – Reducing Risks, Promoting Healthy Life.* Geneva: World Health Organization, 2002.

7. World Bank. *World Development Indicators, 2012.* Washington, DC: World Bank, 2012.

8. McCord C, Freeman H. Excess mortality in Harlem. *New England Journal of Medicine* 1990;322(3):173–7.

9. Australian Bureau of Statistics. *Experimental Life Tables for Aboriginal and Torres Strait Islander Australians, 2005–2007.* Canberra: Australian Bureau of Statistics, 2009.

10. Cooke M, Mitrou F, Lawrence D, Guimond E, Beavon D. Indigenous well-being in four countries: An application of the UNDP'S Human Development Index to Indigenous Peoples in Australia, Canada, New Zealand, and the United States. *BMC International Health and Human Rights* 2007;7(9). Online.
11. Scitovsky T. *The Joyless Economy: The Psychology of Human Satisfaction and Consumer Dissatisfaction.* New York: Oxford University Press, 1977.
12. Diener E, Biswas-Diener R. Will money increase subjective well-being? *Social Indicators Research* 2002;57(2):119–69.
13. Blanchflower D, Oswald A. Well Being Over Time in Britain and USA. Mimeo, Warwick University, 1999.
14. Diener E. Subjective well-being. *Psychological Bulletin* 1984;95:542–75.
15. Frey B, Stuzter A. *Happiness and Economics: How the Economy and Institutions Affect Human Well-Being.* Princeton, NJ: Princeton University Press, 2002.
16. Graham C, Pettinato S. *Happiness and Hardship: Opportunity and Insecurity in New Market Economies.* Washington, DC: Brookings Institution Press, 2002.
17. Cummins R. Personal income and subjective well-being: A review. *Journal of Happiness Studies* 2000;1(2):133–58.
18. Easterlin R. Income and happiness: Towards a unified theory. *The Economic Journal* 2001;111(473):465–84.
19. Myers D. The funds, friends and faith of happy people. *American Psychologist* 2000;55(1):56–67.
20. Easterlin R. Will raising the incomes of all increase the happiness of all? *Journal of Economic Behavior and Organization* 1995;27(1):35–47.
21. Diener E, Oishi S. Money and happiness: Income and subjective wellbeing across nations. In: Diener E, Suh E, editors. *Subjective Wellbeing Across Cultures.* Cambridge, MA: MIT Press, 2000.
22. Wilkinson R. Health, redistribution and growth. In: Glyn A, Miliband D, editors. *Paying for Inequality: The Economic Cost of Social Injustice.* London: Rivers Oram Press, 1994.
23. Easterlin R. Does economic growth improve the human lot? In: Abramovitz M, David P, Reder M, editors. *Nations and Households in Economic Growth: Essays in Honor of Moses Abramovitz.* New York: Academic Press, 1974.
24. Ahuvia A, Friedman D. Income, consumption, and subjective well-being: Toward a composite macromarketing model. *Journal of Macromarketing* 1998;18(2):153–68.
25. Veenhoven R. Is happiness relative? *Social Indicators Research* 1991;24:1–34.
26. Wilkinson R. *Unhealthy Societies: The Affliction of Inequalities.* London: Routledge, 1996.
27. Diener E, Oishi S. Money and happiness: income and subjective well-being across nations. In: Diener E, Suh E, editors. *Culture and Subjective Wellbeing.* Cambridge, MA: MIT Press, 2000.
28. Myers D, Diener E. The pursuit of happiness. *Scientific American.* May, 1996:54–6.
29. Lane R. *The Loss of Happiness in Market Democracies.* New Haven, CT: Yale University Press, 2000.
30. Clark A. Born to be mild: Cohort effects in subjective well-being. Working Paper N 2006 – 35. JEL: C23, I3, J11. Paris: Paris-Jourdan Sciences Economiques, 2006.
31. Easton M. Britain's happiness in decline. BBC News May 2, 2006.
32. Pusey M. The Impact of Restructuring on Quality of Life in Middle Australia. First Annual Meeting of the International Society of Quality of Life Studies. Charlotte NC, 1997.
33. D'Andrea SS. Italian quality of life. *Social Indicators Research* 1998;44(1):5–39.
34. Krass P. *Carnegie.* Hoboken, NJ: John Wiley & Sons, 2002:98.

35. Inglehart R, Foa R, Peterson C, Welzel C. Development, freedom and rising happiness: A global perspective (1981–2007). *Perspectives on Psychological Science* 2008;3(4):264–85.
36. Spencer-Rodgers J, Peng K, Wang L, Hou Y. Dialectial self-esteem and East–West differences in psychological well-being. *Personality and Social Psychology Bulletin* 2004;30(11):1416–32.
37. Lee Y, Seligman M. Are Americans more optimistic than the Chinese? *Personality and Social Psychology Bulletin* 1997;23(1):32–40.
38. Demyttenaere K, et al. Prevalence, severity and unmet need for treatment of mental disorders in the World Health Organization World Mental Health Surveys. *JAMA* 2004;291:2581–90.
39. James O. *Affluenza: How To Be Successful and Stay Sane*. London: Vermilion, 1997.
40. Meyers L. Deceiving others or deceiving themselves? *The Psychologist* 2000;13(8):400–3.
41. Freud S. *Civilization and Its Discontents*. New York: Cape & Smith, 1949:123.
42. Murray C, Lopez A. The global burden of disease: A comprehensive assessment of mortality and disability from diseases, injuries and risk factors in 1990 and projected to 2020. Global Burden of Disease and Injury Series: Harvard School of Public Health, 1996.
43. Fromm E. *The Sane Society*. London: Macmillan, 1955/1990:201.
44. Layard R. *Happiness: Lessons from a New Science*. London: Penguin, 2005.
45. Hagnell O, Lanke J, Rorsman B, Ojesjö L. Are we entering an age of melancholy? Depressive illnesses in a prospective epidemiological study over 25 years: the Lundby Study, Sweden. *Psychological Medicine* 1982;12(2):279–89.
46. Cross-National Collaborative Group. The changing rate of major depression: cross-national comparisons. *JAMA* 1992;268(1):3098–105.
47. Diener E, Seligman M. Beyond money: Towards an economy of well-being. *Psychological Science in the Public Interest* 2004;5(1):1–31.
48. Department of Health and Human Services. *Mental Health, A Report of the Surgeon General*. Rockville, MD: Department of Health and Human Services, 1999.
49. Klerman G, Weissmann M. Increasing rates of depression. *JAMA* 1989;261:2229–35.
50. Lewinsohn P, Rhode P, Seeley J, Fischer S. Age-cohort changes in the lifetime occurrence of depression and other mental disorders. *Journal of Abnormal Psychology* 1993;102(1):110–20.
51. Kessler R, McGonagle K, Nelson C, Hughes M, Swartz M, Blazer D. Sex and depression in the National Comorbidity Survey II: Cohort effects. *Journal of Affective Disorders* 1994;30(1):15–26.
52. Murphy J, Laird N, Sobol A, Leighton A. A 40-year perspective on the prevalence of depression: The Stirling County Study. *Archives of General Psychiatry* 2000;57(3):209–15.
53. Horwitz A, Wakefield J, Spitzer R. *The Loss of Sadness: How Psychiatry Transformed Normal Sorrow into Depressive Disorder*. Oxford: Oxford University Press, 2007.
54. Brown J, Boardman J, Elliott S, Howay E, Morrison J. Are self-referrers just the worried well? A cross-sectional study of self-referrers to community psycho-educational Stress and Self-Confidence workshops. *Social Psychiatry and Psychiatric Epidemiology* 2005;40(5):396–401.
55. Compton W, Conway K, Stinson F, Grant B. Changes in the prevalence of major depression and comorbid substance use disorders in the United States between 1991–1992 and 2001–2002. *The American Journal of Psychiatry* 2006;163(12):2141–7.
56. ONS. *Psychiatric Morbidity Among Adults Living in Private Households*. London: Her Majesty's Stationary Office, 2001.

57. WHO. *The Global Burden of Disease: 2004 Update.* Geneva: World Health Organization, 2008.

58. WHO. *The World Health Report 2001: Mental Health – New Understanding, New Hope.* Geneva: World Health Organization, 2001.

59. Rosen B. *Winners and Losers of the Information Revolution: Psychosocial Change and Its Discontents.* Westport, CT: Praeger, 1998.

60. Sloan T. *Damaged Life: The Crisis of the Modern Psyche.* New York: Routledge, 1996.

61. Twenge J. The age of anxiety? Birth cohort change in anxiety and neuroticism, 1952–1993. *Journal of Personality and Social Psychology* 2000;79(6):1007–21.

62. Spielberg C, Rickman R. Assessment of state and trait anxiety. In: Sartorius N, Andreoli V, Cassano G, Einsenberg L, Kielkolz P, Pancheri P, et al., editors. *Anxiety: Psychobiological and Clinical Perspectives.* New York: Hemisphere Publishing, 1990.

63. Somers J, Goldner E, Waraich P. Review: Worldwide lifetime prevalence of anxiety disorders is 16.6%, with considerable heterogeneity between studies. *Evidence Based Mental Health* 2006;9(4):115.

64. Woods D. Rising workplace stress levels set to cost millions. *HR Magazine* May 22, 2009.

65. Marmot M. *Status Syndrome: How Your Social Standing Directly Affects Your Health and Life Expectancy.* London: Bloomsbury, 2004.

66. Korman A, Wittig-Berman U, Lang D. Career success and personal failure: Alienation in professionals and managers. *The Academy of Management Journal* 1981;24(2):342–60.

67. Board B, Fritzon K. Disordered personalities at work. *Psychology, Crime and Law* 2005;11(1):17–32.

68. Cass A. Casualties of Wall Street: An Assessment of the Walking Wounded. American Psychological Association Convention. Washington, DC, 2000.

69. Sahadi J. How Wall Street can wreck your life. CNNMoney.com. New York, 2006.

70. Rutter M, Smith D. *Psychosocial Disorders in Young People: Time Trends and Their Causes.* Chichester, West Sussex: John Wiley and Sons, 1995.

71. Robins L. A 70-year history of conduct disorder: Variations in definition, prevalence, and correlates. In: Cohen P, Slomkowski P, Robins L, editors. *Historical and Geographical Influences on Psychopathology.* Mahwah, NJ: Lawrence Erlbaum Associates, 1999.

72. Twenge J, Gentile B, DeWall C, Ma D, Lacefield K, Schurtz D. Birth cohort increases in psychopathology among young Americans, 1938–2007: A cross-temporal meta-analysis of the MMPI. *Clinical Psychology Review* 2010;30(2):145–54.

73. The Nuffield Foundation. Time trends in adolescent well-being. London: The Nuffield Foundation, 2004.

74. Collishaw S, Maughan B, Natarajan L, Pickles A. Trends in adolescent emotional problems in England: A comparison of two national cohorts twenty years apart. *Journal of Child Psychology and Psychiatry* 2010;51(8):885–94.

75. CAMHS. National CAMHS dataset. Supporting information needs for child and adolescent mental health services. Child and Adolescent Mental Health Services (CAMHS) Outcomes Research Consortium. Dunstable: Durocobrivis Publications, 2004.

76. Eckersley R. Psychosocial disorders in young people: On the agenda but not on the mend. *Medical Journal of Australia* 1997;166(8):423–4.

77. O'Connor E. *The Essential Epicurus: Letters, Principal Doctrines, Vatican Sayings, and Fragments.* New York: Prometheus Books, 1993.

78. McClelland D. *Motivational Trends in Society.* Morristown, NJ: General Learning Press, 1978.

79. Becker G. *The Economic Approach to Human Behaviour.* Chicago: University of Chicago Press, 1976.
80. Becker G. A theory of marriage: Part 2. *The Journal of Political Economy* 1974;82(2):S11–S26.
81. Weber M, Henderson A, Parsons T. *The Theory of Social and Economic Organization.* New York: Oxford University Press, 1947.
82. Nisbet R. *The Sociological Tradition.* New York: Basic Books, 1966.
83. Christie R, Geis F. *Studies in Macchiavellianism.* New York: Academic Press, 1970.
84. Guterman S. *The Machiavellians: A Social Psychological Study of Moral Character and Organizational Milieu.* Lincoln, NE: University of Nebraska Press, 1970.
85. Webster R, Harmon H. Comparing levels of Machiavellianism of today's college students with college students of the 1960s. *Teaching Business Ethics* 2002;6(4):435–45.
86. Veroff J, Douvain E, Kulka R. *The Inner American: Self-Portrait from 1957 to 1976.* New York: Basic Books, 1981.
87. Olds J, Schwartz R. *The Lonely American: Drifting Apart in the Twenty-first Century.* Boston: Beacon Press, 2009.
88. Cacioppo J, Patrick W. *Loneliness: Human Nature and the Need for Social Connection.* New York: W.W. Norton & Co, 2008.
89. McPherson M, Smith-Lovin L, Brashears M. Social isolation in America: Changes in core discussion networks over two decades. *American Sociological Review* 2006;71(3):353–75.
90. Hamilton C. *Growth Fetish.* London: Pluto Press, 2004.
91. Tawney R. *The Acquisitive Society.* New York: Harcourt, Brace and World, 1920:188.
92. Putnam RD. Bowling alone: America's declining social capital. *Journal of Democracy* 1995;6(1):65–78.
93. Easton M. Life in UK "has become lonelier." BBC News December 1, 2008.
94. Ferri E, Bynner J, Wadsworth M. *Changing Britain, Changing Lives: Three Generations at the Turn of the Century.* London: Institute of Education, 2003.
95. National Family and Parenting Institute. *Teenagers' Attitudes to Parenting.* London: National Family and Parenting Institute, 2000.
96. Sartorious N, Davidian H, Ernberg G, Fenton F, Fujii I, et al. *Depressive Disorders in Different Cultures: Report of the World Health Organization Collaborative Study in Standardized Assessment of Depressive Disorders.* Geneva: World Health Organization, 1983.
97. Putnam R. The strange disappearance of Civic America. *The American Prospect* 1996;7(24):34–48.
98. Rahn W, Transue J. Social trust and value change: The decline of social capital in American youth, 1976–1995. *Political Psychology* 1998;19(3):545–65.
99. Uchitelle L. Defying forecast, job losses mount for a 22nd month. *New York Times* September 6, 2003.
100. Jackson T. *Prosperity Without Growth? The Transition to a Sustainable Economy.* London: Sustainable Development Commission, 2009.
101. UNEP. Decoupling Natural Resource Use and Environmental Impacts from Economic Growth, Panel IR, editor. New York: United Nations Environment Programme, 2011.
102. Weizsäcker Ev, Weizsäcker E, Lovins A, Lovins L. *Factor Four: Doubling Wealth – Halving Resource Use: The New Report to the Club of Rome.* London: Earthscan, 1998.
103. Daly H. Sustainable growth: An impossibility theorem. In: Daly H, Townsend K, editors. *Valuing the Earth: Economics, Ecology, Ethics.* Cambridge, MA: MIT Press, 1993.
104. Fromm E. *The Sane Society.* London: Routledge, 1955/1991:3.

105. Meadows D, Meadows D, Randers J. *The Limits to Growth*. New York: University Books, 1972.
106. Mill JS. *Principles of Political Economy With Some of their Applications to Social Philosophy*. London: John W Parker and Son, 1848:316–19.
107. Daly H. *Steady-State Economics: Second Edition With New Essays*. Washington, DC: Island Press, 1991.
108. Victor P. *Managing Without Growth*. London: Sustainable Development Commission, 2008.
109. Bosch G. Working time reductions, employment consequences and lessons from Europe. In: Figart D, Golden L, editors. *Working Time: International Trends, Theory and Policy Perspectives*. London: Routledge, 2002.
110. Durning A. *How Much Is Enough? The Consumer Society and the Future of the Earth*. New York, London: W W Norton & Company, 1992.
111. Kondo N, Subramanian S, Kawachi I, Takeda Y, Yamagata Z. Economic recession and health inequalities in Japan: Analysis with a national sample, 1986–2001. *Journal of Epidemiology and Community Health* 2008;62(10):869–75.
112. Valkonen T, Martikainen P, Jalovaara M, Koskinen S, Martelin T, Makela P. Changes in socioeconomic inequalities in mortality during an economic boom and recession among middle-aged men and women in Finland. *European Journal of Public Health* 2000;10(4):274–80.
113. Franco M, Orduñez P, Caballero B, Tapia-Granados J, Lazo M, Bernal J, et al. Impact of energy intake, physical activity, and population-wide weight loss on cardiovascular disease and diabetes mortality in Cuba, 1980–2005. *American Journal of Epidemiology* 2007;166(12):1374–80.
114. Cited in Mofid K. *Business Ethics, Corporate Social Responsibility and Globalisation for the Common Good*. London: Shepheard-Walwyn, 2003:3.
115. Brooks A. *Gross National Happiness: Why Happiness Matters for America – and How We Can Get More of It*. New York: Basic Books, 2008.
116. Cobb C, Cobb J. *The Green National Product: A Proposed Index of Sustainable Economic Welfare*. Lanham, MD: University Press of America, 1994.

Chapter 3: United we spend

1. Hume D. Of Refinement in the Arts. *Essays: Moral, Political, and Literary*. London: Longmans, Green, and Co., 1752/1875.
2. Hume D. *Essays and Treatises on Several Subjects*. London: A. Millar, 1752:25.
3. Smith A. *The Theory of Moral Sentiments*. London: A. Millar, 1759/1790:IV.I.10.
4. Mandeville B. *The Fable of the Bees and Other Writings*. Indianapolis, IN: Hackett Publishing, 1724/1997:154.
5. Lasch C. The age of limits. In: Melzer A, Weinberger J, Zinman M, editors. *History and the Idea of Progress*. Ithaca, NY: Cornell University Press, 1995.
6. Veblen T. *The Theory of the Leisure Class*. Charleston, SC: Forgotten Books, 1899/2008.
7. Wilde O. *The Picture of Dorian Gray*. London: Plain Label Books, 1890/2007:197.
8. Nystrom P. *Economics of Fashion*. New York: The Ronald Press Company, 1928.
9. Schor J. *The Overspent American: Upscaling, Downshifting, and the New Consumer*. New York: Basic Books, 1998.
10. Williams R. *Dream Worlds: Mass Consumerism in Nineteenth-Century France*. Berkeley, CA: University of California Press, 1982.

11. Frank R. *Luxury Fever: Why Money Fails to Satisfy in an Era of Excess.* New York: The Free Press, 1999.
12. Gramsci A. *Prison Notebooks.* New York: Columbia University Press, 1992.
13. Hume D. Of the First Principles of Government. *Essays: Moral, Political, and Literary.* London: Longmans, Green, and Co., 1875:109.
14. Marx K, Engels F. *The German Ideology.* London: International Publishers, 1947:64.
15. Scitovsky T. *The Joyless Economy: The Psychology of Human Satisfaction and Consumer Dissatisfaction.* New York: Oxford University Press, 1977.
16. Heath R. Life on Easy Street: Rich Americans do a lot of what you'd expect – ski, sail, and go to art auctions. *American Demographics* 1997;19(4):32–9.
17. Carrier J. Sailing the high-end seas: Luxury craft are back and prices are bigger than ever. *New York Times* January 24,1998.
18. Snead E. For younger patients, aging is an unkinder cut. *USA Today* July 1, 1996.
19. Peck D. Cosmetic surgery numbers sag, but Americans are still spending billions on it. *The Oregonian* May 27, 2009.
20. Press A. Americans are spending more on cars. *Chicago Tribune* March 15, 1998.
21. Davis S, Truett L. *An Analysis of the Impact of Sport Utility Vehicles in the United States.* Oak Ridge, TN: Oak Ridge National Laboratory, 2000.
22. Rogoski R. Recession not a roadblock for luxury-car sales. *Triangle Business Journal* Friday, November 28, 2008.
23. Laurance J. Cosmetic surgeons demand ban on advertising their own trade. *The Independent* November 16, 2009.
24. Speth JG, Haas PM. *Global Environmental Governance: Foundations of Contemporary Environmental Studies.* Washington, DC: Island Press, 2006.
25. Downey K. Basics, not luxuries, blamed for high debt. *Washington Post* May 12, 2006.
26. McGuire B. *Seven Years to Save the Planet: The Questions . . . and Answers.* London: Weidenfeld & Nicolson, 2008.
27. UNDP. *Human Development Report 1998.* New York: United Nations Development Programme, 1998.
28. Cha A. China's cars, accelerating a global demand for fuel. *Washington Post* July 28, 2008.
29. US News. SUV sales soaring . . . in Russia. *US News and World Report* September 24, 2008.
30. Kahneman D. A psychological perspective on economics. *The American Economic Review* 2003;93(2):162–8.
31. Frederick S, Lowenstein G. Hedonic adaptation. In: Kahneman D, Diener E, Schwarz N, editors. *Well-Being: The Foundations of Hedonic Psychology.* New York: Russell Sage Foundation, 1999.
32. Graham C, Pettinato S. *Happiness and Hardship: Opportunity and Insecurity in New Market Economies.* Washington, DC: Brookings Institution Press, 2002.
33. Cummins R, Nistico H. Maintaining life satisfaction: The role of positive cognitive bias. *Journal of Happiness Studies* forthcoming.
34. Brickman P, Coates R, Janoff-Bulman R. Lottery winners and accident victims: Is happiness relative? *Journal of Personality and Social Psychology* 1978;36(8):917–27.
35. Carver C, Lawrence J, Scheier M. A control process perspective on the origins of affect. In: Martin L, Tesser A, editors. *Striving and Feeling: Interactions Among Goals, Affect and Self-Regulation.* Mahwah, NJ: Erlbaum, 1996.
36. Niemi R, Mueller J, Smith T. *Trends in Public Opinion: A Compendium of Survey Data.* New York: Greenwood Press, 1989.

37. Wilde O. *The Importance of Being Earnest: And Other Plays*. New York: Random House, 2003:52.
38. Schumacher E. *Small is Beautiful: A Study of Economics As If People Mattered*. London: Harper Perennial, 1973:34.
39. de-Botton A. *Status Anxiety*. New York: Pantheon Books, 2004.
40. Hamilton C. Overconsumption in Australia: The Rise of the Middle-Class Battler. Discussion Paper Number 49. Canberra: The Australian Institute, 2002.
41. Taylor P, Morin R, Parker K, Cohn D, Wang W. *Luxury or Necessity? The Public Makes a U-Turn. A Social & Demographic Trends Report*. Washington, DC: Pew Research Center, 2009.
42. Darwin C. *The Descent of Man and Selection in Relation to Sex*. London: John Murray, 1871.
43. Bauman Z. *Consuming Life*. London: Polity Press, 2007.
44. Cronin H. *The Ant and the Peacock*. New York Cambridge University Press, 1991.
45. Chambers R, Taylor J, Potenza M. Developmental neurocircuitry of motivation in adolescence: A critical period of addiction vulnerability. *The American Journal of Psychiatry* 2003;160(6):1041–52.
46. Naish J. *Enough: Breaking Free from the World of Excess*. Edinburgh: Hodder & Stoughton, 2009.
47. Smith K, Berridge K. Opioid limbic circuit for reward: Interaction between hedonic hotspots of nucleus accumbens and central pallidum. *The Journal of Neuroscience* 2007;27(7):1594–605.
48. Galbraith JK. *The Affluent Society*. Harmondsworth, UK: Pelican Books, 1969.
49. Ekins P. The sustainable consumer society: A contradiction in terms? *International Environmental Affairs* 1991;3:243–58.
50. Klein N. *No Logo: Taking Aim at the Brand Bullies*. New York: Picador, 2000.
51. Buckley K. The selling of a psychologist: John Broadus Watson and the application of behavioral techniques to advertising. *Journal of the History of the Behavioral Sciences* 1982;18(3):207–21.
52. Moschis G, Moore R. A longitudinal study of television advertising effects. *Journal of Consumer Research* 1982;9(3):279–86.
53. Kasser T, Ryan R. Be careful what you wish for: Optimal functioning and the relative attainment of intrinsic and extrinsic goals. In: Schmuck P, Sheldon K, editors. *Life Goals and Well-Being: Towards a Positive Psychology of Human Striving*. Goettingen, Germany: Hogrefe & Huber, 2001.
54. Cheung C, Chan C. Television viewing and mean world value in Hong Kong's adolescents. *Social Behavior and Personality* 1996;24(4):351–64.
55. Scott-Clark C, Levy A. Fast forward into trouble. *Guardian Weekend*, June 14, 2003.
56. Belk R. Possessions and the extended self. *Journal of Consumer Research* 1988;15(2):139–68.
57. Kasser T. *Family, Community, and the Earth: The High Price of Materialism*. Cambridge, MA: MIT Press, 2002:91.
58. Gorz A. *Capitalism, Socialism, Ecology*. London: Verso, 1994.
59. Ruskin G. Why they whine: How corporations prey on our children. *Mothering* 1999;97:41–50.
60. Twitchell J. *Branded Nation: The Marketing of Megachurch, College, Inc., and Museumworld*. New York: Simon & Schuster, 2004.
61. Keynes JM. Economic possibilities for our grandchildren. In: Keynes J, editor. *Essays in Persuasion*. New York: WW Norton, 1931/1963.

62. Marx K. *Wage-labour and Capital* and *Value, Price, and Profit.* New York: International Publishers, 1849/1933:33.

63. Smith A. *The Theory of Moral Sentiments.* London: A. Millar, 1759:85–6.

64. Luttmer E. Neighbors as negatives: Relative earnings and well-being. *Quarterly Journal of Economics* 2005;20(3):963–1002.

65. Easterlin R. Does economic growth improve the human lot? In: Abramovitz M, David P, Reder M, editors. *Nations and Households in Economic Growth: Essays in Honor of Moses Abramovitz.* New York: Academic Press, 1974.

66. Hirschman A. An alternative explanation of contemporary harriedness. *Quarterly Journal of Economics* 1973;87(4):634–7.

67. Smith A. *The Theory of Moral Sentiments.* London: A. Millar, 1759:83–4.

68. Sullivan A, Gilbert W. *The Gondoliers; or, The King of Barataria.* London, 1889.

69. Bronk R. *Progress and the Invisible Hand: The Philosophy and Economics of Human Advance.* London: Warner Books, 1998.

70. Deci E, Ryan R. The "what" and "why" of goal pursuits: Human needs and the self-determination of behavior. *Psychological Inquiry* 2000;11(4):227–68.

71. Baumeister R, Leary M. The need to belong: Desire for interpersonal attachments as a fundamental human motivation. *Psychological Bulletin* 1995;117(3):497–529.

72. Carver C, Baird E. The American dream revisited: Is it what or why you want it that matters? *Psychological Science* 1998;9(4):289–92.

73. Fromm E. *To Have or To Be?* London: Continuum, 1976/1997.

74. Jessop B, Wheatley R. *Karl Marx's Social and Political Thought.* New York: Routledge, 1999:342.

75. Russell B. *Political Ideals.* London: Unwin Books, 1917.

76. Russell B. *Political Ideals.* London: Unwin Books, 1917:12.

77. Pryor J. *The American Freshman: Forty-Year Trends, 1966–2006.* Los Angeles, CA: Higher Education Research Institute, 2007.

78. Meyers DG. What is the Good Life? *Yes! A Journal of Positive Futures* Summer 2004:14.

79. Myers D. The secret to happiness. *Yes! Magazine* June 18, 2004:13–16.

80. Engardio P. Nice dream if you can live it. *BusinessWeek* September 13, 2004.

81. Reynolds J, Stewart M, MacDonald R, Sischo L. Have adolescents become too ambitious? High school seniors' educational and occupational plans: 1976–2000. *Social Problems* 2006;53(2):186–206.

82. Naim A, Omrod J, Bottomley P. *Watching, Wanting and Wellbeing: Exploring the Links.* London: National Consumer Council, 2007.

83. Marmot M. *Status Syndrome: How Your Social Standing Directly Affects Your Health and Life Expectancy.* London: Bloomsbury, 2004.

84. Ryan R, Chirkov V, Little T, Sheldon K, Timoshina E, Deci E. The American Dream in Russia: Extrinsic aspirations and well-being in two cultures. *Personality and Social Psychology Bulletin* 1999;25(12):1509–24.

85. Sheldon K, Kasser T. Pursuing personal goals: Skills enable progress, but not all progress is beneficial. *Personality and Social Psychology Bulletin* 1998;24(12):1319–31.

86. Diener E, Oishi S. Money and happiness: Income and subjective wellbeing across nations. In: Diener E, Suh E, editors. *Subjective Wellbeing Across Cultures.* Cambridge, MA: MIT Press, 2000.

87. Belk R. Three scales to measure constructs related to materialism: Reliability, validity and relationships to measures of happiness. In: Kinnear T, editor. *Advances in Consumer Research.* Provo, UT: Association for Consumer Research, 1984.

88. Belk R. Materialism: Trait aspects of living in the material world. *Journal of Consumer Research* 1985;12:265–80.

89. Hamilton C, Mail E. Downshifting in Australia: A sea-change in the pursuit of happiness. Discussion Paper Number 50. Canberra: The Australian Institute, 2003.
90. The Harwood Group. *Yearning for Balance: Views of Americans on Consumption, Materialism and the Environment.* Milton Village, MA: Merck Family Fund, 1995.
91. Kasser T. *The High Price of Materialism.* Cambridge, MA: MIT Press, 2002.
92. Kubey RW, Csikszentmihalyi M. *Television and The Quality Of Life: How Viewing Shapes Everyday Experience.* Hillsdale, NJ: Erlbaum, 1990.
93. Della-Fave A, Bassi M. The quality of experience in adolescents' daily lives: Developmental perspectives. *Genetic, Social and General Psychology Monographs* 2000;126(3):347–67.
94. Stendhal. *On Love.* New York: Penguin, 1822/1975.
95. Belk R. Three scales to measure constructs related to materialism: Reliability, validity and relationships to measures of happiness. In: Kinnear T, editor. *Advances in Consumer Research.* Provo, UT: Association for Consumer Research, 1984.
96. Belk R. Materialism: Trait aspects of living in the material world. *Journal of Consumer Research* 1985;12(3):265–80.
97. Kasser T. Two versions of the American dream: Which goals and values make for a high quality of life? In: Diener E, Rahtz D, editors. *Advances in Quality of Life Theory and Research.* Dordrecht, Netherlands: Kluwer, 2000.
98. Saunders S, Munro D. The construction and validation of a consumer oriented questionnaire (SCOI) designed to measure Fromm's (1955) marketing character in Australia. *Social Behavior and Personality* 2002;28:219–40.
99. Richins M, Dawson S. A consumer values orientation for materialism and its measurement: Scale development and validation. *Journal of Consumer Research* 1992;19(3):303–16.
100. Sheldon K, McGregor H. Extrinsic value orientation and "the tragedy of the commons." *Journal of Personality* 2000;68(2):383–411.
101. Ryan R, Sheldon K, Kasser T, Deci E. All goals are not created equal: An organismic perspective on the nature of goals and their regulation. In: Gollwitzer P, Bargh J, editors. *The Psychology of Action: Linking Cognition and Motivation to Behavior.* New York: Guilford, 1996.
102. Kernis M, Paradise A. Distinguishing between secure and fragile forms of high self-esteem. In: Deci E, Ryan R, editors. *Handbook of Self-Determination Research.* Rochester, NY: University of Rochester Press, 2002.
103. Deci E, Ryan R. Human autonomy: The basis for true self-esteem. In: Kernis M, editor. *Efficacy, agency, and self-esteem.* New York: Plenum Press, 1995.
104. Kernis M, Brown A, Brody G. Fragile self-esteem in children and its associations with perceived patterns of parent–child communication. *Journal of Personality* 2000;68(2):225–52.
105. Raskin R, Terry H. A principal-components analysis of the Narcissistic Personality Inventory and further evidence of its construct validity. *Journal of Pesonality and Social Psychology* 1988;54(5):890–902.
106. Kasser T, Ryan R, Zax M, Sameroff A. The relations of maternal and social environments to late adolescents' materialistic and prosocial values. *Developmental Psychology* 1995;31(6):907–14.
107. Cohen P, Cohen J. *Life Values and Adolescent Mental Health.* Mahwah, NJ: Erlbaum, 1996.
108. Williams G, Hedberg V, Cox E, Deci E. Extrinsic life goals and health risk behaviors in adolescents. *Journal of Applied Social Psychology* 2000;30(8):1756–71.

109. Twenge J, Foster J. Birth cohort increases in narcissistic personality traits among American college students, 1982–2009. *Social Psychological and Personality Science* 2010;1(1):99–106.

110. Suttie I. *The Origins of Love and Hate.* London: Free Association Books, 1988.

111. Galbraith JK. *The Affluent Society.* Harmondsworth, UK: Pelican Books, 1969:284.

112. Bentham J. *The Rationale of Reward.* London: John and HL Hunt, 1825:206.

113. Mill JS. *Utilitarianism.* London: Parker, Son, and Bourn, 1863:14.

114. Keynes JM. *Economic Possibilities for Our Grandchildren. Essays in Persuasion.* New York: WW Norton, 1931/1963:365–73.

115. Adbusters. Work, buy, consume and die. Vancouver, 2010.

116. Bush G. Excerpts from the president's remarks on the war on terrorism. *New York Times* October 12, 2001.

117. Swann C. Consuming concern: Why the stamina of shoppers will be crucial for global growth. *Financial Times* January 20, 2006:11.

118. Bell D. *The Cultural Contradictions of Capitalism.* New York: Basic Books, 1978.

119. O'Connor E. *The Essential Epicurus: Letters, Principal Doctrines, Vatican Sayings, and Fragments.* New York: Prometheus Books, 1993.

120. Belk R. Wordly possessions: Issues and criticisms. In: Bagozzi R, Tybout A, editors. *Advances in Consumer Research.* Ann Arbor, MI: Association for Consumer Research, 1983.

121. Lama D, Cutler H. *The Art of Happiness: A Handbook for Living.* New York: Penguin, 1998.

122. Thoreau HD. *Walden: or, Life in the Woods.* Philadelphia: Henry Altemus Company, 1900:94.

123. Aurelius M. *Meditations: With Selected Correspondence.* New York: Oxford University Press, 2011.

124. Emmons R, McCullogh M. Counting blessings versus burdens: An experimental investigation of gratitude and subjective well-being in daily life. *Journal of Personality and Social Psychology* 2003;84(2):377–89.

125. Center for a New American Dream. New American Dream: A Public Opinion Poll, 2004.

126. Hamilton C, Mail E. Downshifting in Australia: A sea-change in the pursuit of happiness. Discussion Paper Number 50. Canberra: The Australian Institute, 2003.

127. Schor J. *The Overworked American: The Unexpected Decline of Leisure.* New York: Basic Books, 1991.

128. George S. *Another World Is Possible If . . .* London: Verso, 2004:226.

129. Pudor J. *Consumption, Complicity and SUVs.* Online: ZNet Commentary, 2001.

130. Schor J. *The Overworked American.* New York: Basic Books, 1991:120.

131. Cohen L. *A Consumer's Republic: The Politics of Mass Consumption in Postwar America.* New York: Knopf, 2003.

132. Hamilton C. *Growth Fetish.* London: Pluto Press, 2004.

Chapter 4: Chains of the free world

1. Bronk R. *Progress and the Invisible Hand: The Philosophy and Economics of Human Advance.* London: Warner Books, 1998.

2. Sen A. *Development As Freedom.* Oxford: Oxford University Press, 1999.

3. Friedman B. *The Moral Consequences of Economic Growth.* New York: Knopf, 2005.

4. Marcuse H. The closing of the political universe. *One-Dimensional Man: Studies in the Ideology of Advanced Industrial Society.* New York: Routledge, 1964/2002:36.

5. Friedman M, Friedman R. *Free to Choose: A Personal Statement.* London: Secker and Warburg, 1980.

6. Twenge J, Zhang L, Im C. It's beyond my control: A cross-temporal meta-analysis of increasing externality in locus of control, 1960–2002. *Personality and Social Psychology Review* 2004;8(3):308–19.

7. Rotter J. External control and internal control. *Psychology Today* 1971;5:37–59.

8. Brofenbrenner U, Mcclelland P, Ceci S, Moen P, Wethington E. *The State of Americans: This Generation and the Next.* New York: Free Press, 1996.

9. Friedman T. Foreign affairs: Angry, wired and deadly. *New York Times* August 22, 1998.

10. Marcuse H. *One-Dimensional Man: Studies in the Ideology of Advanced Industrial Society.* New York: Routledge, 1964/2002.

11. Mumford L. *The Conduct of Life.* New York: Harcourt Brace Jovanovich, 1970:16.

12. Fromm E. *The Sane Society.* London and New York: Routledge, 1955/1991:222.

13. Fromm E. *The Sane Society.* London and New York: Routledge, 1955/1991:263.

14. Bell D. *The Cultural Contradictions of Capitalism.* London: Heinemann, 1976.

15. Neville R. The business of being human. *Amerika Psycho: Behind Uncle Sam's Mask of Sanity.* New York: Ocean Press, 2003:6.

16. Koran L, Faber R, Aboujaoude E, Large M, Serpe R. Estimated prevalence of compulsive buying behavior in the United States. *The American Journal of Psychiatry* 2006;163:1806–12.

17. McFadden R, Macropoulus A. Wal-Mart employee trampled to death. *New York Times* November 28, 2008.

18. Williamson J. *Decoding Advertisements: Ideology and Meaning in Advertisements.* New York: Marion Boyars, 1978.

19. Porter R. Addicted to modernity: Nervousness in the early consumer society. In: Melling J, Barry J, editors. *Culture in History: Production, Consumption and Values in Historical Perspective.* Exeter: University of Exeter Press, 1992.

20. Friedman G. *Reigniting the Labor Movement: Restoring Means to Ends in a Democratic Labor Movement.* New York: Routledge, 2008:65.

21. OECD. *Special Focus: Measuring Leisure in OECD Countries. Society at a Glance 2009: OECD Social Indicators.* Paris: Organization for Economic Cooperation and Development, 2009.

22. Wallich P. A workaholic economy. *Scientific American.* 1994;271(2):89.

23. European Foundation for the Improvement of Living and Working Conditions. Fourth European Working Conditions Survey. Dublin, Ireland, 2007.

24. Schor J. *The Overworked American: The Unexpected Decline of Leisure.* New York: Basic Books, 1991.

25. Taylor R. Britain's World of Work – Myths and Realities. ESRC Future of Work Programme Seminar. Swindon, UK, 2002.

26. Department of Trade and Industry. *Department of Trade and Industry's Work–Life Balance Campaign and Management Today Survey.* London: Department of Trade and Industry, 2002.

27. Fox L, Han W-J, Ruhm C, Waldfogel J. Time for Children: Trends in the Employment Patterns of Parents, 1967–2009. NBER Working Paper Series. Bonn: National Bureau of Economic Research, 2011.

28. Belsky J, Vandell DL, Burchinal M, Clarke-Stewart KA, McCartney K, Tresch Owen M. The NICHD Early Child Care Research Network. *Child Development* 2007;78(2):681–701.

29. Burke R. Work motivations, satisfactions, and health: Passion versus addiction. In: Burke R, Cooper C, editors. *The Long Work Hours Culture: Causes, Consequences and Choices*. Bingley, UK: Emerald, 2008.
30. Bakker AB, Demerouti E, Burke R. Workaholism and relationship quality: A spillover-crossover perspective. *Journal of Occupational Health Psychology* 2008;14(1):23–33.
31. Iso-Ahola S, Weissinger E. Perceptions of boredom in leisure: Conceptualization, reliability, and validity of the Leisure Boredom Scale. *Journal of Leisure Research* 1990;22(1):1–17.
32. Aristotle. *The Nicomachean Ethics*. London: Wordsworth, 350 BC/1996.
33. Kasser T, Brown K. On time, happiness and ecological footprint. In: Graaf Jd, editor. *Take Back Your Time: Fighting Overwork and Time Poverty in America*. San Francisco, CA: Berrett-Koehler, 2003.
34. Hayden A, Shandra JM. Hours of work and the ecological footprint of nations: An exploratory analysis. *Local Environment* 2009;14(6):575–600.
35. Hunt J, Kernan J, Chatterjee A, Florsheim R. Locus of control as a personality correlate of materialism: An empirical note. *Psychological Reports* 1990;67(3f):1102–3.
36. Carver C, Baird E. The American dream revisited: Is it what or why you want it that matters? *Psychological Science* 1998;9(4):289–92.
37. Richins M. Social comparison, advertising, and consumer discontent. *American Behavioral Scientist* 1995;38(4):593–607.
38. Thoreau HD. *Life Without Principle*. Charleston, SC: Forgotten Books, 1863/2008:2.
39. Festinger L. A theory of social comparison process. *Human Relations* 1954;7(2):117–40.
40. Lieberman M, Eisenberg N. A pain by any other name (rejection, exclusion, ostracism) still hurts the same: The role of dorsal anterior cingulate cortex in social and physican pain. In: Cacioppo J, Visser P, Pickett C, editors. *Social Neuroscience: People Thinking About People*. Cambridge, MA: MIT Press, 2005.
41. Lascu D, Zinkhan G. Consumer conformity: Review and applications for marketing theory and practice. *Journal of Marketing Theory and Practice* 1999;7(3):1–12.
42. Cova B. The postmodern explained to managers: Implications for marketing. *Business Horizons* 1996;39(6):15–23.
43. Kashdan T, Breen W. Materialism and diminished well-being: Experiential avoidance as a mediating mechanism. *Journal of Social and Clinical Psychology* 2007;26:521–53.
44. Fromm E. *The Sane Society*. London and New York: Routledge, 1955/1991:352.
45. Antonovsky A. *Health, Stress and Coping: New Perspectives on Mental and Physical Well-being*. San Francisco, CA: Jossey-Bass, 1979.
46. Burton RP. Global integrative meaning as a mediating factor in the relationship between social roles and psychological distress. *Journal of Health and Social Behavior* 1988;39:201–15.
47. Plato. *Apology*. In: *Five Dialogues: Euthyphro, Apology, Crito, Meno, Phaedo*. Claremont, CA: Coyote Canyon Press, 2009:39.
48. O'Connor E. *The Essential Epicurus: Letters, Principal Doctrines, Vatican Sayings, and Fragments*. New York: Prometheus Books, 1993.
49. Russell B. *In Praise of Idleness and Other Essays*. Crows Nest, New South Wales: Allen & Unwin, 1935.
50. Aquinas T. *On Prayer and the Contemplative Life*. General Books LLC, 2010.
51. Becker E. *The Denial of Death*. New York: Free Press, 1973.
52. Becker E. *The Denial of Death*. New York: Free Press, 1973:133.
53. Arndt J, Solomon S, Kasser T, Sheldon K. The urge to splurge: A terror management account of materialism and consumer behavior. *Journal of Consumer Psychology* 2004;14(3):198–212.

54. Jonas E, Martens A, Kayser D, Fritsche I, Sullivan D, Greenberg J. Focus theory of normative conduct and terror-management theory: The interactive impact of mortality salience and norm salience on social judgment. *Journal of Personality and Social Psychology* 2008;95(6):1239–51.

55. Frey B, Oberholzer-Gee F. The cost of price incentives: An empirical analysis of motivation crowding-out. *American Economic Review* 1997;87(4):746–55.

56. Rifkin J. *The Empathic Civilization: The Race to Global Consciousness in a World in Crisis.* New York: Penguin, 2009.

57. Solomon S, Greenberg J, Jeffrey L, Pyszczynski T. Lethal consumption: Death-denying materialism. In: Kasser T, Kanner A, editors. *Psychology and Consumer Culture: The Struggle for a Good Life in a Materialistic World.* Washington, DC: American Psychological Association, 2004.

58. Arndt J, Greenberg J, Simon L, Pyszczynski T, Solomon S. Terror management and self-awareness: Evidence that mortality salience provokes avoidance of the self-focused state. *Personality and Social Psychology Bulletin* 1998;24(11):1216–27.

59. Mandel N, Heine S. Terror management and marketing: He who dies with the most toys wins. *Advances in Consumer Research* 1999;26:527–32.

60. Kasser T, Sheldon K. Of wealth and death: Materialism, mortality salience and consumption behavior. *Psychological Science* 2000;11(4):348–51.

61. Faber R. Self-control and compulsive buying. In: Kasser T, Kanner A, editors. *Psychology and Consumer Culture: The Struggle for a Good Life in a Materialistic World.* Washington, DC: American Psychological Association, 2004.

62. Moskalenko S, Heine S. Watching your troubles away: Television viewing as a stimulus for subjective self-awareness. *Personality and Social Psychology Bulletin* 2003;29(1):76–85.

63. Jonas E, Schimel J, Greenberg J, Pyszczynski T. The Scrooge Effect: Evidence that mortality salience increases prosocial attitudes and behavior. *Personality and Social Psychology Bulletin* 2002;28(10):1342–53.

64. Yalom I. *Existential Psychotherapy.* New York: Basic Books, 1980.

65. Noyes R. Attitude change following near-death experiences. *Psychiatry: Journal for the Study of Interpersonal Processes* 1980;43(3):234–41.

66. Russell B. A free man's worship. *Mysticism and Logic: And Other Essays.* Harlow: Longmans, Green and Company, 1919:54–5.

67. Spinoza B. *Ethics.* London: Everyman's Library, 1677.

68. Mill JS. *The Autobiography of John Stuart Mill.* Sioux Falls, SD: NuVision Publications, 1997:152.

69. Frankl V. *Man's Search For Meaning.* London: Random House, 1946/1992:12.

70. Fromm E. *The Sane Society.* London and New York: Routledge, 1955/1991.

71. Sartre J-P. *L'existentialisme est un humanisme.* Paris: Editions Nagel, 1946.

72. Maslow A. A theory of human motivation. *Psychological Review* 1943;50:370–96.

73. Fromm E. *Man for Himself: An Inquiry into the Psychology of Ethics.* London: Routledge, 1947/2003:117.

74. Sheldon K, Ryan R, Deci E, Kasser T. The independent effects of goal contents and motives on well-being: It's both what you pursue and why you pursue it. *Personality and Social Psychology Bulletin* 2004;30(4):475–86.

75. Frankl V. *Man's Search For Meaning.* London: Random House, 1946/1992:87.

76. Rousseau JJ. *Discourses on the Origins of Inequality.* Indianapolis, IN: Hackett, 1755.

77. Peck J. *The Chomsky Reader.* London: Serpent's Tail, 1987:148–50.

78. Einstein A. *Out of My Later Years.* New York: Citadel Press, 1995:19.

79. Schwartz S. Cultural and individual value correlates of capitalism: A comparative analysis. *Psychological Inquiry* 2007;18(1):52–7.
80. Smith A. *An Inquiry into the Nature and Causes of the Wealth of Nations: Volume 3.* Edinburgh: Mundell, Doig and Stevenson, 1809:194.
81. Marx K. *Capital: An Abridged Edition.* Oxford: Oxford University Press, 1999:293.
82. De Toqueville A. In: Dwight T, Hawthorne J, editors. *The World's Great Classics: Democracy in America.* London: Wordsworth, 1899:169.
83. de-Botton A. *Status Anxiety.* New York: Pantheon Books, 2004:111.
84. Mill JS. *Principles of Political Economy: With Some of Their Applications to Social Philosophy.* London: Longmans, Green and Co., 1848:751.
85. Keynes JM. *Economic Possibilities for Our Grandchildren. Essays in Persuasion.* New York: WW Norton, 1931/1963:329.
86. Keynes JM. *Economic Possibilities for Our Grandchildren. Essays in Persuasion.* New York: WW Norton, 1931/1963:362.
87. Collins RM. *More: The Politics of Economic Growth in Postwar America.* New York: Oxford University Press, 2000:63.
88. Russell B. *In Praise of Idleness and Other Essays.* New York: Routledge, 1935/2004:6.
89. Scitovsky T. *The Joyless Economy: The Psychology of Human Satisfaction and Consumer Dissatisfaction.* New York: Oxford University Press, 1977.
90. Solnick S, Hemenway D. Is more always better?: A survey on positional concerns. *Journal of Economic Behavior and Organization* 1997;37(3):373–83.
91. Elrich P, Kennedy D. Millenium assessment of human behavior. *Science* 2005;309(5734):562–3.
92. Senge P, Scharmer C, Jaworski J, Flowers B. *Presence: Human Purpose and the Field of the Future.* New York: Doubleday, 2005.
93. Tucker M, Grim J. Daring to dream: Religion and the future of the Earth. *Reflections – The Journal of the Yale Divinity School* 2007;4:4–9.
94. Raskin P, Banuri T, Gallopin G, Gutman P, Hammond A. *Great Transition: The Promise and Lure of the Times Ahead.* Boston, MA: Stockholm Environment Institute, 2002.
95. Korten DC. *The Great Turning: From Empire to Earth Community.* San Francisco, CA: Berrett-Koheler, 2006.
96. Ray PH, Anderson SR. *The Cultural Creatives: How 50 Million People Are Changing the World.* New York: Three Rivers Press, 2001:44.

Chapter 5: Market mediocracies

1. Schell J. *The Unfinished Twentieth Century: The Crisis of Weapons of Mass Destruction.* London: Verso, 2001.
2. Tang M. Examining the lagged effect of economic development on political democracy: A panel-VAR model. *Democratization* 2008;15(1):106–22.
3. Freedom House. Democracy's Century: A Survey of Global Political Change in the 20th Century. Press Release. New York: Freedom House, 1999.
4. Barber BR. *Strong Democracy: Participatory Politics for a New Age.* Berkeley, CA: University of California Press, 2003.
5. Dewey J. *The Public and its Problems.* Athens, OH: Swallow Press, 1954.
6. Twain M. Chapter XX. *Following the Equator: Journey Around the World.* Charleston, SC: Forgotten Books, 1899/2010:195.
7. IDEA. *Voter Turnout.* Stockholm: International IDEA Voter Turnout Website, 2010.
8. Putnam R. The strange disappearance of Civic America. *The American Prospect* 1996;7(24):34–48.

9. Macedo S, Alex-Assensoh Y. *Democracy At Risk: How Political Choices Undermine Citizen Participation and What We Can Do About It.* Washington, DC: The Brookings Institution Press, 2005.

10. Putnam R. *Bowling Alone: The Collapse and Revival of American Community.* New York: Simon & Schuster, 2000.

11. OECD. *OECD Stats Extract – Labour.* Paris: Organization for Economic Co-operation and Development, 2009.

12. IDEA. *Voter Turnout Since 1945: A Global Report.* Stockolm, Sweden: International Institute for Democracy and Electoral Assistance (IDEA), 2002.

13. Marshall J. Globalization and the Turnout Decline in Advanced Industrialized Democracies, 1960–2000. Elections, Public Opinion and Parties 2008 Annual Conference. Manchester, 2008.

14. Park A, Curtice J, Thomson K, Phillips M, Johnson M, Clery E. *British Social Attitudes: The 26th Report.* British Social Attitudes Survey series. Thousand Oaks, CA: Sage Publications, 2007.

15. Klingemann H, Fuchs D. *Citizens and the State.* New York: Oxford University Press, 1995.

16. Burnham WD. The appearance and disappearance of the American voter. In: Rose R, editor. *Electoral Participation: A Comparative Analysis.* Thousand Oaks, CA: Sage Publications, 1980:40.

17. Lijphart A. Unequal participation: Democracy's unresolved dilemma. *American Political Science Review* 1997;91(1):1–14.

18. Niemi R, Weisberg H. *Controversies in Voting Behavior,* 4th ed. Washington, DC: CQ Press, 2001.

19. International Institute for Democracy and Electoral Assistance (IDEA). Voter Turnout, 2010. Online.

20. Inglehart R. *Modernization and Postmodernization: Cultural, Economic and Political Change in 43 Societies.* Princeton, NJ: Princeton University Press, 1997.

21. Fieldhouse E, Tranmer M, Russell A. Something about young people or something about elections? Electoral participation of young people in Europe: Evidence from a multilevel analysis of the European Social Survey. *European Journal of Political Research* 2007;46:797–822.

22. Department for Business Enterprise and Regulatory Reform. *Trade Union Membership 2008.* London: Department for Business Enterprise and Regulatory Reform, 2009.

23. Glyn A. *Capitalism Unleashed: Finance Globalization and Welfare.* New York: Oxford University Press, 2006.

24. Weeks J. Have workers in Latin America gained from liberalization and regional integration? In: Harris R, Seid M, editors. *Critical Perspectives on Globalization and Neoliberalism in the Developing Countries.* Leiden, Netherlands: Brill, 2000.

25. Davenport D, Skandera A. Civic associations. In: Berkowitz P, editor. *Never a Matter of Indifference: Sustaining Virtue in a Free Republic.* Stanford, CA: Hoover Press, 2003.

26. Skopol T. United States: From membership to advocacy. In: Putnam R, editor. *Democracies in Flux: The Evolution of Social Capital in Contemporary Society.* New York: Oxford University Press, 2002.

27. Marmot M, Wilkinson R. Psychosocial and material pathways in the relation between income and health: A response to Lynch et al. *BMJ* 2001;322(7296):1233–6.

28. Paxton P. Social capital and democracy: An interdependent relationship. *American Sociological Review* 2002;67(2):254–77.

29. Rodrik D. Institutions for high quality growth draft: What they are and how to acquire them. International Monetary Fund Conference on Second-Generation Reforms. Washington, DC, 1999.

30. Uslaner E, Brown M. Inequality, trust and civic engagement. *American Politics Research* 2005;33(6):868–94.
31. Lister R. The real egalitarianism? Social justice "after Blair." In: Hassan G, editor. *After Blair: Politics After the New Labour Decade.* London: Lawrence Wishhart, 2007.
32. Bookchin M. *The Ecology of Freedom: The Emergence and Dissolution of Hierarchy.* Oakland, CA: AK Press, 2005.
33. Lukács G. *History and Class Consciousness: Studies in Marxist Dialectics.* Cambridge, MA: MIT Press, 1972.
34. Putnam RD. Bowling alone: America's declining social capital. *Journal of Democracy* 1995;6(1):65–78.
35. Bennett W. Ithiel De Sola Pool Lecture: The uncivic culture: Communication, identity, and the rise of lifestyle politics. *Political Science and Politics* 1998;31(4):741–61, 750.
36. Kasser T. Foreword. *The High Price of Materialism.* Cambridge, MA: MIT Press, 2002:ix.
37. Einstein A. Why socialism? *Monthly Review* 1949;I(1):9–15.
38. Rahn W, Rudolph T. A tale of political trust in American cities. *Public Opinion Quarterly* 2005;69(4):530–60.
39. Bromley C, Curtice J, Seyd B. *Is Britain Facing a Crisis of Democracy?* London: UCL Constitution Unit, 2004.
40. Powell GB. American voter turnout in comparative perspective. *The American Political Science Review* 1986;80(1):17–43.
41. Russell D. The social transformation of trust in government. *International Review of Sociology* 2005;15(1):133–54.
42. Ladd E. The 1994 congressional elections: The postindustrial realignment continues. *Political Science Quarterly* 1995;110(1):1–23.
43. The Pew Research Center For The People and The Press. *The People and Their Government: Distrust, Discontent, Anger and Partisan Rancor.* The Pew Research Center For The People and The Press, 2010.
44. Korten D. *When Corporations Rule the World.* San Francisco, CA: Berrett-Koehler Publishers, 1995.
45. Coleman S. The lonely citizen: Indirect representation in an age of networks. *Political Communication* 2005;22(2):197–214.
46. Bernstein A, Arndt M, Zellner W, Coy P. Too much corporate power? *Business Week* September 11, 2000.
47. Nikolayenko O. Social capital in post-communist societies: Running deficits? Annual Meeting of the Canadian Political Science Association. University of West Ontario, 2005.
48. Kettering Foundation and Harwood Group. *Citizens and Politics: A View from Main Street America.* Dayton, OH: Kettering Foundation, 1991.
49. Hastings E, Hastings P. *Index to International Public Opinion, 1992–1993.* Westport, CT: Greenwood Press, 1994.
50. American National Election Studies. *The ANES Guide to Public Opinion and Electoral Behavior: Is the Government Run For the Benefit of All, 1964–2004.* Ann Arbor, MI: American National Election Studies, 2005.
51. Globescan. *Research Findings: Trust in Institutions and Growing Pessimism.* Toronto: Globescan, 2006.
52. Alesina A, Wamiarg R. The economies of civic trust. In: Pharr S, Putnam, R, editors. *Disaffected Democracies: What's Troubling the Trilateral Countries?* Princeton, NJ: Princeton University Press, 2000.

53. Brecher J, Costello T, Smith B. *Globalization From Below: The Power of Solidarity*. Brooklyn, NY: South End Press, 2000.

54. Nye J, Zelikow P, King D. *Why People Don't Trust Government*. Cambridge, MA: Harvard University Press, 1997.

55. Mettler S. Bringing the State back in to civic engagement: Policy feedback effects of the G.I. Bill for World War II veterans. *American Political Science Review* 2002;96(2):351–65.

56. Truman D. *The Governmental Process: Political Interests and Public Opinion*. Chicago, IL: Alfred A Knopf, 1951.

57. Campbell AL. *How Policies Make Citizens: Senior Political Activism and the American Welfare State*. Princeton, NJ: Princeton University Press, 2003.

58. Reich R. The road to supercapitalism. *Supercapitalism: The Battle for Democracy in an Age of Big Business*. Cambridge: Icon Books, 2007:50.

59. Faux J. *The Global Class War: How America's Bipartisan Elite Lost Our Future – and What It Will Take to Win It Back*. Hoboken, NJ: Wiley, 2006.

60. Gill S. Theorizing the interregnum: The double movement and global politics in the 1990s. In: Amoore L, editor. *The Global Resistance Reader*. London: Routledge, 2005.

61. Friedman M. Nobel Speech. Stockholm, 1976.

62. Dreher A, Gaston N. Has globalisation really had no effect on unions? *Kyklos* 2007;60(2):165–86.

63. Faber H, Westera B. *Round Up the Usual Suspects: The Decline of Unions in the Private Sector, 1973–1998*. Industrial Relations Section, Working Paper #437. Princeton, NJ: Princeton University, 2000.

64. Prosten R. The rise in NLRB election delays: Measuring business' new resistance. *Monthly Labor Review* 1979;102(2):38.

65. Cavanagh J, Leaver E. *Controlling Transnational Corporations*. Washington, DC: Foreign Policy In Focus, 1996.

66. Sagafi-Nejad T, Dunning J. *The UN and Transnational Corporations: From Code of Conduct to Global Impact*. Bloomington, IN: Indiana University Press, 2008.

67. Duffy J. Bilderberg: The ultimate conspiracy theory. BBC News Online June 3, 2004.

68. Archer J. *The Plot to Seize the White House*. New York: Hawthorn Books, 1973.

69. Balkan J. Democracy Ltd. *The Corporation: The Pathological Pursuit of Profit and Power*. New York: Free Press, 2004:95.

70. Chomsky N. *Democracy Promotion at Home. Failed States: The Abuse of Power and the Assault on Democracy*. New York: Owl Books, 2006:207.

71. Crozier M, Huntington S, Watanuki T. *The Crisis of Democracy: Report on the Governability of Democracies to the Trilateral Commission*. New York: The Trilateral Commission, 1975.

72. Chomsky N. *Necessary Illusions: Thought Control in Democratic Societies*. New York: South End Press, 1989.

73. Chomsky N. *Profit over People: Neoliberalism and Global Order*. New York: Seven Stories Press, 1999.

74. Lippman W. *Public Opinion*. New York: Macmillian, 1922/1998:xx.

75. Niebuhr R. *Moral Man and Immoral Society: A Study in Ethics and Politics*. Westminster: John Knox Press, 1932/2002:xxv.

76. Hume D. *Of the First Principles of Government. Essays: Moral, Political, and Literary*. London: Longmans, Green, and Co., 1875:109.

77. Bernays EL. The engineering of consent. *The Annals of the American Academy of Political and Social Science* 1947;250(1):113–20.

78. Curtis A. *The Century Of The Self*. BBC, 2002:240 minutes.

79. Bernays E. *Organizing Chaos. Propaganda.* New York: Ig Publishing, 1928/2005:37.
80. Marcuse H. The closing of the universe discourse. *One-Dimensional Man: Studies in the Ideology of Advanced Industrial Society.* New York: Routledge, 1964/2002:88.
81. McChesney R. *Corporate Media and the Threat to Democracy.* New York: Seven Stories Press, 2003.
82. Schulz W. Media change and the political effects of television: Americanization of the political culture? *Communications* 1998;23(4):527–43.
83. Negrine R, Papathanassoloulos S. The "Americanization of Political Communication": A Critique. *The Harvard International Journal of Press/Politics* 1996;1(2):45–62.
84. Lapham L. Tentacles of rage: The Republican propaganda mill, a brief history. *Harper's Magazine* 2004;309(1852):31–41.
85. McChesney R. The global media giants: We are the world. Extra! New York: FAIR (Fairness and Accuracy in Reporting), 1997.
86. Hermann E, McChesney R. *The Global Media: The New Missionaries of Corporate Capitalism.* London: Continuum International, 1997.
87. Norris P. *Public Sentinel: News Media & Governance Reform.* Washington, DC: World Bank, 2009.
88. Orwell G. *1984.* New York: Bloom's Guide, 1948/2004.
89. Herman ES, Chomsky N. Worthy and unworthy victims. *Manufacturing Consent: the Political Economy of Mass Media.* London: Vintage, 1994:ix.
90. Monbiot G. *The Age of Consent: A Manifesto for a New World Order.* London: Harper Perennial, 2004.
91. von-Goethe JW. *Goethe's Opinions on the World, Mankind, Literature, Science, and Art.* London: John W Parker and Son, 1853:3.
92. Fearn R. *Amoral America: How the Rest of the World Learned to Hate America:*539.
93. Postman N. *Entertaining Ourselves to Death.* New York: Viking, 1985.
94. Gabler N. *Life the Movie.* New York: Alfred A. Knopf, 1998.
95. Fallows J. *Breaking the News.* New York: Pantheon Books, 1996.
96. Magnuson E. Anyone listening? *The Nation* May 23, 2005.
97. Robinson M. Public affairs television and the growth of political malaise: The case of "the selling of the president." *American Political Science Review* 1976;70(3):409–32.
98. Entman R. *Democracy without Citizens: Media and the Decay of American Politics.* Oxford: Oxford University Press, 1989.
99. Dautrich K, Hartley T. *How the News Media Fail American Voters: Causes, Consequences and Remedies.* New York: Columbia University Press, 1999.
100. Blumler J. Origins of the crisis of communication for citizenship. *Political Communication* 1997;14(4):395–404.
101. PIPA/Knowledge Networks Poll. Misperceptions, the Media and the Iraq War: Program on International Policy Attitudes and Knowledge Networks, 2003.
102. Rampton S, Stauber J. *Weapons of Mass Deception: The Uses of Propaganda in Bush's War on Iraq.* New York: Tarcher/Penguin, 2003.
103. Greenwald R. *Outfoxed: Rupert Murdoch's War On Journalism.* USA: MoveOn.org Brave New Films, 2004:77 minutes.
104. Schechter D. *The More You Watch, the Less You Know: News Wars/(sub)Merged Hopes/Media Adventures.* New York: Seven Stories Press, 1998.
105. Glasgow University Media Group. *TV News and Public Understanding of the Israeli/Palestinian Conflict.* Dublin: Causeway Press, 2002.
106. Dalton R. *The Good Citizen. How a Younger Generation is Reshaping American Politics.* Washington, DC: CQ Press, 2008.

107. Deschouwer K, Hooghe M, Delwit P, Walgrave S, Andeweg R. Changing Patterns of Participation and Representation in Contemporary Democracies. Ex-post Evaluation Report for IAP network. Brussels: Interuniversity Attraction Pole, 2009.

108. Hooghe M, Marien S. *Political Trust, Political Efficacy and Forms of Participation: A Comparative Analysis of the Relation between Political Trust and Different Forms of Participation.* Oxford: Nuffield College, 2010.

109. Bennett W. Communicating global activism: Strengths and vulnerabilities of networked politics. *Information, Communication, and Society* 2003;6(2):143–68.

110. Bennett W. Global media and politics: Transnational communication regimes and civic cultures. *Annual Review of Political Science* 2004;7:125–48.

111. Hawken P. *Blessed Unrest: How the Largest Movement in the World Came Into Being and No One Saw It Coming.* New York: Viking, 2007.

112. Falk R. Resisting "globalisation-from-above" through "globalisation-from-below." *New Political Economy* 1997;2(1):17–24.

Chapter 6: The market greed doctrine

1. Polanyi K. *The Great Transformation: The Political and Economic Origins of Our Time.* Boston: Beacon Press, 1944/2001.

2. Polanyi K. The hundred years' peace. *The Great Transformation: The Political and Economic Origins of Our Time.* Boston: Beacon Press, 1944/2001:3.

3. Smith A. *The Wealth of Nations: Complete and Unabridged.* New York: The Modern Library, 1776.

4. Smith A. Of restraints upon the importation from foreign countries, of such goods as can be produced at home. *An Inquiry into the Nature and Causes of the Wealth of Nations Vol II.* London: Printed for W. Strahan and T. Cadell, 1776:35.

5. Smith A. *The Theory of Moral Sentiments.* London: A. Millar, 1759/1790:I.I.1.

6. Coats A. *The Classical Economists and Economic Policy.* New York: Methuen, 1971:9.

7. Smith A. *The Theory of Moral Sentiments.* London: A. Millar, 1759/1790:VII.II.92.

8. Baum S. Poverty, inequality and the role of government: What would Adam Smith say? *Eastern Economic Journal* 1992;18(2):143–56.

9. Malthus T. Effects of the knowledge of the principal cause of poverty on civil liberty. *An Essay on the Principle of Population, Volume II.* Cambridge: Cambridge University Press, 1798/1989:127.

10. Malthus T. Continuation of the same subject. *An Essay on the Principle of Population, Volume II.* Cambridge: Cambridge University Press, 1798/1989:181.

11. Hobsbawm E. *Industry and Empire: From 1750 to the Present Day.* Harmondworth: Penguin, 1990.

12. Ricardo D. *On the Principles of Political Economy and Taxation.* London: John Murray, 1817:110–11.

13. Polanyi K. Antecedents and consequences. *The Great Transformation: The Political and Economic Origins of Our Time.* Boston: Beacon Press, 1944/2001:106–7.

14. Darwin C. *On the Origin of Species by Means of Natural Selection, or the Preservation of Favoured Races in the Struggle for Life.* London: John Murray, 1859.

15. Spencer H. *Principles of Biology.* London: Williams and Norgate, 1864.

16. Darwin C. Comparison of the mental powers of man and the lower animals – continued. *The Descent of Man and Selection in Relation to Sex.* Princeton, NJ: Princeton University Press, 1871/1981:77.

17. Darwin C. *The Descent of Man, and Selection in Relation to Sex.* Princeton, NJ: Princeton University Press, 1871/1981:101.

18. Huxley T. *Method and Result: Collected Essays.* Whitefish, MT: Kessinger, 1983/2005.

19. Spencer H. Poor-laws. *Social Statics: Or The Conditions Essential to Human Happiness Specified and the First of Them Developed.* London: John Chapman, 1851:324.

20. Spencer H. National education. *Social Statics: Or The Conditions Essential to Human Happiness Specified and the First of Them Developed.* London: John Chapman, 1851:354.

21. Spencer H. Sanitary supervision. *Social Statics: Or The Conditions Essential to Human Happiness Specified and the First of Them Developed.* London: John Chapman, 1851:380.

22. Sumner W. *The Challenge of Facts: and Other Essays.* New Haven, CT: Yale University Press, 1914.

23. Russell B. *Freedom Versus Organization: the Pattern of Political Changes in the 19th Century European History.* New York: The Norton Company, 1934:111.

24. Antonio R. The cultural construction of neoliberal globalization. In: Ritzer G, editor. *The Blackwell Companion to Globalization.* Hoboken, NJ: Blackwell Publishing, 2007.

25. Foner E. *The Story of American Freedom.* New York: WW Norton and Company, 1998.

26. Phillips K. *Wealth and Democracy: A Political History of the American Rich.* New York: Broadway Books, 2002.

27. Doherty B. Objectivism, anarcho-capitalism, and the effects of psychedelics on faith and freedom. *Radicals for Capitalism: A Freewhelming History of the Modern American Libertarian Movement.* New York: Public Affairs, 2007:246.

28. Hill JJ. Industrial and railroad consolidations. *Highways of Progress.* New York: Doubleday, 1910:126, 37.

29. Carnegie A. Wealth. *North American Review* 1889;148(391).

30. Bright J, Rogers JT. *Richard Cobden, Speeches on Questions of Public Policy by Richard Cobden.* London: Macmillan & Co, 1880:35.

31. Hofstadter R. *Social Darwinism in American Thought.* New York: George Braziller, 1959:45.

32. Daily Mail. Goldman Sachs chief says "we do God's work" as he defends the bank's mega profits. *Daily Mail* November 8, 2009.

33. Ranelagh J. *Thatcher's People: An Insider's Account of the Politics, the Power, and the Personalities.* New York: Fontana, 1992:ix.

34. George S. We know what we're talking about. *Another World Is Possible If . . .* London: Verso, 2004:10.

35. Time. The rising risk of recession. *Time.* New York: Time Warner, 1969.

36. Williamson J. What Washington means by policy reform. In: Williamson J, editor. *Latin American Adjustment: How Much Has Happened?* Washington, DC: Institute for International Economics, 1990.

37. Ha-Joon Chang H-J. *Rethinking Development Economics.* London: Anthem Press, 2006:197.

38. Friedman T. *The Lexus and the Olive Tree.* London: Harper Collins, 1999:103.

39. The Economist. *Globalisation: Making Sense of an Integrating World.* London: St Edmundsbury Press, 2001:40.

40. Dollar D. Is globalization good for your health? *Bulletin of the World Health Organization* 2001;79(9):827–33.

41. Feachem R. Globalisation is good for your health, mostly. *BMJ* 2001;323(7311):504–6.

42. Ozdemir Y. With or without the IMF? A comparison of the role of the IMF in Argentina and Turkey's recovery from the 2001 financial crises. The American Political Science Association 2008 Annual Meeting. Boston, Massachusetts, 2001.

43. Dreher A. IMF and economic growth: The effects of programs, loans, and compliance with conditionality. *World Development* 2006;34(5):769–88.

44. Cornia A. Globalization and health: Results and options. *Bulletin of the World Health Organization* 2001;79(9):834–41.
45. World Bank. *Better Health in Africa: Experience and Lessons Learned*. Washington, DC: World Bank, 1994.
46. Chen S, Ravallion M. The developing world is poorer than we thought, but no less successful in the fight against poverty. *Quarterly Journal of Economics* 2008;125(4):1577–625.
47. Dollar D. *Globalization: Who wins, who loses and what the world can do about it*. Washington, DC: World Bank, 2001.
48. World Bank. *The East Asian Miracle: Economic Growth and Public Policy*. Washington, DC: World Bank, 1993.
49. Schrecker T, Labonté R, De Vogli R. Globalization and health: The need for a global vision. *Lancet* 2008;372(9650):1670–6.
50. Wolf M. Incensed about inequality. *Why Globalization Works*. New Haven, CT: Yale University Press, 2004:146.
51. The Economist. *Globalisation: Making Sense of an Integrating World*. London: St Edmundsbury Press, 2001:60.
52. UNCTAD. Structural adjustment, economic growth and the aid–debt service system. *The Least Developed Countries Report, 2000 – Aid, Private Capital Flows and External Debt: The Challenge of Financing Development in the LDCs*. Geneva: United Nations Conference on Trade and Development, 2000.
53. Stein H. *The World Bank and the IMF in Africa: Strategy and Routine in the Generation of a Failed Agenda*. Ann Arbor, MI: Center for Afro-American and African Studies (CAAS), University of Michigan, 2004.
54. Summers L. Comment. In: Blanchard O, Froot K, Sachs J, editors. *The Transition in Eastern Europe. Volume 1: Country Studies*. Chicago, IL: University of Chicago Press, 1994.
55. Passell P. Dr. Jeffrey Sachs, Shock Therapist. *New York Times* June 27, 1993.
56. Sachs J. Accelerating Privatization in Eastern Europe: The Case of Poland. World Bank Annual Conference on Development Economics. Washington, DC: World Institute for Development Economics Research of the United Nations University, 1991:1.
57. The Economist. Don't give up now: A survey of business in Eastern Europe. *The Economist* September 21, 1991:5.
58. Walberg P, McKee M, Shkolnikov V, Chenet L, Leon D. Economic change, crime, and mortality crisis in Russia: Regional analysis. *BMJ* 1998;317:312–18.
59. De Vogli R. Neoliberal globalisation and health in a time of economic crisis. *Social Theory and Health* 2011;9:311–25.
60. Cornia G, Rosignoli S, Tiberti L. Globalization and Health: Impact Pathways and Recent Evidence. Working Paper Number RP2008/74. Helsinki, Finland: United Nations University World Institute for Development Economic Research 2007.
61. Moser K, Shkolnikov V, Leon D. World mortality 1995–2000: Divergence replaces convergence from the late 1980s. *Bulletin of the World Health Organization* 2005;83(3):202–9.
62. McMichael A, McKee M, Shkolnikov V, Valkonen T. Mortality trends and setbacks: Global convergence or divergence? *Lancet* 2004;363(9415):1155–9.
63. Machenbach J, Bos V, Andersen O, Cardano M, Costa G, Harding S, et al. Widening socioeconomic inequalities in mortality in six Western European countries. *International Journal of Epidemiology* 2003;32(5):830–7.
64. Minujin A, Delamonica E. Mind the gap! Widening child mortality disparities. *Journal of Human Development* 2003;4(3):397–418.

65. De Vogli R, Schrecker T, Labonte R. Neoliberal globalisation and health inequalities. In: Monaghan L, Gabe J, editors. *Key Concepts in Medical Sociology*, 2nd ed. London: Sage, forthcoming.
66. Jerzmanowsky M, Malhar N. Financial Development and Wage Inequality: Theory and Evidence. MPRA Paper N. 9841. Munich, Germany: University Library, 2008.
67. Milanovic B, Ersado L. Reform and inequality during the transition: An analysis using panel household survey data, 1990–2005. Policy Research Working Paper 4780. Washington, DC: The World Bank Development Research Group, 2007.
68. Hanson G, Harrison A. Trade liberalization and wage inequality in Mexico. *Industrial and Labour Relations Review* 1999;52(2):271–88.
69. Shaffer E, Waitzkin H, Brenner J, Jasso-Aguilar R. Global trade and public health. *American Journal of Public Health* 2005;95(1):23–34.
70. Blouin C, Chopra M, van-der-Hoeven R. Trade and social determinants of health. *The Lancet* 2009;373(9662):502–7.
71. Hopkins S. Economic stability and health status: Evidence from East Asia before and after the 1990s economic crisis. *Health Policy* 2006;75(3):347–57.
72. Stuckler D, Meissner C, King L. Can a bank crisis break your heart? *Globalization and Health* 2008;4(1):1–12.
73. Stuckler D. Understanding privatisation's impacts on health: Lessons from the Soviet experience. *Journal of Epidemiology and Community Health* 2008;62(7):664.
74. Naterop E, Wolffers I. The role of the privatization process on tuberculosis control in HoChiMinh City Province, Vietnam. *Social Science and Medicine* 1999;48(11):1589–98.
75. Bettcher D. Tobacco control in an era of trade liberalisation. *Tobacco Control* 2001;10(1):65–7.
76. Hogstedt C, Wegman D, Kjellstrom R. The consequences of economic globalization on working conditions, labor relations, and workers' health. In: Kawachi I, Wamala S, editors. *Globalization and Health*. Oxford: Oxford University Press, 2007.
77. Evans M, Sinclair R, Fusimalohi C, Liava'a V. Globalization, diet, and health: An example from Tonga. *Bulletin of the World Health Organization* 2001;79(9):856–62.
78. Hawkes C. Uneven dietary development: Linking the policies and processes of globalization with the nutrition transition, obesity and diet-related chronic diseases. *Globalization and Health* 2006;2(4).
79. Stuckler D, King L, Basu S. International Monetary Fund programs and tuberculosis outcomes in post-communist countries. *PLoS Medicine* 2008;5(7):1079–90.
80. Jayarajah C, Branson W, Sen B. *Social Dimensions of Adjustment: World Bank Experience 1980–93*. Washington, DC: World Bank 1996.
81. World Bank. *Adjustment in Africa: Reform, Results and the Road Ahead*. Washington, DC: World Bank, 1993.
82. Breman A, Shelton C. Structural adjustment and health: A literature review of the debate, its role-players and presented empirical evidence. Working Paper WG6. Geneva: WHO, Commission on Macroeconomics and Health, 2001.
83. Cornia G, Jolly R, Stewart F. *Adjustment with a Human Face: Volume 1: Protecting the Vulnerable and Promoting Growth*. Oxford: Oxford University Press, 1987.
84. Alarcón-González D, McKinley T. The adverse effects of structural adjustment on working women in Mexico. *Latin American Perspectives* 1999;26(3):103–17.
85. Ekwempu C, Maine D, Olorukoba M, Essien E, Kisseka M. Structural adjustment and health in Africa. *Lancet* 1990;336(8703):56–7.
86. Wakhweya A. Structural adjustment and health. *BMJ* 1995;311(6997):71–2.
87. Dao H, Waters H, Le Q. User fees and health service utilization in Vietnam: How to protect the poor? *Public Health* 2008;122(10):1068–78.

88. Gilson L, McIntyre D. Removing user fees for primary care in Africa: The need for careful action. *BMJ* 2005;331(7591):762–5.

89. Breman A, Shelton C. Structural adjustment and health: A literature review of the debate, its role-players and presented empirical evidence Cambridge, MA: Commission on Macroeconomics and Health, 2001.

90. De Vogli R, Birbeck G. Potential impact of adjustment policies on vulnerability of women and children to HIV/AIDS in sub-Saharan Africa. *Journal of Health, Population, and Nutrition* 2005;23(2):105–20.

91. Stiglitz J. The promise of global institutions. *Globalization and Its Discontents*. New York: W.W. Norton & Company, 2002:13.

92. Williamson J. Did the Washington Consensus Fail? Outline of Speech at the Center for Strategic & International Studies Washington, DC, 2002.

93. Bhagwati J. *In Defense of Globalization*. Oxford, New York: Oxford University Press, 2004.

94. Antweiler W, Copeland B, Taylor M. Is free trade good for the environment? *American Economic Review* 2001;9:877–908.

95. World Bank. *World Development Report: Development and the Environment. World Development Indicators.* Oxford: World Bank, 1992.

96. Sachs W. *For Love of the Automobile: Looking Back into the History of our Desires.* Berkeley, CA: University of California, 1992.

97. Schreuder Y. *The Corporate Greenhouse: Climate Change Policies in a Globalizing World.* London: Zed Books, 2008.

98. Glomsrod S, Monge M, Vennemo H. Structural adjustment and deforestation in Nicaragua. *Environment and Development Economics* 1999;4(1):19–43.

99. Angelsen A, Shitindi E, Aarrestad J. Why do farmers expand their land into forests? Theories and evidence from Tanzania. *Environment and Development Economics* 1999;4(3):313–31.

100. Shandra J, Shor E, London B. Debt, structural adjustment, and organic water pollution: A cross-national analysis. *Organization Environment* 2008;21(1):38–55.

101. Reed D. *Structural Adjustment, the Environment, and Sustainable Development.* London: Earthscan, 1996.

102. Neumayer E. Pollution havens: An analysis of policy options for dealing with an elusive phenomenon. *The Journal of Environment and Development* 2001;10(2):147–77.

103. Daly H. Globalization versus internationalization: Some implications. *Ecological Economics* 1999;31:431–55.

104. Kessler J, van-Dorp M. Structural adjustment and the environment: The need for an analytical methodology. *Ecological Economics* 1998;27(3):267–81.

105. Gueorguieva A. A critical review of the literature on structural adjustment and the environment. Environment Department Working Paper (draft). Washington, DC: World Bank Environment Department, 2000.

106. Pet R. *The Unholy Trinity: The IMF, World Bank and WTO.* London: Zed Books, 2003.

107. Stigliz J. *Globalization and Its Discontents.* London: Penguin, 2002.

108. Gray J. Occidental twilight and the rise of Asia's capitalisms. *False Dawn: The Delusions of Global Capitalism.* London: Granta Books, 1998:187.

109. Chang H-J. *Bad Samaritans: The Myth of Free Trade and the Secret History of Capitalism.* New York: Blooomsbury Press, 2008.

110. Chang H-J. *Bad Samaritans:*13.

111. Rodrik D. *The Global Governance of Trade: As if Development Really Mattered.* New York: United Nations Development Programme, 2001:5, 24.

112. Chang H-J. *Kicking Away the Ladder: Development Strategy in Historical Perspective.* London: Anthem Press, 2002.

113. Chang H-J. *Kicking Away the Ladder: The "Real" History of Free Trade.* Silver City, NM: Foreign Policy in Focus, 2003.

114. Komiya R, Okuno M, Suzumura K. *Industrial Policy of Japan.* Tokyo: Academic Press, 1988.

115. Chomsky N. *Year 501: The Conquest Continues.* Boston, MA: South End Press, 1993:101.

116. Mészáros I. *Beyond Capital: Towards a Theory of Transition.* London: Merlin Press, 1995.

117. Boxer C. War and Trade in the Indian Ocean and the South China Sea, 1600–1650. *The Great Circle, Journal of the Australian Association for Maritime History* 1:1979:3.

118. Hobsbawm E. *The Age of Empire, 1875–1914.* New York: Pantheon Books, 1987:45.

119. Zinn H. *The Twentieth Century: A People's History.* Cambridge: Harper and Row, 1984:3.

120. Huntington S. Why international primacy matters. *International Security* 1993;17(4):68–83.

121. Vidal G. *Perpetual War for Perpetual Peace: How We Got to be So Hated: Causes of Conflict in the Last Empire.* New York: Clairview, 2002:158.

122. Friedman T (quoting from Talbot K. Backing Up Globalization with Military Might). What the World Needs Now. *New York Times* March 28, 1999.

123. Machiavelli N. Of cruelty and clemency, and whether it is better to be loved or feared. *The Prince.* London: Grant Richards, 1903:66.

124. Hobbes T. Of the differences of manner. *Leviathan; or, The matter, Form and Power of a Commonwealth, Ecclesiastical and Civil.* London: Routledge, 1886:64.

125. Nietzsche F. The genealogy of morals. *The Birth of Tragedy and The Genealogy of Morals.* New York: Doubleday Anchor Books, 1956.

126. Dawkins R. Preface. *The Selfish Gene.* New York: Russell Sage Foundation, 2002:xvi.

127. Blakeslee S. Cells that read minds. *New York Times* January 10, 2006.

128. Bowlby J. *The Making and Breaking of Affectional Bonds.* London: Tavistock Publications, 1979.

129. Kohut H. *The Restoration of the Self.* New York: International Universities Press, 1977.

130. Suttie I. *The Origins of Love and Hate.* London: Free Association Books, 1988.

131. Levy D. Primary affect hunger. *American Journal of Psychiatry* 1937;94:643–52.

132. Dawkins R. *Unweaving the Rainbow: Science, Delusion and the Appetite for Wonder.* London: Penguin, 1998.

133. Boehm C. Impact of the human egalitarian syndrome on Darwinian selection mechanics. *The American Naturalist* 1997;150(Suppl.):S100–21.

134. Bekoff M. Wild justice and fair play: Cooperation, forgiveness and morality in animals. *Biology and Philosophy* 2004;19(4):489–520.

135. Gross R. *Psychology: The Science of Mind and Behaviour.* London: Hodder & Stoughton, 1996.

Chapter 7: Divided we fail

1. Pareto V. The new theories of economics. *The Journal of Political Economy* 1897;5(4):485–502.

2. Woodburn J. Egalitarian societies. *Man* 1982;17(3):431–51.

3. Orrell D. *Economyths: Ten Ways That Economics Gets It Wrong.* London: Icon Books, 2010.

4. Davies J. *Personal Wealth from a Global Perspective.* Oxford: Oxford University Press, 2008:20.

5. Maddison A. *The World Economy: A Millennial Perspective*. Paris: Development Center of the Organisation for Economic Cooperation and Development, 2001.

6. Wolf M. The "magic" of the market. *Why Globalization Works*. New Haven, CT: Yale University Press, 2004:43.

7. von Hayek F. *The Road to Serfdom*. London: University of Chicago Press/Routledge, 1944/2007:212.

8. Harris F. Oscar's growth to originality about 1890. *Oscar Wilde: His Life and Confessions*. London: Wordsworth, 2007:67.

9. Ruttan W. *Is War Necessary for Economic Growth?* New York: Oxford University Press, 2006.

10. Ferguson D. Free Market Capitalism and the Pentagon System. Online: ZNet, Z Communications 2010.

11. Friedman M. Milton Friedman on slavery and colonization. Milton Friedman Speaks: Freedom Channel, 2007.

12. Smith A. *An Inquiry into the Nature and Causes of the Wealth of Nations: Volume I*. London, 1776/1804:343.

13. Smith A. *An Inquiry into the Nature and Causes of the Wealth of Nations: Volume II*. London, 1776:26.

14. Chomsky N. The great work of subjugation and conquest. *Year 501: The Conquest Continued*. Boston, MA: South End Press, 1993:5.

15. Shillington K. *British Made: Abolition and the Africa Trade History Today*. London: Andy Patterson, 2007:20–7.

16. Mancke E, Shammas C. *The Creation of the British Atlantic World*. Baltimore, MD: JHU Press, 2005.

17. Galeano E. *Open Veins of Latin America: Five Centuries of the Pillage of a Continent*. New York: Monthly Review Press, 1973:11–12.

18. Diamond J. *Guns, Germs and Steel: The Fates of Human Societies*. London: W.W Norton & Company, 1997.

19. Parker P. *Brazil and the Quiet Intervention, 1964*. Austin, TX: University of Texas Press, 1979.

20. Marx K. Capital/Genesis of the industrial capitalist. *Marx, Engels Collected Works*. London: Lawrence & Wishart, 2005:738.

21. Caute D. *Essential Writings of Karl Marx*. New York: Macmillian, 1967:113.

22. Galeano E. *Open Veins of Latin America: Five Centuries of the Pillage of a Continent*. New York: Monthly Review Press, 1973:79.

23. Inikori J. Slave-based commodity production and the growth of Atlantic commerce. In: Inikori J, editor. *Africans and the Industrial Revolution in England: A Study in International Trade and Economic Development*. Cambridge: Cambridge University Press, 2002:157.

24. Williams E. *Capitalism and Slavery*. Chapel Hill, NC: University of North Carolina Press, 1944.

25. Cuautemoc G. Carta de un Efe Indio A Los Gobiernos De Europa: La Verdadera Deuda Externa. Revista Renacer Indianista 2000:7.

26. Mandel E. *Marxist Economic Theory*. New York: Monthly Review Press, 1968.

27. Keay J. *The Honourable Company: A History of the English East India Company*. New York: Macmillan, 1994:281.

28. Smith A. *An Inquiry into the Nature and Causes of the Wealth of Nations Vol II*. London, 1776:190.

29. Zinn H. *A People's History of the United States*. New York: Harper Perennial Modern Classics, 1980:3–4.

30. de Las-Casas B. *Short Account of the Destruction of the Indies*. London: Penguin, 1999.

31. de Las Casas B, Sullivan F. *Indian Freedom: The Cause of Bartolome de Las Casas: A Reader*. Lanham, MD: Rowman & Littlefield, 1995:146.

32. Nietzsche F. *Beyond Good and Evil*. Chicago, IL: Gateway Editions, 1955:50.

33. Nietzsche F. *The Genealogy of Morals*. London: Macmillan, 1897:79.

34. Hume D. *The Philosophical Works*, Green T and Grose T, editors. London, 1882:253.

35. Hegel F. Geographical basis of history. *The Philosophy of History*. New York: Dover, 1956:93.

36. Chomsky N. *World Orders, Old and New*. London: Pluto Press, 1997:30–1.

37. Roosevelt T. *The Winning of the West*, Vol. III. New York: GP Putnam's Sons, 1894.

38. Gilbert M. *Winston S. Churchill*. London: Heinemann, 1976.

39. Lindqvist S. *"Exterminate All the Brutes": One Man's Odyssey into the Heart of Darkness and the Origins of the European Genocide*. New York: The New Press, 1996.

40. The Economist. In Defense of Columbus: The Trouble With Eden. *The Economist*, December 21, 1991.

41. Singer DW. *Giordano Bruno: His Life and Thought*. New York: Schuman, 1950:179.

42. Friedman TL. While I was sleeping. *The World Is Flat: A Brief History of the Twenty-First Century*. New York: Picador, 2005:8.

43. Dollar D, Kraay A. Trade, growth, and poverty. *The Economic Journal* 2002;114(493):F22–F49.

44. Wolf M. Doing more harm than good. *Financial Times* May 8, 2002.

45. Sala-i-Martin X. The world distribution of income: Falling poverty and . . . convergence, period. *Quarterly Journal of Economics* 2006;121(2):351–97.

46. Giddens A. Globalisation: Good or Bad? London School of Economics. London, 2000.

47. Smeeding T. Globalization, inequality and the rich countries of the G-20: Evidence from the Luxembourg Income Study (LIS). Working paper No. 48. Syracuse, NY: Syracuse University Center for Policy Research, 2003.

48. Dorling D, Shaw M, Davey-Smith G. Global inequality of life expectancy due to AIDS. *BMJ* 2006;322:662–4.

49. Birdsall N. The World Is Not Flat: Inequality and Injustice in Our Global Economy. WIDER Annual Lecture 2005. Helsinki: World Institute for Development Economics Research, 2006.

50. Wade RH. Winners and losers: The global distribution of income is becoming more unequal: That should be a matter of greater concern than it is. *The Economist*, 2001;359(8219):93–7.

51. Wade RH. Is globalisation reducing poverty and inequality? *World Development* 2004;32(4):567–89.

52. Bosmans K, Decancq K, Decoster A. The evolution of global inequality: Absolute, relative and intermediate views. JEL Classification. D31 D63 I31 O5. Department of Economics, Maastricht University, 2010.

53. Milanovic B. Global inequality recalculated: The effect of new 2005 PPP estimates on global inequality. Policy Research Working Paper: World Bank Research Department Group, 2009.

54. Hartmann B, Boyce JK. *A Quiet Violence: View from a Bangladesh Village*. London: Zed Books, 1983.

55. Chomsky N. *Year 501: The Conquest Continues*. Boston, MA: South End Press, 1993.

56. Cobden R. *The Political Writings of Richard Cobden*. London: W Ridgway, 1878.

57. World Bank. *Global Development Finance 2005: Mobilizing Finance and Managing Vulnerability*. Washington, DC: World Bank, 2005.

58. National Catholic Reporter. Millions of the world's children are desperate. *National Catholic Reporter* December 22, 2000.

59. George S. *The Debt Boomerang: How Third World Debt Harms Us All.* London: Pluto Press, 1993.

60. UN DESA. *World Economic Situation and Prospects 2006.* New York: United Nations Department of Economic and Social Affairs, 2006.

61. Public Agenda. Majorities say the U.S. is doing more than its share of helping less fortunate countries and we should focus on problems at home. Online 2011.

62. Public Agenda. More than half of Americans say the U.S. spends too much on foreign aid, but support sharply increases for specific types of aid such as food, medical assistance and education. Online 2011.

63. UNCTAD. *Economic Development in Africa: Debt Sustainability: Oasis or Mirage?* Geneva: United Nations Conference on Trade and Development, 2004.

64. Caney S. Global justice: From theory to practice. *Globalizations* 2006;3(2):121–37.

65. Lekomola M. The African debt dilemma: An overview of magnitude, causes, effects and policy options. *Journal of American Science* 2010;6(3):63–9.

66. Oxfam. Debt relief and the HIV/AIDS crisis in Africa: Does the Heavily Indebted Poor Countries (HIPC) Initiative go far enough? Oxfam Briefing Paper 25. London: Oxfam, 2002.

67. New Economic Foundation. *Debt Relief As If Justice Mattered: A Framework for a Comprehensive Debt Relief that Works.* London: New Economic Foundation, 2007.

68. Henwood D. Impeccable logic: Trade, development and free markets in the Clinton era. *NACLA Report on the Americas* 1993;26(5):25.

69. Mackenzie S. Systematic crimes of the powerful: Criminal aspects of the global economy. *Social Justice* 2006;33(1):162–82.

70. South Commission. *The Challenge to the South.* Oxford: The South Commission, 1990.

71. Danaher K. *50 Years Is Enough: The Case Against the World Bank and the International Monetary Fund.* Boston, MA: South End Press, 1994:6.

72. Wolf M. *Why Globalization Works.* New Haven, CT: Yale University Press, 2004.

73. Boushey H, Weller C. What the numbers tell us. In: Lardner J, Smith D, editors. *Inequality Matters: The Growing Economic Divide In America And Its Poisonous Consequences.* New York: New Press, 2005:36.

74. Sherman A, Aron-Dine A. *New CBO Data Show Income Inequality Continues to Widen.* Washington, DC: Center on Budget and Public Priorities, 2007.

75. Shnayerson M. The champagne city. *Vanity Fair* December 1997:182–202.

76. Frydman C, Saks R. *Historical Trends in Executive Compensation, 1936–2003.* Working Paper. Boston, MA: Harvard University, 2005.

77. Hacker A. The rich: Who they are. *New York Times Magazine* November 19, 1995:70–1.

78. Reich R. *Supercapitalism: The Battle for Democracy in an Age of Big Business.* Cambridge: Icon Books, 2007.

79. Truell P. Another year, another bundle: Billions in bonuses are expected to fall on Wall Street. *New York Times* December 5, 1997.

80. Kohonen M, Mestrum F. *Tax Justice: Putting Global Inequality on the Agenda.* London: Pluto Press, 2009.

81. Farrell G, O'Connor S. Goldman Sachs staff set for record pay. *Financial Times* July 15, 2009.

82. Moore M, Harper C. Goldman Sachs stock bonus plan to defer compensation expense. *Bloomberg* December 11, 2009.

83. von Hayek FA. *The Fatal Conceit: Errors of Socialism*. Chicago, IL: University of Chicago Press, 1991.

84. Clark S, Binham C. Profit "is not satanic," Barclays CEO Varley says. *Bloomberg* November 3, 2009.

85. Corning P. The future of fairness: The fair society. *The Fair Society: The Science of Human Nature and the Pursuit of Social Justice*. Chicago, IL: University of Chicago Press, 2011:189.

86. Kuznets S. Economic growth and income inequality. *The American Economic Review* 1955;45(1):1–28.

87. Nissanke M, Thorbecke E. Channels and policy debate in the globalization–inequality–poverty nexus. *World Development* 2006;34(8):1338–60.

88. De Vogli R, Mistry R, Gnesotto R, Cornia G. Has the relation between income inequality and life expectancy disappeared? Evidence from Italy and top industrialised countries. *Journal of Epidemiology and Community Health* 2005;59(2):158–62.

89. Babones S. Income inequality and population health: Correlation and causality. *Social Science & Medicine* 2008;66(7):1614–26.

90. WHO Commission on Social Determinants of Health. *Closing the Gap in a Generation: Health Equity through Action on the Social Determinants of Health*. Geneva: World Health Organization, 2008.

91. Rousseau J. Book II. *The Social Contract*. New York: Cosimo Classics, 1762/2008:30.

92. Plato. *The Dialogues of Plato, Vol. 4*, Jowett B, editor. London: MacMillan & Co., 1871:263.

93. Cornia G. *Liberalization, Globalization and Income Distribution*. Helsinki: UN World Institute for Development Economic Research (WIDER), 1999.

94. Lynch J, Smith GD, Kaplan J, House J. Income inequality and mortality: Importance to health of individual income, psychosocial environment, or material conditions. *BMJ* 2000;320(7243):1200–4.

95. Wilkinson R, Pickett K. Income inequality and population health: A review and explanation of the evidence. *Social Science and Medicine* 2006;62(7):1768–84.

96. Davey-Smith G. Income inequality and mortality: Why are they related? *BMJ* 1996;312:987–8.

97. Wilkinson R, Pickett K. *The Spirit Level: Why Greater Equality Makes Societies Stronger*. New York: Bloomsbury Press, 2009.

98. Lee K, Jung W, Youm Y. A multilevel analysis of the effect of household income equality in classes on adolescent stresses in South Korea. American Sociological Association Annual Meeting. Boston, MA, 2008.

99. Pickett K, James O, Wilkinson R. Income inequality and the prevalence of mental illness: A preliminary international analysis. *Journal of Epidemiology and Community Health* 2006;60(7):646–7.

100. De Vogli R, Santinello M. Unemployment and smoking: does psychosocial stress matter? *Tobacco Control* 2005;14(6):389–95.

101. Hsieh C-C, Pugh MD. Poverty, income inequality, and violent crime: A meta-analysis of recent aggregate data studies. *Criminal Justice Review* 1993;18(2):182–202.

102. Marmot M, Wilkinson R. Psychosocial and material pathways in the relation between income and health: A response to Lynch et al. *BMJ* 2001;322(7296):1233–6.

103. Kawachi I, Kennedy B. Income inequality and health: Pathways and mechanisms. *Health Services Research* 1999;34(1):215–27.

104. Uslaner E, Brown M. Inequality, trust and civic engagement. *American Politics Research* 2005;33(6):868–94.

105. Collins C, Yeskel F. *Economic Apartheid In America: A Primer On Economic Inequality & Insecurity*. New York: The New Press, 2005.
106. Baer P, Harte J, Haya B, Herzog A, Holdren J, Hultman N, et al. Equity and greenhouse gas responsibility. *Science* 2000;289(5488):2287.
107. Huntingford C, Gash J. Climate equity for all. *Science* 2005;309:1789.
108. Athanasiou T, Baer P. *Dead Heat: Global Justice and Global Warming*. New York: Seven Stories Press, 2002.
109. Roberts J, Parks B. *A Climate of Injustice: Global Inequality, North–South Politics and Climate Policy*. Cambridge, MA: MIT Press, 2006.
110. Schreuder Y. *The Corporate Greenhouse: Climate Change Policies in a Globalizing World*. London: Zed Books, 2008.
111. Schelling T. What makes greenhouse sense? Time to rethink the Kyoto Protocol. *Foreign Affairs* 2002;81(3):2–9.
112. George S. *The Debt Boomerang: How Third World Debt Harms Us All*. London: Pluto Press, 1993:1.
113. Harris P. Fairness, responsibility and climate change. *Ethics and International Affairs* 2003;17(1):149–56.
114. Paavola J, Adger W. Fair adaptation to climate change. *Ecological Economics* 2006;56(4):594–609.
115. Agyeman J, Bullard R, Evans B. *Just Sustainabilities: Development in an Unequal World*. Cambridge, MA: MIT Press, 2003.
116. Meyer A. The fair choice for climate change. BBC News. London: BBC, 2006.
117. World Bank. *The Little Green Data Book. World Development Indicators*. Washington DC: The World Bank, 2003.
118. Speth JG. The limits of today's environmentalism. *The Bridge at The Edge of the World: Capitalism, the Environment, and Crossing from Crisis to Sustainability*. New Haven, CT: Yale University Press, 2008:73.
119. Bookchin M. The concept of social ecology. *The Ecology of Freedom: The Emergence and Dissolution of Hierarchy*. Oakland, CA: AK Press, 2005:107.
120. Barkan E. *The Guilt of Nations: Restitution and Negotiating Historical Injustices*. Baltimore, MD: Johns Hopkins University Press, 2001.
121. Chakrabarty D. The climate of history: Four theses. *Critical Inquiry*, 2009;35(2):221.
122. Goldenberg S, Stratton A. Barack Obama's speech disappoints and fuels frustration at Copenhagen. *The Guardian* December 18, 2009.
123. Alinsky SD. *Rules for Radicals: A Practical Primer for Realistic Radicals*. New York: Random House, 1971.
124. Titmuss R. War and social policy. In: Titmuss R, editor. *Essays on "The Welfare State."* New Haven, CT: Yale University Press, 1959.
125. Douthwaite R. *The Growth Illusion: How Economic Growth Has Enriched the Few, Impoverished the Many, and Endangered the Planet*. Tulsa, OK: Council Oak Books, 1993.
126. Hoffman ML. *Empathy and Moral Development: Implications for Caring and Justice*. New York: Cambridge University Press, 2000.
127. Batson C. How social an animal? The human capacity for caring. *American Psychologist* 1990;45(3):336–46.
128. Gowdy J. Behavioral economics and climate change policy. *Journal of Economic Behavior & Organization* 2008;68(3–4):632–44.
129. Curtis A. The Lonely Robot. Part 2 of *The Trap: What Happened to Our Dream of Freedom?* London: BBC, 2007:180.
130. Wilson EO. *Biophilia*. Cambridge, MA: Harvard University Press, 1984.

131. Sanfey A. Social decision-making: Insights from game theory and neuroscience. *Science* 2007;318(5850):598–602.
132. Rifkin J. *The Empathic Civilization: The Race to Global Consciousness in a World in Crisis.* New York: Penguin, 2009.
133. Range F, Horn L, Viranyi Z, Huber L. The absence of reward induces inequity aversion in dogs. *Proceedings of the National Academy of Sciences* 2009;106(1):340–5.
134. Fehr E, Fischbacher U. The nature of human altruism. *Nature* 2003;425:785–91.
135. Dawes C, Fowler J, Johnson T, McElreath R, Smirnov O. Egalitarian motives in humans. *Nature* 2007;446:794–6.
136. Jefferson T. Thomas Jefferson to William Johnson, 1823. *Writings,* HA Washington editor. New York: HW Derby 1861, 15:441.
137. Johnson D, Stopka P, Knights S. Sociology: The puzzle of human cooperation *Nature* 2003;421:911–12.
138. Kahneman D, Knetsch J, Thaler R. Fairness and the assumptions of economics. *Journal of Business* 1986;59(4):S285–S300.
139. Schmidt M, Sommerville J. Fairness expectations and altruistic sharing in 15-month-old human infants. *PlosOne* 2011;6(10):e23223.
140. Dickens C. *Great Expectations.* London: Collector's Library, 1860/2003:83.
141. Henrich J, Boyd R, Bowles S, Camerer C, Fehr E, Gintis H, et al. "Economic man" in cross-cultural perspective: Behavioral experiments in 15 small-scale societies. *Behavioral and Brain Sciences* 2005;28(6):795–815.
142. OECD. *Social Justice in the OECD: How Do the Member States Compare? Sustainable Governance Indicators 2011.* Paris: Organization for Economic Cooperation and Development, 2012.
143. Alesina A, Angeletos G-M. Fairness and redistribution. *The American Economic Review* 2005;95(4):960–80.
144. Svalford S. Worlds of welfare and attitudes to redistribution: A comparison of eight Western nations. *European Sociological Review* 1997;13(3):283–304.
145. Hills J. *Inequality and the State.* Oxford: Oxford University Press, 2004.
146. Pierson P. When effect becomes cause: Policy feedback and political change. *World Politics* 1993;45(4):595–628.
147. Orton M, Rowlingson K. *Public Attitudes to Economic Inequality.* York: Joseph Rowntree Foundation, 2007.
148. Tawney R. *The Acquisitive Society.* Harcourt: Brace and Howe, 1920:188.
149. Lorde A. Age, race, class, and sex: Women redefining difference. In: Rothenberg P, editor. *Racism and Sexism: An Integrated Study.* New York: St. Martin's Press, 1988.
150. Harman O. *The Price of Altruism: George Price and the Search for the Origins of Kindness.* New York: WW Norton & Company, 2010:127.

Chapter 8: Out of control

1. Bloomberg. Bringing down Wall Street as ratings let loose subprime scourge. *Bloomberg* September 24, 2008.
2. Buffett W. Buffett warns on investment "time bomb." BBC News March 4, 2003.
3. Atlas J. The conservative origins of the sub-prime mortgage crisis: Everything you ever wanted to know about the mortgage meltdown but were afraid to ask. *The American Prospect* December 18, 2007.
4. Smith A, Bax EB. *An Inquiry into the Nature and Causes of the Wealth of Nations.* London: G. Bell & Sons, 1896:418.

5. Conway E. WEF 2009: Global crisis "has destroyed 40pc of world wealth." *The Telegraph* January 28, 2009.

6. ILO-IMF. The Challenges of Growth, Employment and Social Cohesion. Oslo: Joint ILO-IMF Conference in Cooperation with the Office of the Prime Minister of Norway, 2010.

7. Stuckler D, Basu S, Suhrcke M, McKee M. The health implications of financial crisis: A review of the evidence. *The Ulster Medical Journal* 2009;78(3):142–5.

8. Stuckler D, Basu S, Suhrcke M, Coutts A, McKee M. The public health effect of economic crises and alternative policy responses in Europe: An empirical analysis. *Lancet* 2009;374(9686):315–23.

9. Kentikelenis A, Karanikolos M, Papanicolas I, Basu S, McKee M, Stuckler D. Health effects of financial crisis: Omens of a Greek tragedy. *Lancet* 2011;378(9801):1457–8.

10. De Vogli R, Marmot M, Stuckler D. Excess suicides and attempted suicides in Italy attributable to the Great Recession. *Journal of Epidemiology and Community Health*, forthcoming.

11. De Vogli R, Gimeno D. Changes in income inequality and suicide rates after "shock therapy": Evidence from Eastern Europe. *Journal of Epidemiology and Community Health* 2009;63(11):956.

12. WHO. *The Financial Crisis and Global Health: Report of a High-Level Consultation.* Geneva: World Health Organization, 2009.

13. Baird S, Friedman J, Schady N. Aggregate Income Shocks and Infant Mortality in the Developing World. Harmonizing Health and Economics. Beijing: World Bank, 2009.

14. Conway E. IMF puts total cost of crisis at £7.1 trillion. *The Telegraph* August 8, 2009.

15. Cho D, Dennis B. Bailout king AIG to pay millions in bonuses. *Washington Post* March 15, 2009.

16. Jackson T. *Prosperity Without Growth? The Transition to a Sustainable Economy.* London: Sustainable Development Commission, 2009.

17. BBC News. Wall Street giant Goldman Sachs fined £17.5m by FSA. *BBC Business News* September 9, 2010.

18. New York Times. The Never-Ending Bailout. *New York Times* March 3, 2009.

19. Guba K, Luce E. Greenspan backs bank nationalisation. *Financial Times* February 18, 2009.

20. Krugman P. Money for nothing. *New York Times* April 27, 2009.

21. New York Times. Major Parts of the Financial Regulation Overhaul. *New York Times* May 20, 2010.

22. Fox News. As finance bill passes, GOP calls for repeal. Fox News July 16, 2010.

23. G20 Meeting. London Summit Communiqué. Leaders Statement: The Global Plan for Recovery and Reform. London, 2009.

24. George S. We know what we're talking about. *Another World Is Possible If. . .* London: Verso, 2004:10.

25. Stiglitz J. Capital-market liberalization, globalization, and the IMF. *Oxford Review of Economic Policy* 2004;20(1):57–71.

26. Krugman P. *The Return of Depression Economics.* London: Allen Lane: Penguin, 1999.

27. Press TV interview. Chomsky: No change coming with Obama. Press TV January 24, 2009.

28. Chang H-J. *Bad Samaritans: The Myth of Free Trade and the Secret History of Capitalism.* New York: Bloomsbury Press, 2008.

29. Makridakis S, Hogarth R, Gaba A. Forecasting and uncertainty in the economic and business world. *International Journal of Forecasting* 2009;25(4):794–812.

30. Cooper Ramo J. The Three Marketeers. *Time Magazine* February 15, 1999.

31. Nichols M, Hendrickson J, Griffith K. Was the financial crisis the result of ineffective policy and too much regulation? An empirical investigation. *Journal of Banking Regulation* 2011;12:236–51.
32. Calabria M. Did deregulation cause the financial crisis? *Cato Policy Report* 2009;31(4).
33. Kaminsky C, Reinhart K. Banking Crises: An Equal Opportunity Menace. Working Paper 14587. Cambridge, MA: National Bureau of Economic Research, 2008.
34. Eichengreen B, Fishlow A. Contending with capital flows: What is different about the 1990s? In: Kahler M, editor. *Capital Flows and Financial Crises*. Manchester: Manchester University Press, 1998.
35. Klein N. *The Shock Doctrine: The Rise of Disaster Capitalism*. New York: Metropolitan Books, 2007.
36. Rodrik D, Velasco A. Short-Term Capital Flows. 1999 ABCDE Conference at the World Bank. Washington, DC, 1999.
37. Edsall T. Alan Greenspan: The oracle or the master of disaster? *Huffington Post* March 22, 2009.
38. Risk Management and Challenges in the U.S. Financial System. Global Association of Risk Professionals 7th Annual Risk Management Convention and Exhibition, February 26, 2008, New York.
39. Kroszner R, Strahan P. What drives deregulation? Economics and politics of the relaxation of bank branching restrictions. *The Quarterly Journal of Economics* 1999;114(4):1437–67.
40. Moss D. An ounce of prevention: Financial regulation, moral hazard and the end of "too big to fail." *Harvard Magazine* September–October 2009.
41. Eichengreen B, Bordo MD. Crises Now and Then: What Lessons from the Last Era of Financial Globalisation. National Bureau of Economic Research (NBER). Working Paper N.8716. Cambridge, MA, 2002.
42. Bordo M, Eichengreen B, Klingebiel D, Martinez-Peria M. Financial crises: Lessons from the last 120 years. *Economic Policy* 2001;April:53–82.
43. Patomäki H, Teivainen T. *A Possible World: Democratic Transformations of Global Institutions*. London: Zed Books, 2004.
44. BIS. Triennial Central Bank Survey. Foreign Exchange and Derivative Market Activity in 2007. Basel, Switzerland: Bank for International Settlements (BIS), 2007.
45. Philips K. *Bad Money: Reckless Finance, Failed Politics, and the Global Crisis of American Capitalism*. New York: Viking, 2008.
46. Anderson S, Cavanagh J. *Field Guide to the Global Economy*. New York: New Press, 2000.
47. BIS. Semi-Annual OTC Derivatives Statistics: Bank for International Settlement, 2010.
48. Tett G. *Fool's Gold: How the Bald Dream of a Small Tribe at J.P. Morgan Was Corrupted by Wall Street Greed and Unleashed a Catastrophe*. New York: Free Press, 2009.
49. Johnson S, Kwak J. *13 Bankers: The Wall Street Takeover and the Next Financial Meltdown*. New York: Panthen Books, 2010.
50. The Economist. *Globalisation: Making Sense of an Integrating World*. London: St Edmundsbury Press, 2001:284.
51. Friedman T. *The Lexus and the Olive Tree*. New York: Farrar, Straus and Giroux, 1999:432.
52. Philippon T, Resheff A. Wages and Human Capital in the US Financial Industry: 1909–2006. Working Paper 2008.
53. Reich R. *Aftershock: The Next Economy and America's Future*. New York: Random House, 2010.

54. Rajan R. *Fault Lines: How Hidden Fractures Still Threaten the World Economy*. Princeton, NJ: Princeton University Press, 2010.
55. Kumhof M, Ranciere R. Inequality, Leverage and Crises. IMF Working Paper. Washington, DC: International Monetary Fund, Research Department, 2011.
56. Kindleberger C. *The World in Depression, 1929–1939*. Berkeley, CA: University of California Press, 1986.
57. Obstfeld M, Rogoff K. Global Imbalances and the Financial Crisis: Products of Common Causes. Federal Reserve Bank of San Francisco Asia Economic Policy Conference. Santa Barbara, CA, 2009.
58. Keys B, Mukherjee T, Seru A, Vig V. Did securitization lead to lax screening? Evidence from subprime loans. *Quarterly Journal of Economics* 2010;125(1):307–62.
59. Taylor J. *Getting Off Track: How Government Actions and Interventions Caused, Prolonged and Worsened the Financial Crisis*. Stanford, CT: Hoover Institution Press, 2009.
60. Anderson K. International perspectives on household wealth. *Comparative Economic Studies* 2009;51(2):274–7.
61. Gills B. The swinging of the pendulum: The global crisis and beyond. *Globalizations* 2008;5(4):513–22.
62. Cassidy J. *How Market Fails: The Logic of Economic Calamities*: Farrar, Straus and Giroux, 2009.
63. Duménil G, Levy D. *Capital Resurgent: Roots of the Neoliberal Revolution*. Cambridge, MA: Harvard University Press, 2004.
64. Wade R, Veneroso F. The Asian crisis: The high debt model versus the Wall Street-treasury-IMF complex. *New Left Review* 1998;228:3–23.
65. Luhnow D. The secrets of the world's richest man. *Wall Street Journal* August 4, 2007.
66. Time. The committee to save the world. *Time Magazine* February 15, 1999.
67. Bruno M. Deep Crises and Reform: What Have We Learned So Far? Conference of the International Economics Association. Tunis, 1996:4.
68. Rahm Emanuel. You never want a serious crisis to go to waste. Interview with the *Wall Street Journal*. January 28, 2009. http://www.youtube.com/watch?v=1yeA_kHHLow
69. Williamson J, Haggard S. The political conditions of economic reform. In: Williamson J, editor. *The Political Economy of Policy Reform*. Washington, DC: Institute for International Economics, 1994:565.
70. Williamson J. In search of a manual for technopols. In: Williamson J, editor. *The Political Economy of Policy Reform*. Washington, DC: Institute for International Economics, 1994:20.
71. Friedman M. Preface, 1982. *Capitalism and Freedom*. London: The University of Chicago Press, 1962/1982/2002:xiii–ix.
72. Lynn B. *Cornered: The New Monopoly of Capitalism and the Economics of Destruction*. Hoboken, NJ: John Wiley & Sons, 2010.
73. Chossudovsky M, Marshall AG. *The Global Economic Crisis. The Great Depression of the XXI Century*. Montreal: Global Research Publishers, 2010.
74. Business Week. Another year in bank heaven? *Bloomberg Business Week* January 10, 1994:103.
75. Krebs A. *The Corporate Reapers: the Book of Agribusiness*. Washington DC: Essential Books.
76. Foster JB, McChesney RW, Jonna RJ. Monopoly and competition in twenty-first century capitalism. *Monthly Review* 2011;62(11).
77. Merger Waves in the 19th, 20th and 21st Centuries. The Davies Lecture Osgoode Hall Law School York University, 2006, Toronto, Canada.

78. Lynn B. Cornered: *The New Monopoly of Capitalism and the Economics of Destruction.* Hoboken, NJ: John Wiley & Sons, 2010.

79. Hollander S. Engels's early contribution. *Friedrich Engels and Marxian Political Economy.* Cambridge: Cambridge University Press, 2011:31.

80. Vogel D. *The Market for Virtue: The Potential and Limits of Corporate Social Responsibility.* Washington, DC: Brookings Institution, 2005:3–4.

81. Friedman M. The social responsibility of business is to increase profits. *New York Times Magazine* September 13, 1970.

82. Wolf M. The "magic" of the market. *Why Globalization Works.* New Haven, CT: Yale University Press, 2004:49.

83. Reich R. *Supercapitalism: The Battle for Democracy in an Age of Big Business.* Cambridge: Icon Books, 2007:75.

84. Bowles S. American capitalism: Accumulation and change. *Understanding Capitalism: Competition, Command and Change.* New York: Oxford University Press, 2005:148–9.

85. Sweezy P. More (or less) on globalization. *Monthly Review* 1997;49(4):1–4.

86. Magdoff H. *Imperialism: From the Colonial Age to the Present.* New York: Monthly Review Press, 1978:187.

87. Balkan J. Business as usual. *The Corporation: The Pathological Pursuit of Profit and Power.* London: Constable, 2005:50.

88. Balkan J. Business as usual. *The Corporation: The Pathological Pursuit of Profit and Power.* London: Constable, 2005:35.

89. Minsky H. *Can "It" Happen Again?: Essays on Instability and Finance.* Armonk, NY: M. E. Sharpe, 1982.

90. Kindelberger C. *Manias, Panics and Crashes: A History of Financial Crises.* London: John Wiley and Sons, 2001.

91. Marx K. Wage labor and capital. In: Marx K, Engels F, Elliott J, editors. *Marx and Engels on Economics, Politics, and Society.* Santa Monica, CA: Goodyear, 1980.

92. Marx K, Engels F. *The Communist Manifesto: A Modern Edition.* London: Verso, 1848/1998:38–9.

93. Marx K. *Grundrisse: Foundations of the Critique of Political Economy.* New York: Vintage, 1973:334, 408.

94. Schumpeter JA. *Capitalism, Socialism and Democracy.* London: George Allen & Unwin, 1943.

95. Marx K. *Capital.* New York: New World Paperbacks, 1967:615.

96. Kliman A. *The Failure of Capitalist Production: Underlying Causes of the Great Recession.* New York: Pluto Press, 2011.

97. Marx K, Engels F. *The Communist Manifesto: A Modern Edition.* London: Verso, 1848/1998:41.

98. Santayana G. *Reason in Common Sense: The Life of Reason Volume 1.* New York: Dover Publications, 1905/1980:310.

99. Greenspan A. Testimony of Dr Alan Greenspan to the Committee of Government Oversight and Reform, 2008.

100. Luce E, Freeland C. Summers calls for boost to demand. *Financial Times* March 8, 2009.

101. Simms A, Pettifor A, Lucas C, Secrett C, Hines C, Leggett J, et al. *A Green New Deal: Joined-up Policies to Solve the Triple Crunch of the Credit Crisis, Climate Change and High Oil Prices.* London: New Economics Foundation (NEF) on behalf of the Green New Deal Group, 2007:12.

102. Volcker P. Statement Before the Committee on Banking and Financial Services of the House of Representatives. Washington, DC: United States House of Representatives, 2009.

103. Skidelsky R. *Keynes: The Return of the Master.* New York: Public Affairs, 2009.
104. Ferguson N. Introduction. *The Ascent of Money: A Financial History of the World.* New York: Penguin, 2008:10.
105. Patman W. *The Robinson-Patman Act: What You Can and Cannot Do Under This Law.* New York: Ronald Press, 1938.
106. Eatwell J, Taylor L. *Global Finance at Risk: The Case for International Regulation.* New York: The New Press, 2000.
107. O'Grady S. Hundreds of economists call for tax on currency speculation. *The Independent* Monday, February 15, 2010.
108. Ramonet I. Désarmer les marchés. *Le Monde Diplomatique* December 1997.
109. Speth JG. *The Bridge at The Edge of the World.* New Haven, CT: Yale University Press, 2008:90.

Chapter 9: State of political inertia

1. The Economist. *Globalisation: Making Sense of an Integrating World.* London: St Edmundsbury Press, 2001:9.
2. Friedman T. *The Lexus and the Olive Tree.* London: Harper Collins, 1999.
3. Thoreau D. Civil disobedience. In: Thomas O, editor. *Walden and Civil Disobedience.* New York: WW Norton and Company, 1849/1966:224.
4. Zhan J. *World Investment Report 2011: Non-Equity Modes of International Production and Development.* Geneva, Switzerland: United Nations Conference on Trade and Development (UNCTAD), 2011.
5. UNCTAD. *World Investment Report, 1996: Investment, Trade and International Policy Arrangements.* Geneva, Switzerland: United Nations Conference on Trade and Development (UNCTAD), 1996.
6. Anderson S, Cavanagh J. *Top 200: The Rise of Corporate Global Power.* Washington, DC: Institute for Policy Studies, 2000.
7. UNCTAD. *Are Transnationals Bigger Than Countries?* Geneva, Switzerland: United Nations Conference on Trade and Development, 2002.
8. Patomäki H, Teivainen T. *A Possible World: Democratic Transformations of Global Institutions.* London: Zed Books, 2004.
9. Kohonen M, Mestrum F. *Tax Justice: Putting Global Inequality on the Agenda.* London: Pluto Press, 2009.
10. Edsall T. Alan Greenspan: The oracle or the master of disaster? *Huffington Post* March 22, 2009.
11. Coghlan A, MacKenzie D. Revealed: the capitalist network that runs the world. *New Scientist* October 24, 2011.
12. George S. We know what we're talking about. *Another World Is Possible If . . .* London: Verso, 2004:10.
13. Gray J. *False Dawn: The Delusions of Global Capitalism.* London: Granta Books, 1998.
14. Rodrik D. *Has Globalization Gone Too Far?* Washington, DC: Institute for International Economics, 1997:75.
15. Sassen S. Immigration tests the new order. *Losing Control? Sovereignty in an Age of Globalization.* New York: Columbia University Press, 1996:67–86.
16. Schrecker T. The power of money: Global financial markets, national politics, and social determinants of health. In: Kay A, Williams O, editors. *Global Health Governance: Crisis, Institutions and Political Economy.* Houndmills, UK: Palgrave Macmillan, 2009.
17. Mandel M. Can anyone steer the economy? *Bloomberg Business Week* November 20, 2006:56–8.

18. Reich R. *The Work of Nations*. New York: Alfred A Knopf, 1991.

19. Black WK. *The Best Way to Rob a Bank Is to Own One: How Corporate Executives and Politicians Looted The S&L Industry*. Austin, TX: University of Texas Press, 2005.

20. Hertz N. Let them eat cake. *The Silent Takeover: Global Capitalism and the Death of Democracy*. London: Arrow Books, 2001:60.

21. Shaw M, Smith GD, Dorling D. Health inequalities and New Labour: How the promises compare with real progress. *BMJ* 2005;330(7498):1016–20.

22. Rubin R, Weisberg J. *In an Uncertain World: Tough Choices from Wall Street to Washington*. New York: Random House, 2004.

23. The White House. Remarks by the president to business leaders and officials and employees of Gateway Computers. Dublin, Ireland: The White House Office of the Press Secretary, 1998.

24. Greider W. The soul of capitalism. *The Soul of Capitalism: Opening Paths to a Moral Economy*. New York: Simon and Schuster, 2003:29.

25. Friedman T. *The Lexus and the Olive Tree*. London: Harper Collins, 1999:103.

26. Brittain-Catlin W. *Offshore: The Dark Side of the Global Economy*. New York: Farrar, Straus and Giroux, 2005.

27. World Wealth Report. *World Wealth Report, 2007*, 12th ed. Merryll Lynch and Capgemini, 2007.

28. General Accounting Office. *Comparison of the Reported Tax Liabilities of Foreign and US-Controlled Corporations, 1996–2000*. Washington, DC: General Accounting Office (GAO), 2004.

29. The Economist. Rupert laid bare. *The Economist*. March 18, 1999.

30. Shaxson N. *Treasure Islands: Uncovering the Damage of Offshore Banking and Tax Havens*. New York: Palgrave Macmillan, 2011.

31. Nader R. *Cutting Corporate Welfare*. New York: Seven Stories Press, 2000.

32. Ganghof S. *The Politics of Income Taxation: A Comparative Analysis*. Colchester, UK: ECPR Press, 2006.

33. Citizens for Tax Justice. *United States Remains One of the Least Taxed Industrial Countries*. Washington, DC: Citizens for Tax Justice Publications 2007.

34. Institute on Taxation and Economic Policy. State Corporate Tax Disclosure: Why It's Needed. Policy Brief #16. Washington, DC: Institute on Taxation and Economic Policy, 2005.

35. Internal Revenue Service. *Individual Income Tax Data of Taxpayers with the Top 400 Adjusted Gross Income*. Washington, DC: Internal Revenue Service, 2007.

36. Chomsky N. Neoliberalism and global order. *Profit Over People: Neoliberalism and Global Order*. New York: Seven Stories Press, 1999:38.

37. Galbraith J. *The New Industrial State*. Boston, MA: Houghton Mifflin, 1967.

38. Slivinski S. *The Corporate Welfare State: How the Federal Government Subsidizes U.S. Businesses*. Washington, DC: CATO Institute, 2007.

39. Myers N, Kent J. *Perverse Subsidies: How Tax Dollars Can Undercut the Environment and the Economy*. Washington, DC: Island Press, 2001.

40. Galbraith JK. *The Affluent Society*. Harmondsworth, UK: Pelican Book, 1969.

41. Cooper M, Wakin DJ. Archdiocese leaves Kerry and president off guest list. *New York Times* September 17, 2004.

42. Jefferson T. Thomas Jefferson to John Taylor, 1816, *Writings*, HA Washington editor. New York: HW Derby 1861.

43. Jackson A (1830). Cited by Charles Sellers, *The Market Revolution: Jacksonian America 1815–1846*. New York: Oxford University Press, 1991:62.

44. Davidson D. *The Wisdom of Theodore Roosevelt*. New York: Citadel Press, 2003:47.
45. Woodrow Wilson, William Bayard Hale. *The New Freedom: A Call for the Emancipation of the Generous Energies of a People*. New York: Doubleday, 1918:57.
46. Wolf TP, Daynes BW. *Franklin D. Roosevelt and Congress: The New Deal and Its Aftermath*. New York: ME Sharpe 2001:33.
47. Dilliard I. *Mr. Justice Brandeis, Great American 1856–1941: Press Opinion & Public Appraisal*. St. Louis, MI: Modern View Press, 1941:42.
48. Ferguson T. *Golden Rule: The Investment Theory of Party Competition and the Logic of Money-Driven Political System*. Chicago, IL: University of Chicago Press, 1995.
49. Jacobs LR, Skocopl T. *Inequality and America Democracy: What We Know and What We Need to Learn*. New York: Russell Sage Foundation, 2005.
50. Dahl RA. *On Political Equality*. New Haven, CT: Yale University Press, 2006:x.
51. Ansolabehere S, de-Figueiredo J, Snyder J. Why is there so little money in U.S. politics? *The Journal of Economic Perspectives* 2003;17(1):105–30.
52. Repetto R. Best Practice in Internal Oversight of Lobbying Practice. Working Paper Number 200601: Yale Center for Environmental Law and Policy, 2006.
53. Brennan Center for Justice, Common Cause, Democracy Matters, Public Campaign, Public Citizen, US-PIRG. *Breaking Free with Fair Elections: A New Declaration of Independence for Congress*. New York: The Brennon Center for Justice, 2007.
54. *Citizens United v Federal Elections Commission*. No. 130 US 876. Supreme Court of the United States, 2010.
55. Overton S. The donor class: Campaign finance, democracy, and participation. *University of Pennsylvania Law Review* 2004;152:73–118.
56. Verba S, Schlozman KL, Brady H. *Voice and Equality: Civic Voluntarism in American Politics*. Cambridge, MA: Harvard University Press, 1995.
57. Hertsgaard M. *Earth Odyssey: Around the World in Search of Our Environmental Future*. New York: Broadway Books, 1999:82.
58. Francia P, Herrnson P. Begging for bucks. *Campaigns & Elections* 2001;22(2):51–2.
59. The Economist. Politicians for rent. *The Economist*, February 8, 1996.
60. Institute on Taxation and Economic Policy. Buy Now Save Later: Campaign Contributions and Corporate Taxation. Washington, DC: Institute on Taxation and Economic Policy, 2001.
61. Essential Information and Consumer Education Foundation. *Sold Out: How Wall Street and Washington Betrayed America*. Washington, DC: Essential Information and Consumer Education Foundation, 2009.
62. Doster A. *Durbin on Congress: The Banks Own the Place*. Online: Progress Illinois 2009.
63. Center for Responsive Politics. *Money Is the Victor in 2002 Midterm Elections*. Washington, DC: Center for Responsive Politics, 2002.
64. Center for Responsive Politics. *2004 Election Outcome: Money Wins*. Washington, DC: Center for Responsive Politics, 2004.
65. Gloudeman N. Barack Obama: Marketer of the Year. Online: Mother Jones October 20, 2008.
66. Rove K. McCain couldn't compete with Obama's money: America affirms Chicago's golden rule. *Wall Street Journal* December 4, 2008.
67. Schouten F, Korte G. Conservatives outspent liberals 2–1 in elections. *USA Today* November 4, 2010.
68. Raber P. Plutocracy in action: Corporate lobbyists write anti-environmental legislation. *Sierra Magazine* July 1, 1995.
69. Drutman L. Perennial lobbying scandal. Online: TomPaine.com February 28, 2007.
70. Hirsh M. Why is Barney Frank so effing mad? *Newsweek* December 4, 2009.

71. Pell M, Eaton J. Five lobbyists for each member of Congress on financial reforms. Online: iWatch News August 2, 2011.

72. Domhoff GW. *Who Rules America? Challenges to Corporate and Class Dominance.* Boston, MA: McGraw-Hill, 2006:xi–xiv.

73. Public Citizen. *Blind Faith: How Deregulation and Enron's Influence Over Government Looted Billions from Americans.* Washington, DC: Public Citizen, 2001.

74. Weissman R, Donahue J. *Sold Out: How Wall Street and Washington Betrayed America.* Washington, DC: Essential Information and Consumer Education Foundation, 2009.

75. Cited in Reich R. *Supercapitalism: the Battle for Democracy in an Age of Big Business.* Cambridge: Icon Books, 2007:139.

76. Ignatius D. When the gurus flinched. *Washington Post* Sunday, March 1, 2009.

77. Scheiber N. Obama's choice: The next Larry Summers . . . or Larry Summers. *The New Republic* November 5, 2008.

78. Taibbi M. Obama's big sellout: The president has packed his economic team with Wall Street insiders intent on turning the bailout into an all-out giveaway. *Rolling Stone* December 13, 2009.

79. Interview with Noam Chomsky. What next? The elections, the economy, and the world. *Democracy Now* November 24, 2008.

80. Revolving doors, accountability and transparency: Emerging regulatory concerns and policy solutions in the financial crisis. Discussion paper, Global Forum on Public Governance: Building a Cleaner World. Paris: OECD, 2009.

81. Balot RK. *Greed and Injustice in Classical Athens.* Princeton, NJ: Princeton University Press, 2001.

82. Jayapalan N. Plato's conception of justice. *Plato.* New Delhi: Atlantic Publishers and Distributors, 1999:16.

83. Kagan D. *The Fall of Athenian Empire.* Ithaca, NY: Cornell University Press, 1987.

84. UNESCO and World Radio and Television Council. Public Broadcasting: Why? How? 2000. Online.

85. Dummett K. Drivers for corporate environmental responsibility. *Environment, Development and Sustainability* 2006;8(3):375–89.

86. Levy DL, Newell P. Oceans apart? Business responses to global environmental issues in Europe and the United States. *Environment* 2000;42(9):8–21.

87. Speth JG. *Red Sky at Morning: America and the Crisis of the Global Environment.* New Haven, CT: Yale University Press, 2005.

88. Derber C. *Corporation Nation.* New York: St. Martin Griffin, 1998.

89. Hartmann T. *Unequal Protection: The Rise of Corporate Dominance and the Theft of Human Rights.* Emmaus, PA: Rodale Press, 2004.

90. Dresser C. Vanderbilt in the West. *New York Times* October 9, 1882.

91. White AL. Transforming the Corporation. GTI Paper Series n°5. Boston, MA: Great Transition Initiative and Tellus Institute, 2006:7–8.

92. White AL. Transforming the corporation. GTI Paper Series n°5. Boston, MA: Great Transition Initiative and Tellus Institute, 2006:6.

93. Barsky RF. *The Chomsky Effect: A Radical Works Beyond the Ivory Tower.* Boston, MA: MIT Press, 2007:209.

94. Voltaire. *Candide.* Sioux Falls, SD: NuVision Publications, 2005:8.

95. Leibniz G. *Essais de Théodicée sur la bonté de Dieu, la liberté de l'homme et l'origine du mal.* Whitefish, MA: Kessinger Publishing, 1710/2010.

96. Evans EJ. Thatcher triumphant, 1982–8. *Thatcher and Thatcherism.* London: Routledge, 1997:35.

97. Hayek F. *The Road to Serfdom.* London: University of Chicago Press/Routledge, 1944/2007:212.

98. Fukuyama F. By way of an introduction. *The End of History and the Last Man*. New York: Free Press, 1992:1.

99. Friedman T. *The Lexus and the Olive Tree: Understanding Globalization*. London: Macmillan, 2000:102.

100. Wolf M. The "magic" of the market. *Why Globalization Works*. New Haven, CT: Yale University Press, 2004:49.

101. Giddens A. *The Third Way: The Renewal of Social Democracy*. Hoboken, NJ: Wiley, 1998.

Chapter 10: Progress or collapse

1. Diamond J. *Collapse: How Societies Choose To Fail or Survive*. London: Penguin, 2005.

2. Diamond J. Prologue: A tale of two farms. *Collapse: How Societies Choose To Fail or Survive*. London: Penguin, 2005:23.

3. Tainter JA. *The Collapse of Complex Societies*. Cambridge: Cambridge University Press, 1990.

4. Huber P. Externality: Pollution on a chip. *Hard Green: Saving the Environment from the Environmentalists: A Conservative Manifesto*. New York: Basic Books, 1999:29.

5. Malthus T. Effects of the knowledge of the principal cause of poverty on civil liberty. *An Essay on the Principle of Population, Volume II*. Cambridge: Cambridge University Press, 1798/1989:127.

6. Beckerman W. *Small Is Stupid: Blowing the Whistle on the Greens*. London: Duckworth, 1995.

7. Huber P. Eschatology: From Malthus to Faust. *Hard Green: Saving the Environment from the Environmentalists: A Conservative Manifesto*. New York: Basic Books, 1999:81.

8. The Economist. Sui genocide. *The Economist* December 19, 1998.

9. Kahn H, Brown W, Martel L. *The Next 200 Years: A Scenario for America and the World*. New York: William Morrow and Company, 1976.

10. Larry Summers, recorded at the 1991 Bangkok meeting in an interview with Kirsten Garrett. Background Briefing, ABC, November 10, 1991.

11. Moytl A. *Imperial Ends: The Decay, Collapse, and Revival of Empires*. New York: Columbia University Press, 2001:41–5.

12. Diamond J. The last Americans: Environmental collapse and the end of civilization. *Harper's Magazine* June 2003:43.

13. Latouche S. *Farewell to Growth*. Cambridge: Polity Press, 2008.

14. Firth N. Human race "will be extinct within 100 years," claims leading scientist. *Daily Mail* June 19, 2010.

15. Rees M. *Our Final Century: Will the Human Race Survive the Twenty-first Century?* London: Heineman, 1993.

16. University of York. Fossil record supports evidence of impending mass extinction. *ScienceDaily* May 27, 2007.

17. Benton M. *When Life Nearly Died: The Greatest Mass Extinction of All Time*. London: Thames and Hudson, 2003.

18. Sahney S, Benton M. Recovery from the most profound mass extinction of all time. Proceedings of the Royal Society: *Biological Sciences* 2008;275(1636):759–65.

19. Ward PD. *Under a Green Sky: Global Warming, the Mass Extinctions of the Past, and What They Can Tell Us About Our Future*. New York: Harper Collins, 2007.

20. Parry M, Arnell N, McMichael T, Nicholls R, Martens P, Kovats S, et al. Millions at risk: Defining critical climate change threats and targets. *Global Environmental Change* 2001;11:181–3.

21. Derber C. *Greed to Green: Solving Climate Change and Remaking the Economy.* Boulder, CO: Paradigm Publishers, 2010.

22. Kunstler JH. *The Long Emergency: Surviving the Converging Catastrophes of the 21st Century.* London: Atlantic Books, 2005.

23. Wright R. *A Short History of Progress.* Edinburgh, New York, Melbourne: Canongale, 2004.

24. Homer-Dixon T. Catagenesis. *The Upside of Down: Catastrophe, Creativity and the Renewal of Civilisation.* Washington, DC: Island Press, 2006:289.

25. Homer-Dixon T. Disintegration. *The Upside of Down: Catastrophe, Creativity and the Renewal of Civilisation.* Washington, DC: Island Press, 2006:254.

26. IPCC. *Climate Change 2007: The Physical Science Basis – Summary for Policymakers.* Geneva: Intergovernmental Panel on Climate Change, 2007.

27. Hare B. Relationship between increases in global mean temperature and impacts on ecosystems, food production, water and socio-economic systems. In: Schellnhuber H, Cramer W, Nakicenovic N, Wigley T, Yohe G, Pachauri R, et al., editors. *Avoiding Dangerous Climate Change.* Cambridge: Cambridge University Press, 2006.

28. Grassl H, et al. Climate Protection Strategies for the 21st Century: Kyoto and Beyond. WBGU Special Report. Berlin: WBGU German Advisory Council on Global Change, 2003:11.

29. Pearce F. What Tallberg taught me. *The Telegraph* July 10, 2007.

30. Weaver A, Zickfeld K, Montenegro A, Eby M. Long term climate implications of 2050 emission reduction targets. *Geophysical Research Letters* 2007;34(L19703).

31. Stern N. *The Economics of Climate Change: The Stern Review.* Cambridge: Cambridge University Press, 2007.

32. Foster JB, Clark B, York R. *The Ecological Rift: Capitalism's War on the Earth.* New York: Monthly Review Press, 2010.

33. Broecker W. CO_2 arithmetic. *Science* 2007;315(5817):1371.

34. Morton O. Climate change: Is this what it takes to save the world? *Nature* 2007;447:132–6.

35. Raupach M, Marland G, Ciais P, Quéré CL, Canadell JG, Klepper G, et al. Global and regional drivers of accelerating CO_2 emissions. *PNAS* 2007;104(24):1028–93.

36. Harrabin R. China building more power plants. BBC News June 19, 2007.

37. FAO. *Global Forest Resources Assessment 2005: Progress Towards Sustainable Forest Management.* Rome: Food and Agriculture Organization of the United Nations, 2006.

38. Homer-Dixon T. On the threshold: Environmental changes as causes of acute conflict. *International Security* 1991;16(2):76–166.

39. Farrington S. Oil over a barrel: Good-bye to cheap oil from 2010? Dow Jones Newswires. New York: Bloomberg, 2004.

40. Monbiot G. A sudden change of state. *The Guardian* July 3, 2007.

41. Von Weizacker E, Lovins A and Lovins L. *Factor Four: Doubling Wealth, Halving Resource Use.* London: Earthscan Publications, 1998: 211.

42. Greenpeace. *Energy [R]evolution: A Sustainable China Energy Outlook.* Brussels, Belgium: Greenpeace European Renewable Energy Council, 2007.

43. Brown LR. *Plan B 3.0: Mobilizing to Save Civilisation,* 3rd ed. New York: WW Norton and Company, 2008.

44. Lowe C. EU sees solar power imported from Sahara in 5 yrs. *Reuters* June 21, 2010.

45. Douthwaite R. *The Growth Delusion: How Economic Growth Has Enriched the Few, Impoverished the Many and Endangered the Planet.* Green Books, 1999.

46. Holdren J. Environmental change and the human condition. *Bulletin of the American Academy of Arts and Sciences* 2003;Fall 2003:24–31.

47. World Bank. *World Development Indicators, 2010*. Washington, DC: World Bank, 2010.

48. REN21. *Renewables 2011: Global Status Report*. Paris: REN21 Secretariat, 2011.

49. Renner M. *Jobs in Renewable Energy Expanding*. Washington, DC: WorldWatch Institute, 2008.

50. Myers N, Kent J. *Perverse Subsidies: How Tax Dollars Can Undercut the Environment and the Economy*. Washington, DC: Island Press, 2001.

51. Bradsher K. Green power takes root in the Chinese desert. *New York Times* July 3, 2009.

52. US Department of Energy. Alternative Fuel Vehicles (AFVs) and Hybrid Electric Vehicles (HEVs): Trend of sales by HEV models from 1999–2009. Alternative Fuels and Advanced Vehicle Data Center (U.S. DoE), 2010.

53. Martin J. *The Meaning of the 21st Century: A Vital Blueprint For Ensuring Our Future*. London: Eden Projects Books, 2006:149.

54. Sachs J. The spread of economic prosperity. *The End of Poverty: Economic Possibilities of Our Time*. New York: Penguin, 2005:34–7.

55. Schrecker T, Labonté R, De Vogli R. Globalization and health: The need for a global vision. *Lancet* 2008;372(9650):1670–6.

56. Cheru F. Structural adjustment, primary resource trade and sustainable development in sub-Saharan Africa. *World Development* 1992;20(4):497–512.

57. Rosenblum M, Williamson D. *Squandering Eden: Africa at the Edge*. New York: Harcourt Brace, 1987.

58. Corning P. *The Fair Society: The Science of Human Nature and the Pursuit of Social Justice*. Chicago, IL: University of Chicago Press, 2011:189.

59. Wilkinson R, Pickett K, De Vogli R. Equality, sustainability, and quality of life. *BMJ* 2010;341:1138–40.

60. Halstead S, Walsh J, Warren K. Good Health at Low Cost: Proceedings of a Conference Held at the Bellagio Conference Center. New York: Rockefeller Foundation, 1985.

61. Clark MA. *Gradual Economic Reform in Latin America: The Costa Rican Experience*. New York: State University of New York Press, 2001.

62. Segura-Ubiergo A. Costa Rica: Globalization, gradual reform and the politics of compensation, 1973–2002. *The Political Economy of the Welfare State in Latin America: Globalization, Democracy, and Development*. Cambridge: Cambridge University Press, 2007:207–28.

63. Véron R. The "new" Kerala model: Lessons for sustainable development. *World Development* 2001;29(4):601–17.

64. UNDP. *Human Development Report 2011: Sustainability and Equity: A Better Future For All*. New York: United Nations Development Programme, 2011.

65. Harris P. Beyond Bush: Environmental politics and prospects for US climate policy. *Energy Policy* 2008;37(3):966–71.

66. Brown L. *Plan B 2.0: Rescuing a Planet Under Stress and a Civilization in Trouble*. Washington, DC: WW Norton and Company, 2006.

67. Franco M, Orduñez P, Caballero B, Tapia-Granados J, Lazo M, Bernal J, et al. Impact of energy intake, physical activity, and population-wide weight loss on cardiovascular disease and diabetes mortality in Cuba, 1980–2005. *American Journal of Epidemiology* 2007;166(12):1374–80.

68. McKibben B. The year of eating locally. *Deep Economy: The Wealth of Communities and the Durable Future*. New York: Times Books, 2007:73.

69. Simms A, Pettifor A, Lucas C, Secrett C, Hines C, Leggett J, et al. *A Green New Deal: Joined-up Policies to Solve the Triple Crunch of the Credit Crisis, Climate Change and High*

Oil Prices. London: New Economics Foundation (NEF) on behalf of the Green New Deal Group, 2007:12.

70. Sen A. Mortality as an indicator of economic success and failure. *Royal Economic Society Economic Journal* 1998;108(446):1–25.

71. Winter J. *The Great War and the British People*. London: Macmillian, 1986.

72. Tobin J. A currency transactions tax, why and how? *Open Economies Review* 1996;7(1):493–9.

73. Toynbee P. Bring on the Robin Hood tax. *The Guardian* March 13, 2010.

74. Kohonen M, Mestrum F. Introduction. *Tax Justice: Putting Global Inequality on the Agenda*. London: Pluto Press, 2009:14.

75. Ikenberry G. A world economy restored: Expert consensus and the Anglo-American postwar settlement. *International Organisation* 1992;46(1):289–321.

76. Patomäki H, Teivainen T. *A Possible World: Democratic Transformations of Global Institutions*. London: Zed Books, 2004.

77. Havana Charter. *Havana Charter for an International Trade Organization*. Havana: Globefield Press, 1948.

78. Sogge D. *Give and Take: What's the Matter With Foreign Aid?* London: Zed Books, 2002.

79. Danaher K, Mark J. *Insurrection: Citizen Challenges to Corporate Power*. New York: Routledge, 2003.

80. Monbiot G. The mutation. *The Age of Consent: A Manifesto for a New World Order*. London: Harper Perennial, 2004:1.

81. Held D. Democracy, the nation-state and the global system. In: Held D, editor. *Political Theory Today*. Cambridge: Polity Press, 1991.

82. Archibugi D, Held D. *Cosmopolitan Democracy: An Agenda for a New World Order*. Cambridge: Polity, 1995.

83. Falk R. *On Humane Governance: Toward a New Global Politics*. Cambridge: Polity Press, 1998.

84. Monbiot G. *The Age of Consent: A Manifesto for a New World Order*. London: Harper Perennial, 2004.

85. Patomäki H, Teivainen T. Introduction. *A Possible World: Democratic Transformations of Global Institutions*. London: Zed Books, 2004:3.

86. South Centre. *For a Strong and Democratic United Nations: A South Perspective on UN Reform*. London: Zed Books, 1997.

87. Teivainen T. International organizations and the architecture of world power: A conference synthesis. In: Fisher W, Ponniah T, editors. *Another World Is Possible: Popular Alternatives to Globalisation at the World Social Forum*. London: Zed Books, 2003.

88. Russell B. *Political Ideals*. London: Unwin Books, 1917.

89. Derber C. *People Before Profit: The New Globalization in an Age of Terror, Big Money*. New York: Picador, 2002:142.

90. Kovel J. *The Enemy of Nature: The End of Capitalism or the End of the World?* London: Zed Books, 2002.

91. Schumpeter JA. *Capitalism, Socialism and Democracy*. London: George Allen & Unwin, 1943.

92. Meszaros I. *Beyond Capital: Towards a Theory of Transition*. London: Merlin Press, 1995:994.

93. Baumol WJ. Introduction: The engine of free-market growth. *The Free-Market Innovation Machine: Analyzing the Growth Miracle of Capitalism*. Princeton, NJ: Princeton University Press, 2002:1.

94. Bookchin M. *Remaking Society*. Montreal & Cheektowaga, NY: Black Rose Books, 1989:93–4.

95. Sachs J. New members please apply. *Time* July 7, 1997.

96. Mittelman J, Chin C. Conceptualising resistance to globalization. In: Amoore L, editor. *The Global Resistance Reader*. London: Routledge, 2005.

97. Stiglitz J. Another world is possible. *Making Globalisation Work: The Next Steps to Global Justice*. London: Penguin Books, 2006:7.

98. Antonio R. The cultural construction of neoliberal globalization. In: Ritzer G, editor. *The Blackwell Companion to Globalization*. Hoboken, NJ: Blackwell, 2007.

99. Rupert M. *Ideologies of Globalization: Contending Visions of a New World Order*. London: Routledge, 2000.

100. Amoore L. *The Global Resistance Reader*. London: Routledge, 2005.

101. Birchfield V. Contesting the hegemony of market ideology: Gramsci's "Good Sense" and Polanyi's "Double Movement." *Review of International Politcal Economy* 1999;6(1):27–54.

102. Anheier H, Glasius M, Kaldor M. Introducing global civic society. In: Anheier H, Glasius M, Kaldor M, editors. *Global Civic Society 2001*. Oxford: Oxford University Press, 2001.

103. Klein N. Farewell to end of history: Organisation and vision in anti-corporate movements. In: Amoore L, editor. *The Global Resistance Reader*. London: Routledge, 2005.

104. Bhagwati J. Anti-globalization: Why? *Journal of Policy Modeling* 2004;26:439–63.

105. Friedman TL. Foreign affairs: Senseless in Seattle. *New York Times* December 1, 1999.

106. Rory C, Vidal J, Pallister D, Bowcott O. Men in black behind chaos: Hardliners plan "actions" away from main protesters. *The Guardian* July 23, 2001.

107. World Social Forum. Porto Alegre call for mobilization. In: Lechner FJ, Boli J, editors. *The Globalization Reader*. Oxford: Blackwell Publishing, 2004:435.

108. George S. Europe wins the war within the west. *Another World Is Possible If . . .* London: Verso, 2004:116.

109. Bernard E. The battle in Seattle: What was that all about? *Washington Post* December 5, 1999.

110. Monbiot G. *The Age of Consent: A Manifesto for a New World Order*. London: Harper Perennial, 2004:23.

111. Hawken P. *Blessed Unrest: How the Largest Movement in the World Came Into Being and None Saw It Coming*. New York: Viking, 2007:12.

112. Achbar M. *Manufacturing Consent: Noam Chomsky and the Media*. The Companion Book to the Award-Winning Film by Peter Wintonick and Mark Achbar. Montreal: Institute for Policy Alternatives, 1994:221.

113. Russell B. Capitalism and the wage system. *Political Ideals*. London: Unwin Books, 1917:53–7.

114. Xie J, Sreenivasan S, Korniss G, Zhang W, Lim C, Szymanski B. Social consensus through the influence of committed minorities. *Physical Review E* 2011;84(1).

115. Lutkehaus N. *Margaret Mead: The Making of an American Icon*. Princeton, NJ: Princeton University Press, 2008:261.

116. Russell B. *Roads to Freedom*. London and New York: Routledge, 1993.

117. Clarke A. *Profiles of the Future: An Inquiry into the Limits of the Possible*. New York: Harper & Row, 1962.

ACKNOWLEDGMENTS

By and large, this book has been a solitary project. Nevertheless, it involved the emotional and intellectual support of wise and generous colleagues, advisers, friends, and persons I love.

I owe special thanks to my research assistant Jocelynn Owusu for double-checking every single sentence and reference of this book, and for the excellent feedbacks and editing suggestions she provided. I feel very grateful to the editors of Routledge/Francis & Taylor for reviewing the entire manuscript with unusual dedication. My fond appreciation to Richard Wilkinson, for having believed in me and in this project from the very beginning. Aida Sanchez deserves special mentioning for having taken the pain of reading an early draft of the entire book and for providing useful editing feedbacks. I owe a special thank to Roberto Gnesotto that read some of the chapters of this book and provided precious suggestions. Above all, I thank him for his boundless support, humor and generosity. Gianni Martini deserves a special thank for having encouraged me not to give up during the very first years of writing. A huge "gracias" goes to David Gimeno for inspiring me with his unique, irreverent desire to challenge power and for his wonderful jokes! Valuable inputs were also provided by Ritesh Mistry, Katherine Smith, Damita Abayaratne, Paolo Vineis, David Woodward, David Stuckler and Isaac Prilleltensky. This book has also benefited indirectly from conversations I had with Frank Anderson.

There are some authors I have actually never met that shaped some of the ideas contained in this book without even knowing it. My writing has been partly inspired by the works of Bertrand Russell, Noam Chomsky, Gore Vidal and Susan George.

The book has also drawn inevitably from my research and teachings at the Department of Epidemiology and Public Health, University College London and at the Department of Health Behavior and Health Education, University of Michigan. Special thanks go to my colleagues for putting up with my lateral, critical way of looking at health issues and the world. I also thank some of my students for their feedbacks and enthusiasm.

A word of appreciation goes to the Economic and Social Research Council (ESRC) that provided me with financial support to study globalization and health (Grant# – RES-070-27-0034.) Needless to say, the views expressed in this book are only mine and do not represent those of any of the people or institutions I have thanked here. I feel grateful to all of them, especially those that have suggested, without much success, to tone down my writing style.

And now I want to thank Paulina Duda. She has not only provided fresh, genuine insights throughout the entire manuscript. She has also put up with me, and my temper, during moments of frustration that bordered desperation. Her daily doses of kindness, truthfulness and sympathy helped this project beyond measure. Finally, a word of gratitude goes to my mother Rosalia Molon that helped me to write this book without even knowing it. Of course, she bears no blame for any of the lines written in it, though she must surely feel responsible for having shaped the way I am.

INDEX